3-3-68

Hist.

FRENCH PUBLIC OPINION
AND
FOREIGN AFFAIRS,
1870–1914

FRENCH PUBLIC OPINION
AND FOREIGN AFFAIRS
1870-1914

BY

E. MALCOLM CARROLL

ARCHON BOOKS
Hamden, Connecticut
1964

De
58
.C37F7
1964

To

ULRICH BONNELL PHILLIPS

PREFACE

The historical development of public opinion in its relation to foreign affairs is a comparatively new field of investigation. This volume is the result of the first exploration of a considerable section of this field. If it shows that the history of international relations before 1914 requires a broader treatment than is possible with the traditional methods of diplomatic history, if it suggests a more intensive study of certain problems which could not be examined here in detail, and if it encourages similar studies for the other Great Powers, it will not have been in vain. The present writer, at least, has found the problem of absorbing interest, and he ventures to hope that something of this interest may be communicated to others.

The author does not pretend to have accomplished the impossible. The mass of printed material which to a degree influenced or expressed public opinion defies a completely exhaustive study. Nor is it, in fact, necessary, for there were usually a comparatively few opinions whose repetition was limited only by the capacity of the press and by the number of politicians who were interested in these questions. The author believes that he has traced the more important currents of public opinion, and that he has indicated with a measure of accuracy their influence or lack of influence, as the case may be, upon the official policy.

The use of material from the newspaper press involved certain technical difficulties. Two methods were possible. A few editorials could be quoted at some length on each question, following the example of the diplomatic historian who wishes to give each important statement in its context; the alternative was the quotation of a phrase, or of a few sentences, from a larger number of newspapers. The latter procedure has been followed in this study. It permits a more complete, and therefore more satisfactory, presentation of the evidence. It has the merit of reproducing something of the mass effect of the press. The plan does not, it is believed, require the sacrifice of essential material. The editorial is most frequently the elaboration of a fairly definite point of view which may be suggested perhaps more effectively by a brief than by a long quotation.

The idea which developed into this study had its inception during the summer of 1925. While examining the files of the Paris *Temps* for the last years of the Second Empire with a different question in mind, the author's interest was increasingly aroused by the comparatively moderate attitude of this liberal and opposition newspaper toward Germany. His original purpose was adjourned when he noticed the absence of the emotional reaction to the Ems despatch in July, 1870, which the usual accounts had led him to expect. The results of his investigation as to the influence of public opinion upon the declaration of war by France appeared in an article, "French Public Opinion on War with Prussia in 1870" in the *American Historical Review*, July, 1926. Rewritten and with some new evidence, this article is the basis of the first two sections of the second chapter.

The author's obligations are numerous. His work was facilitated by a grant from the John Simon Guggenheim Memorial Foundation, in coöperation with Duke University, of the year 1927–1928. It was renewed by the Foundation for a period of three months. A long and interesting conversation with M. Charles Seignobos, Professor Emeritus of the University of Paris, is remembered with gratitude. M. Michel L'Hèritier, the secretary of the International Committee of Historical Sciences, and Professor Émile Bourgeois, of the University of Paris, offered suggestions, and the former gave assistance in locating material. Professor Sidney B. Fay kindly read portions of the manuscript. None of these gentlemen, however, are responsible for the interpretations of this book or any errors which may appear in it. A reader whose requirements were numerous recalls with appreciation the services of the staffs of the Bibliothèque Nationale and of the Archives Nationales (Paris), of the Bibliothèque Nationale et Universitaire (Strassburg), of the Preussische Staatsbibliothek (Berlin), of the British Museum (London), and of the Library of Congress (Washington, D. C.).

E. M. C.

Durham, North Carolina
December 15, 1930.

CONTENTS

63 digits

CHAPTER		PAGE
I	THE PROBLEM	3
II	THE FRANCO-PRUSSIAN WAR, 1870–1871	15
III	RECONSTRUCTION AND READJUSTMENTS, 1871–1875 .	44
IV	OPPORTUNISM IN FOREIGN AFFAIRS, 1875–1881 . . .	66
V	COLONIAL EXPANSION AND THE ENTENTE WITH GERMANY, 1881–1885	84
VI	THE *REVANCHE* AND THE CRISIS OF 1887	109
VII	THE FRANCO-RUSSIAN ALLIANCE	136
VIII	ENGLAND OR GERMANY?	162
IX	THE PARTING OF THE WAYS, 1899–1904	183
X	MOROCCO AND THE BALANCE OF POWER, 1905–1908 . .	206
XI	THE FRANCO-GERMAN ACCORD OF 1909 AND THE AGADIR CRISIS, 1911	231
XII	THE NEW NATIONALISM, RUSSIA, AND THE BALKANS .	252
XIII	THE FAILURE OF THE EQUILIBRIUM, JULY, 1914 . .	285
	INDEX	313

voir p 336 pour "Nationalism"

FRENCH PUBLIC OPINION AND FOREIGN AFFAIRS, 1870–1914

CHAPTER I

The Problem

La presse, par les nouvelles qu'elle divulge aussitôt, par la manière, dont elle discute publiquement toutes les données d'une question, par les dispositions enfin qu'elle engendre ou propage dans la nation, devient chaque jour davantage, si nous osons ainsi dire, une puissance diplomatique de premier ordre.

Temps, April 5, 1900.

The place of public opinion in the relations between the European Powers during the half-century which preceded the World War has been comparatively neglected. The first need was, of course, for a better understanding of the foreign policy and diplomacy of each country. Much still remains to be done in this direction, but a disproportionate emphasis upon purely diplomatic history leads to a one-sided view of international relations. The balance needs to be adjusted by a due consideration of a number of general forces, of which public opinion is not the least important. The absence of adequate machinery for the popular or parliamentary control of foreign policy in the most democratic of countries [1] is not a satisfactory reason for its omission, for there is abundant evidence that public opinion was a fairly constant factor in the conduct of foreign affairs. Page after page of diplomatic correspondence was written in regard to its reactions. It served as a reason for resistance in crises and for insisting upon certain demands. Frequently specious, these arguments at least show that public opinion was almost always a factor in the calculations of diplomats and of governments. Finally, its reaction to the conditions and events which eventually aligned peoples against each other upon the battlefield has an interest and importance that is independent of its influence upon the conduct of foreign affairs.

Historians of international relations have rarely concerned themselves in detail with any phase of public opinion. Its intangible character, and the difficulty of establishing satisfactory conclusions, have

---

[1] S. R. Chow, *Le Contrôle Parlementaire de la Politique Étrangère en Angleterre, en France et aux Etats-Unis* (Paris, 1920), p. 200.

3

persuaded them to leave the field to the psychologist, the political scientist, and the publicist. This is unfortunate, for the relation between public opinion and a definite question in foreign affairs is essentially an historical problem. The need in this connection is not so much for a theory of public opinion as for sound information as to its formation, expression, and influence. The purpose of this study is to meet this need with reference to France. Before taking up the complicated threads of this story, a preliminary discussion of the point of view from which it is considered and of the sources seems desirable.

The representation of the state of mind of a people at a given moment is one of the most difficult of all problems in the reconstruction of the past. The task, especially if it is undertaken by one who is not a native of the country in question, requires a certain humility, and it need scarcely be said that impartiality is an essential prerequisite. It rarely happens that the several currents which contribute to the main stream of public opinion fuse into one; it is therefore almost always necessary to select those which are the more important. The pressure of a crisis sometimes creates a practical unanimity, but even then it is not always easy to be certain as to the predominant point of view. If the witnesses of a definite event usually differ as to what they have seen or heard, how much greater is the risk of error when a question of opinion is involved! The diplomat urging his case with every weapon at his command, the minister explaining his policy in parliament, the editor seeking to influence the government or his public were all interested in representing public opinion as in agreement with their own respective points of view.[2] These difficulties do not justify, however, a surrender to the counsel of despair, for it is possible, by comparing the expression of opinion in a wide range of material, to arrive at an approximately correct conclusion. When this has been done, the more delicate questions relating to the determining forces remain, and these require an evaluation of traditions, of political, social, and even of economic influences.

Public opinion is one of those vague terms which elude precise definition. In its common use, it refers to the composite reactions of the general public, but, as a rule, the only tangible evidence of these tendencies is to be found in the opinions of the more influen-

[2] Walter Lippmann has pointed out the frequency with which private interests are identified with the public good, a somewhat similar confusion. W. Lippmann, *The Phantom Public. A Sequel to Public Opinion* (New York, 1927), pp. 110–114.

tial leaders. It is therefore often impossible in practice to draw a clear distinction between the leaders and the rank and file; and, to a considerable extent, it will be the task here to discover those leaders who were the most effective in shaping and expressing the opinions, prejudices, passions, and aspirations of the general public. The man in the street in France, as elsewhere, had at best an inadequate understanding of the questions involved in the foreign affairs of his country, and he was usually content to leave them to the experts. Perhaps this resignation was due as much to a feeling of powerlessness as to indifference, for he became intensely concerned when there was a danger of war.

It is more difficult to explain the origins of the passions which moved the French people even in more normal times than it seems at first sight. It is not sufficient to say that they were the inevitable result of France's defeat in 1871 and of the loss of Alsace-Lorraine, for they would probably have been forgotten if specific efforts had not been made to give new life to them. The veterans of the war of 1870, and those who retained a vivid memory of its scenes, sometimes used their influence for this purpose. Textbooks in history and civics, although the permanent influence of impressions acquired in the schools may perhaps be exaggerated, were of influence in keeping hatred of Germany alive. The appeal was often upon a high plane, and therefore the more effective. The duty of loyalty to Alsace-Lorraine, for example, was sometimes urged as required by the unwavering loyalty of these provinces to France. The newspaper press helped to confirm these impressions, although there were always moderate journals whose circulation was larger than that of chauvinist organs. The frequent use of standardized phrases, which have been described as stereotypes,[3] in regard to Alsace-Lorraine, Germany, and England indicated the importance of these phrases not only in the formation of popular sentiment but also in its expression. The problem of the lost provinces was rarely discussed without the frequent use of such vivid terms as *le plaie saignant,* and *la blessure toujours douloureuse.* For a number of years after 1871, the German soldier was pictured in numerous caricatures as leaving France laden with stolen clocks, and Germany's "brutality" and her "appetite for conquest" figured in innumerable editorials. The old phrase, "perfidious Albion," was revived against England when the colonial interests of the two countries clashed. The tend-

[3] Walter Lippmann, *Public Opinion* (New York, 1922), pp. 111, 112.

ency of the press in every country to adopt stock expressions which take no account of shades of meaning doubtless explains in part the origin of these terms, and in time, particularly at the close of the nineteenth century,[4] they tended to become mere phrases. Their effectiveness was never the same with all groups, for hatred of Germany declined among the moderate Republicans in the decade 1875–1885, when they turned to colonial expansion as a means of national recovery.[5] Even the extreme nationalists modified their point of view under the influence of the animosity against England caused by the Fashoda incident in 1898.[6] The affirmation that France desired peace, which almost always accompanied a discussion of grievances against Germany, was not merely intended to impress opinion abroad, for there was in fact a real passion for peace among the French people.

Leadership in the formation of public opinion in regard to foreign affairs came, for the most part, from the executive, the administration, parliament, and the newspaper press. The influence of each of these authorities varied at different times. Napoleon III's pronouncements were understood as indicating the government's policy, while the Presidents of the Republic rarely discussed foreign affairs in public. It was the President of the Council, or the Minister of Foreign Affairs, who used the executive power to the greatest effect under the Empire as well as after 1870. Perhaps the best example was Gramont's declaration, as Minister of Foreign Affairs, on July 6, 1870, to the *Corps Législatif,* for it was clearly intended as an appeal to the nation for its support in resisting the Hohenzollern candidature.[7] On October 27, 1912, Poincaré, then the President of the Council and the Minister of Foreign Affairs, appealed to public opinion even more directly in a speech at Nantes when he was about to invite the Powers to declare their disinterestedness in the Balkan War.[8]

Only exceptional circumstances led to the active intervention of the chiefs of state, and when it occurred, its effect can be measured with some exactness. It is more difficult to weigh the influence of the prefects under the direction of the Minister of the Interior, for it was exerted in a less dramatic fashion. During the Second Em-

---

[4] See below, p. 184.
[5] See below, chapter V.
[6] See below, p. 176.
[7] See below, pp. 27–29.
[8] See below, pp. 260, 266.

pire, it was used to inspire confidence in the government's policy and to prepare for its decisions.[9] The numerous contacts between these officials and the people of their departments furnished many opportunities for this purpose, but it was also one of their functions to inform the government in Paris as to the prevailing state of mind in regard to foreign affairs. At least once a month, and occasionally at the specific order of the Minister of the Interior, reports were submitted which, it appears, were given serious attention. In view of the tendency of some to please their superiors by the nature of their observations, this evidence is not always entirely trustworthy. It may be noted that these reports, now kept in the *Archives Nationales,* although a mine of information as to public opinion upon a wide variety of subjects, have been little used. Unfortunately they are not available after 1870, but the prefects presumably continued to serve the same functions.

Circumstances gave more influence to parliamentary speeches and debates during the last years of the Empire than under the Republic. In 1860, the press was permitted to publish them without comment, and this privilege was used with effect by the leaders of the liberal opposition to present their views to the nation. Thiers's speech of May 3, 1866, attacking the government's Italian and German policies from the point of view of France's traditional policy of the balance of power, was an example.[10] Few debates upon foreign affairs after 1870 equaled that of March 15–18, 1867, upon the German question in the variety of opinions expressed.[11] It was felt under the Republic that it would be unpatriotic to reveal differences of opinion in the open chamber as to France's foreign policy.[12] Years passed with scarcely any formal interpellations of the Minister of Foreign Affairs, and when a more active interest was shown, as in the annual discussion of the budget for the Ministry of Foreign Affairs, it was usually by the opposition groups. Political motives were therefore involved, as in the attack upon Ferry's colonial policy in March, 1885. The comparative silence of the chamber encouraged silence

[9] See below, pp. 18, 19.
[10] See below, p. 17.
[11] See below, pp. 20, 21.
[12] "Since the war of 1870, silence upon foreign policy was a duty." E. Vacherot, *La Politique Extérieure de la République* (Paris, 1881), p. 5. Cf. Paul de Cassagnac in the *Annales de la Chambre des Députés* (1890), I, 584. *France Militaire,* May 11, 1887.

on the part of the government. Nor was there any sustained criticism of this state of affairs by the press.[13]

The newspaper press was by all odds the most effective instrument for influencing public opinion and the most important medium for its expression. It rapidly attained its present position early in the period covered by this study. In 1868, many of the restrictions which had been placed upon it by Napoleon III, who had a wholesome respect for public opinion, were removed. The liberal and radical opposition again was the first to take advantage of this comparative freedom by increasing the number of its organs.[14] After 1871, the clash between the Monarchists and Republicans gave a further stimulus to the growth of the press as a means of securing popular support for their ideas. The number of newspapers rapidly multiplied. Paris had not more than a dozen of any importance before 1868; by 1873 the Parisian could choose between fifteen morning and forty evening newspapers.[15] In 1876 alone, fifteen were founded.[16] Many had only a short life, but there were normally about fifty of some significance. Each political group and many individual leaders had one or more press organs.

The most significant change in the character of the press during this period was the appearance of the *journaux d'information,* whose chief function was the distribution of news. It had been made possible in 1836 when Émile de Girardin used commercial advertising as the chief source of income for his newspaper, the *Presse,* but more than a generation passed before the full possibilities of this innovation were exploited. In 1867, Marignani founded the *Petit Journal* as a commercial enterprise. By avoiding controversial subjects, he kept upon good terms with the government and avoided offense to possible readers. He was the first in France to rely largely upon the sale of separate numbers in the streets instead of upon subscribers. For nearly a decade, the *Petit Journal* remained the only newspaper of its kind in Paris. Then occurred a number of mechanical improvements, such as the invention of the rotary press, the lino-

---

[13] A certain amount of criticism was occasioned in 1905 by the Moroccan crisis. *Journal de Rouen,* May 7, June 7. *Petit Provençal* (Marseilles), June 16. *Humanité,* July 10. *Gaulois,* Dec. 18. *Aurore,* April 14, 1906.

[14] Among them were the *Électeur, Réveil, Tribune, Rappel,* and Rochefort's famous *Lanterne.* Georges Weill, *Histoire du Parti Républicain en France (1814–1870)* (Paris, 1928), pp. 382–386.

[15] *Correspondant,* Old Series, vol. 90, p. 747.

[16] *Ibid.,* O. S., vol. 106, pp. 397, 398.

type, the manufacture of paper from wood-pulp, and improved facilities for the collection and distribution of news, which prepared the way for the modern newspaper of wide circulation. The *Petit Parisien,* which was later to rival and to surpass the *Petit Journal* as the most popular newspaper, was founded in 1876. In 1883, the *Matin* was established by the Englishman Edwards upon the model of American newspaper practice. The *Journal* began publication in 1889 as an attempt to popularize the literary style and smartness of the aristocratic *Figaro.* Directing their appeal to as many groups as possible, these newspapers were distinctly more independent than the *journaux d'opinion* which frankly acknowledged their propagandist purposes, yet in foreign affairs some of them adopted a definite point of view. The *Matin,* for a number of years, printed articles by leaders of each political group ranging from Jaurès for the Socialists to Jules Delafosse for the Monarchists, but John Lemoinne, formerly an important contributor to the *Journal des Débats* and a member of the Académie Française, usually wrote its editorials upon international questions. His place was later taken by Stéphane Lauzanne and Jules Hedemann, whose opinions were strongly nationalist. Ernest Judet began his stormy career about 1890 with his anti-British editorials in the *Petit Journal.*

From the first, the Paris press maintained a leading position for the entire country.[17] The government of the Second Empire had used the provincial newspapers for the control of public opinion in its own interests by distributing the contracts for the printing of official notices. Only a few, like the *Progrès* of Lyon, the *Progrès de la Côte d'Ôr* of Dijon, and the *Phare de la Loire* of Nantes, retained their independence. The war of 1870 and the Commune, by separating Paris from the provinces, gave an impulse to the provincial press,[18] but it was the increased use of the telegraph in bringing the news to the most remote section which made its fortune. By the end of the century, almost all of the large cities had at least one

---

[17] A report of the prefect of Vaucluse in 1859 named the liberal *Siècle* of Paris as the most widely circulated newspaper. "Its clientèle is especially the habitués of cafés. I have never been able to find a remedy for this unfortunate state of affairs. The influence of this newspaper upon the masses of the city of Charpentras . . . is incontestable and bad." Avignon, July 13, 1859. Archives Nationales. Administration Générale. Esprit Publique et Elections. Série Départmentale, F1c. III Vaucluse 6.

[18] Arthur Meyer, *Ce Que Mes Yeux Ont Vu* (Paris, 1911), p. 365. Meyer was for many years the editor of the bonapartist and monarchist *Gaulois.*

newspaper which compared favorably with the Paris press. The more important were the *Dépêche* of Toulouse, the *Petit Marseillais,* the *Lyon Républicain,* the *Petite Gironde* of Bordeaux, the *Journal de Rouen,* and the *Écho du Nord* of Lille. In spite of their local or regional character, the capital continued to exert a strong influence upon them through the leading articles, which were often written in Paris, and through their correspondents. A rather extensive examination of the above mentioned provincial newspapers and others failed to show any great difference in their reactions to foreign affairs from those of the Paris press. If some, like the *Lyon Républicain,* the *France de Bordeaux et du Sud-Ouest,* and the *Progrès de la Côte d'Ôr* of Dijon were distinctly moderate, so also were some of the Paris newspapers of the same political opinions, while the *Petit Marseillais,* and the *Écho du Nord* of Lille were strongly nationalist. The *Petit Comtois* of Besançon, like Senator Bérenger's *Action* in Paris, combined a support of radical reforms in France with a nationalist attitude in foreign affairs. Nevertheless, there is need of a more careful comparison between the Paris press and the provincial newspapers than has been possible in this study. In its absence, the latter cannot safely be neglected.

This astonishing development of the press made the public "newspaper conscious." More than ever, editorials became the chief medium for the discussion of France's relations with other countries. It was from the hundreds of daily newspapers throughout France whose total circulation numbered into the millions that the public's immediate impressions were secured. There was a noticeable increase of attention to these questions in the press at the beginning of the twentieth century. It was shown by every section, but most of all by the moderate republican and conservative newspapers. Except the socialist *Humanité,* whose policy was determined by Jaurès, the radical press was too concerned with political and social questions at home to give much attention to the international situation. It was the *Temps,* whose daily bulletin upon foreign affairs was established in 1901, the *Journal des Débats,* the nationalist and clerical *Écho de Paris,* the conservative. *Figaro,* and the other newspapers of like character that commented most frequently even after the beginning of the decade of crises in 1905. The influence of one article was probably slight, but the chief weapon of the editorial and of the press in general was the power of repetition. The *Temps,* after 1904, was perhaps the most expert in its use. André Tardieu, who became

its foreign editor in that year,[19] interpreted each event in foreign
affairs as to its bearing upon the policy of the balance of power.
Repeated almost daily in the *Temps*'s "Bulletin de l'Etranger," this
point of view, aided by circumstances and the weight of tradition,
was accepted by the press as a whole.[20]

The influence of a given newspaper depended upon its character,
but its character was, in large measure, determined by its public.
Because the *Temps* and the *Journal des Débats* were the favorites
of the upper middle classes whose opinions counted for most under
the Third Republic, they were more important, for example, than
either the monarchist *Gaulois* or the socialist *Humanité*. It is also
dangerous to use a newspaper in showing the reaction of public
opinion without accounting for its political connections for they
frequently explain its point of view. The importance of its opinions
then depended largely upon the importance of the group which it
represented, and it frequently depended upon the personal following
of the writer. Signed editorials were the rule, and if they were anonymous, as in the case of the *Temps,* their author was usually known.
The extent of a newspaper's circulation was not conclusive evidence
as to its influence, for those which were the most popular usually
gave the least attention to foreign affairs. The wide public to which
they appealed was sometimes, however, an attraction to officials who
wished to influence public opinion.

Although it is difficult, in the absence of adequate information,
to determine the extent of official influence upon the press, that it
existed is certain. The Quai d'Orsai, like other foreign offices, had
its division of the press which probably served other functions than
those of a clipping bureau, but its secrets have never, to the writer's
knowledge, been disclosed. Other ministries were involved, it is evident, for the distribution of the Russian press-fund in 1912–1913,
described in Chapter XII, was placed under the direction of the
Minister of Finance, and the press as a whole came within the jurisdic-
tion of the Minister of the Interior. There are few subjects in regard
to which governments are more secretive. It is well known that Bismarck constantly practised the manipulation of the press,[21] and his suc-

[19] His predecessor, Francis de Pressensé, was dismissed on the ground that
his socialist inclinations were not in accord with the *Temps*'s policy. *Temps,*
Jan. 21, 1914.
[20] See below, pp. 222, 223.
[21] Moritz Busch, *Bismarck: Some Secret Pages of His History,* 2 vols. (London, 1898), especially vol. I. Cf. Heinrich Wuttke, *Le Fonds des Reptiles* (Paris,

cessors followed his example, but the forty volumes of the *Grosse Politik* throw little or no light upon the details of this policy. The publication of Russian documents has shown that Russian money was spent upon the French press with the knowledge and coöperation of the French government, and it is commonly supposed that the secret-funds included in each annual budget were in part used for this purpose.[22] But important as this evidence is, this influence may easily be exaggerated. Other methods were more frequently used. Semi-official communications were given to selected newspapers or to the Havas Agency, whose relations with the government have never been fully explained.[23] This practice permitted a prompt and easy correction if the result proved unsatisfactory. The first volumes to appear of the French pre-war diplomatic correspondence show that the Minister of Foreign Affairs was sometimes asked by the French diplomatic agents abroad, especially in Berlin, to influence newspaper opinion in favor of moderation.[24] These documents are silent as to the results, if any, of this advice. Indeed, there was no exact parallel in France under the Republic to the *Norddeutsche Allgemeine Zeitung* which was generally admitted to be the official organ of the German Foreign Office, but it was understood that certain newspapers possessed the government's confidence. Those which occupied this favored position changed with the varying tendencies of the numerous cabinets and with individual ministers. Although the *Temps* and the *Journal des Débats* perhaps most frequently reflected the official point of view, they were sometimes critical, especially if the min-

1877), for the use made of the proceeds from the confiscation of the King of Hanover's estates. This is a translation from the German. Wuttke, *Die Deutschen Zeitscriften und die Entstehung der Öffentlichen Meinung. . . .* (Leipzig, 1875). Information concerning the relations between the government of the Second Empire and the press may be found in *Les Petits Papiers Secrets des Tuileries et de Saint-Cloud, étiquetés par un Collectionneur* (Paris, 1870).

[22] See Camille Pelletan's remarks in the *Justice,* Dec. 15, 1883. Cf. Robert de Jouvenel, *La République des Camarades* (Paris, 1914), pp. 210, 211. Jouvenel discounts the influence of these subsidies in his interesting discussion of the press.

[23] For a brief sketch of the history of this important news agency see A. de Chambure, *À Travers la Presse* (Paris, 1914), pp. 518, 519. The Ministry of Foreign Affairs, according to the radical Delaisi, controlled its despatches. Francis Delaisi, *La Guerre Qui Vient* (Paris, 1911).

[24] *Documents Diplomatiques Français (1871-1914)*, Ist Series (1871-1900), I (Paris, 1929), pp. 284, 287, 327 note. On Nov. 17, 1911, the Service of Communications was instructed that the press should not interpret the departure of the *Berlin* from Agadir as a diplomatic victory. *Ibid.,* 3d Series (1911-1914), I (Paris, 1929), p. 210.

istry depended upon a radical majority. Delcassé used the *Matin* for the expression of his opinions, and in 1911 the *Petit Parisien* was said to have been close to Caillaux. There is a dearth of specific evidence as to the control of the press, but it is at least true that the authority of certain newspapers was increased by the assumption that they spoke in the name of the government.

Successful publicists and journalists were more frequently appointed to high offices in France than elsewhere.[25] This was a distinct departure from the practice of the Second Empire, when they were usually either henchmen of the government or in complete opposition. Later, the transition between the press and even the Ministry of Foreign Affairs and the diplomatic service was often made. Prior to his first ministry in 1881, Jules Ferry had been a contributor to the *Temps,* and Gambetta had founded in 1871 the *République Française* whose policy he directed. Delcassé, Stephen Pichon, and the Cambon brothers, who were later to impress their influence upon French foreign policy, began their careers as journalists. After leaving the Quai d'Orsai in 1911, Pichon became the editor of the *Petit Journal.* Clemenceau was in turn the editor of the *Justice,* the editor of the *Aurore,* the Minister of the Interior, President of the Council, and the editor again of the *Homme Libre.* Gabriel Hanotaux wrote occasionally for the press, and before 1912 Poincaré contributed a few articles upon foreign affairs. It does not follow by any means that these men applied in office the point of view which they had expressed as irresponsible journalists, for they at once came under the influence of the traditions of French foreign policy. As an editor, for example, Clemenceau had never been an enthusiastic friend of the Russian alliance, but his government, 1906–1909, remained steadfastly loyal to it.[26] While it cannot safely be said that France's foreign policy was determined by this factor, nevertheless it probably strengthened the importance of public opinion in the calculations of the government.

The support of a favorable public opinion was appreciated by officials with a background of experience in journalism. Useful in a diplomatic crisis, it was indispensable in the event of war.[27] To secure it

---

[25] Paul Elzbacher, *Die Presse als Werkzeug der Auswärtigen Politik* (Jena, 1918), p. 34.

[26] See below, p. 226.

[27] Writing in the *Gaulois,* Dec. 20, 1905, General Zurlinden pointed out that the reservists would bring the prevailing temper of public opinion into their regiments in the event of mobilization. It need scarcely be said that universal military service greatly increased the need of confidence in the government's policy.

was therefore one of the main preoccupations of the government, and for this purpose it was necessary to take the public, to a certain degree, into the government's confidence. Martin Spahn, the German historian, has ventured the opinion that "the scholar who knows how to read, may find everything in the newspapers which the documents contain."[28] This statement contains the exaggeration common to most generalizations. Nevertheless, it is submitted that the aims of French foreign policy in their broad outlines may be found in the press. To pretend to write a history of diplomacy from press clippings would be absurd. Any serious study of public opinion in relation to foreign affairs must always make use of newspapers in connection with the diplomatic correspondence. Only in this way is it possible to be certain that governments were seeking the same objectives which were acknowledged in parliament and in the press.

[28] Karl Otto Herkenberg, *The Times und das Deutsch-Englische Verhältnis im Jahre, 1898* (Berlin, 1925) (Introduction by Martin Spahn), p. 13. A recent German minister was responsible for this statement, which was first applied to domestic policy.

CHAPTER TWO

THE FRANCO-PRUSSIAN WAR, 1870–1871

Nous sommes persuadés que les Français, pris en masse, sont parfaitement d'avis qu'il convient de laisser les Allemands se débrouiller chez eux; que l'Allemagne doit appartenir aux Allemands . . . comme la France aux Français.

Charles Dollfus, *Temps*, March 25, 1869.

I

An inevitable conflict, it is often said and more frequently assumed, divides the French and German peoples. The accident which had placed them along a frontier "that nature had not drawn deeply enough" [1] is represented as the cause of a thousand years of rivalry and war. A philosophy based upon historical determinism may accept this alleged fatality, but the modern form of the Franco-German problem, upon which the peace of Europe and of the world so largely depends, arose from more tangible origins. It began when the French kings and ministers of the sixteenth and seventeenth centuries established the policy of maintaining the political divisions of Germany and of extending France's eastern frontier to the Rhine. Although designed to guarantee the security of France against the ambitions of the Hapsburg princes and to advance her influence in Europe, it is probable that public opinion had no part in the origins of this policy. Its results in the enhancement of the nation's glory, and the weight of tradition, later insured its tacit approval by the French people and the active support of the minority which concerned itself with foreign affairs. Modified in detail according to circumstances and the ambitions of individuals, it was changed in no essential respect during the Revolution, nor by Napoleon I, and if it was temporarily suspended after 1815, that was due to France's weakness. It continued to dominate the opinion of the conservative parties during the Second

---

[1] Hermann Oncken, *Die Rheinpolitik Kaiser Napoleons III, von 1863 bis 1870 und der Ursprung des Krieges von 1870–71,* 3 vols. (Stuttgart, 1926), I, 2. The introduction has been translated. H. Oncken, *Napoleon III and the Rhine. The Origin of the War of 1870–1871* (New York, 1928).

15

Empire when Prussia, under Bismarck, assumed control of the movement for the unification of Germany.

A new factor appeared with Napoleon III's ambitious plan for
the reorganization of Europe along the lines of nationalism. Foreshadowed in his pamphlet, *Des Idées Napoliennes* (London, 1839), its
first application in 1859 to the Italian question at once showed that he
was not prepared to discard France's traditional policy completely. His
hands were tied, to a certain degree, by public opinion at home. While
the liberals had approved his policy of nationalism as in accord with
their interpretation of the ideals of the Revolution, they condemned
his desertion of the Italian cause in his separate peace with Austria,
and the conservatives considered any support of Italian nationalism
as a betrayal of the policy which had served the interests of France
so well under the monarchy. The clash between Napoleon's support
of nationalism and its results was especially clear in regard to Germany. His refusal to accept her complete unification, which was
shared by many leaders of public opinion in France, became "a fundamental cause of the Franco-Prussian War." [2]

It was not generally believed in France that a real desire for unity
existed in Germany. Public opinion was assured that the majority
of her people were attached to the separate States. Influenced by
their own criticism of centralization in France, some liberals, like Jules
Ferry,[3] were ready to believe that the Germans would be happier under the old German Confederation. French intervention, it was said,
would create a feeling of nationalism where it would not otherwise
have existed. "Fear of Austria united Italy," wrote a student of German affairs in 1867, "and fear of France will unite Germany." [4] Renan
wrote during the Franco-Prussian War that there would have been
no German nationalism without France's hostility.[5] Accurate information as to the desires of the German people was less important,
however, in the formation of public opinion upon this question than
the prevailing views and sentiments as to France's legitimate rôle in

[2] Adolphe Guéroult, "La République en France," *Rev. des Deux Mondes,*
1870, VI, 107.

[3] *Lettres de Jules Ferry* (*1846–1896*) (Paris, 1914), p. 39.

[4] Émile de Laveleye, "L'Allemagne depuis la Guerre de 1866," *Rev. des Deux
Mondes,* 1867, I, 808.

[5] Ernest Renan, "La Guerre entre la France et l'Allemagne," *Ibid.,* 1870, V,
267. Cf. *Temps,* Aug. 12, 1867. The liberal Prévost-Paradol argued that the
existence of opposition to unification in Germany justified France's attitude.
Lucien A. Prévost-Paradol, *La France Nouvelle* (Paris, 1868), pp. 375–377.

European affairs. "France has always aspired," wrote a candid patriot during the siege of Paris, "to preponderant power in Europe as the due of her superior civilization." [6] The leaders of all groups assumed in different ways France's right to a predominant influence. The moderate and radical Republicans believed that France should assume the leadership of liberal movements. The clerical party was eager for France to exercise supreme power in the interests of the Church, while the Monarchists and conservatives were not to be shaken in their devotion to the traditional policy of the monarchy.[7] Many liberals declared that they had no objection in principle to German unity and that they merely claimed the right to prefer the democratic to the Prussian movement.[8] It is unfortunate that events did not test their sincerity.

Napoleon's policy of nationalism, strengthened by a desire to tear up the treaties of 1815 as a reminder of his uncle's failure and of France's defeat, induced him on the eve of the Austro-Prussian War in 1866 to consider an alliance with Prussia. His approval of a moderate development of Prussia's influence in northern Germany, however, was to be given in return for territorial compensations upon the Rhine.[9] An alliance with Prussia was supported by a section of the press, which included the Opinion Nationale, the Journal des Débats, and the Siècle, even in the face of a later charge of being in Bismarck's pay.[10] Comparatively little was said in the press as to territorial compensations, and the opponents of the proposed alliance refused to tolerate the suggestion of a bargain. Thiers, who was then a determined opponent of German unity,[11] declared in the Corps Législatif, May 3, 1866, that France's true interests were in the maintenance of the treaties of 1815. Prussia's ambitions, he predicted, would lead to the reëstablishment of the Empire of Charles V in a close union with Italy. He reminded the German people that their "organization as a union of independent States is the funda-

[6] Alfred Maury, "Les Guerres entre des Français et des Allemands," Rev. des Deux Mondes, 1871, I, 579.

[7] Émile Bourgeois, Manuel Historique de Politique Étrangère, 4 vols. (Paris, 1906–1927), III (1927), pp. 614, 615.

[8] Temps, May 1, 1861; Apr. 16, May 21, 1862; Jan. 27, 1864; Aug. 12, 1865.

[9] He suggested this possibility as early as 1854. Albert Pingaud, "La Politique Extérieure du Second Empire," Revue Historique, vol. 156, p. 49.

[10] Anatole Claveau, Souvenirs Politiques et Parlementaires d'un Témoin, 2 vols. (Paris, 1913, 1914), I, 200.

[11] Daniel Halévy, Le Courrier de M. Thiers (Paris, 1921), pp. 381, 382.

mental principle of European politics." [12] Jules Ferry wrote, at the same time, that the creation of a greater Prussia would be "productive of dangers to our country, such as hitherto have been unknown in her history." [13] Heedless of these warnings and without an assurance of compensations, Napoleon announced his approval of a moderate extension of Prussian territory, June 11, 1866, in a letter to parliament. A counterbalance, he said, would be necessary in the union of the South German States and by the maintenance of Austria's "great influence" in German affairs. Discreetly silent in regard to compensations, he implied France's neutrality unless the *status quo* should be altered to the advantage of one Power. He closed with the comforting assurance that "whatever the results of the war might be, none of the questions which interest France would be settled without her approval." [14]

In no mood for heroic measures after the Crimean and Italian wars, and especially since the Mexican adventure, public opinion approved this policy of neutrality. [15] Like the government, it was not prepared, however, for the rapidity of Prussia's successes. Within six weeks, she was in a position to dictate terms of peace. Drouhyn de Lhuys, the Minister of Foreign Affairs, advised the concentration of the army upon the Rhine, July 4–5, on hearing the news of Sadowa. On the verge of a breakdown, Napoleon was not clear in his own mind as to the proper policy, and his hesitation was confirmed by the War Minister's warning that the army was not prepared. [16] Instead of authorizing decisive measures, the government chose to pretend a satisfaction which it obviously did not feel. The official *Moniteur Universel* (July 5) proclaimed Napoleon's purely formal rôle in handing Venitia over to Italy as a notable recognition of his influence, and the public buildings of Paris were illuminated that night. [17] Administrative officials throughout the country were instructed

[12] *Annales du Sénat et du Corps Législatif,* 1866, V, 78.

[13] *Temps,* May 4, 1866.

[14] *Annales,* 1866, VIII, 24, 25.

[15] See the author's article, "French Public Opinion on War with Prussia in 1870," *Amer. Hist. Rev.,* vol. XXXI (4), p. 681, for citations from the reports of the prefects. Cf. A. de Castarède, *Considérations sur la Guerre en 1866* (Paris, 1866), pp. 22–24. *Temps,* June 10, July 2, 1866.

[16] The Emperor's cousin, Prince Jérôme, also advised against intervention. Metternich to Beust, Paris, July 7, 1866. Oncken, *Die Rheinpolitik Napoleons III,* I, 315.

[17] Alfred Stern, *Geschichte Europas seit den Verträgen von 1815 bis zum Frankfurter Frieden von 1871,* 10 vols. (Stuttgart), IX (1923), p. 528.

to represent the Emperor's policy as entirely successful.[18] A plausible explanation was furnished by Adolphe Guéroult, one of the friends of an alliance with Prussia, in the *Opinion Nationale* (Aug. 3, 1866). The German Confederation, he declared, with Austria's support, had united a population of seventy-five millions in a defensive union against France. In providing for a North German Confederation and for the independence of the South German States, and in excluding Austria, the preliminary peace of Nikolsburg, he declared, had divided this formidable *bloc* into three separate parts. France was, therefore, in a better position than she had been before the Austro-Prussian War.[19] This theory, received as it was later observed "with Homeric laughter," was given official sanction in a public circular, September 16, 1866, to the diplomatic representatives of France,[20] and by Rouher, the chief minister, in the *Corps Législatif*.[21] As late as the fall of 1868, a colored map was widely circulated as a graphic illustration of the alleged three-fold division of Germany,[22] and the Emperor contributed to this campaign of misrepresentation in his address at the opening of parliament, February 14, 1867. "I did not advance a single regiment," he declared, "and yet the voice of France halted the victor at the gates of Vienna." [23]

Critical observers were not satisfied with this shallow pretense. The *Temps* (July 24, 1866) predicted the formation of *"le grand empire allemand,"* and ten days later, it described the preliminary peace of Nikolsburg as the most significant event in the history of Europe since the treaties of Westphalia. "We must consider these events," it declared, "as to their effects upon the preponderance and perhaps the security of our country." It was observed that the gov-

[18] Archives Nationales. Administration Générale. Esprit Publique et Élections. Série Départmentale, F1c. III. Haute Garonne 9, July 6, 1866; Gironde 6, Aug. 6, 1866; Nord 8, Aug. 7, 1866.

[19] Cf. Alphonse de Calonne, *Le Rôle de la Prusse et de l'Allemagne du Nord dans l'Équilibre Européen* (Paris, 1866), p. 21. Le Comte de la Guéronnière, *La France et l'Europe* (Paris, 1867), p. 19. Radowitz, who was an official in the Prussian embassy at this time, testifies to Guéroult's disinterestedness in comparison with other publicists who were in Prussia's pay. *Aufzeichnungen und Erinnerungen aus dem Leben des Botschafters Joseph Maria von Radowitz*, H. Holborn, ed. 2 vols. (Berlin, 1925), I, 76.

[20] *Les Origines Diplomatiques de la Guerre de 1870–1871*, A. Aulard, ed., (1910–   ), XII, 301–307. *Constitutionnel*, Sept. 19, 1866.

[21] *Annales*, 1867, II, 226, 227. (March, 1867.)

[22] *Opinion Nationale*, Oct. 30, 1868. *Corresp.*, Old Series, vol. 76, pp. 557, 558. See the report of Baden's agent in Paris, Oct. 30, 1868. Oncken, *Die Rheinpolitik Napoleons III*, p. 49 (note).

[23] *Annales*, 1867, I, 3.

ernment's public statements were not in accord with its actions. Sadowa was followed almost immediately by the consideration of a plan for the reorganization of the army modeled upon the Prussian system of universal service.[24] In May, 1867, the Luxemburg crisis revealed fully, for the first time, the government's fruitless efforts to secure compensations for changes which it had identified as entirely satisfactory. Public opinion would doubtless have approved a substantial extension of French territory if it had been secured without trouble,[25] but it was not in favor of war as a means of attaining it.[26] Although from the theory of the threefold division of Germany it was evident that the government wished to limit the extension of Prussia's influence to the Main River [27] (as is now known from the secret negotiations with Austria and Italy [28]), the implicit contradictions in the government's attitude inspired a growing suspicion that it had no clearly defined policy either of peace in accepting the prospect of German unity or of resistance to this prospect at the price of war.

The absence of coherent leadership from official sources encouraged the development of a variety of opinions as to the proper policy. For five days, March 14–18, 1867, the problem was debated in the *Corps Législatif*. Several speakers believed that the existing situation should be accepted, and others implied that France should not resist the further development of German unity. If Rouher obstinately repeated the official theory of the threefold division of Germany, Granier de Cassagnac, the imperialist editor of the *Pays,* declared that Prussia's victories could not be condemned without repudiating those of France in her struggle for unity. "I see only one policy," affirmed Émile Ollivier, a recent convert to the cause of a liberal empire, "that is worthy and wise, and that is to accept a situation which . . . is not directed against us." But Thiers again defended France's traditional policy in a speech which was, by all odds,

[24] Pierre de la Gorce, *Histoire du Second Empire,* 6 vols. (Paris, 1900) (13th ed.), V, 317–346.

[25] Archives Nationales, F1c- III Haute-Garonne 9, July 6, Aug. 6, 1866; Haut-Rhin 7, Aug. 1, Sept. 1, 1866; Bas-Rhin 8, Sept. 4, 1866; Meurthe 8, Oct. 5, 1866; Côte d'Ör 7, June 4, 1866. *Temps,* Aug. 14, 15, 1866. A. de Calonne, *La Politique de la France dans les Affaires de l'Allemagne et de l'Italie* (Paris, 1866), p. 16.

[26] *Temps,* May 4, 1867, Aug. 30, 1868. A. de Calonne, *La Politique de la France,* pp. 16, 17. Cf. *Amer. Hist. Rev.,* XXXI (4), p. 681.

[27] *Temps,* Sept. 20, 1868.

[28] Oncken, *Die Rheinpolitik Napoleons III,* III, 65–219.

the ablest and the most influential. French policy, he said, had never been successful except in supporting the balance of power based upon the division of the German people. In his opinion, the peace of Europe and the interests of France were threatened by the Empire's support of nationalism. *"Pour l'Europe, c'est le chaos; pour la France, c'est la troisième rang."* But war, he declared, would be the one mistake which the Empire had not yet made.[29]

On March 19, the day after the conclusion of this discussion, the press announced the existence of offensive and defensive alliances between Prussia and the South German States.[30] Perhaps no single event between Sadowa and the crisis of July, 1870, had a comparable effect upon public opinion. "It has been interpreted," wrote a publicist who accepted the prospect of German unity, "as a challenge to France . . . and as a confirmation of M. Thiers's gloomy predictions."[31] Prussia had obviously crossed the Main, and it was not long before other indications pointed to the tightening of the bonds between Prussia and the South German States. Concern for the security of France greatly increased,[32] and some of the newspapers which had formerly urged an alliance with Prussia began to clamor for war.[33] Even the opposition parties, partly to score a political success, represented Sadowa as the equivalent of a French defeat. They capitalized the increasing discontent with the official policy as a bond of union between such widely separated groups as the Monarchists and the Republicans. It was a dangerous practice, for it could be interpreted as pressure in favor of an aggressive policy.[34] In fact, the Liberal Union, the misleading name adopted by the opposition parties, was bitterly hostile to a war for the purpose of retrieving the government's blunders. It caused the delay of the proposed mili-

---

[29] *Annales,* 1867, II, 148–169, 191–277.

[30] These treaties were printed by the *Staats-Anzeiger* (Berlin), March 19, and the *Bayerische Zeitung* (Munich), March 19. Bismarck had foreseen that this announcement would arouse a furor in France. Bismarck to Goltz, Berlin, Mar. 15, 1867. Oncken, *Die Rheinpolitik Napoleons III,* III, 248. G. Halévy, *Le Courrier de M. Thiers,* p. 376.

[31] *Revue Contemporaine,* vol. 91, p. 371.

[32] Duc de Broglie, "Le Corps Législatif, le Mexique et la Prusse," *Corresp.,* O. S., vol. 75, p. 728.

[33] The following newspapers and editors, who were the most eager for war, were closely associated with the Court: B. A. and Granier de Cassagnac, the *Pays;* Clément Duvernois, the *Peuple Français,* and Émile de Girardin, the *Liberté.* Cf. *Amer. Hist. Rev.,* XXXI (4), p. 680.

[34] Marquis de Gricourt, *Les Relations de la France avec l'Allemagne.* (Brussels, 1870), p. 32.

tary reforms and their eventual revision. In the provinces, the unpopularity of these changes among the peasants and middle classes was exploited against the Empire. A considerable section of the opposition believed, however, that German unity was inevitable. France, according to an anonymous pamphleteer, should pronounce "the final word for peace by a sincere, complete and sympathetic acceptance of the changes already made or about to be made in Germany in all that concerns her internal organization." [35] It was the war party in the press, not the opposition newspapers, which raised the cry of "Revenge for Sadowa," and which urged the acquisition of the Rhine as France's natural frontier.

The details of these problems were, of course, unknown to the peasants who constituted a large majority of the nation. In some departments the rate of illiteracy exceeded 50 per cent, and such schools as existed for the masses scarcely taught more than the fundamentals.[36] Nor was the provincial press an adequate substitute for formal instruction, since it was to a large extent under government influence. Even the peasants whose interests were normally limited to their immediate commune, were gradually affected by the general feeling of uncertainty, and the opposition skilfully exploited their dislike of universal military service, as well as the fears aroused by the persistent rumors of war.[37] Manufacturers and merchants were more immediately affected by the chronic economic depression after 1867 caused by the prevailing sense of insecurity. A few prefects, but only a few, reported that even war was preferred to a prolonged crisis with its limited investments, restricted production and unemployment. From the department of Vaucluse came the report in August, 1867, that "the stagnation of business is as serious as ever. . . . War is believed to be inevitable, and an immediate conflagration would be preferred to an indefinite period of waiting." [38]

[35] *Napoléon III et l'Europe en 1867* (Paris, 1867). The Prussian ambassador reported, Mar. 23, 1867, that many believed it to be too late to oppose German unity. Oncken, *Die Rheinpolitik Napoleons III*, II, 257.

[36] Charles Douniol, "De l'Instruction Primaire en France," *Corresp.*, O. S., vol. 78, pp. 623, 624.

[37] Archives Nationales, F1c. III Puv-de-Dôme 7. Oct. 31, 1866; Rhône 5, Dec. 15, 1866; Haut-Rhin 7, Nov. 30, 1866; Feb. 4, 1868; Vaucluse 6, May, 1867; Haute-Garonne 9, Jan. 8, 1868. Claveaux, *Souvenirs Politiques*, I, 205. G. Isambert, P. Coffenhal-Laprade. *La Loi Militaire de 1868 expliquée par Demandes et par Résponses (Catéchismes des Familles)* (Paris, 1868). There were at least ten printings of this pamphlet in 1868.

[38] Archives Nationales, F1c. III Vaucluse 6. Cf. Seine-Inférieure 9, Apr. 30, 1867; Rhone 5, April, 1867; Bas-Rhin 8, Mar. 6, May 5, 1868. A delegation of

The fear of an inevitable war gradually prepared public opinion to accept it without effective protest, and the government was assured that if the Emperor decided that war was necessary, his decision would be approved.[39] But the acceptance of a conflict as inevitable testified to the docile character of public opinion rather than to a desire of war. "Public opinion," declared the *Temps* a liberal opposition newspaper (Jan. 24, 1868), "remains convinced that the government harbors secret purposes in spite of its assurances of peace. . . . The country fears war because it feels that the government has committed grave faults, that it has need of *une grande revanche*." At least until 1870, no incident created a passion for war. Chauvinists became excited by Bismarck's alleged duplicity during the Luxemburg crisis, and by the development of Prussia's influence, but the nation in general saw no reason to go to war because of political changes in Germany. The war party, however, was not discouraged by these pacific tendencies. "The press is moderate," wrote Émile de Girardin, the veteran journalist, in the *Liberté* (July 20, 1868), "the trend of opinion is pacific. But in 1859 public opinion was also opposed to war . . . and a moment sufficed for opinion to favor it. It will be the same again." [40]

II

The attention of public opinion was concentrated almost exclusively upon domestic politics for more than a year before the July crisis of 1870. There seemed to be no justification for alarm as to the Empire's security at home. The gains won by the opposition in the elections of May, 1869, were not sufficient to weaken seriously its disciplined majority in parliament, and the Empire's victory in the plebiscite of the following spring (May 8, 1870) apparently adjourned the hopes of its enemies to the distant future. Nevertheless, the partisans of the Empire, and especially the Empress Eugénie, who was concerned for the succession of the Prince Imperial, were not entirely satisfied. The government had no defenders who could

French merchants to a Commercial Congress meeting in Egypt (1869) expressed this point of view. Robert von Kendell, *Fürst und Fürsten Bismarck, Erinnerungen aus den Jahren 1846 bis 1872* (Berlin, 1901), p. 419.

[39] *Ibid.*, Fle. III Loire-Infèrieure 8, Apr. 9, 1867; Rhône 5, Apr. 26, 1867; Gironde 6, May 5, 1867; Sarthe 7, May 5, 1867; Haute Garonne 9, May 6, 1867; Côtes-du-Nord II, May 28, 1867.

[40] É. de Girardin, *La Guerre Fatale Prévue et Annoncée en 1868* (Paris, 1870), pp. 41, 42.

approach Thiers and Gambetta in political genius, nor could it count upon the services of a propagandist like Rochefort. Every test of strength since the parliamentary election of 1863 had demonstrated the opposition's control of Paris and most of the larger cities, while the passive rural population, for which the Napoleonic legend no longer had any attraction,[41] continued to give its support to the Empire in preference to a possible revolution. By 1870, measures were being considered for the purpose of persuading the peasants that their interests would be protected under the Republic.[42] Some had anticipated that the Empire's success in the plebiscite would encourage the government to adopt an aggressive policy,[43] but there was no clear evidence known to the public as to a definite plan for this purpose. The appointment of the Ollivier ministry in January, 1870, was not, however, an endorsement of his earlier support of German unity, for the Emperor described him to the Austrian Ambassador, Prince Metternich, as incapable in foreign affairs, and for this reason he had not been permitted to take permanent charge of this department.[44] Gramont's appointment as Minister of Foreign Affairs after the plebiscite was a more serious indication of an aggressive policy. It was understood to be an endorsement of his anti-Prussian activities while ambassador in Vienna,[45] and he was scarcely installed in office before he informed Prussia that there must be no thought of crossing the Main River if good relations were to continue between the two countries.[46]

It is by no means certain that war would have come over a question relating directly to the political situation in Germany, for it would have been difficult to arouse sentiment in France in support of a direct intervention in the affairs of another people. Bismarck furnished an occasion, in his encouragement of the candidature of Prince Leopold of Hohenzollern-Sigmaringen for the Spanish throne, for a quarrel that would not be immediately connected with the question of German unity. This occasion was not prepared in

[41] *Progrès de la Côte d'Ôr* (Dijon), May 27, 1870.

[42] Léopold de Gaillard, *La Léçon du Plébiscite* (Paris, 1870), pp. 15, 16, *Mémorial des Deux Sèvres* (Niort), June 17, 1870.

[43] *Mémorial des Deux Sèvres* (Niort), May 21, 1870.

[44] Metternich to Beust, Paris, Nov. 25, 1869. Oncken, *Die Rheinpolitik Napoleons III*, III, 266.

[45] Duc de Broglie, "Mémoires—La Fin de l'Empire," *Rev. des Deux Mondes*, 1929, I. 201.

[46] Werther to Bismarck, Paris, July 1, 1870. Oncken, *Die Rheinpolitik Napoleons III*, III, 384, 385.

complete secrecy, as has often been said, for it had been noted by several newspapers as early as 1868 [47] and by the *Journal des Débats* as late as June 17, 1870. Benedetti, the French ambassador to Prussia, had also called it to the attention of his government.[48] However, until Leopold's acceptance, it was only one of several candidatures, and it was doubtless in good faith that Ollivier assured the Chamber on June 30 that not a cloud threatened the peace of Europe.[49] Parliament's decision to reduce the number of annual recruits to be called to the colors in 1870 was another indication that the government was not planning aggressive action.[50] The government and public opinion were both surprised by the announcement in the press, July 3, that Leopold had accepted the invitation of the Spanish parliament to become the King of Spain. Twelve days later, war was virtually declared against Prussia.

This study is not concerned with the question of the ultimate responsibility for the war, but it is necessary to deal in some detail with the rôle of public opinion during the crisis. In France, diametrically opposed views have been expressed upon this question. Officials of the Empire attempted to shift the responsibility to the nation, while the leaders of the opposition as eagerly attributed it to the government. The tendency among historians under the Third Republic has been to accept the latter point of view,[51] but one of the latest to discuss this problem insists that public opinion was the determining factor.[52] The present writer ventures to differ. If the evidence is examined impartially, it becomes clear that the government called upon the nation to resent the alleged insult and aggression in the Hohenzollern candidature, that the response was not nearly so unanimous as it has been supposed, that Bismarck's version of the Ems despatch was not primarily responsible for the excitement along the boulevards of Paris, July 14–15, and that the government did not use the text of this famous document to secure a

---

[47] Henry Salomon, *L'Incident Hohenzollern* (Paris, 1922), p. 24.
[48] Comte Vincent de Benedetti, *Ma Mission en Prusse* (Paris, 1871), pp. 302–304.
[49] *Annales*, 1870, V, 311.
[50] *Ibid.*
[51] For bibliographical references, see *Amer. Hist. Rev.*, XXXI (4), p. 679, notes 2, 3. Numerous references to the need of giving satisfaction to public opinion appear in Gramont's despatches to Benedetti during the crisis. Duc de Gramont, *La France et la Prusse avant la Guerre* (Paris, 1872), pp. 74, 80, 131, 132, 189, 190. Léon de Montesquiou, *1870—Les Causes Politiques du Désastre* (Paris, 1916), pp. 152–159.
[52] Bourgeois, *Manuel Historique*, III, 717, 718.

declaration of war from parliament, or to justify its action to public opinion.

The news of Leopold's acceptance caused much excited talk of a possible restoration of the empire of Charles V, but public opinion as reflected by the press did not immediately see in it a danger of war. Returning from the country on the evening of July 3, Ollivier found a note on his desk from Gramont: "Beginning tomorrow, we will commence a *prudent* but efficacious campaign in the Press." [53] The results of that campaign are to be found in the *Constitutionnel* (July 4), which first expressed moderate irritation and which later (July 6) announced the government's determination to oppose the candidature, and in a group of newspapers which later were to demand war. As if to give a free hand to the government, the latter declared that the necessity of consulting the Spanish parliament would permit a peaceful solution of the crisis by the usual diplomatic methods, intervention by France alone or in coöperation with other Powers.[54] It was even pointed out that the Spanish people might make any action by France unnecessary by refusing to accept Leopold as their king.[55] The majority of the opposition press at once declared in favor of neutrality and for a peaceful arrangement, but individual newspapers made use of the occasion for another attack upon the government.[56] The republican *Phare de la Loire* of Nantes (July 5) declared that the Empire was about to suffer the most bitter of its humiliations, and the liberal *Progrès* of Lyons (July 7) arraigned the Empire's entire foreign policy. Napoleon's support of nationalism, declared the clerical *Univers* (July 7), would prevent any effective measures against the impending danger to France. An imperialist journal, but a bitter critic of the Ollivier ministry, the

[53] Ollivier, *L'Empire Libéral*, XIV, 27.

[54] *Pays*, July 5; *France*, July 6. *Presse*, July 6. It was not known in Paris until July 7 that the *Cortes* was to meet July 30. R. H. Lord, *The Origins of the War of 1870* (Cambridge, 1924), p. 46.

[55] *Liberté*, July 5. Several of the newspapers which at once discounted the fear that the government would not be equal to the occasion had received money from the government. *Les Petits Papiers Secrets des Tuileries et de Saint Cloud, étiquetés par un Collectionneur* (Brussels, 1870), p. 38.

[56] *Temps*, July 6; *Journal des Débats*, July 6. *Siècle*, July 5, 6. *Presse*, July 5. *Français*, July 7. "The truth is . . . ," Émile de Girardin, editor of the *Liberté*, wrote later (*République Française* February 6, 1878), "that in July, 1870, it required all of the influence of M. Chevandier de Valdrôme, then Minister of the Interior, to persuade the political press of Paris to give any importance to the choice of the Prince of Hohenzollern by Spain and to declare against it." Girardin, nevertheless, was one of the more ardent advocates of war in 1870.

Public (July 6), agreed that the government's faults should not be remedied by war.

"A declaration of war against Prussia? That would be monstrous . . . public opinion should not be incited to hatred and rage against the instigators of the Hohenzollern project: they have merely done their duty . . . It is from our constitutional ministers that we should demand an accounting." [57]

Although convinced that a day of reckoning with Prussia was inevitable,[58] Thiers was equally certain that France should wait until Prussia assumed the aggressive by an overt act. He therefore inspired a colleague of the opposition to interpellate the government, July 5, in order to introduce the check of parliamentary control.[59] The council of ministers met with the Emperor the next morning with the determination, as Gramont told the Austrian ambassador, to resist the Hohenzollern candidature "even at the cost of war." [60] After the council had listened to optimistic reports as to the condition of the army and of the international situation, a declaration was prepared which precipitated a crisis with Prussia. It committed the nation to a policy from which retreat was difficult, if not impossible, without a diplomatic defeat. As read by Gramont to the *Corps Législatif*, July 6, amid the frantic applause of the majority and the consternation of the opposition, the declaration expressed a hope that the "friendship of the Spanish and the wisdom of the German people" would remove the danger to the interests and honor of France. "But should it be otherwise," it concluded, "strong in your support and in that of the nation, we should know how to do our duty without

[57] The Belgian ambassador, however, reported, July 5, that public opinion was in advance of the government. Baron Beyens, *Le Second Empire,* 2 vols. (Paris, 1924–1926), II, 421, 422. Later events changed this opinion, for he wrote after the declaration of war, July 15, that the nation had been led into war. *Ibid.,* II, 444, 445.

[58] For material as to Thiers's attitude, see Pierre Lehautcourt (General Palat), *Les Origines de la Guerre de 1870* (Paris, 1912), pp. 642–648. Halévy, *Courrier de M. Thiers,* p. 410.

[59] Thiers did not explain his motives in his testimony before the parliamentary investigating committee after the war. *Enquête Parlementaire sur les Actes du Gouvernement de la Défense Nationale* (1872), I. Déposition de M. Thiers, p. 6. Cochery, however, later explained his interpellation by the reason given above. *Annales de la Chambre des Députés,* 1878, VI, 223, 224.

[60] Metternich to Beust, Paris, July 8, 1870. Oncken, *Die Rheinpolitik Napoleons III,* III, 846. Metternich's reports dealing with the attitude of leaders of the French government at this time were first published by H. Temperley, "Three Despatches of Prince Metternich on the Origins of the War of 1870," *English Historical Review,* XXXVIII, 93, 94.

hesitation and without weakness." Only the years of humiliating inaction since Sadowa explain the exaltation of the leaders who were responsible for this declaration. "We have had enough humiliations at the hands of Prussia," Ollivier exclaimed. "No more hesitation, no more wavering, the council is unanimous . . . we have won the Chamber, and we will win the nation."[61] The Emperor spoke of the crisis as "notre affaire,"[62] and Eugénie is reported to have expressed the hope that "Prussia will not give in."[63]

Its position defined, the government refused to permit a discussion in the Chamber, although the opposition condemned Gramont's statement as a virtual declaration of war.[64] It is unlikely, in view of the steps immediately taken to secure the intervention of the other Powers for the withdrawal of Leopold's acceptance, that even Gramont was determined at this time upon war at any price. He assured Lyons, the British ambassador, that he would be satisfied by this conclusion of the crisis,[65] but events were to show that he, in contrast to Ollivier, was determined to achieve a diplomatic victory rather than merely Leopold's withdrawal.

The declaration was not only a challenge to Prussia, it was also an appeal to public opinion for its support in an effort to secure a diplomatic victory, or, if necessary, for war. "It was a preparation for an attack," wrote Ollivier many years later, "and not the first blow; it was not a signal gun for the beginning of a battle, but an alarm calling for aid."[66] It was so interpreted by the press. "The word of France has been publicly given," declared the liberal Catholic Français (July 8), "it must be kept; her honor has been engaged, it must be defended; her flag has been unfurled, we must rally to it."

"It was war that dominated the debate," affirmed the chauvinist Presse (July 8). "The government's resolutions are so formal . . . that it may be said; we have no control over the future. We have bound our will, our honor . . . to an ultimatum which we will be enable to withdraw without shame. . . ."

[61] Metternich to Beust, Paris, July 8. Oncken, op. cit., III, 402, 403. "What a page in history will be mine!" Ollivier is said to have exclaimed to a friend. "The plebiscite, war, and then the crown which I shall myself place on the head of the imperial child." Henri Welschinger in the Journal des Débats, Aug. 23, 1913.

[62] Metternich to Beust, Paris, July 8. Oncken, op. cit., III, 400.

[63] Metternich to Beust, Paris, July 7. Oncken, op. cit., III, 396.

[64] Annales, 1870, V, 449.

[65] Lyons to Granville, Paris, July 9, 1870. British and Foreign State Papers, 1869–1870, LX (London, 1876), p. 799.

[66] Ollivier, L'Empire Libéral, XIV, iii.

The *Public* (July 8) likewise abandoned its criticism of the Ollivier ministry on the ground that the issue was no longer concerned with its mistakes. "The question is higher: the dignity of France is engaged, and that is all we see." Throwing aside all restraint, the chauvinists declared that the probable withdrawal of the Hohenzollern candidature would not be an adequate satisfaction for the grievances that had been accumulating against Prussia during the preceding four years.[67] Their agitation, however, affected only the less solid elements of the nation, for reports began to arrive from the prefects on July 9 testifying to a general desire of peace.[68] Even in Paris, according to the correspondent of the London *Times* (July 9), the war party was noisy out of all proportion to its numbers. The great majority of the people, he wrote, would be satisfied if "Prussia caves in and Leopold is withdrawn." The opposition in the press and in parliament of course refused to be stampeded by Gramont's declaration.[69]

When Benedetti, on urgent instructions from Paris, attempted to secure a definite statement from the King of Prussia directing Prince Leopold to withdraw,[70] he was told that the question was a family matter that did not concern the Prussian sovereign. William, however, was unwilling to furnish the occasion for a war which he did not desire, and in order to avoid it, without publicly yielding to France's demands, he sent a confidential agent to Sigmaringen with the advice that Leopold's name should be withdrawn.[71] On July 12, Prince Anthony, Leopold's father, wired Madrid and the Spanish ambassador in Paris that his son's name was withdrawn. The reactions of the French ministry to this substantial victory were to throw a flood of light upon their real purpose. Without consulting his colleagues, Ollivier at once declared in the lobbies of parliament that the crisis was at an end. Gramont, however, was not satisfied, for he had failed to secure definite proof that William had yielded at his command. In consultation with Werther, the Prussian ambassador, when he heard the news from Sigmaringen, he at once sketched a

[67] *Amer. His. Rev.*, XXXI (4), 687.
[68] Jules Pointu, *Histoire de la Chute de l'Empire* . . . (Paris, 1874), pp. 61, 62. These reports were analyzed in the *Journal Officiel*, Oct. 20, 1870. Eighteen departments were reported as desiring war, fifty-three as asking for peace, and the remainder as hesitating. With rare exceptions these reports are not now in the cartons of the Archives Nationales.
[69] *Amer. Hist. Rev.*, XXXI (4), pp. 688, 689.
[70] Benedetti, *Ma Mission en Prusse*, pp. 331, 341, 349, 352.
[71] Lord, *Origins of the War of 1870*, pp. 56, 65.

note of apology which he proposed to have the Prussian King sign.[72] Rumors current in Berlin that France would not be satisfied with Leopold's renunciation certainly influenced Bismarck that evening,[73] but Werther's report of this incident did not arrive at Ems in time to influence the King's attitude during his historic interview with Benedetti on the morning of July 13.[74] In the meantime, Gramont had changed his tactics, and with Napoleon's approval, although Ollivier was not consulted until the new instructions had been sent,[75] he informed Benedetti that he should insist upon a promise that Leopold would never again become a candidate for the Spanish throne. If Gramont's decision had any relation to public opinion, it was merely in anticipation of its eventual reactions, for the demand for guarantees was sent only a few hours after the arrival in Paris of Leopold's renunciation. During the next two days, the chauvinist press denounced this event as the work of *"le père Antoine,"* as *"un succès dérisoire,"* and the ministry which would accept it as the *"ministère de la honte,"* but a majority of the Paris newspapers, including at least two which had formerly stood for war, advised the government to be satisfied.[76]

"The truth is," Gramont declared later, "that after the refusal of our first demands we formulated others." [77] It is scarcely possible that Gramont seriously expected the King to yield after he had refused the less drastic demand. The story of the interview between the King and Benedetti on the promenade at Ems, July 13, of William's firm but courteous refusal of the demand for guarantees, of the famous dinner at Berlin that evening when Bismarck, to the joy of Moltke and Roon, abbreviated the despatch from Ems in order to make it appear that a sharp break had occurred between the two

---

[72] Ollivier, *L'Empire Libéral,* XIV, 245, 246. Gramont, *La France et la Prusse,* p. 122.

[73] Stern, *Geschichte Europas,* X (1924), 341–342. According to Stern, Bismarck heard from the Russian ambassador at Berlin that France would not be satisfied with Leopold's renunciation. Lord contends, however, that Bismarck was not informed of Gramont's new demand until midnight of July 13. Lord, *Origins of the War of 1870,* p. 81. Stern doubtless refers to Oubril's communication in which France was represented as about to present additional demands.

[74] Lord, *Origins of the War of 1870,* p. 81. Stern anticipated Lord's conclusions on this latter point. Stern, *op. cit.,* X, 341.

[75] P. Murat, "Émile Ollivier et le Duc de Gramont les 12 et 13 Juillet 1870," *Revue d'Histoire Moderne et Contemporaine,* XIV, 181.

[76] *Amer. Hist. Rev.,* XXXI, 690, note 67.

[77] *Enquête Parlementaire, I. Déposition de M. Gramont,* pp. 100, 101.

protagonists, of the communication of his version to the press and to Prussia's diplomatic representatives need not be repeated here. The decisive importance usually attributed to this document in arousing a passion for war in the Paris press and in securing a majority for war in the French parliament requires careful attention to its reception in Paris. When Gramont received a copy of the famous extra-edition of the *Norddeutsche Allgemeine Zeitung* (July 13) on the morning of July 14, he told Ollivier: "I have just received an insult." [78] Nevertheless, during the afternoon of the same day, the ministry decided to call a congress of the Powers, and Ollivier was commissioned to prepare a statement announcing this decision for peace to parliament.[79] A new meeting, unfortunately, was summoned late that evening at St. Cloud where it was then decided to order the mobilization of the army and to ask parliament for a virtual declaration of war.

Those who attribute this sudden change of policy to the Ems despatch and to the pressure of public opinion are able to marshal apparently impressive evidence in support of this conclusion. Lyons reported that the wire from Berlin had turned the government toward war.[80] "Public opinion," according to Metternich, "is beginning to weigh upon the government to the point that peace appears henceforth to be impossible." [81] But the Austrian ambassador was no friend of peace, and he expressed this opinion before the Ems despatch appeared in the evening newspapers. Ollivier makes a great deal of the *Soir*'s violent reaction in his vindication, without pointing out that it was perhaps the one newspaper on the evening of July 14 to declare specifically that France had been insulted.[82] Moreover, it had been urging war for several days,[83] and it was the last newspaper to appear that evening upon the boulevards. "A public affront," it declared, "has been given our ambassador. There is no Frenchman who will not resent this injury." The *Times*'s correspondent (July 14) thought that the alleged affront was doubtful and at any rate, not very serious, but he reported that "the thousands who read the

[78] Ollivier, *L'Empire Libéral*, XIV, 355.
[79] La Gorce, *Histoire du Second Empire*, VI, 292, 293.
[80] *British and Foreign State Papers*, LX, 835.
[81] Metternich to Beust, Paris, July 14. Oncken, *Die Rheinpolitik Napoleons III*, III, 437.
[82] Ollivier, *L'Empire Liberal*, XIV, 368.
[83] *Soir*, July 10.

paper tonight were prepared to accept the *Soir's* views, and true or false the story has done incalculable mischief." Crowds thronged the boulevards shouting "À Berlin!"

This evidence may be accepted if it is not interpreted as explaining the action of the ministry that night at St. Cloud. Even Ollivier, whose apology is chiefly based upon the alleged pressure of public opinion, never argued that the street demonstrations changed his point of view between the afternoon and evening meetings of the ministry. He attributed it to the unfavorable reaction of his family circle when he read his statement announcing the decision to call a congress. This was, he writes, a sufficient test of public opinion! [84] Many contemporary witnesses, and they included foreign observers as well as members of the opposition, were convinced that the demonstrations were inspired by government agents, for they saw evidence of concerted action on the part of the leaders.[85] The police remained neutral until after the declaration of war, and the Emperor personally authorized the singing of the *Marseillaise* at the Opera, although it had been forbidden since 1852.[86] A rumor was abroad on the night of July 14–15 that France had been insulted, but the supposed insult was not definitely associated with the Ems despatch. That document was amended as it appeared in several newspapers by a second paragraph which moderated the effect it might otherwise have had. "According to other information from Ems," it declared, "the King informed Benedetti that he had approved his cousin's renunciation and that henceforth he considered that every occasion for conflict had been eliminated." [87] It is probable that this statement was added in Paris after the ministry had decided that afternoon to call a con-

[84] Ollivier, *L'Empire Liberal*, XIV, 386.

[85] *Réveil*, July 16. *Progrès* (Lyon), July 17. *Morning Post* (London), July 18. Jules Simon, *Souvenirs du Quatre-Septembre et Chute du Second Empire* (Paris, 1874), p. 174. Garnier-Pagès, *L'Opposition et l'Empire* (Paris, 1872), pp. 137, 138. L. Drapeyron-Séligmann, *Les Deux Folies de Paris, Juillet 1870, Mars, 1871* (Paris, 1872), p. 20.

[86] Ollivier, *L'Empire Libéral*, XIV, 286. Thiers later declared that the mass of the population did not approve these demonstrations, *Enquête Parlementaire*, I. 9.

[87] *Patrie, Liberté, Univers, Journal des Débats*, July 14. France, July 15. I have found a reference to the publication of the Ems despatch in this form in only two books dealing with the origins of the War of 1870. Alfred Darimon, *Notes pour servir a l'Histoire de la Guerre de 1870* (Paris, 1888), p. 3. It also appears in the same author's *Histoire d'un Jour. La Journée du 12 Juillet 1870* (Paris, 1888), pp. 175, 176. The second paragraph is here explained either as an attempt to moderate the effect of the first or as that part of the original despatch from Ems which Bismarck had eliminated.

gress of the Powers.[88] The apparent contradiction between the two paragraphs was noted by the press, and some observed that this uncertainty as to its meaning required an official confirmation of the alleged insult.[89] When the *Mémorial Diplomatique* appeared on the afternoon of the next day, it declared that this confirmation had not yet been received. The conclusion is therefore warranted that the Ems despatch had little or no influence upon the ministry's decision for war at St. Cloud. It was rather the result of pressure by the war party, supported by Eugénie,[90] with the possibly decisive aid of a wire from the inexperienced French ambassador in Vienna representing Austria as prepared to join France.[91] A plausible justification for this drastic decision was furnished by reports of Bismarck's communication to the European courts, which had arrived from French agents in southern Germany and Switzerland.

Ollivier based his case upon these reports when he asked the *Corps Législatif* on the afternoon of July 15 for its approval of a war policy, but he said nothing of the Ems despatch as it had appeared in the press.[92] The majority received this statement with enthusiasm, but Thiers, Gambetta, Jules Favre, and other leaders of the opposition denied that it justified war. They demanded that the alleged insulting circular should be read, and Ollivier at length read a report from an unnamed South German court containing the text of the Ems despatch as it had appeared in the press, but without the second paragraph which had probably been added in Paris. It was not identified, however, either as the incriminating circular or as an insult to

---

[88] The first paragraph, which is the document known to history, is distinguished by quotes from the second as it appears in the *Journal des Débats,* July 15. The second part does not appear in the *Indépendance Belge* (Brussels), July 15.

[89] *France, Liberté, Patrie, Journal des Débats.*

[90] Marie Thérèse Ollivier, "L'Épouse de l'Empereur," *Revue de Genève,* Feb., 1921, p. 179.

[91] Bourgeois, *Manuel Historique,* III, 716. The facilities enjoyed by Professor Bourgeois in the use of the archives of the Quai d'Orsay give much weight to his opinion on this point. The Belgian ambassador reported that Austria's friendly assurances influenced the decision for war. Beyens, *Le Second Empire,* II, 445.

[92] We have the testimony of Darimon, one of the original members of the parliamentary opposition, that members of the ministry, including Ollivier, were not aware of the publication of the despatch by the Paris press. Alfred Darimon, *Histoire d'un Parti. Les Cent Seize et le Ministère du 2 janvier (1869–1870)* (Paris, 1889), pp. 400–403. Darimon, *L'Agonie de l'Empire . . .* (Paris, 1891), p. 113. For a criticism of Darimon's credibility, see Ollivier, *L'Empire Libéral,* XIV, 233, 244 (note). Cf. *Amer. Hist. Rev.,* XXXI (4), note 2.

France. The opposition continued to call for the circular, assuming, with the government's tacit approval, that the ministry had in its possession a more serious document. After more than eighty members had voted in favor of its communication, Ollivier agreed that the ministry would submit all of the facts in its possession to a committee. No record has survived of this committee's proceedings,[93] but it is known that Gramont misrepresented the government's policy by asserting that its demands had not varied from the beginning of the crisis. Talhouët, its reporter, later testified that Bismarck's circular was known only as it appeared in the report read to the Chamber, and he added, "we were told that the government was disposed to keep the peace if a newspaper article had alone been in question." [94] The committee, nevertheless, affirmed its complete satisfaction with the government's case when the Chamber met again that evening. The opposition continued to call for the circular until the decisive vote was taken, when only ten members refused to approve war.[95]

The reports of these stormy sessions show that Ollivier, perhaps as a result of the form in which the Ems despatch had appeared in the press, gave the impression that Bismarck's communication to the European courts was a much more serious document. Opposition newspapers continued to call for its publication after the declaration of war, arguing that every cause for secrecy had disappeared.[96] A statement claiming to describe its substance was in fact given to the Havas, Wolff, and Reuter news agencies which served the French, German, and British presses respectively, sometime during July 15. "The government announced," according to this document as it appeared in the *Times* (July 16), "that this declaration [of war] is precipitated by the circular of the King to the Prussian agents abroad, which firstly confirms the affront to M. Benedetti, secondly refuses to guarantee the renunciation of Prince Leopold, and thirdly restores to him his liberty to accept the throne of Spain." [97] Of more

[93] Comte É. de Kératry, *Petits Mémoires* (Paris, 1898), p. 159. Kératry was a member of the committee.

[94] *Enquête Parlementaire*, I, 4.

[95] *Annales*, 1870, VI, 68–99. Benedetti, who was in the diplomatic gallery, was not called upon to testify. A. Sorel, *Histoire Diplomatique de la Guerre Franco-Allemande,* 2 vols. (Paris, 1875), I, 186.

[96] *Siècle,* July 17.

[97] *Journal de Marseille,* July 16. *Progrès* (Lyons), July 17. *Indépendance Belge* (Brussels), *Kölnische Zeitung, Daily Telegraph, Daily News, Morning Post,* July 16. (The last three were London newspapers.) This document, identified as a Wolff despatch, is among the documents from the Berlin archives in Lord, *Origins of the War of 1870,* p. 256. There is sufficient resemblance be-

than a score of Paris newspapers examined, only the *Peuple Fran-çais* (July 15), whose editor, Clément Duvernois, had been responsible for an inflammatory interpellation on July 13,[98] printed the essential point of this statement. "King William," it declared, "affirms in this document, which is without precedent in the annals of diplomacy, that . . . he withdraws his former declarations, and that he authorizes the Hohenzollern prince to accept the throne of Spain." The circular, in fact, differed in no essential respect from the Ems despatch as it had appeared in the press,[99] and the government had no reason to believe that it did. An attempt had therefore been made to justify war by a distortion of Bismarck's own version of the original wire from the King's secretary at Ems.

III

After war had been declared, little was said of an insult either in connection with the Ems despatch or with Bismarck's circular. Chauvinists admitted that France had struck the first blow in order to gain the advantage in military preparations.[100] Public opinion had not desired war, but it was accepted, once declared, as inevitable.[101] Even the most advanced radicals yielded to none in their zeal for victory.[102] The fortune of arms, turning against France, prevented a public announcement of the government's war-aims, but it is improbable that any effective opposition could have been made to its plans for dismembering Prussia.[103] The attempt to conceal the news of the first defeats gave new strength to the opposition. The Empire fell with scarcely any resistance, September 4, after the news of Sedan with the capture of Napoleon and of France's last organized army.

tween this communication to the press and Gramont's own comments in a letter to the French minister at Munich on July 14 to suggest the possibility of his connection with it. ". . . Sa majesté," he wrote, "non seulement a repoussé cette démarche d'une manière absolue, mais Elle a témoigné qu' Elle entendait se réserver pour toutes les circonstances sa liberté d'action . . ." Gramont to Cadore, Paris, July 14, 1870. Oncken, *Die Rheinpolitik Napoleons III*, III, 438, 439.

[98] In June, 1870, Duvernois was excused from repaying certain advances from the government in return for "the excellent services which you have rendered in this journal." Conti to Duvernois, Palais des Tuileries, June 20, 1870. *Les Petits Papiers Secrets*, pp. 58, 59.

[99] Lord, *Origins of the War of 1870*, pp. 231–233.

[100] *Opinion Nationale*, July 17.

[101] *Indépendance Belge* (Brussels), July 18.

[102] *Réveil*, July 16, 17, 20. *Progrès* (Lyons), Aug. 10.

[103] Oncken, *Die Rheinpolitik Napoleons III*, III, 526–528.

Later public opinion was even more profoundly influenced by the second period of the war, which began with the organization of the Government of National Defense, than by the first. More clearly than before, the war became a life-and-death struggle for national existence. Tragic memories were left by the siege and bombardment of Paris, and the bitterness caused by the terms of peace was intensified by the sufferings of the civilian population.[104] The continuation of the war after Sedan was therefore of great consequence in view of the later development of public opinion. After the conclusion of peace, Bonapartists charged that the Government of National Defense had prolonged the war in order to establish the Republic upon firm foundations.[105] This political consideration was not without influence upon republican leaders, like Gambetta, who felt that it would be fatal to begin with a shameful defeat; but at the moment, leaders of every party favored a war of desperation to prevent the cession of French territory. On September 3, Marshal Palikao, on behalf of the Imperial government, as well as Jules Favre and Thiers for the opposition, proposed the organization of a committee of national defense. The next morning, Paris was placarded with the announcement that new armies would soon be gathered under its walls.[106]

The attention of the crowds on September 4 was not, however, upon thoughts of war. The prevailing sentiment was one of relief at the fall of the Empire. "The joy of these people," said Gambetta to a companion on his way to the Hôtel de Ville, where the Republic was to be proclaimed, "makes me deathly sad! They do not hear the approaching German legions." [107] The librarian of the Quai d'Orsay later described his impressions of the crowds that thronged the main avenues on this beautiful Sunday of early fall. "Joy shone upon every countenance. After so much unhappiness, there was a revival of hope. The Republic was not responsible for the war, it would make peace. This opinion was shared by all." [108] On September 7,

[104] The passage of German soldiers and of a convoy of French prisoners through his native village left an indelible impression upon the mind of the young Maurice Barrès, later a brilliant leader of French nationalism. F. Duhoureau, "La Voix Intérieure de Barrès, d'après ses Cahiers," *Rev. des Deux Mondes,* Sept. 15, 1928, p. 251.

[105] *Temps,* Aug. 1872. *Siècle,* Mar. 30, 1872. In a review of Reinach's edition of Gambetta's speeches, Albert Sorel wrote in 1887: "Gambetta confused in his thoughts the country which he wished to save and the Republic which he wished to establish. . . ." *Temps,* Jan. 1, 1887.

[106] *Journal des Débats,* Sept. 4. *Pays,* Sept. 5.

[107] Paul Deschanel, *Gambetta* (Paris), p. 54.

[108] *Journal,* Sept. 4, 1909.

Louis Veuillot, the editor of the clerical *Univers,* was not certain that hope for a prompt victory or for a prompt peace was the dominant sentiment. "A pretense of menaces," wrote an official of the Austrian embassy, September 12, "and at heart an immoderate desire of peace, if I am not mistaken . . . represents the real state of public opinion. People wish to lay down their arms, without having the courage to avow it." [109]

It is an axiom in France that the continuation of the war was caused by the advance of the German armies into France after Sedan, on the ground that if Prussia had desired peace she would have initiated negotiations. Bismarck and the Berlin press, however, believed that it was France, as the defeated Power, who should ask for terms of peace.[110] Prussia was by this time determined to insist upon the cession of Alsace and of German Lorraine, but even this need not have prevented the Government of National Defense from affirming at once a desire to end the war upon reasonable terms. It is not impossible, in view of the general tendency of public opinion, that a courageous initiative in this direction might have gained public approval, but only political questions were discussed during the sessions of the new government on September 4.[111] Inexperienced in the conduct of diplomacy, Jules Favre, the Minister of Foreign Affairs, made few changes in the personnel of his department, and his first step was to prepare a circular to the diplomatic representatives of France which was in reality an appeal to the neutral Powers and to public opinion in France rather than an application to Prussia for her terms of peace. Unless Prussia respected her King's earlier declarations that he was making war against the Empire and not against the French people, she would assume the responsibility for a war of desperation. France was determined, he affirmed in terms that were more appropriate for the rostrum than in a State paper, not to yield "an inch of her soil or a stone of her fortresses." [112] The influence of this circular

[109] Hübner, "Siège de Paris, Rapports au Prince de Metternich," *Corresp.,* O. S., 226, p. 1044.

[110] Cf. Bismarck's conversation with an English diplomat, Sept. 15. *Bismarck: die Gesammelte Werke,* 7 vols. Gespräche, I (Berlin, 1924), pp. 344–347. *Norddeutsche Allgemeine Zeitung,* Sept. 24.

[111] *Procès-Verbaux des Sèances du Conseil Publiés d'après les Manuscrits Originaux de M. Dréo* (Paris, 1905), pp. 67–70. These unofficial notes taken by the son-in-law of Garnier-Pagès, were first published in the *Matin,* September, 1903. For a criticism of these notes see J. Simon, *Souvenirs du 4 Septembre. Le Gouvernement de la Défense Nationale* (Paris, 1876), p. 39.

[112] Two witnesses, Jules Brame, General d'Aurelle de Paladines, affirmed to the parliamentary investigating committee in 1872 that this phrase was in-

upon the Paris press was even more decisive than that of Gramont's statement of July 6. It was warmly endorsed by newspapers of every political opinion.[113] "Favre committed an error in writing it," observed Albert Sorel, "but no fault was ever accepted as happier by a nation. It flattered the taste for a theatrical eloquence which the bad teaching of literature continues to maintain in France." [114] Favre's unwise, if eloquent, appeal turned public opinion from its enjoyment of the new political situation to the war. It antagonized neutral Powers and doomed to failure any attempt to negotiate satisfactory terms with Bismarck until France had exhausted every possible means of resistance.

There was more than a suspicion of bluff in the defiant attitude of the Government of National Defense. "The republicans as individuals," wrote the correspondent of the *Times* (Sept. 4), "are among the most desponding of us as regards the chances of the war. As public men, they will go on . . . proclaiming their belief in the inevitable victory of our armies and urging the country to every effort of defense." In October, Chaudordy, the representative of the Ministry of Foreign Affairs at Tours, declared that Favre and his associates were prepared to surrender their posts to other men who were not committed against the cession of territory.[115] Early in September, the services of the Danish agent Jules Hansen were enlisted in an effort to discover Germany's terms.[116]

The danger of revolution in Paris was an obstacle to a peace by negotiation. The fall of the Empire had been followed immediately by the organization of numerous radical clubs where orators nightly renewed the memories of 1792.[117] Innocent of any knowledge of mili-

cluded in the circular because Favre found on his desk after taking office as Minister of Foreign Affairs a communication from St. Petersburg indicating Russia's intention of intervening. *Enquête Parlementaire* (1872), I, 195, 196. Cf. Jules Favre, *Gouvernement de la Défense Nationale*, 3 vols. (Paris, 1871–1875), I, 105. Maurice Reclus, *Jules Favre, 1809–1880* (Paris, 1912), pp. 340–344.

[113] *Temps*, Sept. 10. *Journal des Débats*, Sept. 10. *Pays*, Sept. 13. *Peuple Français*, Sept. 7. Cf. J. Valfrey, *Histoire de la Diplomatie de la Défense Nationale*, 3 vols. (Paris, 1871), I, 11. *Indépendance de la Moselle* (Metz), Sept. 19.

[114] Sorel, *Histoire Diplomatique*, I, 299.

[115] Lord Newton, *Lord Lyons—A Record of British Diplomacy*, 2 vols. (London, 1923), I, 325, 326.

[116] Jules Hansen, *Les Coulisses de la Diplomatie, Quinze Ans à l'Étranger (1864–1879)* (Paris, 1880), pp. 225, 226.

[117] G. Molinari, "Les Clubs de Paris pendant le Siège," *Rev. des Deux Mondes* (1870), VI, 528–542.

tary affairs, these heirs of the Jacobin tradition were confident that
the people only needed to be aroused and armed in order to repel
the invader. "The French of 1870," declared Charles Delescluze, who
was to die upon the barricades of the Commune, in the *Réveil* (Sept.
7), "are the sons of those Gauls for whom battles were holidays, and
who feared only the fall of the Heavens." Blanqui, the veteran revo-
lutionist, was bitterly hostile to peace. In his opinion, the people of
Paris had never been more completely united. "To fight until death,
save Paris and France at any price of its blood, that is its *idée fixe.*"
He warned the government, although he had at first pledged his
unqualified support, that the slightest evidence of weakness would
arouse the people to fury. "It has taken," he declared, "the patriotic
enthusiasm of the press seriously, but the government's actions no
longer seem to measure up to its words." [118] The *Times* (Sept. 13)
was informed that "the fear of our possible next government is
greater than the fear of the Prussians." Fear of revolution does not
alone explain the determination to fight to the end, for patriotic sentiment was deeply aroused by Favre's circular. Germany's remarkable
recovery after 1919 under at least as unfavorable circumstances
shows that the sacrifice of a hundred thousand lives was not essential, as it was often said later, for the recovery of France's self-
respect. The memories of this period of sacrifice in a hopeless cause,
nevertheless, became in later years a source of pride and of consolation,
not only as a proof of the nation's vitality, but also as earning a more
sympathetic consideration from the neutral countries.

Even Favre understood the need of negotiating while preparing
for a desperate resistance. Unfortunately, he sought two unattain-
able purposes, intervention by the neutral Powers, and such terms
from Prussia as would leave France's territorial unity intact. On
September 12, he sent Thiers on a fruitless mission to the European
courts, and a week later, acting upon his own initiative, he attempted
to arrange an armistice with Bismarck in the dramatic interviews
at Ferrières, where his emotional patriotism proved no match for the
Iron Chancellor.[119] Bismarck's insistence upon Alsace and Lorraine
proved immovable.[120] When the result was announced, public opinion
in Paris became more firmly convinced than ever that the war must
continue. It was agreed that if France had assumed the responsibil-

[118] *Patrie en Danger*, Sept. 9.
[119] For a contemporary estimate of Favre's character and capacity see Comte
d'Haussonville, *Mon Journal pendant la Guerre, 1870–1871* (Paris, 1905), p. 380.
[120] Favre, *Gouvernement de la Défense Nationale*, I, 205.

ity for its declaration, Prussia had become the aggressor by insisting upon a cession of territory.[121]

Gambetta's driving energy, and the autocratic powers exercised by his prefects, silenced criticism of the war in the provinces. In Paris, where General Trochu had regarded the siege from the first as an heroic folly, the threat of revolution continued to be a serious obstacle to peace. Favre's negotiations with Bismarck in September aroused Blanqui to fury. "Since September 4," he wrote, "the government's one thought has been peace, not a victorious nor even an honorable peace, but peace at any price." [122] Rumors that Thiers was about to make a new effort to arrange an armistice led to an attack by the radicals, October 31, upon the Hôtel de Ville, where members of the government remained prisoners of the mob for a few hours. After this revolutionary demonstration, Favre rejected the terms which Thiers personally believed should have been accepted, although the plebiscite of November 2 proved that the radicals could muster less than an eighth of the voters.[123] In the meantime, moderate opinion was turning in favor of an arrangement that would make it possible to hold an election for a national assembly. The unprecedented separation between Paris and the provinces, news of revolutionary disturbances in the South, the fall of Metz and Strassburg created a desire of peace by the end of October which, as a witness noted in his diary, became almost dangerous.[124]

Hunger was the decisive argument in favor of an armistice. At midnight, January 28, 1871, Favre listened from the balcony of the Quai d'Orsay to the reverberations of the last cannon shot which the French, due to his efforts, had the honor of firing.[125] In the election of February 8 for a National Assembly, which was held under circumstances that did not permit Paris to exercise her usual leadership, the issue of continued war or of an immediate peace overshadowed the differences between the Monarchists and the Repub-

[121] *Journal des Débats*, Sept. 24. *Opinion Nationale*, Sept. 24. Fustel de Coulanges in the *Temps*, Nov. 2. Guèroult, "La République en France," *Rev. des Deux Mondes* (1870), V, 108.

[122] *Patrie en Danger*, Sept. 22.

[123] Charles Seignobos, *Le Déclin de l'Empire et l'Établissement de la 3e République* (Paris, 1921), p. 269.

[124] Haussonville, *Mon Journal*, pp. 286, 287.

[125] Comte d'Herisson, *Journal d'un Officer d'Ordonnance, Juillet 1870–Février 1871* (Paris, 1885), p. 364 (33d ed.). The author was present during the negotiation of the armistice, as Favre's military aid, and even secured some slight changes in Bismarck's conditions.

licans. The election of a decisive majority of Monarchists, pledged to peace, decided the question. Thiers was plainly indicated as the leader of the nation in its extremity, for he had been elected by more than thirty constituencies, receiving more than two million votes. Never a friend of Germany, and convinced that a war was inevitable, he had nevertheless opposed war in July, 1870, on the ground that the government was not prepared and that it did not have a good case. He had favored a prompt peace after September 4, refusing to become a member of the Government of National Defense.[126] He now undertook the negotiation of preliminary terms of peace, after receiving his commission as Chief of the Executive Power, with the determination to liquidate as quickly as possible the results of an unfortunate experience.[127] He might have obtained somewhat more favorable terms if he had used the possible resumption of war as a threat, but in any event, his desire for peace was undoubtedly in accord with public opinion. He thought that the terms were relatively moderate:[128] the cession of Alsace and of German Lorraine, an indemnity of five billions of francs, the occupation of sixteen departments until its payment, and the privilege of entering Paris accorded to the German army, until the ratification of the preliminary terms of peace by the National Assembly.

The terms were received by the press, however, with a cry of rage, and not a single newspaper appeared during the brief presence in Paris of the German troops. The radical Rappel (March 4) called upon the Paris delegation in the National Assembly to resign rather than to ratify the terms of peace.[129] "The peace of to-day," it declared, "is the war of to-morrow." The moderate Republican Siècle (March 3) protested that "the odious fate inflicted upon us will never be accepted by the French nation." The liberal Catholic Français (March 2, 3, 4) proclaimed that "it is Prussia who condemns us to appeal to a future vengeance." According to the Orleanist Gazette de France (March 2, 3, 4), the moving protest of the Alsatian deputies[130] "im-

---

[126] Haussonville, Mon Journal, pp. 89, 90.

[127] See Thiers's statement of his policy as Chief of the Executive Power, Feb. 19, 1871. Annales de l'Assemblée Nationale, 1871, I, 74, 75.

[128] Hans Herzfeld, Deutschland und das Geschlagene Frankreich, 1871–1873 (Berlin, 1924), p. ii. According to Lyons, Thiers even had "a sort of liking for Bismarck" (Mar. 6, 1871). Newton, Lyons, I, 374–375.

[129] Five deputies, Rochefort, Ranc, Malon, Tridon, and Pyat, followed this advice. Journal des Débats, Mar. 8, 1871.

[130] Gambetta is said to have prepared this eloquent affirmation of loyalty to France. H. Galli [Henri Gallichet], Gambetta et l'Alsace-Lorraine (Paris,

poses upon us an imperious duty . . . and from to-day all our efforts must tend to hasten its coming." Time was to moderate the bitterness of this first impression, but even then, more temperate voices were heard. The Government of National Defense, according to the Bonapartist *Patrie* (March 2, 3) shared with Germany the responsibility for the nation's disasters. The *Temps* (March 2, 3, 4) held that there was no shame in accepting the treaty "when every effort had been made to avert it." If there was any disgrace, it should go to the "frivolous and fatal authors of the war." The *Journal des Débats* (March 1, 2, 3) was chiefly concerned for the future and its tasks.

"France's right arm has been amputated and she has been bled white. And yet we must arouse ourselves. We must again take up the rude pilgrimage of life and labor . . . The future, however, is not ours to dispose of. . . . We do not have the right . . . to dispose of the blood and lives of those who come after us; our whole duty is to enable them to think and to act freely . . . and they alone will have the right to decide one day if they wish to seek vengeance for the blood of their fathers. . . . And who knows? Who knows if the horrible bitterness which oppresses reflective and serious men to-day will survive the passage of several years?"

The development of public opinion under the Republic was to be conditioned by a heritage of hatred for which it was not, in any real sense, responsible. Although misled by some of its leaders as to the desires of the German people, it had opposed war as a means of preventing the unification of Germany. It was only as a result of a legend that public opinion was later believed to have been responsible for the decision which made the Hohenzollern candidature an occasion for war. It was not the pressure of public opinion in its broader sense, it was the determination of the government of the Second Empire and the war party to achieve a diplomatic victory and to prevent the further development of German unity which were the determining factors. Political power passed into more serious, but scarcely abler hands, with the formation of the Government of National Defense. Favre's circular was no more the result of popular

1911), p. 21 (note). "We declare," replied a group of Republican deputies, "that the National Assembly and the French people are incompetent to make a single one of your constituents a Prussian subject; like you, we hold in advance as *nul et non avenu* every act or treaty, every note or plebiscite which cedes any part of Alsace or of Lorraine." Among those signing this statement were Victor Hugo, Louis Blanc, Edgar Quinet, Georges Clemenceau, A. Ranc, H. Brisson, Sadi Carnot. *Rappel*, Mar. 4, 1871.

demand, in spite of its enthusiastic reception, than Gramont's declaration had been. If the minority of chauvinists played an important part in the declaration of war, the minority of radicals were almost equally influential in the decision to continue the war under hopeless conditions. In both cases, moderate opinion could present no effective defense against extremists who claimed to speak in the name of patriotism, and against those in control of the machinery of government.

CHAPTER III

RECONSTRUCTION AND READJUSTMENTS, 1871–1875

Nous ignorons ce que l'avenir nous réserve, et nous ne sommes pas presser de l'interroger, mais il est permis de le penser, l'histoire de France n'est pas finie.
Journal des Débats, June 26, 1871.

The problem which faced public opinion after the war was essentially one of readjustment. It was necessary to take account of the burdens imposed upon France by the Treaty of Frankfort, and at the same time, to revise the ante-bellum point of view in accordance with her new position in Europe. The most serious difficulty did not come from the indemnity, nor from the indirect costs of the war, for these charges, if there had been nothing else, might have been accepted, as according to the rules of the game. France had experienced and recovered from other disasters. But, facing the harsh reality after 1871, public opinion suffered from the infection which came from the open wound left by the cession of Alsace-Lorraine. Nor was this all. The new eastern frontier, which shortened the distance to Paris, was felt to be a constant menace to France's security. Two hundred years of almost uninterrupted cultural and political ascendancy in Europe, moreover, had established habits of thought and emotional reactions which were not justified by the nation's present influence. The unity of Germany had been consummated against the determined hostility of the French government, and military defeat, with the disruption of her armies, deprived France of the usual means of restoring her prestige.

For several years, Bismarck did his part to discourage the development of moderate opinion in France. He inflicted an unnecessary humiliation upon her by proclaiming the new German Empire at Versailles, January 18, 1871, and the terms of peace were in part the result of his belief that France would seize the first favorable opportunity for revenge, even without a cession of territory. The German people were told that the possession of Alsace-Lorraine was a necessary bulwark against this certain attack, and that it was a merited punishment of a nation which had been responsible for the war.[1] Even Bismarck, who sometimes professed a certain contempt for public opinion and who was skilled in its manipulation,[2] found it convenient to attribute the declaration of war to the pressure of French public opinion.[3] In more candid moments, he acknowledged that the masses were peaceful, but he insisted that the influence of the chauvinist minority would always prevail against the desires of the majority.[4] It was a simple matter for him to find evidence in support of this theory in the French press and in the difficulties of the German ambassador and of German travelers in France. Accordingly, he listened to France's repeated assurances of peaceful intentions with open skepticism, and his treatment of her representatives was harsh and abrupt. "I seemed to see," wrote de Gabriac after his first interview with Bismarck as the French *chargé d'affaires* in August, 1871, "Arminius receiving the envoys of the conquered after the defeat of the Roman legions." [5]

If Bismarck could support his theory by citing events in Paris on the eve of the war of 1870, the more serious question concerned the future. He strengthened the extremist elements in France by shaping his policy to conform with this theory. Gambetta, however, denied that the chancellor understood France. "M. de Bismarck," he wrote in 1874, "is a German, and nothing more. He judges us with more jealousy than perspicacity." [6] A passionate desire of revenge, of course, existed in France, and it sometimes went with a bitter hatred of everything that was German. "The German," declared a pamphleteer, "is only a monstrosity of nature." [7] If Gambetta did not share this unreasoning passion, he was, however, at this time an ardent advocate of the *revanche*. In November, 1871, he founded the *République Française,* in part with Alsatian capital for the purpose "of daily calling the attention of Europe to our rights and to

---

[1] *Berliner Post,* Aug. 28, 1870. *Volks-Zeitung* (Berlin), Aug. 31, 1870. *Provinzialkorrespondenz* (Berlin), Aug. 31, 1870.

[2] Busch, *Bismarck: Some Secret Pages of His History.* See especially the first volume.

[3] Favre, *Gouvernement de la Défense Nationale,* I, 166.

[4] Cf. his conversation with Blum, Oct. 20, 1892. *Bismarck: Gesammelte Werke,* Gespräche, III (Berlin, 1926), p. 276.

[5] Marquis de Gabriac, *Souvenirs Diplomatiques de Russie et de l'Allemagne, (1870–1872)* (Paris, 1896), pp. 151–152.

[6] Gambetta to A. Ranc, Paris, Dec. 16, 1874. [Arthur Ranc] *Souvenirs, Correspondance de Ranc, 1831–1908* (Paris, 1913), pp. 264–266.

[7] Étienne Vattier, *La France devant l'Allemagne et devant Elle-Même* (Paris, 1872). Cf. de Gabriac, *Souvenirs,* p. 127.

those of our ravished provinces." [8] He promised an Alsatian that his political activity in France would always have for its "public or secret purpose the recovery of our honest and heroic populations of the East." [9]

Almost immediately after the close of the war, a variety of influences began to work for the development of a more moderate point of view. It was not humanly possible for the explosion of rage that had greeted the terms of peace to continue indefinitely, and the conflict between the Republicans and Monarchists diverted attention to political questions. At times Germany was almost forgotten in the contest which divided the nation into two irreconcilable camps. The tragic and bloody struggle between Paris and the central government during the Commune (March–May, 1871), with its revival of the specter of revolution, convinced many that an attitude of reserve was necessary.[10] Decazes, the Foreign Minister, did not exaggerate when he assured the German ambassador during the crisis of 1875 that the Commune had persuaded France of the necessity of peace.[11] When defeat was followed by this bitter social upheaval, a mood of pessimism and self-criticism became current that was inconsistent with aggressive designs. "It is not against Prussia that we must make war," declared a liberal Catholic, "it is against ourselves. One of the most dangerous, as well as one of the most seductive of our illusions, is our unlimited confidence in the strength and resources of France." [12] Republicans saw the need of a greater sense of realities, "that much must be learned and much forgotten. We must begin the new period with a spirit chastened by defeat." [13]

Even sentiment in regard to Alsace-Lorraine felt this influence. Each of the two parties occasionally yielded to the temptation of using it for political purposes, but the Republicans did this in the interest of moderation. The *Temps* (Mar. 31, 1871) declared that the people of the lost provinces were prepared to wait indefinitely for their deliverance. The eagerness with which some suggested that Alsace-

[8] This is quoted from a circular which was prepared for circulation in Alsace. Galli, *Gambetta et l'Alsace-Lorraine*, pp. 47, 48.

[9] *Ibid.*, pp. 48, 49.

[10] *Rev. des Deux Mondes*, 1871, III, 556. *Siècle*, June 20, 1871.

[11] Hohenlohe to Bismarck, Paris, May 5, 1875. *Die Grosse Politik der Europäischen Kabinette 1871–1914, Sammlung der Diplomatischen Akten des Deutschen Auswärtigen Amts*, 40 vols. (Berlin, 1922–1927), I, 270. This work will henceforth be cited as *G. P.*

[12] G. A. Heinrich, *La France, l'Étranger et les Partis* (Paris, 1873), p. 25.

[13] *Rev. des Deux Mondes*, 1871, II, 201.

Lorraine might be recovered by peaceful means testified to a profound distaste for the thought of another war. There were worthier expressions of patriotism, according to the Bonapartist *Journal de Marseille* (July 27, 1871), than appeals to the desire of revenge. "As for Prussia, her hour will come, whatever happens. She will suffer the fate of every State that has abused its power. . . . When it shall have attained its maximum, the German Empire will dissolve of its own weight." One of the rare publicists who discussed foreign affairs at any length urged the need of caution in regard to this question.

How much tact will be needed! To recover our property with Germany's consent, or if necessary without it; to prove to the German nation, at the same time, that France, in spite of the interpretation of history in Bismarck's speeches, is not its born enemy, that she has not always threatened it in the past, and that she will not necessarily threaten it in the future.[14]

Republican leaders were prepared to go even further in private conversation. Jules Grèvy, then president of the National Assembly, and in 1879 the President of the Republic, declared that "France must not dream of war. She must renounce Alsace." [15] The fiery patriot, Paul Déroulède, resigned his commission in the army when he was told that he would never have an opportunity to fight for the recovery of the lost provinces, " 'for our conservative . . . Republicans will never risk this gamble.' " Thiers is also reported to have assured an advocate of the *revanche*: " 'You may witness Bismarck's death, you will never see his humiliation.' " [16] This exceptional point of view was rarely stated in public by responsible leaders, for loyalty to the memory of the lost provinces at once became a test of patriotism. Political considerations also worked against an open approval of renunciation, for Bismarck's well-known preference for the republican form of government in France,[17] as a guarantee of her weakness, was exploited by the Monarchists. For this as well as for patriotic reasons, only a minority, estimated by Von Arnim as one hundred thousand,[18] believed that France should recog-

[14] [T. Colonna Ceccaldi], *Lettres Diplomatiques* . . . (Paris, 1872), pp. 14, 15.

[15] A. Scheurer-Kestner, *Souvenirs de Jeunesse* (Paris, 1905), p. 262.

[16] Galli, *Gambetta et l'Alsace-Lorraine*, p. 28.

[17] Cf. Georg Rosen, *Der Stellungnahme der Politik Bismarcks zur Frage der Staatsform in Frankreich von 1871 bis 1890* (Detmold, 1924). For the revelations resulting from the von Arnim affair, see E. Figurey, D. Corbier, *Le Procès d'Arnim, Recueil Complet des Document Politiques* . . . (Paris, 1875).

[18] Arnim to Bismarck, Paris, Oct. 3, 1872. *G. P.*, I, 150, 151.

nize the eastern frontier as permanent. Moderate opinion, however, would adjourn the Alsace-Lorraine question to a later date. In January, 1875, a republican in the National Assembly attacked the Bonapartist party on the ground that a restoration of the Empire would result in a new war.[19] The *Ordre* (Jan. 31), a Bonapartist newspaper, at once replied that "any one who would precipitate an immediate war would be as culpable as one who would renounce the two provinces. Reason, and an experience of political changes warrant the belief that they can one day be recovered by peaceful means with the aid of friendly combinations, or of reciprocal concessions." A section of public opinion was beginning to hope that at some future time the two provinces might be recovered by peaceful means. The right to cherish this hope was defended as an inalienable right of independence.

'Does Germany pretend,' asked a moderate observer, 'to determine the measure of our regrets and of our hopes . . . to impose upon us . . . a love of the peace under which we are suffering, sympathy for the Germans, forgetfulness of the past and the abandonment of the future? . . . As for France her policy is simple: she remains within the unhappy limits imposed upon her by circumstances and she keeps her liberty, her inviolability.' [20]

The lines of Thiers's policy were clearly indicated by the Treaty of Frankfort and by his own determination to liquidate the war as soon as possible.[21] In May, 1872, however, he told the German ambassador quite frankly that France would seek the return of Alsace-Lorraine as a price for her neutrality in the event that Germany should go to war with another Power.[22] Bismarck was finally convinced that a continuation of the Thiers government would be Germany's best guarantee for the prompt payment of the indemnity.[23] It was to this end that Thiers acted during the two years of his power

---

[19] *Annales,* 1875, I, 341.

[20] *Rev. des Deux Mondes,* 1872, II, 227, 228.

[21] Thiers retained close control of foreign affairs, even insisting that the nominal head of that ministry should live in the same house with him at Versailles. Jules Simon, *Thiers, Guizot, Rémusat* (Paris, 1885), p. 202.

[22] Von Arnim to Bismarck, Paris, May 6, 1872. *G. P.,* I, 114.

[23] Bismarck to William, Varzin, Oct. 14, 1872. *Ibid.,* I, 154. The Chancellor, however, was almost as suspicious of the radical Republicans as of the Monarchists. H. Doniol, *M. Thiers, le Comte de Saint-Vallier, le Général de Manteuffel, la Libération du Territoire (1871–1873)* (Paris, 1897), pp. 277, 288.

(Feb., 1871–May, 1873). With a country divided between rival parties, he secured united support in paying the charges incumbent upon France. This support was not, however, always given cheerfully. The Republicans were eager for an immediate payment in order to demand a new election as well as to secure the early evacuation of the occupied districts,[24] but the Monarchists, hoping to prolong the life of the National Assembly and their own power, were not eager for the prompt payment of the indemnity.[25] Nevertheless, the Assembly always voted by large majorities the necessary credits to meet the payments Thiers had arranged, and the nation responded splendidly to the loans which were placed in France. Thiers also proceeded with the reorganization of the army, based upon compulsory service of five years. "You will see," he told the Assembly in July, 1871, "that we are going to devote all our energies to the reorganization of the French army." Bismarck interpreted this feverish activity as evidence of the *revanche,* but Thiers declared that "it is our right as a great nation which deserves to keep her grandeur, it is not the astute policy of those who would, at the first pretext, recommence an untimely war." [26] These reforms were well under way when a combination of the Monarchist parties, May 23, 1873, forced his resignation, but he had already signed in March an agreement with Germany fixing the last payment and the withdrawal of the last German soldiers for September of that year.

The apparent swing toward the monarchy, with the support of the Catholic party, in the formation of the Broglie ministry, and MacMahon's election as President, presaged a new period of tension in Franco-German relations. Involved as Bismarck was in a bitter conflict with the Church in Germany, his ill-will was assured for any government in France which was supported by the clericals. His animosity was not without justification, for the French clericals, since the war of 1870, had advocated a distinctly aggressive policy. Encouraged by the revival of religious sentiment which had been inspired by the nation's disasters, they used the ecclesiastical ma-

---

[24] *République Française,* May 15, 1873.

[25] The *Assemblée Nationale* quoted in the *Journal des Débats,* March 14, 1873. Cf. *Notes et Souvenirs de M. Thiers, 1870–1873* (Paris, 1903), pp. 287–289.

[26] *Annales,* 1871, IV, 250 (July 22). Cf. Thiers's statement of his policy in a letter to Le Flô, French ambassador to St. Petersburg, Trouville, Aug. 22, 1872. *Documents Diplomatiques Français,* 1st series, I, 177. Cf. Von Arnim to Bismarck, Paris, Jan. 15, 1872. *G. P.,* I. 108, 109.

chinery of the Church, and an effective press led by the ably edited
Univers, for a nation-wide campaign for the restoration of France
to her former position as the protector of the Church. That the
war had been supported by some Catholics as a kind of crusade
against protestant Prussia [27] did not keep them from representing
France's defeat as a divine punishment for the free-thinking tendencies of her people. "We have been more punished than defeated,"
declared the *Univers* (Sept. 7, 1872). "Certainly Prussia would not
have vanquished a nation ten times stronger and richer than herself,
if France had not merited punishment." It was remarked that the
divine displeasure had been shown in the dry summer and harsh
winter of 1870, which, it was said, had contributed to the defeat.
After using Prussia as an instrument, God was ready to turn against
her for abusing her victory, and France, if she would again serve
the Church, would regain her formerly favored position.[28]

Hostilities had scarcely ceased when a systematic campaign was
undertaken in favor of intervention in Italy on behalf of the temporal power of the Papacy. The highest dignitaries of the Church
secured thousands of signatures to petitions which they sponsored
for this purpose. When these petitions were presented to the National
Assembly in July, 1871, their reporter declared that only diplomatic
action in coöperation with other Powers was desired. Thiers, still opposed in principle to Italian unity, pointed out that "there is an Italian
kingdom which has taken a place among the considerable Powers of
Europe . . . you must not impose a policy upon us the result of which
you would repudiate publicly, that is to say, war." Although the
formal satisfaction of referring the petitions to the Minister of Foreign Affairs was granted,[29] it was understood that this action was
equivalent to their rejection. This reverse did not, however, discourage the clerical leaders. The next few years witnessed the amazing pilgrimages to Lourdes, and the *Gazette de France* (Sept. 27,
1871) openly proclaimed that France should seek to destroy the
unity of Italy. "What remains to us of influence must be used to
break, to annihilate, to destroy it. . . ." This policy, it was said,
would gain for France the alliance of all Catholic nations, and the

[27] Abbé Desorges in the *Monde,* July 20, 1870.

[28] The R. P. Jean Baptiste Caussette, *Dieu et les Malheurs de la France*
(Toulouse, 1871), p. 17.

[29] *Annales* (1871), IV, 248, 249. The Vatican was reported as pleased by
this vote. D'Harcourt to Jules Favre, Rome, July 27, 1871. *Documents Diplomatiques Français,* 1st series, I, 52.

return of the conservative parties to power would be rewarded by Russia's friendship.[30]

High hopes were placed in the Broglie ministry, when it was organized in May, 1873. "The impression," observed the *Univers* (May 31) "has been religious. . . . Every one understood that God had at last remembered his chosen people." It was against Germany as well as against Italy that the clericals would have France act. "If France were to become a monarchy again, and especially a Catholic monarchy, M. de Bismarck would believe that his work was seriously compromised. He would be a hundred times correct. . . . The religious war . . . in fact would permanently and speedily destroy the artificial and lying unity of the new empire." [31] The new ministry, although its clericalism could not be questioned, refused to commit the nation to the certain dangers of this policy. The circumstances which had largely dictated Thiers's policy remained unchanged, and in the main the precedents which he had established were followed. No other course, according to the opposition press, was possible. "If M. de Broglie and his cabinet undertake a Roman campaign," declared the *Journal des Débats* (May 31, 1873), "it will only be in France." "The ministry would not last an hour," according to a moderate observer, "if it should dare to commit the nation to an adventurous policy." [32] Broglie, in fact, immediately urged the need of convincing Europe that France desired peace, that her military reforms were due alone to "the desire of conserving France's legitimate rank." [33] The French ambassador in Berlin, Gontaut-Biron, was informed that he should continue to follow the instructions he had received from the Thiers government,[34] while a diplomatic circular explained that the recent political changes had no connection with foreign affairs.[35] The one notable concession to the clerical point of view was the maintenance of the *Orénoque,* a warship which had remained after the recall of the French garrison, August, 1870, at Civita-Vecchia for the Pope's use if he should decide to leave Rome. Even this gunboat, the presence of which in

[30] A. de Richecour, *Ce Que Doit être l'Alliance des Races Latines, Réponse de la France à l'Entrevue de Gastein.* (Paris, 1871), pp. 27–35.

[31] *Univers,* June 20, 1873.

[32] *Rev. des Deux Mondes,* 1873, II, 958, 959.

[33] *Annales,* 1873, IV, 78 (May 26).

[34] E. Bourgeois, J. Pagès, *Les Origines et les Résponsabilités de la Grande Guerre* (Paris, 1922), p. 159. Broglie to Gontaut-Biron, Paris, May 28, 1873. *Documents Diplomatiques Français,* 1st series, I, 238–240.

[35] *Français,* June 11, 1873.

Italian waters became a source of friction with Italy, was withdrawn Oct. 12, 1874, by Decazes, who succeeded Broglie as the Minister of Foreign Affairs.[36] The optimistic impression among the more extreme clericals in May, 1873, was soon followed by doubt and disappointment. Within a month after the formation of the Broglie ministry, the *Univers* (June 20) was not certain that the new government would be an improvement upon its predecessor, and a year later (May 31, 1874) it referred to the anniversary of the Broglie ministry as *"un jour de martyrs."*

The moderate foreign policy of the monarchist ministries did not, however, mean the end of the dangerous clerical campaign. The German Catholics were openly encouraged in their resistance to Bismarck by the clerical press [37] and by pastoral letters from the French bishops. All this was most irritating to the Chancellor. When the Bishop of Nancy went so far as to instruct the clergy of his diocese, some of whom were officiating in parishes under German rule, to offer public prayers for the return of Alsace-Lorraine to France, Bismarck called upon France to discipline the bishops.[38] The government naturally refused to undertake a public prosecution, but the Bishop had already been reprimanded by the Minister of Public Worship, and the prefects were quietly instructed to advise moderation. At length the *Univers* was ordered to suspend publication for two months. "War was in the air at Paris a few days ago," the *Norddeutsche Allgemeine Zeitung* announced. Germany could not live in peace, it added, with a French government which served Rome by encouraging the press in its sympathy for the German Catholics. The liberal *Temps* (Jan. 21, 1874) denied that there was any occasion for alarm because "the country, at this time, could not, if it would, follow the policy which certain people hope to force upon it." According to the anti-clerical *Presse* (Jan. 18, 1874), the only bond of union between the *Univers,* which received its inspiration from Rome, and the nation was its language. Sensitive as Bismarck was to the encourage-

---

[36] Decazes to Noailles, Versailles, Oct. 12, 1874. *Documents Diplomatiques,* 1st Series, I, 357. See Nigra's insistent request for the *Orénoque's* recall before the Italian elections in November, 1874. Nigra to Decazes, Aix-les-Bains, Aug. 21, 1874. *Ibid.,* 1st Series, I, 349, 350.

[37] *Univers.* Jan. 10, July 6, 1873. *Français.* April 8, 1873.

[38] Decazes to the French ambassadors at London, St. Petersburg, Vienna. Versailles, Jan. 18, 1874. *Documents Diplomatiques Français,* 1st Series, I, 298, 299. For this first phase of Bismarck's international campaign against the Church, see George Goyau, *Bismarck et l'Église,* 4 vols. (Paris, 1922), II, 106–117.

ment given the German Catholics, he was more seriously concerned with France's capacity to form alliances. Numerous references to her *Bündnisfähigkeit* occur in the German diplomatic correspondence of this period. The Chancellor's rather prompt acceptance, January 26, 1874, of France's explanation in the affair of the Bishops [39] was probably due to his confidence that she was not yet able to find allies. "I am convinced," he wrote in February, 1874, "that the French danger will begin with the moment when she is able to form alliances with the monarchical courts of Europe. She did not have that ability under Thiers, and she has not acquired it under Mac-Mahon." [40]

Nevertheless, Bismarck remained suspicious of the clerical and monarchist parties in France even after the enactment of the Organic Laws of February, 1875, had pointed to the eventual triumph of the Republic. In a state of nervous irritation as a result of his conflict with the Church in Germany,[41] he was also oppressed by the "nightmare of coalitions" because of recent evidence of Russia's restlessness in the League of the Three Emperors.[42] Few incidents in diplomatic history have been studied with the care that has been given his part in the War-Scare of 1875, and the conclusion is now well established that he had no intention of forcing a war with France.[43] Yet it is equally clear that he decided early in 1875 to impress upon her the dangers involved in her military reforms and in her desire for allies. Almost exclusively concerned with domestic politics as they were, neither the attitude of the press nor that of public opinion in France justified his alarm, and there is no reason to believe that the government had any intention of departing from its usual reserve.

[39] Gontaut-Biron to Decazes, Berlin, Jan. 26, 1870. *Documents Diplomatiques Français*, 1st Series, I, 304. André Dreux, *Les Dernières Années de l'Ambassade en Allemagne de M. de Gontaut-Biron, 1874–1877* (Paris, 1907), p. 34.

[40] Bismarck to Prince Heinrich VII Reuss, Berlin, Feb. 28, 1871. *G. P.*, I, 239.

[41] *Journal des Débats*, Feb. 22, 1875. Charles Gavard, *Un Diplomat à Londres; Lettres et Notes (1871–1877)* (Paris, 1895), p. 250. Bourgeois, Pagès, *Origines et Résponsabilités*, p. 163 (note). Adalbert Wahl, *Vom Bismarck der 70er Jahre* (Tübingen, 1920), p. 98.

[42] Russia had refused to follow Germany's lead in 1874 in the recognition of Marshal Serrano's government. Hajo Holborn, *Bismarcks Europäische Politik zu Beginn des Siebzieger Jahre und die Mission Radowitz* (Berlin, 1925), p. 53.

[43] S. B. Fay, *The Origins of the World War*, 2 vols. (New York, 1928), I, 58, 59. The recently published French documents bearing upon the war-scare add comparatively little to our knowledge of it. *Documents Diplomatiques Français*, 1st Series, I, 370–497.

The first evidence of tension arose in connection with incidents of comparatively minor importance. In January, Bismarck ordered an embargo upon the export of horses after receiving information of alleged orders placed in Germany by the French War Ministry.[44] Regret was expressed in the French press that Germany did not credit France's assurances of peace,[45] and it, in general, refused to become alarmed. The enactment of article 3 of the new military law, March 12, without discussion [46] had more serious consequences, for it could be given a war-like interpretation in Germany. It was not easy to determine the exact effect of this measure upon the strength of the French army. It added a fourth battalion to each infantry regiment, but the number of companies in each battalion was reduced, and the normal strength of each company was increased. The explanation offered in France that it was intended to take care of twelve hundred captains who would otherwise be placed upon the retired list [47] was probably as far wrong as the assertion in the German press that it would at once add 144,000 men to the French army. The German attaché in Paris, Von Bülow, was probably nearer the truth in reporting that its chief effect would be to provide for the mobilization of a larger number in the first-line army in the event of war.[48] In any case, more than two weeks elapsed before the supposed dangerous character of this law was appreciated in Germany. On March 31, the *National Zeitung* declared that France was preparing for an immediate attack, and the *Kölnische Zeitung* (April 1) added that the French army had attained sufficient strength to be a serious danger under the direction of an able leader.

It was, however, the French press which first raised the question of alliances in connection with the interview between the Austrian and Italian monarchs in Venice on April 5. This event, indicating Austria's renunciation of her losses of Italian territory in 1859 and 1866, caused a vague unrest in Germany,[49] but it was welcomed in France with scarcely veiled joy. At first, Gambetta's *République Française* (March 19) had reported a rumor that Austria was about to es-

---

[44] Bismarck to Hohenlohe, Berlin, Feb. 26, 1875. *G. P.,* I, 245.

[45] *Journal des Débats,* March 10, 1875. Hans Herzfeld, *Die Deutsch-Französisch Kriegsgefahr* (Berlin, 1922), pp. 18–22.

[46] *Annales,* 1875, II, 185, 186.

[47] Duc de Broglie, *La Mission de Gontaut-Biron à Berlin* (Paris, 1896). pp. 185, 186.

[48] Report of Major von Bülow, Paris, April 11, 1875. *G. P.,* I, 250–253.

[49] Herzfeld, *Die Deutsch-Französisch Kriegsgefahr,* p. 28.

cape from Germany's influence with a warning that it should be read "with extreme reserve," but the *Berliner Post* (April 4) noted that Gambetta had forgotten his recent moderation in his claim that Germany was rapidly being isolated. The Bonapartist *Patrie* (March 22) declared that Germany had not been able to prevent the meeting and that it was a defeat for her policy. Blowitz, the correspondent of the *Times,* wrote that "the temptation to exult over the real or imaginary checks German diplomacy may encounter" caused the press to forget "that reserve which is best suited to the position of France." The *Dépêche* of Toulouse (April 8) was one of those which could not restrain its satisfaction at "this first step in a new path. Perhaps it means the beginning of a new Holy Alliance against the menace of pan-Germanism."

Although Bismarck was confident that France would not be able to make an alliance with Austria, the dangerous features of the diplomatic situation were of more concern to him than the new French military law. The *Kölnische Zeitung's* (April 4) famous letter, dated from Vienna, but in reality written in Berlin, emphasized the possibility of a Catholic League including France, Austria, Italy, and the Papacy rather than the military preparations in France.[50] The equally famous and more influential *Berliner Post's* (April 9) article, "Is War in Sight?" balanced the account by elaborating the improbable theme that the conservative majority of the National Assembly would declare war before it was compelled to dissolve. It is known now that this alarmist article, the effect of which was to demonstrate the power of the press, was written without any suggestion from Bismarck, but in accordance with what was assumed to be the Chancellor's point of view.[51] In reply to a definite question, Bismarck assured the German ambassador in Paris, Prince Hohenlohe, that he had been surprised by these articles. Nevertheless, they were not to be specifically repudiated, for their effect might be salutary, and in addition Hohenlohe was to cite an article in the *Norddeutsche Allgemeine Zeitung* (April 11), discounting the prospect of a league of Catholic States but pointing out in a general way the dangerous character of France's military preparation.[52]

A chorus of denials in the French press greeted this press cam-

---

[50] It was sent from the press bureau of the Foreign Office without any indication of Bismarck's attitude. Nicolaas Japikse, *Europa und Bismarcks Friedenspolitik* . . . (Berlin, 1927), pp. 40, 41, citing the *Kölnische Zeitung,* Oct. 28, 1922.
[51] Radowitz, *Aufzeichnungen und Erinnerungen,* I, 326.
[52] Bismarck to Hohenlohe, Berlin, April 10, 1875. *G. P.,* I, 254.

paign. Moderate opinion discounted the seriousness of the crisis on the ground that it had been precipitated in order to restore unity in a Germany that was disrupted by the conflict between the State and the Church.[53] Édouard Hervé's *Journal de Paris* (April 12) called upon the entire press to be prudent. "The government is wise . . . we have no doubt on that score. The press and public opinion must follow its example. The *Post*'s article must be taken as a warning." This advice was followed even by the Catholic press. The *Univers* (April 14) agreed with the *Berliner Post*'s opinion that the conservative majority in the Assembly was more patriotic than the republicans. "But because it is more patriotic, it is also more prudent. Everybody in France is aware of our weakness. . . ." The *Patrie* (April 11) characterized the *Post*'s article as *"une fable,"* and the clerical *Monde* (April 25) declared that France had "every interest in the maintenance of peace." Nevertheless, the Monarchists resented the tendency of the republican press to question the danger of an attack by Germany: "In reading republican newspapers," according to the *Gazette de France* (April 14), "one would not suspect that any excitement had been aroused in Europe by M. de Bismarck's claims." [54] The moderation of the French press was acknowledged in Germany, but it was attributed chiefly to governmental influence. "When its attitude in regard to foreign affairs departs from the government's point of view," declared the *National Zeitung, "un personnage en habit noir* visits the newspaper offices and reëstablishes complete agreement, thanks to patriotism and official influence." Official influence may well have played a part, but moderation after all, was the normal reaction of the press in view of the difficulties of France's situation in Europe.

The first phase of the crisis ended almost as quickly as it had arisen.[55] Even the *Berliner Post*'s Paris correspondent (April 14; Paris, April 10) reported that "No one desires war . . . I can as-

---

[53] *Temps,* April 11. *Courrier de France,* April 11. *Figaro,* April 12. Much attention was given to a collection of excerpts from the French press in the *Norddeutsche Allgemeine Zeitung,* April 18, which attempted to prove that its moderation represented a sudden conversion. However, many of the newspapers selected were obscure provincial sheets, and some dated back to 1871. Dreux, *Les Dernières Années,* pp. 88, 89. H. Heinrich Geffcken, *Frankreich, Russland, und der Dreibund* (Berlin, 1893), p. 91. *Temps,* May 1, 1875. *Patrie,* May 2, 1875.

[54] Cf. *Monde,* April 14.

[55] Wahl thinks that, down to April 15, Bismarck was sounding Europe as to its reaction to a demand to France for a limitation of her armament. A. Wahl, *Vom Bismarck der 70er Jahre,* pp. 101–112.

sure you, that even the official and military circles are far from bellicose, and that the word *revanche* has never been less heard than now." On April 14, the official *Provinzialkorrespondenz* published an unqualified assurance that peace was not endangered, and the *Post* (April 15) attempted to explain its alarmist article as a justifiable stratagem for the purpose of preventing the formation of a hostile coalition. In Paris, Decazes went into the country,[56] and Gontaut-Biron, hastening back to Berlin, was told April 14, by an official of the German Foreign Office: "May peace reign between us for a century! that is all I desire!" The French military attaché, Polignac, was given similar assurances by the Emperor. " 'They have tried to bring about a quarrel between us. Everything is now settled. I give you my word for it.' " [57] The Emperor's pronouncement was not immediately communicated to the press, and then in France earlier than in Germany,[58] but the new tone of the German press was accepted as an indication that the period of tension was over.

In the meantime, Bismarck had asked Belgium to change her laws relating to the press so that she could control the expression of clerical opinion. The moderation which had characterized the reaction to the alarmist articles in the German press yielded to indignation at this intervention in the affairs of another country. The *Dépêche* of Toulouse (April 14) declared that the summons was in reality directed against France, and the orleanist *Gazette de France* (April 11) affirmed: "His purpose is evidently to destroy us." Gambetta's *République Française* (April 11), and the republican *Journal de Paris* (April 22) followed with interest the unfavorable reaction in England to Bismarck's new move, but the moderate press rarely ventured openly to attack his policy. "We cannot, we do not wish to be," declared the *République Française* (April 14), "other than observers. This rôle is forced upon us." The *Journal de Paris* (April 22) protested that "Europe will do what she pleases: France agrees in advance to the decision of the Congress." A ray of hope was seen by the *Radical* (April 11) in England's attitude. "Our patriotism can only hope to see Germany become completely involved in the policy which she appears to favor." The reaction to this incident suggests that public opinion was more alarmed than was apparent from the moderate comments in the press.

---

[56] *Dépêche* (Toulouse), April 15; Paris Corresp., April 13.
[57] Dreux, *Les Dernières Années,* p. 85.
[58] *Times* (London), April 24. Paris Corresp., April 23.

Public opinion, however, like the press, was satisfied that the crisis with Germany had apparently ended. No one had any objection to accepting such diplomatic advantages as might come from Bismarck's mistakes, but few would have approved active measures for the purpose of bringing pressure to bear upon him. The conviction that circumstances compelled a policy of reserve was too deeply rooted in moderate opinion. Yet the evidence is clear that Decazes, although he was convinced that France was not in immediate danger of an attack,[59] revived the crisis in order to profit by Bismarck's mistakes to organize Europe against him.

He had reason to believe that the aid of Russia and England could be secured for this purpose. Both had remained neutral during the war of 1870, but it was evident that the formation of a powerful German Empire pleased neither. Russia, and especially Gortchakov, her foreign minister, who resented Bismarck's success, had already shown a willingness to warn Germany that an attack upon France would not be tolerated. During the summer of 1873, Broglie, on Decazes's suggestion,[60] sent an agent to urge the Russian minister, who was then in Switzerland, to intercede on France's behalf. " 'He would say quite plainly to Prince Bismarck' " was the reply, " 'that he could count upon no one's aid in an aggression.' " [61] But Gortchakov was not yet prepared to risk offending Germany, and he passed through Berlin without fulfilling his promise.[62] Nevertheless, as each appeal by the French ambassador, Le Flô, was answered with the friendliest assurances by Gortchakov and the Tsar,[63] Decazes had reason to believe that Russia would act at the proper moment. England's policy of isolation then, as always, made her position more uncertain. Yet evidence was not lacking that she too would act, if nec-

[59] This is the opinion of the French historians who have used the private papers of Gontaut-Biron and Decazes. They are inclined to believe that a demand for the limitation of French armaments was in preparation. Dreux, *Les Dernières Années*, p. 194. G. Hanotaux, *Histoire de la France Contemporaine*, III, 251, 253. It is evident, however, that Decazes was concerned after his interview with Hohenlohe, May 5, with the possibility of a proposal for France's disarmament.

[60] Ernest Daudet, *Histoire Diplomatique de l'Alliance Franco-Russe*, (1873-1893) (Paris, 1894), p. 41. Note by Chaudordy, Aug. 21, 1873. *Documents Diplomatiques Français*, 1st Series, I, 256.

[61] Broglie to Gontaut-Biron, Versailles, Sept. 4, 1873. Vicomte de Gontaut-Biron, *Mon Ambassade en Allemagne (1872-1873)* . . . (Paris, 1906), pp. 388, 389.

[62] Dreux, *Les Dernières Années*, pp. 10, 11. Gontaut-Biron to Decazes, Berlin, Dec. 26, 1873. *Documents Diplomatiques Français*, 1st Series, I, 288.

[63] Broglie, *Mission de Gontaut-Biron*, pp. 46-48.

essary, in the interest of peace. When Von Moltke, in 1874, declared in the Reichstag that Germany was prepared to guard with her sword for fifty years the provinces which she had conquered in five months, Lord John Russell replied in the House of Commons, May 4, that he "did not think any Power would venture to disturb it [peace] if there was a strong alliance between England and the other Powers to preserve the peace of Europe." The foreign minister, Derby, announced that England would "leave no reasonable endeavour untried to preserve peace." [64] Decazes at once called Lyons's attention to the dangerous character of Germany's attitude at the beginning of the crisis in March, 1875.[65]

It was to Russia, because of the approaching meeting between the Russian and German sovereigns in Berlin, May 10, that Decazes first turned when he decided to take advantage of the opening which Bismarck had given him. On April 14, the same day that French representatives in Berlin were receiving peaceful assurances, he confided something of his plans to Le Flô in St. Petersburg. The information which had arrived from London, from St. Petersburg and even from Berlin, he acknowledged, indicated peace rather than war, but the Tsar should be persuaded that a sudden attack was still possible. "This eventuality," he declared, "may perhaps be avoided by *timely* and firm language, spoken preventively, so to speak, and the alarming symptoms which I have just pointed out, will certainly impress Prince Gortchakov. I might even hope that they may persuade him to give wise counsel at Berlin." [66] The success of his project required, however, a more definite proof of aggressive intentions on Bismarck's part. Late in April, the German press again began to emphasize the alleged dangerous character of France's military preparations. But a more effective weapon became available when a curious coincidence placed in Decazes's hands two reports of a clear statement of the preventive war theory by a German diplomat, Radowitz, who was known to be in close contact with the Chancellor. Le Flô wrote from St. Petersburg, April 21, that he had stated it there in February,[67] and Gontaut-Biron reported a similar expres-

---

[64] *Hansard's Parliamentary Debates,* 3d series, vol. 218, pp. 1566, 1567.
[65] Newton, *Lyons,* II, 70, 71.
[66] G. Hanotaux, *Histoire de la France Contemporaine,* III, 245. This letter does not appear in *Documents Diplomatiques Français,* 1st Series, I.
[67] J. V. Fuller, "The War-Scare of 1875," *Amer. Hist. Rev.,* XXIV, 204, quoting E. Flourens, *Alexandre III,* p. 300.

sion of opinion by Radowitz at a dinner that evening, April 21, at the British Embassy in Berlin.[68] A few days later, perhaps anticipating the use which was to be made of this incident, Bismarck had Radowitz write a report of his conversation with the French ambassador which contained no reference to the objectionable statement, nor any context into which it might be fitted.[69] Whether or not Gontaut-Biron's report was accurate, it could be used most effectively in urging action at St. Petersburg, especially in view of similar statements attributed to other German diplomats.

Before springing his trap, Decazes sought to mislead Germany as to his intentions. He proposed to Hohenlohe, April 25, a possible understanding between France and Germany in regard to specific questions.[70] Nevertheless, he instructed Le Flô, April 29, to urge upon Russia the need of prompt action, citing in justification Radowitz's famous statement. Decazes also quoted the first part of the Emperor William's assertion of April 14, "They have tried to make us quarrel," without giving its conclusion wherein it was affirmed that the crisis was over. The Tsar should be persuaded to say the final word for peace in his approaching interview in Berlin with William. "In any case, it is certain," Decazes concluded, "that the Emperor's trip to Berlin is an occasion which it is important that we utilize to the best advantage." Le Flô secured satisfactory assurances from Gortchakov, who was not unwilling to contribute to an unpleasant experience for Bismarck.[71] The French minister communicated his

[68] The essential part of Radowitz's statement follows: "But if revenge is the inmost thought of France—and it can not be otherwise—why wait to attack her until she has recovered her strength and contracted her alliances? You must agree that from a political, from a philosophical, even from a Christian point of view, these deductions are well grounded, and these preoccupations are fitted to guide the policy of Germany." However, it is not always explained that Radowitz at least pretended to interpret in this the point of view of majority leaders in the Reichstag. Nor is it made clear that this informal conversation was initiated by Gontaut-Biron and not by Radowitz. *Documents Diplomatiques Français*, 1st Series, I, 415–421.

[69] *G. P.*, I, 275–277 (May 12, 1875). Such was Gortchakov's impression after being shown this statement. Mrs. Rosslyn Wemyss, *Memoirs and Letters of the Rt. Hon. Sir Robert Morier*, 2 vols. (London, 1911), II, 363, 364.

[70] Hohenlohe to Bismarck, Paris, April 25, 1875. *G. P.*, I, 262. On May 3, the German Foreign Office sent to Paris a memorandum pointing out that nothing stood in the way of an understanding in regard to Africa, the Near East, Spain, or Italy. *Ibid.*, I, 262–264. Decazes, who thought these suggestions were intended to remove the sting from another reference to the disquieting character of French armaments, omitted them from his report to Gontaut-Biron. *Documents Diplomatiques Français*, 1st Series, I, 433–436.

[71] Hanotaux, *France Contemporaine*, III, 251–256.

plans, and their motives, in greater detail in a private letter of the same date, April 29, to Gontaut-Biron. He was trying, he wrote, to exploit Radowitz's statement. "I am doing this with moderation because, thanks to you, the immediate danger has disappeared; I have believed it necessary to crystallize, perhaps to an exaggerated degree, the attitude of the St. Petersburg cabinet. I have done this in order that it will appreciate the importance which I attribute to its position and also for the purpose of giving the cabinets of London and Vienna to understand that their *prudence* was not imitated. Perhaps I will thus spur them to action!" [72]

His circular of April 29 to the European courts, communicating Radowitz's statement, was not inspired, therefore, by serious alarm but rather by a desire to arouse as general a suspicion as possible of Germany's purposes in view of the approaching Berlin interview.

In England, opinion was divided as to the seriousness of the danger. Derby declared, May 2, that if any had existed, it had disappeared, but his chief, Disraeli, thought that "Bismarck is another Old Bonaparte again, and he must be bridled." [73] Queen Victoria shared the Prime Minister's point of view, even quoting him on this point.[74] It was doubtless to arouse public opinion in England, and to crystallize sentiment in Europe on the eve of the Berlin interview, that Decazes enlisted the services of the London press. As early as April 15, he had suggested to Blowitz the idea of an alarmist article in the *Times,* but some time passed before Blowitz secured the permission of its editor, John T. Delane.[75] It appeared, May 6, under the title, "A French War-Scare," and it was signed by "A French correspondent," perhaps to give the impression that its author was not the *Times*'s regular correspondent. The moment had come, it declared, for the truth to be told. The plans of the war party in Germany were responsible for the scare in France: a new invasion, the occupation of a strategic position near Paris from which France would be compelled to cede Belfort, to pay an indemnity of ten billions of francs over a period of twenty years.[76] The

---

[72] Dreux, *Les Dernières Années,* pp. 100, 101. This letter is not printed in *Documents Diplomatiques Français,* 1st Series, I, although a more alarming statement is given in a note either from this or another letter. *Ibid.,* 1st Series, I, 426, 427 (Note).

[73] A. F. Moneypenny, G. E. Buckle, *The Life of Benjamin Disraeli, Earl Beaconsfield,* 6 vols. (New York, 1920), V, 421.

[74] *The Letters of Queen Victoria* (2nd series), 3 vols. (London, 1926), II, 399.

[75] *Memoirs of M. de Blowitz* (New York, 1903), pp. 98–100.

[76] According to Blowitz, Decazes told him that Radowitz had stated these points during his conversation with Gontaut-Biron of April 21. *Ibid.,* 101, 102. This was

article concluded with an appeal for concerted action in order to prevent the war party in Germany from gaining control.

A second communication of similar character, if not from the same pen, appeared in the *Morning Post* of the same date (May 6). It was also dated from Paris, but it contained what purported to be a letter from St. Petersburg of April 30. Unlike Blowitz's article, it referred to the great interest aroused by the Berlin interview. "Every one agrees," it declared, "in attributing to the interview in Berlin great political importance. The future destinies of Europe might almost be supposed to depend on this meeting." The aims of the German war party were described in much the same way as in the *Times's* letter, but where Blowitz was discretely silent as to the Chancellor's connection with the war party, the second letter openly named him as one of its leaders. Its appeal to the Tsar was also more direct. "William I will undertake nothing without the friendly neutrality of Russia. Ought this promise of friendly neutrality to be granted as in 1870, and at what price? Minds here are much divided on this point, but it is none the less flattering to see that the Emperor Alexander has become the arbiter of the destinies of the world scarcely twenty years after the Crimean War." These articles were clearly intended to crystallize public opinion, although neither directly appealed to England for action. Decazes confided this mission to the French *chargé d'affaires* in London. "You may count upon me," Derby replied, "and you may be sure that the government will not fail to do its duty!" [77]

These articles aroused a distinctly unfavorable reaction on the part of the opposition press in France.[78] Certain newspapers, including the *Journal des Débats* (May 7), the *Ordre* (May 9), and the *Progrès* of Lyons (May 9) explained the *Times's* communication as the work of speculators. Almost without exception, the press either denied the existence of a war party in Germany or questioned its influence, and many claimed that there was no "war-scare" in France. "If there are people in Germany who use the language attributed to them by the 'French Correspondent,'" declared the *République Française* (May 10), "no one will listen to them." The radical *Rappel* (May 9) denied that the article was an accurate reflection of public opinion in France.

doubtless an invention, for nothing of this kind appears in Gontaut-Biron's despatch of April 21.

[77] Gavard, *Un Diplomat à Londres,* p. 241.

[78] The simultaneous publication of the above communications in the *Times* and *Morning Post* aroused much speculation. *Ordre,* May 9. *Progrès de la Côte d'Or* (Dijon), May 10. *Patrie,* May 12. *Temps,* May 13.

The *Temps* refused for some days to print it for fear that it would stimulate alarm where none had existed, and it finally declared: *"Que Dieu me protège contre mes amis, je me charge de mes ennemis."* "We do not know the famous politician," protested the republican *Siècle* (May 8), "who sends from Paris these grave reflections, but in any event they will not divert a great nation, whose only desire is to establish a just and liberal government, from its work." [79] The Paris correspondent of the *Kölnische Zeitung* (May 8) noted this unexpected moderation. "Instead of using the occasion for an attack as usual upon Germany's warlike purposes, it is denied that the article has any foundation."

Decazes's plans evidently did not include the use of official influence for the purpose of exciting opinion in France. The semi-official Havas news agency communicated a reassuring statement to the press on the evening of May 5: "Certain rumors were current to-day at the Bourse as to our foreign relations. No news of any kind has reached here, no event has taken place which justifies them." Nevertheless, newspapers in close relation to the government hinted darkly as to possible dangers. The liberal Catholic *Français* (May 7, 8) urged the public "if it were possible" to maintain "an imperturbable coolness." The *Moniteur Universel* (May 9) declared that the situation might become worse. There is reason to believe that the general public in Paris was, in fact, more seriously alarmed than the attitude of the press would suggest. Only the provinces, declared the *Progrès* of Lyons (May 12), refused to share the alarm felt by the capital. "It was a real panic," reported the *Dépêche* of Toulouse (May 9); and it added, "The denials that have come from every direction have had no effect . . . the impulse has been given and every one asks, 'Is it true that we are going to have war?' " These fears, though real, were not the work of the French press but of the general situation and of the articles inspired by Decazes in the London newspapers.

The explanation of the usually moderate tone of the French press is perhaps to be found in its general tendencies since 1871 rather than in official pressure. In any event, it was useful to Decazes because it gave him an excellent case in asking for the diplomatic support of Russia and England. His careful preparations were rewarded. On May 5, Bismarck was told of Russia's desire for peace, and four

---

[79] Many named Decazes as the source of inspiration for the *Times*'s letter. *Dépêche* (Toulouse), May 16, quoting the *Ordre, Liberté, Kölnische Zeitung,* May 10.

days later Derby instructed all of the British ambassadors, and especially Russell in Berlin, to use their influence for a return to normal international relations. Russell acted at once upon these instructions,[80] and Gortchakov the next day presented Austria's as well as Russia's desire for the conclusion of the crisis. Alexander may have disavowed Gortchakov's "comedy," [81] as Bismarck always described the concluding scene of the crisis, but no hint of this was permitted to become known. "My part was not very difficult," wrote the Tsar to Queen Victoria, May 18, "for I found the Emperor, and Bismarck as well quite decided to undertake nothing against France, knowing that she would not be in a condition to think seriously of revenge for many years." [82]

There was no doubt of the sense of relief in France with the peaceful settlement of the crisis. Chief credit of course was given to Russia, but England's part received some recognition. "It is from to-day, definitely established," declared the *Temps* (May 16), "that the Russian government wished to quiet the prevailing nervousness," and it added that England had joined Russia in preventing Germany, if not from launching an attack, at least from addressing a demand for the reduction of the French army. The *Patrie* (May 14) observed "that the English government has not failed in its international duties. . . ." The *Rappel* (June 4) expressed its gratitude for England's coöperation in protecting France. Later, when France turned toward an alliance with Russia, the memory of her aid in 1875 helped to neutralize the dislike of her autocratic institutions, but the services of England were forgotten. French diplomacy had won a notable success, thanks to the support which it had received, but there was little disposition in the press to exult at Germany's expense, for the dangers of France's position were too clear. Public opinion promptly turned its attention to the approaching elections for the first parliament under the new constitution.

The crisis marked the close of a distinct phase in the development of public opinion. In 1871, there had been at least three possible points of view in regard to foreign affairs. The passion for a prompt revenge soon yielded to the force of circumstances. For a time, it seemed pos-

---

[80] *G. P.*, I, 272.

[81] Radowitz, *Aufzeichnungen und Erinnerungen*, I, 320. Bismarck, *Reflections and Reminiscences*, II, 188, 189. Gortchakov's famous telegram, "Now peace is assured," published in the *Karlsruhe Zeitung*, received surprisingly little attention. *Temps*, May 15.

[82] *Letters of Queen Victoria*, II, 398, 399.

sible that the Catholic element, by a systematic campaign, might force the government to adopt a dangerous policy, either by intervening in Italy or by identifying itself with the cause of the Church for the sake of a union of the Catholic Powers against Germany. Again, circumstances were unfavorable; even the governments which followed Thiers could not do other than continue his moderate policy. Public opinion finally chose the path of wisdom, without renouncing Alsace-Lorraine, in spite of the difficulties for which Bismarck was largely responsible. It was convinced that France must, during an indefinite period, aspire to no greater rôle than that of an observer. Determined to protect the nation's independence and its right to choose the kind of an army which best served its needs, public opinion retained, nevertheless, its moderation even when Decazes's maneuvers led to an unexpected success.

CHAPTER IV

Opportunism in Foreign Affairs, 1875–1881

On s'aperçoit aujourd'hui que dans ce retour à une politique plus modeste, l'esprit français, toujours extrême, court le risque de ne pas s'arrêter. Il ne se contente pas à n'étre plus Don Quichotte, il aurait quelque disposition à se faire Sancho Pança.

Joseph Reinach, *La Politique Opportuniste* (Paris, 1890).

The critical years of the Third Republic witnessed the division of the nation into two main groups, each claiming to be the true representative of France. The Monarchists thought of themselves as the appointed guardians of her national traditions, while the Republicans were equally certain that they represented the living France.[1] During this period of intensely bitter political feeling, when every weapon was used, each party drew such arguments from foreign affairs as were calculated to gain popular approval. It is significant that there was a notable absence of appeals to chauvinist sentiment. The need of peace was emphasized by party leaders, and each group insisted that the success of its opponents would mean war. Convincing evidence of the essentially peaceful tendency of public opinion after the war-scare of 1875 may therefore be found in these polemics. Because it was best represented by the Republicans, their success four years later in gaining complete control of the government apparently assured the practice, during a long period, of a distinctly passive policy. Once in power, however, they expressed a somewhat different point of view.

The coup d'état of May 16, 1877, when MacMahon dismissed the republican Simon cabinet, precipitated a crisis in French politics of the first importance. Gambetta and the Republicans used the clerical movement as their chief issue in the campaign leading to the October elections, as a danger not only to France's institutions but also to peace. Already, forgetting their fruitless efforts in 1873, several bishops had written pastoral letters in favor of intervention in Italy. The

[1] Addressing the Monarchists, the *République Française* declared (July 18, 1878), "L'opposition que vous faites est vaine et misérable. La nation passe à côté de vous sans vous reconnaître. Vous la dédaignez; elle vous méprise, en attendant qu'elle vous ignore."

66

Bishop of Vanne declared that "the temporal power will return," and the Bishop of Nevers appealed to the mayors and justices of the peace of his department to use their influence "to change so abnormal a state of affairs." Clerical newspapers in the provinces, the *Emancipateur* of Cambrai, the *Journal* of Mans, the *Impartiale du Finisterre*, were reported as openly speaking of war with Italy. A system of committees was organized in cities with correspondents in the rural districts for the distribution of pamphlets and other propaganda.[2]

Its clerical allies were a source of embarrassment to the foreign policy of the new Broglie ministry, for no one in authority had any intention of following their dangerous advice. It was his intention, MacMahon declared, to continue the existing friendly relations with the Powers.[3] A conversation with Decazes in Paris convinced Crispi, the Italian Minister of the Interior, that the French minister had no aggressive designs against Italy, although Crispi continued to fear the ultimate results of a conservative victory.[4] Decazes, in fact, protested in a letter, June 29, 1877, to Gontaut-Biron against a telegram from Marshal Manteuffel and Ranke, the historian, to Thiers in which hope was expressed for a republican success in the elections. For three years, he had tried to convince Europe "that the conservative party in France . . . could alone guarantee peace, that there was no question upon which France would hesitate to pronounce if it threatened war." He announced that MacMahon was sending General d'Abzac to Berlin, as a personal agent, "with instructions to see as much as possible, to listen and to explain much."[5] Nor was the clerical propaganda, in its bearing upon foreign affairs, permitted to pass unchallenged as the expression of the official point of view. During the summer of 1877, more than a hundred thousand copies of an anonymous pamphlet, *La Politique du Maréchal*, were distributed in the provinces. France, it declared, had to choose between "three years of quiet, which would prepare for the establishment of a definitive government, and three years of trouble which will certainly lead to the Commune and to war. *Voilà pourquoi le mieux à faire est de voter en masse pour les candidats du Maréchal*."[6]

---

[2] *Annales* (1877), III, 214. The *Univers* again printed numerous petitions for action in behalf of the temporal power. *République Française*, April 23, 1877.

[3] *République Française*, May 20, 1877.

[4] *The Memoirs of Francesco Crispi*, 3 vols. (London, 1912), II, 16–19.

[5] Dreux, *Les Dernières Années*, pp. 275, 276. For Manteuffel's telegram see Halévy, *Courrier de M. Thiers*, p. 504.

[6] *Temps*, Aug. 14, 1877.

The Republicans, of course, refused to accept these assurances of peaceful intentions, or more accurately, they insisted that even if the government desired peace, it could not prevent the dangers which its association with the clericals involved. "Europe believes, rightly or wrongly," declared the *Temps* (Oct. 14, 1877), "that the victory of the *seize mai* would be a victory for clericalism and accordingly a menace." Gambetta's *République Française* (May 28, 1877) had reported, immediately after the formation of the Broglie cabinet, that the garrisons of Metz and Strassburg had been strengthened and that French troops were being sent to the frontier. It even enlisted (May 22) the support of Alsatians in this attempt to impress public opinion with the dangers of the situation. "Who knows better than we," wrote a correspondent from Mulhouse, "with what care, what attention Germany watches France, with what impatience she waits for the government to make a mistake. . . . This mistake has been made." The opponents of the Republic pointed to the use of this argument as proof that the Republican press was under German influence.[7] Broglie did not go so far, but he later declared in the chamber that his party had lost the election because of this appeal to fear. "To alarm Europe as to France's disposition, and then to intimidate France by stressing the foreign menace, that was the plan in a nutshell." [8] Bismarck,[9] still at odds with the Church, had caused the danger of a clerical success to be pointed out in Paris. He instructed Hohenlohe to warn not only Decazes, but also political and social leaders, and foreign diplomats, that "ultramontanism means war." "I believe that our chief problem," he wrote, "is to aid in the defeat of MacMahon's coup d'état. It seems possible to do this if the voters are persuaded that the 363 [the Republicans] stand for peace, the reaction for war." [10] The attitude of the republican press, however, was no proof that it had been determined by German influence, for the prevailing fear of complications and the exigencies of politics were a sufficient explanation. In any case, the Republicans succeeded not only in retaining control of the chamber but also in winning a majority in the senate.

Even its opponents recognized that the results of the election meant

---

[7] *Corresp.*, O. S., 107, p. 756.

[8] *Annales* (1877), IV, 158, 159.

[9] He had recently coöperated with France after the murder of the French and German consuls at Salonica. Bourgeois, Pagès, *Origines et Résponsabilités*, p. 179.

[10] Bismarck to Hohenlohe, Berlin, June 29, 1877. *G. P.*, I, 324–327. Hohenlohe's Memoirs contain nothing upon this point. *Memoirs of Prince Chlodwig of Hohenlohe-Schillingfürst*, 2 vols. (New York, 1906).

the triumph of the Republic. "It has nothing more to fear from its adversaries," one admitted in July, 1878.[11] For many years republican control was more certain in domestic legislation than in foreign affairs, for the personnel of the diplomatic service and of the Foreign Office remained, for the most part, monarchist in its sympathies.[12] Little is known of the friction between the conservative bureaucracy and the republican ministers of foreign affairs, but it seems clear that the main objectives of French diplomacy after 1877 were determined by the responsible ministers.

A gradual change had in fact taken place among Republicans as to the character which should be given to France's foreign policy, a change which corresponded with the evolution of their political point of view. Partly to win the peasants,[13] they had abandoned the program of radical reforms, except in regard to the Church, which they had supported under the Second Empire. Thiers had declared that a conservative Republic would be founded or none at all, and even the bohemian Gambetta was converted. The hard-fisted bourgeoisie, accustomed to close bargaining in private life, became the ruling class. It was profoundly suspicious of panaceas,[14] and in foreign affairs, its mood was not at all heroic. Democracy was no longer to be made for exportation, as during the Revolution. The Republic, Gambetta declared at Lyons, February 26, 1876, had renounced "proselytism and cosmopolitanism, understanding that . . . a foreign policy requires respect for the constitutions of other peoples, whatever they may be." [15] The *République Française* (Feb. 7, 1878) added that France should state clearly that "she could no longer be led astray by useless and dangerous attempts at a sentimental and vague propaganda." [16] This point of view was stated even more definitely by the republican *Siècle* (Feb. 15, 1881). "France is not avaricious of her blood but she does not have enough to spill *aux quatre coins*. She cannot spend one drop for others, she needs all of it for herself."

[11] *Corresp., O. S.*, III, p. 192.

[12] Charles Seignobos, *L'Evolution de la Troisième République* (Paris, 1921), pp. 296, 297.

[13] Mary King Waddington, *My First Years as a Frenchwoman* (New York, 1914), p. 208. The author's husband was the Minister of Foreign Affairs, 1877–1879.

[14] J. E. C. Bodley, *Cardinal Manning, The Decay of Idealism in France, the Institute of France* (London, 1913), pp. 70, 71.

[15] *Discours et Plaidoyers Politiques de M. Gambetta*, J. Reinach, ed., 11 vols. (Paris, 1880–1885), II (1882), p. 181.

[16] Cf. E. Vacherot, *La Politique Extérieure de la République* (Paris, 1881), p. 41.

The Monarchists had no quarrel with this concentration upon France's own interests. "Our concern," wrote one, "is not for the constitution or the form of government in Russia or England . . . but for their strength, and their military resources. In regard to foreign affairs, we are neither monarchists, nor republicans . . . we are simply patriots, diplomats or soldiers." [17] Nevertheless, their conception of a proper foreign policy for France differed from the republican point of view in important respects. When in power, circumstances forced the Monarchists to practise a policy of reserve, but their press openly declared that the recovery of Alsace-Lorraine should be the ultimate and avowed goal of the nation's efforts. Bismarck was correct in his opinion that they would have France take advantage of the first favorable opportunity. Yet they held that it would not be necessary to seek it for "there are enough hostilities and causes of trouble in Europe to produce a favorable occasion sooner or later." [18]

The Republicans, while refusing to recognize the loss of Alsace-Lorraine as definitive, felt that it was not even profitable to speculate as to the means by which the lost provinces might be recovered. The immediate task, and the one which should determine France's foreign policy, was the resumption of the broken contacts with the Powers and of a moderate activity abroad. Only in this way could the confidence of Europe be won, and that confidence was essential for the recovery of France's position as a great Power. Once that position had been attained, it was usually assumed that the Alsace-Lorraine question would be revived. E. Littré was one of the few moderate Republicans to examine these questions with a measure of frankness. It would be hypocritical, he admitted, to pretend that France would not use a war for which she was not responsible and in which she was not involved to secure the return of the lost provinces. But her present policy was not concerned with "hazards which cannot be foreseen. It is a question of two policies, one of revenge, the other of acceptance. The first would subordinate everything at home and abroad to give France the maximum of offensive power; the second, while providing amply for the nation's security, would never divert our resources from the amelioration of our economic and moral conditions." [19] It was the second course which he would have France follow. No ministry ever publicly defined its official attitude toward the Alsace-Lorraine question, but if any had ever done so, its point of view would doubtless have been

[17] *Corresp.*, O. S., 116, pp. 114 ff.
[18] *Ibid.*
[19] *Temps,* Jan. 4, 1880.

substantially that of Littré. The Monarchists insisted that this was in fact no policy at all. France, declared the *Gazette de France* (May 9, 1878), must either accept the *fait accompli* of 1871, and her lessened position, without reserve, or she must dream of repairing her faults. Her national pride was too sensitive to permit complete renunciation. "Thus, the republican party cannot have a policy, it cannot declare either for peace or for war." Those who advanced this criticism failed to understand that the opportunist Republicans were not developing a logical policy but a working arrangement which would adapt itself to the circumstances as they developed. "The opportunist point of view," declared a conservative critic, "is felt rather than defined. It is not very clear, nor very definite, but it is by these characteristics that it may be recognized." [20]

In power, Republicans found that even their desire for a gradual development of a moderate diplomatic activity seemed too dangerous to a public which had been taught the need of a policy of reserve. It was prepared to take alarm at the faintest danger of complications. "The country," wrote a thoughtful observer, "concentrated upon its business, its pleasures, its needs, only asks one thing, and that is to be permitted to live, work and to enjoy life in peace." [21] But republican leaders like Gambetta, Freycinet, and Ferry, aware of the nation's rapid recovery in strength and wealth, were not in sympathy with a policy of abdication in foreign affairs. "To advise France," declared Joseph Reinach, who succeeded Gambetta as the editor of the *République Française,* "in such circumstances, to refuse a foreign policy because she was dismembered in 1871 on the Rhine, is to advise a man who has lost an arm to become tuberculous voluntarily. It is equivalent to killing Marseilles because Strassburg has been sacrificed." [22] These men saw that the interests of France under the Republic remained what they had been under the monarchy.[23] An ambitious policy, even if it had been practicable, would not have been accepted by a nervous public opinion, and in its place they proposed to take advantage of minor opportunities to play a part in European affairs and to develop the nation's interests elsewhere.

The decision to inaugurate a policy of moderate activity in foreign

[20] *National,* Jan. 17, 1885.
[21] Vacherot, *La Politique Extérieure de la République,* p. 1.
[22] J. Reinach, *Le Ministère Gambetta, Histoire et Doctrine* . . . (Paris, 1884), p. 384.
[23] J. Reinach, "L'Opinion Publique en France et la Politique Extérieure," *Rev. Politique et Litteraire,* Dec., 1880, p. 559.

affairs was the work of a small group of leaders. Chief among them was Gambetta. Thiers's death in September, 1877, and the republican victory in the October elections placed him in an unrivaled position. "He has the first rôle, if not the first rank, in the State," declared the moderate Catholic *Français* (Sept. 20, 1878), "he is the omnipotent master of the Left, of the Chamber, of the Ministry." [24] His advice, according to Reinach, was at this time constantly asked upon all important questions by members of the cabinet.[25] His influence upon foreign affairs, while more difficult to estimate than the results of his work in political questions, was doubtless important. His point of view was even more significant as an indication of the general tendency of public opinion, for he possessed the gift to an exceptional degree of sensing its general attitude as well as of guiding it. "It cannot be denied," declared the *Temps* (May 26, 1878), "that M. Gambetta more than any other in our history, has the gift . . . of taking into account the state of public opinion, of associating himself with it, of becoming its representative and of crystallizing it." In foreign affairs, he saw the need of leading and educating public opinion as he had in his campaign for the establishment of the Republic. "M. Gambetta," according to Reinach, "held that loyal men should not desert the cause of truth because the mass is at first refractory; . . . their duty is evident: the democracy must be educated in foreign policy as in domestic politics." [26] The kind of education which he had in mind was that of the child in learning to walk by a series of trials, for the time was not yet ripe for the use of the newspaper press in preparing public opinion for an active policy.

After 1871, Gambetta's ideas as to relations with Germany and as to foreign affairs in general became more moderate with those of his party. Yet the warm loyalty to the lost provinces, which won the life-long devotion of the Alsatian Scheurer-Kestner in 1871,[27] was never abandoned. At first, he weighed the possibility of a union with the Pan-Slavic movement, or of an alliance with Austria and Italy, in each case to be directed against Germany.[28] These dangerous schemes, however, were only mentioned in private, for he repeatedly

---

[24] Freycinet wrote later that Gambetta's influence was greatest in 1878–1879. Charles de Freycinet, *Souvenirs, 1873–1893* (Paris, 1913), p. 30. Gambetta was elected, Jan. 31, 1878, to the presidency of the chamber.

[25] Reinach, *Le Ministère Gambetta*, p. 17.

[26] *Ibid.*, pp. 380, 381.

[27] A. Scheurer-Kestner, *Souvenirs de Jeunnesse* (Paris, 1905), pp. 264, 265.

[28] Paul Deschanel, *Gambetta* (New York, 1920), pp. 219, 220.

affirmed in his speeches the need of prudence.[29] Only at St. Quentin, November 16, 1871, did he suggest that this prudence should conceal a determination to achieve the *revanche*. "Let us not speak of the foreigner, but let him ever be in our thoughts. *Alors vous serez sur le chemin de la revanche.*" [30] It was not, however, necessarily the reconquest of Alsace-Lorraine of which he dreamed, for he told Lalance, an Alsatian engineer, in 1871 that "your return to us will be accomplished by peaceful means." [31] As the necessities of the political situation became imperative, he identified the Republic more and more with a policy of peace. "The Republic alone," he declared at Lille, February 6, 1876, before the first elections under the new constitution, "can guarantee peace; it represents a policy of peace under a pacific majority." [32]

The great republican leader, moreover, had developed, perhaps under the influence of Mme. Léon,[33] ambitions in the field of foreign affairs, which he found could be realized only by a policy of moderation. Jules Hansen gave him instruction in the German language,[34] and openly or in secret he made numerous visits to the European capitals and to Germany, where he seems to have established sources of private information. Henckel von Donnersmarck, the German banker residing in Paris, once referred to him as the best informed of French leaders in regard to German affairs.[35] Experience and observation persuaded Gambetta of the danger of seeking alliances upon the continent and even of the futility of another war with Germany. At the last moment, he refused to carry out plans for an interview with Gortchakov, in September, 1875.[36] His growing coolness to an alliance with Russia exasperated his friend Mme. Adam, a passionate advocate of that alliance and of the *revanche,* whose memoirs throw much

---

[29] This was the tone of his first speech, June 26, 1871, after his return from his self-imposed exile at St. Sebastian. *Discours et Plaidoyers,* II, 24.

[30] G. P. Gooch, *Franco-German Relations, 1871–1914* (London, 1923), p. 6.

[31] Auguste Lalance. *Mes Souvenirs, 1830–1914* (Paris, 1914), p. 64.

[32] *Discours et Plaidoyers,* V (1882).

[33] Harold Stannard, *Gambetta and the Founding of the Third Republic* (London, 1921), p. 226. A selection of Gambetta's letters to Mme. Léon may be found in the *Rev. de Paris,* 1906, VI, 419–469, 673–397; 1907, I, 57–75. The entire collection, which she scrupulously guarded, seems to have been disposed of in such a way that it will never be published. Marcellin Pellet, "Souvenirs sur Gambetta," *Revue de France,* Nov. 15, 1927. Pellet was the secretary of the republican majority before the coup d'état of May 16, 1877.

[34] Hansen, *Coulisses de la Diplomatie,* p. 247.

[35] Galli, *Gambetta et l'Alsace-Lorraine,* p. 143.

[36] Mme. Edmond Adam, *Nos Amitiés Politiques avant l'Abandon de la Revanche* (Paris, 1908), pp. 272–275.

light upon his increasing moderation. However great his confidence that the future would bring reparation, he knew that France could not venture to challenge Germany. "After having watched the maneuvers of every branch of her army," he wrote in September, 1876, "I entreat my country more than ever to remain completely apart from the quarrels of Europe, for unfortunately, we do not possess any forces which can compare with the troops which I have just seen." [37] A few weeks later in his Belleville speech, October 27, 1876, he declared that France could only fight or negotiate. "I am for negotiating. I am against war, against violence." [38] A year later, in the midst of the critical campaign in which Bismarck was using his influence in favor of the Republic, Gambetta told a friend that the recovery of Alsace-Lorraine by force of arms would solve nothing: "every German would consider their defeat a national disgrace, and they would devote all their energies to preparing a new war. It would, therefore, never be ended. It would be infinitely preferable to conclude a peaceful agreement between the two countries by which Germany would, in entire freedom, return her conquest to France, in exchange for financial, colonial or tariff concessions. It would be an honorable agreement and the two peoples could thereupon become friends." [39]

In opposition, Gambetta's ideas were important as those of the most influential leader of the republican party. The October election of 1877 gave these ideas, in a sense, an official significance. The time had come, with the fairly safe establishment of the Republic, to put into effect the second part of his program.[40] It was his purpose, as well as that of almost all of the statesmen of the Third Republic, to restore France to her position as a Great Power. Although confused abroad, especially in Germany, with the desire for revenge, the two aspirations were by no means identical, although the lost provinces were frequently the symbol for the more intangible aim. So it was that Gambetta first considered the possibility of negotiating with Bismarck for the solution of the Alsace-Lorraine question. Delighted with Bismarck's speech of February 19, 1878, which he interpreted

[37] Mme. E. Adam, *Après l'Abandon de la Revanche* (Paris, 1911), pp. 71–73. In June, 1875, he wrote to Mme. Léon that "our rôle should be like that of Molière's Sosie the friend of everybody . . . and to delay the ultimate conflict (Near Eastern crisis) as long as possible." *Rev. de Paris* (1906), VI, 681.

[38] *Discours et Plaidoyers*, VI, 160, 161.

[39] Lalance, *Mes Souvenirs*, p. 70.

[40] This decision is implied in his letters to Mme. Léon in 1877–1878.

as an invitation for the opening of negotiations,[41] he accepted Henckel von Donnersmarck's suggestion of a personal interview with the Chancellor.[42] He wrote to Mme. Léon that he was going to see the "monster," the term which they applied to Bismarck in private.[43] In 1882, he told Reinach that it had been his intention to keep his mission a secret until his arrival in Berlin, where arrangements had been made, he thought, for him to meet officially not only the Chancellor, but also all of the ministers and the presidents of the two Chambers of the German parliament.[44] Gambetta suddenly changed his mind, writing to von Donnersmarck that the pressure of official business would prevent him from leaving Paris, although he left the door open for later negotiations by suggesting that the proposal might be revived in the future.[45] This was evidently a pretext. The truth seems to have been that Bismarck was unwilling to do more than to meet him in secret and above all that he had no intention of permitting a discussion of Alsace-Lorraine. Nevertheless, the Chancellor wrote to Hohenlohe, August 28, 1878, of his desire "to reach a political understanding with M. Gambetta." [46] Gambetta had a further reason for changing his plans, for the indiscretion of a confidant [47] led to an attack from the monarchist press.[48] Even this discouraging experience did not cause him to renounce his preference for a reasonable attitude on the Alsace-Lorraine question. "You are wedded to your prejudices," he told Mme. Adam, "you see only what you wish to see, and that is Alsace-

---

[41] Galli, *Gambetta et l'Alsace-Lorraine*, pp. 158 ff. "Voici que se lève," he wrote to Mme. Lèon, "maintenant dans cet hômme l'aurore radieuse du droit: c'est à nous à présent de profiter des circonstances . . . pour poser nettement nos plus légitimes révendications." *Rev. de Paris*, 1906, VI, 694. Gambetta's optimism was clearly exaggerated. Cf. text of Bismarck's speech. *Die Politischen Reden des Fürsten von Bismarck*, Horst Kohl, ed., 13 vols. (1892-1905), VIII, 92, 93. In view of the fact that Gambetta had no official connection with the Ministry of Foreign Affairs, it is not surprising that his proposed negotiation with Bismarck is not mentioned in the recently published French diplomatic documents. *Documents Diplomatiques Français* (1871-1914), 1st series, vol. II.

[42] Thiers, it is said, introduced Gambetta to the salon of La Païva, von Donnersmarck's wife. J. Reinach, "Gambetta et Bismarck, l'Affaire Schnaebelé," *Rev. de Paris* (1917), IV, 749. Claiming the exclusive credit for this plan, Blowitz does not mention von Donnersmarck. Blowitz, *Memoirs*, p. 150.

[43] Gambetta, "Lettres," *Rev. de Paris*, 1917, I, 58 (April 23, 1878). Cf. C. de Roux, *La République de M. de Bismarck* (Paris, 1915), pp. 63-87.

[44] Reinach, "Gambetta et Bismarck," *Rev. de Paris*, 1917, IV, 750.

[45] Gooch, *Franco-German Relations*, p. 18.

[46] *G. P.*, III, 387.

[47] Reinach named Émile de Girardin as responsible. *Rev. de Paris*, 1917, IV.

[48] Où en est l'Alsace-Lorraine," *Corresp.*, O. S. III, p. 716. *Gazette de France*, Apr. 18, 1878. *République Française*, Apr. 24, 1878.

Lorraine. What France needs is precisely an escape from this vicious circle which has been traced by narrow minds; we must above all breathe, live, we must expand, and move forward." [49] Less attention than in the first years after 1871 was given to Alsace-Lorraine in the *République Française*. "Its tone has changed," complained Mme. Adam, "it has become cautious. It is a complete transformation. The glorious air of courage is now sung in a minor key. . . ." [50]

The Congress of Berlin in 1878 was the first occasion for the application of the opportunist point of view in foreign affairs. The few in France who had shown any interest in the Near Eastern crisis and the Russo-Turkish war were agreed that the country must not be involved. [51] The Serbs, as disturbers of the peace, received little sympathy, and Russia was given no encouragement. [52] Gambetta aroused the righteous indignation of Mme. Adam by calling her a Cossack. "There is nothing to gain with Russia," he told her during the Russo-Turkish war," beaten or victorious, only defeat awaits her." [53] France's influence was therefore exerted, in a moderate way, in the interest of harmony between the Great Powers. [54] Even Gambetta was doubtful at first as to the advisability of participating in the Congress, but his approval was gained when it was decided that none of the questions in which France was vitally interested would be discussed. [55] The Monarchists offered little criticism, and the chamber, by a unanimous vote, approved the decision to participate as in keeping with France's neutrality. [56] For a brief moment, the publication of England's secret agreement with Turkey, June 4, 1878, which permitted her to occupy Cyprus, threatened to cause France's withdrawal. Lyons had predicted that it would be most unfavorably received. [57] Although Gambetta had been turning toward close relations with England, the *République Française* (July 11) declared that the Powers would reserve their freedom of action if the Anglo-Turkish pact were not

[49] Mme. Adam, *Après l'Abandon de la Revanche*, pp. 221, 222.

[50] *Ibid.*, p. 51. That this position was shared by the government is clear from the recently published documents, *Documents Diplomatiques Français*, 1st Series, I, II.

[51] "Peace on the Danube," affirmed the *Corresp.* (O. S., 100, p. 1250, Sept., 1875), "is to-day peace on the Rhine and in the Vosges."

[52] Thiers to Simon, Sept. 16, 1876. Simon, *Thiers, Guizot, Rémusat*, pp. 121, 122.

[53] Mme. Adam, *Après l'Abandon de la Revanche*, pp. 71–73.

[54] Bourgeois, Pagès, *Origines et Résponsabilités*, pp. 179, 180.

[55] He told Mme. Léon that she had overcome his reluctance. Gambetta, "Lettres," *Rev. de Paris*, 1907, I, 57 (March 6, 1878).

[56] *Annales*, 1878, VIII, 160 (June 7).

[57] Newton, *Lyons*, II, 144.

submitted to the Congress, and if it were considered by that assembly, it would be the duty of the French delegation to reject it. The *Journal des Débats* (July 12) and the *Temps* (July 12) at once exerted themselves to moderate this unfavorable impression, but Salisbury's assurance to Waddington, the French foreign minister, July 7, of England's good-will if France should decide to establish her influence in Tunis probably was more effective in reconciling Gambetta.[58] Later in July, he dined with the Prince of Wales in Paris,[59] and an interview with Blowitz shows that Gambetta had recovered from the shock of the Cyprus agreement. He was glad, he said, to see that England had abandoned her policy of isolation for the interests of the two liberal Powers required their coöperation. France had no intention, he said, of seeking an alliance with Russia. "A Franco-Russian alliance, an arbitrary, capricious and perilous policy is no longer possible; the new state of affairs turns us naturally towards a policy of reason, of defense, of good results for all, without danger for any one." [60]

It was a source of satisfaction in France that her representatives supported the interests of Greece and Roumania. Russia was accorded little sympathy by the moderate republican press, for the *Journal des Débats* (Aug. 13), generally known as associated with Léon Say, the economist and Minister of Commerce, even took a strong position against her interests in the Balkans. Austria, it declared, should assume the protectorate of Turkey in Europe as England had in Asia. She was advised to subdue Serbia and Roumania in order to protect her position in Bosnia-Herzegovina against the "plots of Pan-Slavism. The true enemies of Austria are not the Mussulman Begs . . . nor the Porte . . . they are the agents of Pan-Slavism and the government which set them against Turkey is ready to-day to turn them against her." Although France rejected Russia's overtures in 1879 and informed Berlin of them,[61] neither the press in general nor the Quai d'Orsay adopted the *Journal des Débats's* openly anti-Russian attitude. With the conclusion of the Congress's work, the Monarchists abandoned their fairly neutral attitude by claiming that France's position was worse than it had been. The support given the Greeks was con-

---

[58] W. L. Langer, "The European Powers and the Occupation of Tunis," *Amer. Hist. Rev.*, XXXI, 66. It is now clear that Salisbury's offer of Tunis, during the Congress of Berlin, preceded Bismarck's suggestion. Waddington to d'Harcourt, Paris, July 21, 1878. *Documents Diplomatiques Français* (1871–1914), 1st Series, II, 360.
[59] *Gazette de France*, July 24, 1878.
[60] *République Française*, July 27, 1878. Cf. *Discours et Plaidoyers*, VIII, 375.
[61] G. P. Gooch, *History of Modern Europe* (New York, 1923), p. 33.

demned. "We have liberated enough peoples," declared the *Correspondant*," and we have enough French people beyond the Vosges to free in the future." [62] The *Français* (July 17) believed that France was more than ever alone in her tête-à-tête with Germany, for Russia had been alienated, Austria's interests henceforth would be in the Balkans, and England, now satisfied, would return to her policy of isolation.[63] In the absence of complications to give them point, these captious arguments were, in the main, of little influence. The first step in the republican program of renewed diplomatic activity had been successful.

In 1879, MacMahon's resignation and Jules Grèvy's election to the presidency drove the Monarchists from their last stronghold in the government. The joy of republican leaders was increased by the excellent results of the reorganization of the army. Gambetta, especially, believed that the time had arrived for more active measures and for a prouder attitude in foreign affairs. After the presentation of the colors to the army, July 14, 1879, he wrote to Mme. Léon that the splendid appearance of France's young soldiers had given him new hope. A year later, on the same occasion, he told the commanding officers: "You should look forward with confidence to the future as I do. Let us never forget." [64] Hitherto these sentiments had always been stated in private; on August 9, 1881, perhaps moved by the ceremony just concluded of presenting the colors to the fleet, he made his famous reference at Cherbourg to an "imminent justice" which is now carved upon the base of his statue in the Place du Carrousel. .

"We may have a full restitution based upon right. . . We who have seen France fall so low must raise her to her feet again and restore her to her rightful place in the world. If our hearts beat, it is for this goal, and not to pursue an ideal of blood and slaughter; it is to insure that not one jot of the France which remains shall be lost; it is to feel that we may count upon the future, and to know that, here below, there is an imminent justice which will come at its appointed day and hour." [65]

If this proud and ringing declaration of faith had any significance, it meant that Gambetta was announcing publicly that the recovery of Alsace-Lorraine, perhaps by peaceful means, was to be associated

---

[62] O. S., 113 (Dec. 25, 1878).

[63] The *Gazette de France* (Aug. 7, 1878) revived the old indictment that the Republicans were appealing to Germany's aid.

[64] *Rev. de Paris*, 1906, VI, 66.

[65] Deschanel, *Gambetta*, pp. 276, 277. In May, 1881, Gambetta told Sir Charles Dilke that his Cherbourg speech "was the first glass of wine given to convalescent France, good for her but somewhat startling to her system. . . ." Newton, *Lyons*, II, 244.

with the nation's efforts to regain her full stature as a C
His critics at once claimed that he was advocating war
view which was endorsed by Rochefort's radical *Intran*
the monarchist *Pays*.[66] Members of Mme. Adam's group
chauvinists welcomed Gambetta's pronouncement, and g;
exaggerated meaning. Once France had become invulnerable, affirmed Émile de Girardin in the *France* (Aug. 16), "We will wait with
grounded arms the inevitable and complete fall of this badly con-
structed Empire which is the oppressor of races and peoples." Bismarck's official organ, the *Norddeutsche Allgemeine Zeitung,* made
of this article, which expressed neither the views of the French government nor those of Gambetta, an occasion for declaring that Gambetta had tired of supporting a policy of peace. For a time, Gambetta
refrained from answering his critics. On August 28, the *République
Française* proudly proclaimed that "France . . . has recovered her
place in the European concert. . . . She has recovered her full
strength." It was not until six months later that Gambetta protested
in the chamber that a mistaken interpretation had been given a phrase
"which like many others lent itself to a double interpretation." [67] In
any event, the German press did not continue the attack, for Bismarck
accepted President Grèvy's and Freycinet's (the Prime Minister)
peaceful assurances.

Gambetta had lost touch with the prevailing tendency of public
opinion in the enthusiasm caused by the nation's renewed military
strength. His Cherbourg speech had won the applause of his audience,
but the public in general was not yet prepared for the luxury of extreme self-confidence. The promptness with which the opposition
urged the danger of war testified to the failure of public opinion to
respond to his appeal. In 1880, the Monarchists were strengthened in
their opposition to the opportunist Republicans by new and strange
allies from the radical left. The Radicals had hitherto concentrated
their efforts upon the enactment of an amnesty in behalf of those who
were still being punished, or who were still in exile, for their participation in the Commune. Although Gambetta was largely responsible
for the success of this effort, once this purpose had been accom-

[66] Reinach, *Le Ministère Gambetta,* pp. 408, 409 Cf. *Univers,* Aug. 12. *Gazette de France,* Aug. 11. The *Temps* (Aug. 21) denied that the speech was an
appeal to the spirit of revenge.
[67] *Annales,* 1881, I, 323 (Feb. 21). He perhaps wished to counteract the effect of a monarchist pamphlet attributing a war policy to him which circulated to
the extent of a hundred thousand copies. *Léon Lavedan* [*Philippe de Grandlieu*],
M. Gambetta et la Guerre (Paris, 1881).

plished, they turned against him, joining the Monarchists in a policy of systematic opposition. The radical and moderate Republicans differed chiefly, it is true, in regard to the questions of domestic politics, and the *République Française* (Dec. 5, 1880) found it difficult to believe that the Republic's foreign policy would be opposed by Republicans. Nevertheless, the Radicals did not agree with the opportunist point of view in foreign affairs. In November, 1880, Reinach identified the foreign policy of the Republic with the traditions of the monarchy. The Republic, he wrote, was the heir of "the foreign policy established by the Valois kings and gloriously continued by Henry IV and Louis XIV. It is these traditions, in their noblest and highest form, which the republican policy continues in the Near East and elsewhere." [68] The extreme left, in Parliament and in the press, represented by Rochefort's *Intransigeant* and Clemenceau's *Justice,* both founded in 1880, drew its inspiration from the Jacobin traditions of the Revolution. Its opinions in regard to foreign affairs at first were determined by a concern for social and political reforms in France. Instead of seeking to resume an active foreign policy, wrote Charles Longuet in the *Justice* (Sept. 16, 1880), France should contribute by a passive attitude to a long period of peace which would help the revolutionary groups in Russia to overthrow the aristocracy. "The best way to accomplish the destruction of reactionary institutions in Russia and elsewhere," declared Camille Pelletan, "is to condemn them to inaction by preventing any occasion for the disturbance of European peace." [69] Even Clemenceau, in spite of his later reputation as a fire-eater, agreed with this point of view. "We desire republican reforms," he said at Marseilles, October 29, 1880, "and consequently peace . . . violence founds nothing. Permit peace to accomplish its work among all of the peoples of Europe, and it will be promptly seen that it is the best ally of France and of the Republic." [70] This point of view differed even more widely from the opinions of the Monarchists than from those of the opportunists, yet the Radicals and Monarchists almost immediately joined forces against the Republic's modest efforts to resume a moderate activity in foreign affairs.

[68] Reinach, "L'Opinion Publique en France et la Politique Extérieure," *Rev. Pol. et Lit.,* Dec., 1880, pp. 563, 564. Cf. Ferry's preface to his "Affaires de Tunisie," *Discours et Opinions de Jules Ferry,* P. Robiquet, ed., 7 vols. (Paris, 1893–1898), V, 522, 523.

[69] *Justice,* Sept. 18, 1880.

[70] *Ibid.,* Nov. 1, 1880. The influence of the extreme left in parliament and in the press should not, however, be exaggerated.

The first occasion for this union arose in connection with the boundary difficulties between Greece and Turkey. Certain leaders held that France had a particular and perhaps sentimental interest in Greece. "She is, so to speak," remarked Reinach, "a creation of France." [71] The French representatives at the Congress of Berlin had been active in securing for Greece the promise of Thessaly in Article 13 of the final treaty, but it was evident by the spring of 1880 that Turkey did not intend to cede this province voluntarily. The way was thereby opened for the common action of the signatory Powers and for an initiative by France. In April, Freycinet, the Minister of Foreign Affairs, suggested to England that the question should be submitted to a conference,[72] and it is said that he hoped that it would meet in Paris.[73] It was Bismarck, however, who issued the invitation, and it was in Berlin that the conference met in June, 1880. A boundary line was agreed upon without, however, providing any specific means for compelling Turkey to yield. In the later negotiations, occasioned by Greece's restlessness and Turkey's inaction, French diplomacy was careful to act in conjunction with the other Powers, and especially with Germany.[74]

No particular opposition was aroused in France until July, when it was rumored that the government contemplated the dispatch of a military mission to Greece upon her invitation, as well as a shipment of thirty thousand rifles, and that Germany was about to send officers to Turkey.[75] "The country was perfectly tranquil," wrote a thoughtful observer of events, "when it suddenly heard that it was engaged in Near Eastern affairs, that a military mission was going to Greece where a campaign against Turkey was in preparation." [76] Even the moderate press joined in the protest aroused by this departure from the policy of reserve which public opinion for years had been told was necessary. "It is the first time in ten years," declared the *Journal des Débats* (Aug. 6), "that a question of foreign policy impassions public opinion; it is the first time that the country is moved by the resolutions of its government and that it apparently desires to control that policy by a serious examination." Even the *Temps* (July 16) at first

[71] Reinach, *Le Ministère Gambetta*, p. 386.
[72] *Livre Jaune: Affaires de Grèce en 1880* (Paris, 1881), pp. 1–4.
[73] Bourgeois, *Manuel Historique*, IV, 71.
[74] É. Driault et M. L'Hèritier, *Histoire Diplomatique de la Grèce*, IV (Paris, 1926), pp. 72–151.
[75] Hanotaux, *Histoire de la France Contemporaine*, IV, 629.
[76] Vacherot, *La Politique Extérieure de la République*, p. 2.

joined the chorus of disapproval, contending that France should take no initiative in favor of the Greeks. "The time does not seem to us to have arrived for France to depart from the reserve from which she has drawn so much strength, and it would seem to us to be doubly regrettable that she should abandon it now to throw herself into one of those sentimental adventures whose disinterestedness is so close to dupery." [77] The nervousness of public opinion furnished an admirable opportunity for the Monarchists and Radicals. Several factors prevented their success in pressing their advantage to secure the government's complete withdrawal. The Thomassin mission never left France, and it was learned that the German mission would not go to Turkey until the boundary dispute had been settled.[78] Both the Freycinet cabinet and the Ferry ministry which succeeded it in September, 1880, repeatedly warned Greece that French public opinion would not tolerate active measures in her defense if she decided to go to war with Turkey. Their policy of coöperation with the other Powers until the question was arranged in May, 1881, by a separate agreement between Greece and Turkey quieted the alarm of the moderate press. The *Temps,* the *Journal des Débats,* and the *République Française* advised resistance to the systematic opposition of the Monarchists and Radicals.[79] On February 3, a vote of confidence was given the government's policy by a considerable majority, but Antonin Proust's defense of it was received coolly by an inattentive chamber.[80]

While in opposition, the opportunist point of view agreed with the prevailing tendencies of public opinion, which, in fact, it had done much to confirm. In power, the determination of the moderate Republicans to resume an active part in foreign affairs was passively accepted, but with the implied condition that there would be no complications. Even Gambetta's strength depended much more upon his support of republican institutions than upon his advocacy of an active foreign policy, or upon his appeal to patriotic sentiment in his Cherbourg speech. The sudden reversal of public opinion during the affair of the Greco-Turkish frontier again revealed the prevailing susceptibility to the slightest danger. It was a source of keen disappointment to Reinach. "It is in vain," he complained, "that men of common sense

[77] See Newton, *Lyons,* II, 229, for Lyons's comments, Oct. 4, 1880.

[78] *Livre Jaune: Affaires de Grèce en 1880,* pp. 88, 89. Cf., Barthélemy Saint-Hilaire, *Diplomatie Française. Fragments pour servir l'Histoire de la Diplomatie Française du 23 Septembre, 1880 au 14 Novembre 1881* (Paris, 1882), p. 10.

[79] Reinach, "L'Opinion Publique en France et la Politique Extérieure," *Rev. Pol. et Lit.* Dec., 1880, p. 556.

[80] *Annales,* 1881, I, 323.

and courage are prodigal of the most pressing warnings. . . . What is it precisely that is feared? No one can say. The true character of fear is its vagueness." It was necessary, he concluded, to form "in this country a firm and reasoned public opinion upon foreign policy."[81] Dependent upon the support of the nation, and none too sure of its tenure in power, the Republic refrained from developing its diplomatic activity upon the Continent when faced by the danger of complications. In this cautious policy, it yielded to the nervousness of public opinion. Nevertheless, opportunism had restored France to a place in the councils of Europe. "France has reëntered the concert of Europe," wrote Barthèlemy Saint-Hilaire, "she has played her part in the great events of the last three years."[82]

---

[81] Reinach, "L'Opinion Publique en France et la Politique Extérieure," *Rev. Pol. et Lit.*, Dec., 1880, pp. 561, 562.
[82] *Livre Jaune: Affaires de Grèce, 1880–1881*, p. XVIII (June 20, 1881).

CHAPTER V

COLONIAL EXPANSION AND THE ENTENTE WITH GERMANY, 1881–1885

Il est nécessaire de se placer devant la réalité des choses et de ne pas se bercer de vains rêves, d'illusions chimériques. . . . je le dis avec douleur mais avec une parfaite sincérité, celui qui dans l'etat présent des choses provoquerait une collision avec un pays que je ne veux pas nommer, celui-là serait non seulement un insensé, mais un criminel. Je trouve donc que le moment est bien choisi pour refaire notre fortune coloniale.
Bishop Freppel, *Annales de la Chambre des Députés* (1884)., II (November 25).

After the settlement of the Greco-Turkish boundary difficulty, no other opportunity was available for the development of France's diplomatic activity in Europe. The formation of Bismarck's alliances, moreover, had increased the sensitiveness of public opinion to the danger of complications. He had assured France that the Dual Alliance with Austria in 1879 was not directed against her,[1] and the moderate Republicans, to check unwarranted alarm, sometimes agreed.[2] Nevertheless, even those who were apparently most optimistic reflected bitterly that the peace which Germany wished to maintain was based in part upon the Treaty of Frankfort,[3] while the Monarchists naturally emphasized the difficulties which the Republic would encounter after the formation of the Triple Alliance in 1882.[4]

Colonial expansion was therefore suggested as a less dangerous and a more profitable way of enhancing the prestige and influence of France and of the Republic. A group of republican leaders, according to the monarchist deputy, Jules Delafosse, held that "France must expand in order to compensate her losses upon the Continent."[5] In comparison with Tunis, wrote Saint-Vallier, the ambassador to Ger-

[1] Hanotaux, *Histoire de la France Contemporaine*, IV, 501, quoting the *Temps*, Sept. 27, 1879. *Documents Diplomatiques Français*, 1st Series, II, 559–564.
[2] *Rev. des Deux Mondes* (1883), III, 471, 472.
[3] *Republique Française*, Sept. 16, 1879. *Temps*, Feb. 10, 1880.
[4] Broglie declared in the Senate, May 1, 1883, that France would have to count upon the hostility of three Powers instead of one in diplomacy as well as war. *Annales du Sénat*, 1883, II, 50–53. Cf. *Corresp.*, O. S., 131, pp. 580, 581.
[5] *Annales*, 1883, II, 299.

many (March 29, 1881), such questions as that of the Greek frontier "are merely platonic affairs for us." [6] Gambetta was unwilling to subordinate France's Continental interests, but it was his opinion that "the colonial policy is the only fruitful policy of recovery." [7] Public opinion was not the cause of this change of policy any more than it explains the war of 1870, Decazes's maneuvers in 1875, or France's initiative on behalf of Greece. Lacking the imperial traditions of England, and Germany's exuberant spirit of expansion supported by her remarkable industrial and commercial development, the French nation of necessity and choice was mostly concerned with problems at home. It was not until the Tunis expedition of 1881 that an active colonial propaganda was organized. Prévost-Paradol's prophetic vision of a French empire in North Africa had aroused little interest in the last years of the Second Empire, when every colonial enterprise was associated with the Mexican adventure of unhappy memory.[8] In 1874, Paul Leroy-Beaulieu published his *Colonisation chez les Peuples Modernes* as an academic exercise without appreciable effect upon public opinion. The "terrible year" was too near for much attention to be given to distant parts of the world.

After France had entered the race for colonies in 1881, propagandists at once busied themselves in an effort to arouse public opinion. Almost all of the moderate republican press used its influence for this purpose, and when such newspapers as the *Temps* and the *Journal des Débats* gave their active support, it meant that the powerful middle classes were sympathetic. The case for colonial expansion was supported by the same arguments that were used in other countries: the need of markets and raw materials, the necessity of avenging insults, strategic considerations, and the nation's *"mission civilisatrice."* [9] France's position after 1871, however, sometimes changed the emphasis and occasionally led to the expression of a distinctive point of view. Jules Ferry, the leading colonial statesman, urged the value of colonies as outlets for France's surplus capital.[10] Other arguments were developed which responsible statesmen could not well avow. France's low birth-rate, it was said, required drastic action, for the close of the twentieth century might find England and Germany

[6] Ernest Daudet, *La Mission de Saint-Vallier* (Paris, 1918), pp. 248, 249.
[7] Reinach, *Le Ministère Gambetta,* pp. 412, 413.
[8] Prévost-Paradol, *La France Nouvelle,* pp. 417–419.
[9] Parker T. Moon, *Imperialism and World Politics* (New York, 1926), pp. 41–47.
[10] A. Rambaud, *Jules Ferry* (Paris, 1903), pp. 390, 391.

with 145 millions (!) while she would have a population of only 50 millions.[11] One of the few advocates of colonial expansion among the Radicals pointed to its military value. "The grandeur of France," he wrote, "is indispensable to the progress of humanity. It is for that reason that I approve a policy which will gather a hundred millions of defenders of the Revolution around the French flag." [12] Gabriel Charmes, an important contributor to the *Journal des Débats*, discussed the question from the point of view of France's general policy. In his opinion, France had sacrificed too much to her Continental policy, and he cited Russia's expansion in the Far East after the Crimean War to show that colonial expansion would contribute to the nation's recovery.[13] Another wrote that "colonization has never weakened us; on the contrary, the Continental policy has caused most of our reverses." [14] The ultimate effect of these arguments was to arouse considerable interest in colonial expansion, but the more general development of this interest was due to the romantic aspects of exploration. Publishers established reviews and printed novels dealing with this theme in expectation of profits.[15] A steady majority in parliament sanctioned Ferry's numerous requests for appropriations and voted resolutions of confidence in his policy.[16] Even the monarchist and radical opposition was embarrassed when valuable territory, like Tunis, was acquired. Nevertheless, events were to show that success and the avoidance of international complications were essential for a favorable reaction of public opinion.

Bismarck's paramount position in Europe required an assurance of his approval in order to be certain of these necessary conditions. His temper in regard to France had improved with the establishment of the Republic and after the conclusion in 1878 of his own conflict with the Church. During a period of several years, he apparently changed his estimate of French psychology by admitting the possibility of reconciling public opinion in France to the loss of Alsace-Lorraine. It was not only to turn her attention away from the Rhine but to encourage the development of a moderate opinion that he sup-

[11] Lefefvre Saint-Ogan, *La Question Sociale et la Crise* (Paris, 1886), p. 13.

[12] Léon Hugonnet, *Le Réveil National* (Paris, 1886), p. 66. The *Temps,* April 15, 1883, recommended the organization of a colonial army of colored troops.

[13] G. Charmes, *Politique Extérieure et Coloniale* (Paris, 1885), pp. 8–10. See the appreciative article by Étienne Lamy upon Charmes in *Le Livre du Centenaire du Journal des Débats* (Paris, 1889), pp. 376–383.

[14] Hugonnet, *Le Réveil National,* V–VII.

[15] E. Wickersheimer, "La Politique Coloniale," *Nouvelle Revue,* vol. 49, p. 563.

[16] Freycinet, *Souvenirs,* pp. 266, 267.

ported almost all of France's aspirations, always excepting Alsace-Lorraine. He was also unwilling to go very far with France in the Egyptian question, for that would endanger his relations with England. "Our understanding," he wrote to Hohenlohe, April 8, 1880, "extends from Guinea to Belgium and covers all latin countries; France must only renounce Germany's conquests in order to remain on friendly terms with us." [17] In April, 1881, during the Tunis affair, he declared that France could have a free hand in much of the Mediterranean, and, according to Busch, he hoped that France would one day see that a friendly German Empire was more important to her than a million Alsace-Lorrainers. [18]

It is easy to say from the point of view of later events that Bismarck was seeking the impossible in attempting to persuade France "to forgive Sedan as she had forgiven Waterloo." Nevertheless, it did not appear to be entirely hopeless at the time. If Saint-Vallier always accompanied his discussion of the questions in which the two countries could coöperate with the warning that Alsace-Lorraine was reserved, [19] he did not adequately interpret public opinion in France. Gambetta's advice of silence, as he must have foreseen, was followed to the extent that the memories of 1871 became less poignant. Alsace-Lorraine was rarely mentioned in the press, almost never in parliament, and concern for the nation's prestige and security in Europe figured more largely in the arguments of the opponents of colonial expansion. "One would say that a century has elapsed since 1871!" exclaimed a moderate observer. "To-day people try to avoid thinking of the past, to throw a veil over its unhappy memories. It is the style to be indifferent to the old wounds and to believe in all sorts of good fortune." [20] It was one of the rare periods after 1871 when even a few responsible publicists ventured to speak openly of the need to accept the *status quo* in regard to the eastern frontier. One would have France, like other Powers, follow a policy of self-interest, instead of cherishing "sterile regrets. The most disastrous mistake we can make is to believe in perpetual hostilities." Her existing boundaries following mountains and rivers were satisfactory, and if Alsatians were dissatisfied with German rule, they should emigrate like the Turks in Bulgaria. [21] The economist, Paul Leroy-

[17] *G. P.*, III, 395, 396.
[18] Busch to Hohenlohe, Berlin, Nov. 15, 1881. *Ibid.*, III, 402.
[19] Bourgeois, Pagès, *Origines et Résponsabilités*, pp. 387, 388.
[20] *Rev. des Deux Mondes*, 1881, III, 467.
[21] Hugonnet, *Le Réveil National*, p. 285.

Beaulieu, was even more explicit. "We must tell our country the truth, we must dispel the illusions which would lead us into new catastrophes. In the presence of a Germany of 45 millions, which will have 60 in twenty years, and 80 in fifty years, the hope of revenge is chimerical." [22]

The great majority of the nation, of course, was not prepared to accept this conclusion when it was stated in unequivocal form. None of the influential newspapers, whose business it was to sense the point of view which would be acceptable to public opinion, ventured to approve it. Yet it was possible in the course of time to create a state of mind which would in practice mean the acceptance of the *status quo,* even if a formal recognition of it were never made. A long stride toward this end might have been taken if the colonial group could have counted upon Germany's support in the friction which its policy was certain to create with England. This support seemed assured in the first phases of French colonial expansion. In 1879, Bismarck persuaded England not to withdraw her approval of France's aspirations in Tunis,[23] and she received his support during the Madrid conference of 1880 in regard to Morocco.[24] Continued throughout the Tunis affair, it was in effect withdrawn in Egypt when it would have been most appreciated in France. However, it was not only Bismarck's refusal to support France there which prevented the development of a more tolerant attitude toward Germany. Politics also played an important part. The opposition parties were ready to use the government's coöperation with Germany to arouse patriotic sentiment against an association with the national enemy. This maneuver was first attempted—without effect, however—upon the government's policy during the Tunis expedition of 1881.

Public opinion had no part in the origins of the plan to establish French influence in Tunis. Decazes had thought of it, as early as 1873,[25] but the first steps were taken by French capitalists who ad-

---

[22] *Économiste Française,* May 7, 1881. Cf. Christian Schefer, *La Crise Actuelle* (Paris, 1901), pp. 22, 23.

[23] Bülow to Bismarck, Berlin, Jan. 2, 1879. Bismarck to Bülow, Friedrichsruh, Jan. 3, 1879. Herbert von Bismarck to Bülow, Jan. 5, 1879. *G. P.,* III, 387–389.

[24] *Ibid.,* III, 398, 399.

[25] W. L. Langer, "The European Powers and the French Occupation of Tunis, 1878–1881," I. *Amer. Hist. Rev.,* XXXI, 58, 59. Decazes, at this time, gave the most formal assurances to England that his government had no such intentions. Decazes to Gavard, Versailles, Dec. 28, 1873. *Documents Diplomatiques Français,* 1st Series, I, 289.

vanced loans to the Bey at exorbitant interest. Waddington said in private on his return from the Congress of Berlin in 1878 that he had brought Tunis home in his pocket, but the friendly press claimed that no bargain had been made, that his hands were clean.[26] France delayed action until 1881, in part because of prospective opposition from the Monarchists and Radicals. This expectation was well founded. When the government used one of the numerous violations of the Algerian frontier, March 30, by the Hroumirs as an excuse for a military expedition,[27] the monarchist *Gazette de France* and the radical *Intransigeant* combined in a protest against a "new Mexican adventure." [28] The government's failure to communicate its intentions to parliament and to public opinion, and the obviously friendly attitude of Germany became the chief grounds of criticism. "Instead of a policy of frankness, carried out in close association with the chamber and public opinion," complained Camille Pelletan, Clemenceau's associate in the *Justice,* "the ministry proceeds without explaining anything and the chamber approves complaisantly." [29] It was Germany's friendly attitude, however, which was used with greatest effect. It was, in fact, Bismarck's support which prevented active opposition to France's plans by Italy, who cherished similar ambitions in Tunis, and by Turkey.[30] The Radicals opposed in principle the acquisition of any colonies, but both factions were equally aroused by Germany's suspicious friendliness. Clemenceau conceded the need of punishing the Hroumirs, but he at once added that if the expedition were not promptly withdrawn after its avowed purpose had been accomplished, the government would confess its complicity with Bismarck. "When gifts are offered by M. de Bismarck, they are particularly suspect in our eyes." [31] The *Gazette de France* (May 16) suspected that the Chancellor was seeking to separate France from England and Italy. This charge was repeated by Clemenceau in the debate, May 23, on the ratification of the Treaty of Bardo. "And what is more serious," he added, "we have this sudden and surprising explosion of friendship. For my part, I find it dangerous. (Applause from the Right and Ex-

[26] *Journal des Débats,* July 20, 1878. *République Française,* July 19, 1878.

[27] Bismarck had renewed his assurance of support. E. Daudet, *La Mission du Comté de Saint-Vallier* (Paris, 1918), pp. 209–213. Blowitz published Salisbury's approval in the *Times,* April 11, 1881.

[28] *Temps,* April 7, 1881.

[29] *Justice,* April 9, 1881.

[30] Langer, "Occupation of Tunis," II. *Amer. Hist. Rev.,* XXXI, 262, 263.

[31] *Justice,* May 5.

treme Left.) I suspect these presents instead of accepting them with the gratitude which I am astonished to find expressed in a document in the newspapers." [32]

It was a letter which Barthélemy Saint-Hilaire, the Minister of Foreign Affairs, was said to have written to the *Deutsche Revue*, to which Clemenceau referred. " *'We have nothing but praise for Germany's attitude* in this important question; I am happy to express the gratitude we owe to the German government and to the important organs of your press. This is but justice.' " [33] This frank acknowledgment of Germany's support was at once exploited by the opposition as a betrayal of the memories of 1871. "We confess that we still remember something of 1871," declared Camille Pelletan in the *Justice* (May 27). "We do not possess the marvelous faculty of forgetting which we see around us. We cannot efface from our memories the impressions of the time when France, invaded, mutilated, and in pain, lay gasping under the German boot. Was the Tunis expedition," he asked, "the first step in the renunciation recommended by Leroy-Beaulieu?" In spite of this campaign, and thanks to the comparative absence of dangerous complications, the Treaty of Bardo was ratified with only one negative vote.[34] Yet the newspapers which had supported the government's policy did little to counteract the revival of bitter memories. The moderate Republican *Siècle* (May 27) was no "passionate admirer of Barthélemy Saint-Hilaire's letter. Whatever MM. Leroy-Beaulieu and Clemenceau may think, it seemed to us that we could have one eye upon Tunis and the other upon the Vosges . . . Cannot a lesson be administered to the Bey of Tunis without being constrained to embrace M. de Bismarck?" The attack upon the Ferry ministry failed in its immediate purpose, the defeat of its Tunis policy, but it created an "unworthy agitation throughout the country," and finally it led to Ferry's defeat in November, 1881.[35]

Long deferred, a Gambetta ministry was clearly indicated by the parliamentary elections of October. The popular imagination in France and abroad had identified him with "the spirit of the bleeding Fatherland"; [36] many therefore anticipated the beginning of a trou-

---

[32] *Annales,* 1881, II, 120–130.

[33] *Gazette de France,* May 23. The italics appear in this newspaper. The letter was not mentioned by the *Temps* or the *Journal des Débats,* nor does it appear in the *Deutsche Revue,* vol. IX (Jan.-June, 1881).

[34] *Annales,* 1881, II, 131 (May 23).

[35] Reinach, *Le Ministère Gambetta,* p. 3.

[36] Henri Boland, *La Prochaine Guerre entre la France et l'Allemagne,* (Paris, 1884), p. 25.

bled period.[37] He at once declared in favor of a protectorate in Tunis,[38] and gave other indications of a firm policy. In reality, his accession to power was something of an anticlimax. His hope of forming *le Grand Ministère* with the coöperation of the outstanding leaders of the Republican party failed on account of political differences, and a cabinet of "camarades" promised an early defeat. Considerable care was taken to reassure Bismarck as to Gambetta's intentions. Some have even spoken of a trip to Varzin in October, 1881, for this purpose.[39] If he was firm in his determination to reject Germany's attempts to attract France within her orbit, he did not believe that the time was ripe for an alliance with either Russia or England, although, in his opinion, they should be held in reserve.[40] "*Gambetta, c'est la guerre*," was the refrain of the Monarchist opposition,[41] but it is of interest that Bismarck did not apparently credit him with warlike purposes.[42] The Chancellor had President Grèvy's assurance that the dangerous activities of any minister would be restrained.[43] Although the Quai d'Orsai was informed that Bismarck's reserve was to be explained by his desire to throw the responsibility for possible trouble upon France, his assurances that Germany's attitude would not be altered were doubtless sincere. At any rate, Gambetta's cabinet was too short-lived to affect the Chancellor's support of France's colonial expansion.

It was during Gambetta's ministry that the nationalist revolt under Arabi Bey precipitated the crisis in Egyptian affairs. Since 1876, France and England had coöperated in a joint control of the Egyptian finances, and those in France who favored colonial expansion also approved coöperation with England if more active measures were necessary. The valley of the Nile aroused more genuine interest in France than any territory which came within the scope of her colonial

---

[37] Hanotaux, *Histoire de la France Contemporaine*, IV, 739.

[38] *Ibid.*, IV, 735.

[39] Stannard, *Gambetta*, pp. 233, 234. According to the *Justice*, Oct. 16, 1881, Bismarck evaded the interview on the plea of illness. Cf. E. de Cyon, *Histoire de l'Entente Franco-Russe* (Paris, 1895), p. 31.

[40] See his conversation with Ferry, Sept. 2, 1881. Freycinet, *Souvenirs*, p. 181. Also his speech at Elysée Ménilmontant, Aug. 12, 1881. Reinach, *Le Ministère Gambetta*, pp. 382, 383.

[41] Grandlieu, *M. Gambetta et la Guerre* (Paris, 1881), pp. 6, 7.

[42] Hatzfeldt to Hohenlohe, Berlin, Nov. 15, 1881. *G. P.*, III, 402, Note by Herbert von Bismarck, Nov. 16, 1881. *Ibid.*, III, 403. Yet Saint-Vallier reported that the government and public opinion were suspicious of Gambetta's intentions. Daudet, *Mission de Saint-Vallier*, pp. 300, 301.

[43] Bourgeois, Pagès, *Origines et Résponsabilités*, pp. 187, 188.

activities.[44] St. Louis's crusade, Napoleon's campaign, France's support of Mehemet Ali against the rest of Europe, and the influence of French culture had created traditions which were difficult to abandon. Gambetta believed that France, whose chief interests were in the Mediterranean, and England, whose concern, he thought, was for the security of her Indian empire, could act together without danger to their respective interests.[45] He therefore took the initiative by suggesting that the Khedive should be assured of their support against the nationalist movement,[46] and he later told Freycinet that he had assembled an expeditionary force in the south of France.[47] In the meantime, Gladstone and Granville, the Secretary of State for Foreign Affairs, were not prepared to intervene by military force until the need was greater, and Germany, Austria, Italy, and Russia preferred action by Turkey as a guarantee against the establishment of either of the western Powers in Egypt.[48]

Public opinion, of course, had no effective comprehension of the details of these complicated negotiations, but there was no doubt as to the main issues involved: independent action by France or England, their coöperation, or intervention by Turkey. No important group was prepared to support separate action by France, especially since Gambetta had been attacked as a danger to peace, nor were those who were attached to the traditions of French influence in Egypt willing to permit England to act alone. The *Temps,* the *Journal des Débats,* and the *République Française* consistently urged close coöperation with England, and Freycinet, who followed Gambetta in January, 1882, would have intervened if he had secured the backing of parliament and of public opinion. Without this assurance, he even considered the possibility of Turkish intervention as a lesser evil than independent action by England.[49] He could not develop this idea, which might have served as the basis for an understanding between the Continental Powers against England, because the press, almost without

---

[44] E. Hippeau, *Histoire Diplomatique de la Troisième République (1870–1889)* (Paris, 1889), p. 408.

[45] *République Française,* April 30, 1879, July 8, 1880.

[46] *Livre Jaune: Affaires d'Égypte, 1881–1882,* pp. 3, 4, 26, 27. P. B. Gheusi, *Gambetta par Gambetta, Lettres Intimes et Souvenirs de Famille . . .* (Paris, 1909), pp. 356–359.

[47] Freycinet, *Souvenirs,* p. 212.

[48] Freycinet wished to block this move by a direct appeal to Bismarck, but was dissuaded by Courcel, the ambassador in Berlin, who argued that it would place France under too great an obligation. Bourgeois, *Manuel Historique,* IV, 130.

[49] *Livre Jaune: Affaires d'Égypte, 1881–1882,* pp. 108–110.

exception, condemned this project. It was feared that the presence of Turkish troops in Egypt would incite a holy war among France's Mohammedan subjects in North Africa.[50] From the first, the Radicals had declared for a policy of complete non-intervention, arguing that Egypt should be left to the Egyptians,[51] but the prevailing point of view in the public at large was that the affair was dangerous. The prospect of isolation created a panic. "What we bitterly deplore," lamented the *Journal des Débats* (June 17, 1882), "is not so much France's weakened position as its spontaneous and satisfied acceptance by public opinion. . . . The head of our government may have been imprudent in declaring openly that France would land no troops in Egypt . . . but we must confess . . . our humiliation and agree that it conforms exactly with the spirit of the chamber and of the country."

Nevertheless, when the bombardment of Alexandria made a decision necessary, the ministry proposed to act with England in defense of the Suez Canal, with the reservation, to quiet the fears of an alarmed public opinion, that the two governments should secure a mandate from the other Powers.[52] On July 8, an appropriation was asked for the vague purpose of "meeting the expenses required by the events in Egypt," [53] with the implication that more extensive operations were contemplated. It was followed by a last effort by Gambetta and the moderate press to gain the support of public opinion for co-operation with England.[54] Freycinet then asked, July 29, for credits for the occupation of the northern end of the Suez Canal with an assurance that the zone would not be extended into Egypt proper. News that the Powers meeting at Constantinople had refused a mandate to England and France caused the defeat of the appropriation by a combination of the two extreme parties in the chamber with the aid of the more timid members of the moderate groups. Many feared that, once installed on the Suez Canal, France would be caught in a chain of circumstances the outcome of which it would be impossible to predict. Clemenceau closed the most important attack upon the government, however, with one of the few references to the general European situation in this debate. "The conclusion to be drawn from these

---

[50] *Temps*, Feb. 12, April 21, May 5, June 2, 6. *Journal des Débats*, Jan. 17. Feb. 5, April 16. *République Française*, March 4, March 31. E. Valaray, *France et ses Intérêts* (Paris, 1882), pp. 16–24.

[51] *Intransigeant*, July 10; *Justice*, July 20.

[52] *Livre Jaune: Affaires d'Égypte, 1882*, pp. 127, 128.

[53] *Annales*, 1882, II, 814.

[54] *Ibid.*, 1882, II, 971, 972 (July 18). *République Française*, July 11, 1882.

events is this : Europe is covered with soldiers; everyone is waiting; every Power is reserving its freedom of action for the future; you must reserve that of France." [55] It was an attack of nerves, rather than a clear-sighted determination to concentrate France's strength for an impending test of strength with Germany that explains the response of public opinion to the agitation against coöperation with England. Public opinion had repudiated a policy which seemed to imply incalculable dangers.

France had herself to blame for her failure to accompany England into Egypt, but the consideration that England had profited by her weakness to act alone in her own interest was sufficient to stimulate a bitter resentment which was shared to a certain extent by all groups. An excellent opportunity presented itself for a union with Germany against England, not only in the general field of colonial expansion but more specifically in the Egyptian question. There had been a relative absence of polemics in the press against Bismarck and Germany during the crisis.[56] At no time had Freycinet been attacked, as Ferry had been during the Tunis expedition, as Bismarck's friend. When Ferry began his second and long ministry in November, 1882, he turned his attention to other regions without, however, abandoning France's claims in Egypt. Until the formation of the Entente Cordiale of 1904, the most important claim was that England should fix a definite date for her evacuation,[57] but until France was prepared to risk a first-rate crisis, she could not openly press this claim. In the meantime, she was prepared to embarrass England's administration of Egypt whenever possible. It was her refusal to approve the reduction of interest upon the Egyptian bonds that led to the London Conference of July, 1884.[58] Many in France hoped that the conference would consider the entire Egyptian question, but it adjourned without accomplishing anything to their satisfaction.

More than ever the need of Germany's support was apparent. Bismarck had been experiencing difficulties of his own with England in the establishment of the colony at Angra Pequena. Granville's long delay in replying to his request for information as to England's at-

[55] *Annales*, 1882, II, 1173–1190.

[56] They were sometimes charged with supporting Turkey for the purpose of encouraging development of the Pan-Islamic sentiment in France's North-African colonies.

[57] Granville wrote Waddington, the French ambassador, that England would evacuate Egypt in 1888 if the Powers then believed that the situation warranted it. *Livre Jaune: Affaires d'Égypte, 1884*, pp. 21–25.

[58] *Ibid.*, pp. 1, 2, 17, 18.

titude, the hostility of the Cape Colony government, and the pressure of the colonial party in Germany were arguments in favor of coöperation with France.[59] He was, of course, animated by no admiration for France's *beaux yeux*,[60] and if he agreed to support her occasionally, and to a limited degree, in Egypt, he expected a return. He acknowledged later that he had been prepared to give England a free hand in Egypt if she had been accommodating toward Germany's interests,[61] but failing that he thought that "it should be our immediate purpose to create difficulties for England in all diplomatic questions." [62] What he desired most of all was a union of the secondary naval powers against England,[63] and the price which he would have France pay for his support was for her to make the first move.[64]

The preparations for the Berlin Conference in October, 1884, which was to consider questions relating to central Africa, furnished an occasion for a Franco-German conversation. It revealed Germany as rather vague as to the essential question of her attitude in Egypt, and France as eager for an assurance of her support. Hohenlohe was instructed to propose a prior understanding between the two countries as to the commercial exploitation of territories in central Africa as a step toward a more general understanding.[65] France made no objection, but Courcel, Saint-Vallier's successor as ambassador in Berlin, hinted that the proposed accord was too narrowly defined: " 'it seems,' " he complained, " 'that our first common action will only deal with the most distant parts of the globe.' " Here was a plain invitation to bring the entire Egyptian question into the discussion, and it was so interpreted: Instead of replying to this broad hint, Germany proposed coöperation in the relatively minor question of the indemnities due as a result of the bombardment of Alexandria. Courcel admitted it to be a "respectable" suggestion, but he was moved to state the French position more clearly than before. " 'France's interest requires . . . that the situation be regarded from a higher point of view, and even from that of the entire future of Egypt.' " France, he promised, " 'will not desert you, if you and

[59] Bismarck to Münster, Berlin, Jan. 25, 1885. *G. P.*, IV, 96.
[60] Daudet, *Mission du Comte de Saint-Vallier*, pp. 217, 218.
[61] Bismarck to Münster, Berlin, Jan. 24, 1886. *G. P.*, IV, 94.
[62] Count Wilhelm von Bismarck's memorandum, Varzin, Aug. 23, 1884. *Ibid.*, IV, 79.
[63] See his annotation of Münster's letter, May 24, 1884. *Ibid.*, IV, 58, 59.
[64] Courcel to Ferry, Berlin, Sept. 23, 1884. Bourgeois, Pagès, *Origines et Résponsabilités*, pp. 383, 384.
[65] Bismarck to Hatzfeldt, Varzin, Aug. 7, 1884. *G. P.*, III, 413, 414.

your allies wish to do something.'" Again, the question was evaded by a counter-suggestion that France should herself precipitate the Egyptian question by calling a conference to meet in Paris. Courcel's reply was non-committal: *"'C'est une idée.'"* [66]

Bismarck was informed after this conversation that the "French could be led to make definite proposals . . . if they believed that they could count upon our support and that of our allies against England." [67] Nevertheless, Germany's slowness to respond to Courcel's hints seems to have increased Ferry's caution. Hohenlohe was told that conditions were not favorable for a definite understanding even in regard to the minor questions relating to the Berlin Conference. [68] On August 18, Courcel returned to Paris to discuss these negotiations, and a few days later, Hohenlohe was told that an arrangement could be made in regard to specific questions relating to West Africa and to Egypt. There could, however, be no thought of a formal alliance. "He, like Courcel, considers that the easily excited public opinion requires caution." [69] On his return to Berlin, Courcel also emphasized the need of considering public opinion. [70] Germany at length agreed to give her own support and to secure that of Austria and Russia for France in regard to questions relating to the Egyptian finances. [71] An understanding was likewise soon arranged as to the work of the Berlin Conference.

According to Bismarck the concern of the French authorities for public opinion was due to their fear of the ministry's possible defeat. It may also be explained by their doubts as to the Chancellor's purposes, but in any event, their reference to public opinion was in anticipation of its future reactions, for no unusual agitation had as yet developed. It was not until early in September, after Courcel's return to Berlin, and after Bismarck had refused to promise complete support in Egypt, that the Monarchist and Radical press launched an attack upon Ferry as representing an alliance with Germany. Rochefort was perhaps the first to sound the alarm in the radical *Intransigeant* (Sept. 3): "Jules Ferry has solemnly renounced the hope of revenge. He has abandoned Alsace-Lorraine for all time to the

---

[66] Hatzfeldt to Bismarck, Berlin, Aug. 11, 1884. *Ibid.*, III, 414–416.
[67] *Ibid.*
[68] Hohenlohe to Bismarck, Paris, Aug. 15, 1884. *Ibid.*, III, 419, 420.
[69] Hohenlohe to Bismarck, Paris, Aug. 23, 1884. *Ibid.*, III, 420, 421.
[70] Hatzfeldt to Bismarck, Berlin, Aug. 25, 1884. *Ibid.*, 421–424. Bismarck to Busch, Varzin, Aug. 30, 1884. *Ibid.*, III, 424–426.
[71] Hatzfeldt's Memorandum, Berlin, Sept. 22, 1884. *Ibid.*, III, 428–430.

fantasies of the Prussian soldiery." Clemenceau's *Justice* (Sept. 22) denounced Ferry's "surrender" to Germany, and later (Sept. 28) it referred to Ferry as the "protégé of M. de Bismarck," claiming that he had yielded equal rights to Germans in all of France's colonies in return for his support in Egypt. On September 29, Clemenceau protested that Ferry's colonial enterprises left Bismarck "the absolute master of Europe; he commands, and the French government obeys . . . everyone knows the price of M. de Bismarck's friendship . . . no tyranny is heavier than his alliance." [72] Alexandre Millerand, then a Socialist, declared at a meeting of a Radical league of Paris that this organization "condemns and censures any compromise with Germany" and that the Radicals would use his foreign policy to defeat Ferry at the next elections.[73] Later, the extreme chauvinists were to divide their hatred between England and Germany, but at the moment they were outraged by the thought of an association with Germany. Mme. Adam, since 1879 the editor of the *Nouvelle Revue,* declared that the German press, notably the *Kölnische Zeitung,* was inciting France against England and that it was describing "the great advantage of renouncing the lost provinces in an alliance with the bombarders of Strassburg." [74] Déroulède denounced Ferry's alleged pact with Bismarck as treasonable at a banquet of the Grand Orient lodge of the Masonic Order, where he was reported to have received "thunderous applause." [75] The socialist *Cri du Peuple* (Oct. 1, 1884) condemned any complicity with Bismarck's colonial ambitions, and the monarchist *Gazette de France* (Sept. 29) was certain that "Ferry had been caught in Prussia's trap."

Several moderate newspapers, who supported the government, did not at first join this hue and cry. In defending a policy of limited coöperation with Germany, they yielded to their bitter resentment against England. Its extreme form was voiced by the short-lived weekly, the *Anti-Anglais,* which declared (Sept. 6–13) that the old phantom of an aggressive Germany no longer existed. When the English press described Germany's friendly attitude as a maneuver to induce France to renounce Alsace-Lorraine, the *République Française* (Aug. 29) replied that equitable sentiments should not be answered by recrimination and disdain. Edmond About's *XIX Siècle*

---

[72] *Justice,* Sept. 29.
[73] *Kölnische Zeitung,* Oct. 7, 1884.
[74] *Nouvelle Revue,* vol. 30, p. 119.
[75] He proposed a toast of "L'alliance français—français contre l'alliance franco-allemande." *Kölnische Zeitung,* Oct. 3, 1884.

(Sept. 30) agreed that there could be no question of an alliance with Germany. "But the question of the day concerns England's ambitions, for she wishes to seize control of the route to India." Even the aristocratic *Figaro* (Sept. 28) approved a Continental union against England. "Continental Europe is camped before her, more firmly decided than ever. It is Germany, not France, who heads the coalition; M. Ferry has wisely ceded the first place to M. de Bismarck." Gabriel Charmes, who earlier had advocated an entente with England, thought that the time had come to re-orient French policy. England's systematic obstruction of France's interests in Egypt, China, and Madagascar was reviving, he said, the old animosity between the two countries. Her conduct was forcing France to consider a union with the Continental Powers. It had produced "the strange result, that an alliance with Germany is openly discussed; it is a political combination to which opinion is adjusting itself." [76] His point of view was significant as that of a zealous advocate of colonial expansion.

On October 8, the *Figaro* noted the presence in Paris of Herbert Bismarck, the Chancellor's son, and it added that his purpose was to arrange the differences between the two countries in regard to Egypt. Germany was interested in a league of the Continental Powers, and Herbert's real mission was to work for France's adherence to it. His conversations with Ferry led to a mutual assurance that no independent action would be taken in Egypt, but the French minister remained cool to the renewed suggestion of a conference to meet in Paris.[77] The suspicion that Franco-German negotiations were in progress found support in Ferry's announcement, during Herbert Bismarck's visit, of an understanding in regard to the work of the Berlin Conference.[78] Courcel's visit to Paris, his journey to Varzin, Bismarck's visit at the French embassy in Berlin, and finally Herbert Bismarck's presence in Paris apparently pointed to momentous decisions, and to more activity than was warranted by "a conference about unappropriated territory in a pestilential climate in equatorial Africa."[79] The storm of protest in France thereupon reached its climax. "The danger is imminent," proclaimed Mme. Adam, "the first step which costs the most has been taken against the wishes of an excited and protesting public opinion." [80] The monarchist *Gazette de*

[76] *Journal des Débats,* Sept. 30.
[77] H. von Bismarck to Bismarck, Paris, Oct. 6, 1884. *G. P.,* III, 431–437.
[78] *Livre Jaune: Affaires du Congo, 1884,* pp. 43, 44 (Oct. 5, 6, 7, 1884).
[79] *Standard* (London), Oct. 13.
[80] *Nouvelle Revue,* vol. 30, p. 875.

France (Oct. 17) observed that few republican newspapers dared to discuss the problem of relations with Germany. This observation was not entirely accurate, for several went to some pains to deny that there was any question of an alliance. The *Temps* (Oct. 10) rejected as unworthy the suspicion that the government would betray the one sentiment which had the sanction of the nation, while the *République Française* (Oct. 11) declared that no alliance could exist where the interests of two countries differed so widely. The *Figaro* (Oct. 14) was able to print a letter from Courcel to Bismarck, dated Sept. 29, before the publication of the *Yellow Book,* showing that the understanding was limited to West Africa. The pressure of public opinion led to official action, for a *Yellow Book* was published on October 14, to show that there was no question of an alliance.[81]

It was Germany's refusal to give France's claims in Egypt her unreserved support, as well as the excited press, that explains this cautious policy. Without this assurance, neither the government nor leaders of public opinion could afford to risk anything more. The attitude of Gabriel Charmes is enlightening. It was his opinion, he wrote in the *Journal des Débats* (Oct. 5), that the government's critics wished to defeat the ministry more than to attack Germany, because they were aware that no one had any desire for a formal alliance with Germany. He was somewhat more indefinite the next day, in an editorial which was probably written before his dinner with Herbert Bismarck. "We have made it a point to speak of an alliance merely as an hypothesis, because in fact it is nothing more at the moment. . . . We have only preferred the language of discussion to the extravagance of the radical sheets." [82] He dined that evening with Herbert, in company with his brother Francis and Pallain, the director of the Ministry of Finance. The three Frenchmen were pleased by the results of Herbert's conversations with Ferry. Pallain believed that a *détente* in the relations between the two countries would soon lead to an *entente,* and one of the Charmes added, " 'This nightmare for France and Germany must stop: we are on the right road.' " [83] Nevertheless, Gabriel's moderate support of an understanding in the *Journal des Débats* was withdrawn. It was not until December 4,

[81] The Paris correspondent of the *Kölnische Zeitung* (Oct. 16) reported the Radical press as unconvinced. "France's little finger had been given to the devil, and he was so unutterably clever that he would draw hand, arm, and body after it."

[82] *Journal des Débats,* Oct. 7.

[83] H. von Bismarck to Bismarck, Paris, Oct. 6, 1884. *G. P.,* III, 437.

1884, that he again discussed the question, and then in a different spirit. He doubted that France would derive any profit from the Conference of Berlin, although the two countries could have arranged an exchange of support without going so far as an alliance. Charmes, it is evident, had turned to a balanced position between England and Germany. He hoped that France would not be driven into complete hostility by the conquest of Egypt. In the meantime, negotiations with Germany should continue, but he doubted "that the French government has the necessary strength and decision to maintain an accord with Germany against the violent attacks . . . which it has inspired since the press began to discuss it." Privately convinced of the value of coöperation with Germany as he was, in public, faced by the violent criticism of the extreme parties and doubting the government's firmness of purpose, he had turned away:

Public opinion had been aroused by the polemics of the radical and monarchist press. The reflections of Freycinet's organ, the *Télégraphe* (Sept. 28) were doubtless correct: "It is generally believed that any intimacy with Germany would be a *jeu de dupe ou un feu de paille* unless it should start with the healing of our real wounds . . . we do not mean the loss of money or of prestige, but the separation from our Alsatian brothers." It is possible that neither the Ferry government nor the friendly press would have been induced to champion courageously an entente with Germany even if a definite assurance of effective support in calling England to account had been given. In any event, the absence of that assurance could only result in their surrender to the clamor of the extremists.

Ferry continued his policy of colonial expansion and accepted Germany's support when it suited his purposes. In January, 1885, Bismarck agreed to back France's demand for an investigation of the Egyptian finances,[84] but the recent eruption of sentiment had taught Ferry the need of caution. When the Chancellor inquired if Germany's attitude had not been satisfactory,[85] Ferry acknowledged that it had been responsible for his recent successes in negotiations with England, thereby evading a direct statement as to his own attitude. Moreover, he hoped that the German press would not discuss the question of coöperation, for the opposition in France would use it

---

[84] Bismarck's note of a conversation with Courcel, Berlin, Jan. 4, 1885, *G. P.*, III, 439, 440.
[85] Hohenlohe to Bismarck, Paris, Jan. 24, 1885. *Ibid.*, III, 440, 441.

against the government.[86] As long as nothing occurred to threaten complications, Ferry was able to proceed with his protracted campaign, which had commenced in October, 1883, for the establishment of French control in Tonkin. He had avoided disturbing public opinion by representing China, who had declared war in 1883, as *"un quantité négligeable,"* by asking parliament's approval for only small if frequent appropriations and by sending troops in *"petits paquets."* War was never declared against China because of consideration for public opinion. These precautions enabled Ferry to secure a safe majority upon every vote and to claim that his policy had the sanction of parliament and of public opinion. In reality, their approval was never more than passive. The *Journal des Débats* (Jan. 7, 1885) denied that the chamber had any clear opinion in regard to the Tonkin affair: "It has been content to follow the government's directions. To speak of a mandate imposed upon the government is nonsense. It is the ministry through its most devoted friends which has prepared the resolutions of confidence."

In October, 1884, even in the midst of the agitation in the French press, Bismarck had promised that he would not create trouble for her in China and that he would intervene in the interest of peace if France so desired.[87] However, Germany was not at first involved in the attack upon Ferry. It was the result of his decision, indicated by the resignation as Minister of War of General Campenon, who had opposed the extension of military operations beyond the delta of the Red River,[88] to undertake a more energetic prosecution of the campaign. For the first time, Ferry explained his purpose to the chamber as "the full, complete and uncontested possession of Tonkin." [89] The *Justice* at once declared that Ferry's decision placed France's "security, her independence in Europe" at the mercy of an accident in this distant province.

By an irony of fate, that accident occurred when negotiations with China had almost reached a successful conclusion. An agreement recognizing France's control in Tonkin was signed on April 4, 1885, but Ferry had already been defeated. On March 26, the press announced

[86] Hohenlohe to Bismarck, Paris, Jan. 27, 1885. *Ibid.,* III, 441–443. Cf. Newton, *Lyons,* II, 341, 342 for the British ambassador's reactions.

[87] H. von Bismarck to Bismarck, Paris, Oct. 6, 1884. *G. P.,* III, 437.

[88] " 'We have only one course to follow,' " Campenon declared in the *Événement* (Jan. 7, 1885), " 'to wait and to struggle, not in distant quarters of the world, but in Europe; you know against whom.' "

[89] *Annals,* 1885, I, 8 (Jan. 14, 1885).

the defeat of a French force with some two hundred casualties in front of Lang-Son, a city in the interior of Tonkin, and its enforced retreat. Ferry pretended that there was no reason for alarm, and three days later he insisted that there were adequate forces in Tonkin.[90] He had the misfortune of seeing his optimism immediately contradicted by a brief telegram announcing a new defeat, the evacuation of Lang-Son, and a retreat to the coast.[91] The storm immediately broke in Paris. His failure to consult parliament, the dispersal of France's soldiers, the danger of complications were flung at him. The opposition press, of course, made full use of the panic. The *Justice* (March 30) predicted: "There will be a single cry of rage and pain throughout France." Under flaring headlines, *"Désastre au Tonkin,"* the Bonapartist *Pays* (March 31), declared that two hundred thousand Chinese troops were pouring into the region. The *Patrie* (March 31) regretted that the people of Paris had lost the habit of insurrection. In vain, the newspapers which remained loyal to the government attempted to stem the current by appealing to the patriotism of the nation.[92] "The life of Paris was suspended," wrote a critic of the government, "the panic was communicated to the nation at large, it was a general stupor, almost a national mourning."[93] A victim was demanded, and Ferry was clearly indicated.

Ferry opened the session of the chamber, March 30, with a request for new credits of two hundred millions as if nothing had happened. Clemenceau from the left and Delafosse from the monarchist right rushed to the attack, but the former gained the floor and launched his scathing indictment. Ferry, he declared, was no longer the premier but an accused man.[94] The mob which thronged the approaches to the Palais Bourbon was more enraged than the chamber. The spirit of revolution was in the air. Members of the ministry, "always prudent and hating the crowd," entered the chamber by the rear doors.[95] Within an hour after the opening of the session, Ferry had resigned, so completely discredited that he was never again to be available for a ministerial office. The indignation of the opposition was not entirely innocent of political motives. "Lang-Son was the

[90] Rambaud, *Ferry,* 361.

[91] *Journal Officiel,* March 29.

[92] *Siècle,* March 30. *Voltaire,* March 31. *Événement,* April 1.

[93] (Anonymous), "A la Recherche de la Vérité sur l'Évacuation de Lang-Son," *Corresp.,* O. S., 141, p. 775.

[94] *Annales,* 1885, I, 804.

[95] (Anonymous), *Le Désastre du Tonkin: Chute du Ministère Ferry* (Epinal, 1885).

pretext," was the opinion of an experienced politician. He reported a meeting of a group of republican deputies on the evening of March 29 in the offices of the *Journal des Débats,* where it was decided "that it had become necessary to defeat Jules Ferry; and it was his domestic rather than his foreign policy which determined this decision."[96] His dry and authoritative personality probably explains in part the desertion of a considerable section of his own party, which decided the vote against him on March 30. But the most important factor was the sudden outburst of passion, intensified if not created by the opposition press, which was not to be resisted. Henceforth, so public opinion decreed, Ferry, the *Tonkinois,* was to be ostracized. "M. Ferry," wrote a friendly journal, "is the leper of Aosta. Do not touch, do not speak to this man, you would be infected by his disease."[97]

If the passion of the mob had prevailed, Ferry's fall would doubtless have been followed by the evacuation of Tonkin. Sufficient time elapsed, however, before the formation of the Brisson cabinet, for cooler counsels to prevail. When attention could be given to the situation, the opposition had divided as to the proper policy. That part of the Radicals which followed the leadership of Clemenceau, with some of the Monarchists, favored the continuation of military operations until the nation's honor had been avenged, while other fractions of these groups held that complete and immediate evacuation should be ordered. Brisson simply continued Ferry's policy, unmoved by its apparent repudiation by public opinion. Adequate credits were voted unanimously.[98] The socialist *Cri du Peuple* (April 9) found no difference between the new ministry and that of "Ferry-le-Cynique." The Bonapartist *Patrie* (April 16) referred to Brisson as Ferry's protégé, and the monarchist *Français* (April 22) wrote of the "advantage of not having lost M. Ferry."

In view of its earlier use in the propaganda against Ferry and colonial expansion, there was a curious absence of the usual charge of guilty relations with Germany. Even Clemenceau's favorite theme, the effect of this policy upon France's Continental position, did not appear in the press or parliament, although it perhaps was implied.

---

[96] E. de Marcère, *Entretiens et Souvenirs,* 2 vols. (Paris, 1894), II, 29, 30. The *Temps,* Jan. 13, 1885, had noted the tendency of a section of the majority party, the *Union Républicaine,* to join the Radicals on the ground that Ferry had abandoned Gambetta's policies.

[97] *Voltaire,* May 14.

[98] *Annales,* 1885, I, 834 (April 7).

It was the definite defeat of a French military force that most impressed a susceptible public opinion. At first, there was no definite indication of a change in the program of limited coöperation between France and Germany. Freycinet, the Minister of Foreign Affairs, was reported as prepared to continue Ferry's policy.[99] The German Foreign Office in fact used its influence, without intervening, to facilitate a diplomatic arrangement between France and China.[100] Nevertheless, the period between Ferry's defeat, March 30, and the elections in October concluded the period of better relations which had lasted since 1878. The repudiation of Ferry and supposedly of colonial expansion meant that France would henceforth give greater attention to European affairs. In May, 1885, Bismarck confessed in substance the failure of his French policy. He was convinced, he wrote, that France could not be depended upon to maintain a stiff opposition to England either in Egypt or in the Congo question, and that her government, intimidated by the chauvinists and the opposition, could not practise a sustained policy of coöperation with Germany.[101] An article in the *Temps* (July 24), recommending the transfer of six cavalry regiments from Paris to the eastern frontier, was the occasion for a sharp warning, although the *Temps* explained that it had merely advised an equality of forces upon the frontier. The official *Norddeutsche Allgemeine Zeitung* (Aug. 3) attributed great importance to this article, in view of the *Temps's* well-known moderation and of its influence in France, as an indication that Germany's policy of conciliation had failed. This pronouncement was by no means the work of an irresponsible journalist, for Hohenlohe was instructed to explain in Paris that it "only had the peaceful purpose of exerting a pacific influence upon the French elections." [102] He was also to say that his government would not be indifferent to anti-German demonstrations.

Only a serious misunderstanding of French psychology explains the hope that good results would follow this warning. It was naturally interpreted as a menace and as an unjustifiable intervention in French affairs. The German press, the Bonapartist *Pays* (Aug. 5) admitted, had been friendly to Ferry and his policy, "but the moment we show signs of greater sense, Germany begins to threaten and to demon-

[99] Note of a conversation with Barère, the French representative upon the Suez Canal Commission. Paris, May 26, 1885. *G. P.*, III, 447, 448.
[100] Hatzfeldt's Memorandum Berlin, April 3, 1885. *Ibid.*, III, 445.
[101] Bismarck to Hohenlohe, Berlin, May 25, 1885. *Ibid.*, III, 446.
[102] Rantzau's Memorandum, Varzin, Aug. 26, 1885. *Ibid.*, III, 451.

strate in brutal ways her superior strength. . . ." The *Figaro* (Aug. 7) thought that the article in question expressed Germany's disappointment at her failure to make of France one of her satellites, while the chauvinist *National* (Aug. 13) interpreted it as a menace against every country which had a grievance against Germany. The Monarchist *Français* (Aug. 9) was one of the few to react according to the anticipation of the German Foreign Office. "Assuredly, we furnish no pretext whatsoever for an aggression, and we do not believe that any party is mad enough to make the *revanche* a part of its platform in the approaching elections." The greater number of the Paris newspapers evaded the question, however, by explaining the *Norddeutsche Allgemeine Zeitung's* article as a maneuver intended to impress upon the German people the need of military increases.[103]

The change in Bismarck's attitude was soon signalized by other incidents. Gustave Rothan, a diplomat of the Second Empire, was excluded from Alsace in August after his election as a vice-president of the Ligue des Patriotes. The Monarchist *Soleil* (Aug. 20) noted the increasing number of frontier incidents, and the Republican and chauvinist *Événement* (Aug. 20) characterized Germany's attitude as "absolutely provocative and aggressive." In September, the Chancellor pretended that all parties in France had made common cause with Spain in his difficulty with her over the Caroline Islands, and that it meant the failure of his efforts during fifteen years to establish a basis for coöperation between the two countries. Hohenlohe was again instructed to warn the friends of peace in France that Germany would be forced to assure the defense of her western frontier in the event of a war with Spain.[104] Bismarck had distorted the facts, for the Paris press, in general, had adopted a studious neutrality in this question.[105] In this irritable temper, Bismarck was prepared to interpret neutrality as hostility. Nor did events warrant his blustering tactics in attempting to influence the October election.

With Ferry eliminated, there was no occasion for the use of the old arguments against an association with Germany during the campaign. No party played upon the national grievance, and the Radicals, whose consistent policy had been to demand renewed zeal in the watch upon the Vosges, identified themselves with the cause of peace. Clemenceau denounced Ferry's defense of the moderate Republican foreign policy, July 28, as a confession that the grandeur of France

---

[103] *Journal des Débats,* Aug. 5. *Justice,* Aug. 5. *Figaro,* Aug. 5. *Patrie,* Aug. 6.
[104] Bismarck to Hohenlohe, Berlin, Sept. 21, 1885. *G. P.,* III, 452.
[105] *Français,* Sept. 7. *Voltaire,* Sept. 8.

could only be served by an adventurous policy. For himself, he stood for peace, and he believed that his party could carry the elections if it adopted a program of social reforms based upon the maintenance of peace.[106] His point of view prevailed in the manifesto of the *Union de la Presse Radicale-Socialiste* on the eve of the elections. After demanding the suppression of the senate, the abrogation of the Concordat, and other radical reforms, it denounced the "policy of adventures" of the opportunist Republicans. "The spirit of the Revolution is quite different. In foreign affairs, it asks for influence only as a consequence of the Republic's peaceful progress and of the spread of ideas. It approves war only in defense of the *patrie*." [107] It was a tribute to the political value of peaceful purposes that the leaders who had condemned an association with Germany should base their campaign upon these arguments. Nor did other groups, the moderate Republicans and Monarchists, profess more dangerous intentions.

The critical significance of the elections was clearly understood, not however in their connection with foreign affairs, but in domestic politics. If the Radicals exploited the passions that had been aroused against Ferry in order to gain power, the Monarchists continued their attack upon colonial expansion as a means of accomplishing the downfall of the Republic.[108] Friends of the government willingly accepted the challenge, for they knew that a defense of the Republic would be easier than a defense of the colonial policy. As the elections approached, little was said of Tonkin. "Where is Tonkin?" asked the *Figaro* (Oct. 5). "The Government is silent. The public is indifferent. . . . It is no longer a question of the Tonkin expedition." The first balloting foreshadowed a victory for the electoral combination between the Radicals and the Monarchists,[109] and it was only when confronted by the most serious danger which the Republic had faced since 1877 that the Radicals joined forces with the Opportunists to save the day in the second voting of October 18.[110] Of more than

[106] *Annales*, 1885, II, 1081 (July 30). Even Mme. Adam expressed this point of view. *Nouvelle Revue*, vol. 35, p. 873.

[107] *Justice*, Oct. 1, 1885.

[108] A coalition of the Monarchist and Bonapartist groups was formed in view of the election. *Pays*, March 4, July 14. *Gazette de France*, May 13. *Gaulois*, July 1, Aug. 1. *République Française*, Sept. 14.

[109] They had, it was said, excellent prospects of winning a clear majority. *Journal des Débats*, Oct. 6, 1885.

[110] It was agreed that all should support the candidate in each instance who had polled the largest vote in the balloting of Oct. 4. *Paris*, Oct. 6, 7. *Voltaire*, Oct. 7. *République Française*, Oct. 7. *Justice*, Oct. 8, 18. *Intransigeant*, Oct. 10. *Pays*, Oct. 12.

270 contests to be decided, the Monarchists won only twenty.[111]

It was not easy to discern the significance of this election, except its clear endorsement of republican institutions. Those who believed that France should not abandon Tonkin insisted that no mandate had been given for its evacuation. The Radicals, however, thought differently, and Camille Pelletan, the chairman of the finance committee, reported against the government's request for credits to organize Tonkin. The chamber, nevertheless, passed the appropriation over his protest, by 274 to 270.[112] A section of the Radicals at the last moment refused to withdraw the French flag from territory where it was firmly established.[113] The narrow escape from complete evacuation was a convincing demonstration that the policy of colonial expansion would be restricted if not abandoned. Tolerated by public opinion rather than actively approved, that policy finally had to yield to the persistent fear of complications.

The rather promising prospects of better feeling between France and Germany suffered an even more decisive defeat. It is not sufficient to say that the result was inevitable without a solution of the Alsace-Lorraine question. No complete reconciliation was of course possible without it, but even in its absence, a working arrangement might in time have replaced the sullen reserve which was represented by extremists as a patriotic duty. It would have been the logical consequence of the opportunist point of view and of the satisfaction derived from colonial expansion. Two main difficulties arose which in the end defeated the moderate policy. The opposition exploited every evidence of Germany's approval for political effect. Although claiming to represent the cause of social reform in France and asserting that the hope for the redress of France's grievances lay in the progress of social justice in Europe, Clemenceau, Pelletan, and other Radicals did not hesitate to play upon the memories of 1871 to score a success against their political opponents. Moderate leaders were able to resist this pressure during the Tunis affair, because Bismarck's support prevented such complications as might have led to a revolt of public opinion. They lacked this assurance in the more dangerous Egyptian question, and without it, they were disarmed when the discussion of an *entente* with Germany reached its climax in October, 1884. With the defeat of the colonial policy, when the ever-present danger of complications became a reality in the Far East, and with

---

[111] *Siècle,* Oct. 20. *Justice,* Oct. 20.
[112] *Annales,* 1885, III, 302.
[113] *Événement,* Dec. 26, 1885.

the prospect of a more intensive concentration upon the eastern frontier, Bismarck abandoned his efforts to conciliate France and turned to a policy that resembled intimidation. Through it all, public opinion remained essentially peaceful.

CHAPTER VI

The *Revanche* and the Crisis of 1887

Nous devons éviter la guerre par tous les moyens honorables qui sont en notre pouvoir, en tout cas, ne jamais la déclarer. M. de Bismarck compte sur une imprudence de notre part pour entraîner l'Allemagne, peu désireuse de nouvelles entreprises militaires, et cela est arrivé en 1870. Ne lui donnons pas cet avantage.
Comte de Chaudordy, La France en 1889 (Paris, 1889).

Since 1871, a minority had never wavered in its hope of a prompt revenge. Advocates of the *revanche* differed, however, in their understanding of the objectives to be attained. For some, the recovery of Alsace-Lorraine was sufficient, while others thought of the return of the lost provinces as inseparably associated with the restoration of France to the place in European affairs which she had lost in 1871. All sections of the minority agreed in resenting the growth of moderate opinion and the policy of colonial expansion as implying the renunciation of Alsace-Lorraine, an association with Germany, the acceptance of France's diminished position in Europe, and a weakened will to dare great things. Untroubled by thoughts of the cost of achieving their aspirations, the extremists were determined to check these tendencies and to convert the nation to their own conception of patriotism. Circumstances at length favored them after Ferry's defeat had led to renewed emphasis upon Continental affairs.

A leader, Paul Déroulède, had been found, and a propagandist agency, the Ligue des Patriotes, had been organized. Born in Paris, September 2, 1846, of middle-class parentage, Déroulède's temperament and the circumstances of his youth formed at an early age the romantic devotion to the glory of France which made of him the most picturesque and best-loved leader of nationalist sentiment for more than thirty years. "His father, mother, and uncle," wrote an admirer, "raised him in the horror of *l'étranger* and in the cult of France." A long residence at Fontainebleau, frequent visits to Versailles, and attendance at a school in a château of the Princes of Condé at Vannes filled his imagination with the pictures of France's ancient glories.[1] At twenty-six, the war of 1870 found him without a

---

[1] Arsène-Jules Claretie, *Paul Déroulède* (Paris, 1883), pp. 4–6. Claretie was a prolific and popular dramatist.

settled place in life, either in the law—his father's profession—or as a poet. He enlisted, was captured at Sedan, and after escaping, served with credit for the duration of the hostilities. Physical disability led in 1878 to his retirement from the army.

Of his literary work, only the *Chants du Soldat,* first published in 1872, which reached 130 editions before his death in 1914, brought him fame of a sort.[2] The "Clairon," the best-known of this collection of patriotic poems, was memorized by successive classes of pupils in all the schools of France. Permeated by the sense of his country's humiliation, Déroulède found his career in that of a popular agitator. His preoccupation with one idea, the *revanche,* his unquestioned sincerity and integrity qualified him admirably for this rôle. Although a Republican by principle, he, like Mme. Adam, condemned the opportunists's anti-clerical policy as sacrificing the Church's friendly interest in France's aspirations, for he believed that patriots needed the moral support of religious sentiment.[3] He was prepared to work for a dictatorship if parliamentary government did not prove to be an adequate instrument for the attainment of the *revanche.* In and out of season, he preached the need of moral and military preparation.[4]

The organization of the Ligue des Patriotes resulted from a difference of opinion between Déroulède and Ferry. A committee, with Déroulède as a member, had been named for the selection of suitable textbooks to be used in the schools under the law of 1882 to prepare boys for military service. When Ferry used his authority as the Minister of Education to annul the committee's selection,[5] Déroulède decided that there was need of an independent source of patriotic instruction, and for this purpose he took a leading part in the establishment of the Ligue. des Patriotes, May 18, 1882.[6] From the first, it was closely associated with existing gymnastic and rifle clubs, while

[2] Camille Ducroy, *Paul Déroulède* (Paris, 1914), p. 105.

[3] His drama, the *Moabite,* was based upon the religious associations of patriotism. *Ibid.,* pp. 131, 132.

[4] He feared that silence would lead to forgetfulness. Cf. Louis Barthou's speech at the unveiling of the monument to Déroulède. *Journal des Débats,* Nov. 21, 1927.

[5] Claretie, *Déroulède,* pp. 25–27. Later Déroulède reproached Ferry for his colonial policy. "I have lost two children, and you offer me twenty domestics." Gooch, *Franco-German Relations,* p. 21.

[6] The idea was suggested to him by the founder of an earlier Ligue which had exerted little influence. A. H. Canu, G. Buisson, *M. Paul Déroulède et sa Ligue des Patriotes* (Paris, 1889), pp. 18, 19.

its patriotic purposes were at once approved by numerous notabilities. Henri Martin, the historian, was chosen as its first president, and the names of Gambetta, Sadi Carnot, Félix Faure, and Victor Hugo appeared among its members.[7] Its purposes were at first defined vaguely as "the development of patriotic and military education" [8] in order to gain the support of all groups without distinction as to political or religious beliefs, for it was not until 1886 that the Ligue announced the revision of the Treaty of Frankfort and the return of Alsace-Lorraine as its purpose.[9] Books, songs, rifle practice, and gymnastic exercises were to be used by the Ligue, and the *Drapeau,* a weekly, became its official organ in 1882.

An active propaganda was at once organized. In 1885, Déroulède reported as its president that more than three hundred lectures had been delivered in thirty different cities, sixty-two regional committees had been organized, and more than two hundred thousand copies of patriotic pamphlets had been distributed. Much attention was given to convincing public opinion that Germany was merely waiting for an opportunity to take several more provinces from France. For this purpose, more than a hundred thousand copies of a map of France taken from a German school atlas were distributed. It represented *Flandre* as *Flandern, Lorraine* as *Lothringen, Franche Comté* as *Freigrafschaft, Bourgogne* as *Burgund.* This maneuver was doubtless of some influence in encouraging the fear of a German attack.[10] The charge of aggressive purposes was only one method used by the Ligue in arousing a war spirit. It was particularly interested in the education of the younger generation. Déroulède once affirmed (1882) the need of " 'keeping alive the memory of the defeat in the minds of young men in order to conserve the idea of revenge.' " [11] The *Drapeau* (March 23, 1882) had defined this conception of patriotic education in brutal terms. "Would not the pitiless recital of our unprecedented disasters be a certain means of planting in these hearts of sixteen and eighteen, the desire, the passion, the rage for ven-

---

[7] H. Galli [H. Gallichet], *Paul Déroulède raconté par Lui-Même* (Paris, 1900), p. 64.

[8] Membership fees varied from twenty-five centimes to two hundred francs. *Drapeau,* Jan. 5, 1884.

[9] *Ligue des Patriotes. Ce qu'ils nous ont pris. Ce qu'ils veulent nous prendre* (Paris, 1887).

[10] *Ligue des Patriotes. Ce qu'ils nous ont pris.* Charles Leven, *Un Exemple à Suivre* (Paris, 1883), p. 102.

[11] Claretie, *Déroulède,* pp. 25–27.

geance? We wish to make this exposition as complete, as cruel as possible."

Other arguments were used to enlist mature and substantial citizens. To gain the approval of business men, little was said of Alsace-Lorraine or of humiliating defeats. They were told that the existing economic depression was due to Article 11 of the Treaty of Frankfort, which gave to Germany the benefit of the most favored nation clause.[12] A wanton attack by members of the Ligue upon a restaurant in Paris where Germans foregathered was described by the *Drapeau* as "The first signal of this defensive economic campaign which we have sought for a year and a half."[13] The attack upon German commerce in France, wrote an official of the Ligue, was as important as military preparation. "Who has shown France that the amputation of two cherished provinces, however serious, is only a minor evil in comparison with the damage to our commerce and industry by this terrible article?"[14] What do we owe to the treaty imposed by Germany, asked a patriot. "A misery beyond comparison . . . it is only France that does not have enough food for her children!"[15] The Ligue proposed to combat Germany's commercial methods by adopting a distinctive trade-mark, and it appealed for a boycott against German goods as well as German labor.[16] When Déroulède announced his candidacy for the Chamber of Deputies in 1885, he promised that he would ask for special taxes upon foreign laborers.[17] But most of all the Ligue dwelt upon Alsace-Lorraine and the need of revenge.

"For four years," wrote a member in 1887, "we have continually appealed to those who were tempted to forget; don't you hear yonder your brothers of Alsace-Lorraine who are weeping! And, like the surgeon who would cauterize a wound in order to heal it, we have turned and turned again the hot iron in the wound from which France is bleeding, renewing

[12] Commerce between France and Germany declined from 1882 to 1886. Imports from Germany fell from 613 to 448 millions, exports from 379 to 320 millions. Émile Worms, *Une Association Douanière Franco-Allemande avec Restitution de l'Alsace-Lorraine* (Paris, 1888), p. 25.

[13] Canu, Buisson, *M. Paul Déroulède et sa Ligue des Patriotes*, p. 27.

[14] A. H. Canu, *La Ligue des Patriotes: Son But et son Oeuvre* (Paris, 1887), p. 7.

[15] C. H.-R., *Réponse d'un Patriot Français aux Défis Continuels de M. de Bismarck* (Paris, 1887), p. 9.

[16] *France Militaire*, July 7, 1886. See *Kölnische Zeitung* (Jan. 3, 1887) for comments upon the economic arguments of the chauvinists. Cf. *France*, Aug. 23. Oct. 12, 1886. *Petite République Française*, Sept. 1, 1886.

[17] Canu, Buisson, *M. Paul Déroulède*, pp. 36, 37.

the pain but reminding the sufferer of the debts she owes and the duties which she must fulfil." [18]

The significance of the Ligue, and the influence it exerted under Déroulède's leadership, are not to be entirely measured by the number of its members. Never more than three hundred thousand at the most,[19] it was only a small minority, but the important test, that which interested Bismarck, was the attitude of the government and of public opinion in regard to the Ligue and to the ideas it represented. During the first three years of its existence, the life of the nation proceeded without serious disturbance. Only the Ligue's spectacular exploits attracted the attention of the press, and then the usual reaction was one of annoyance and of humiliation. After the raid upon the German restaurant in September, 1882, Rochefort observed in the *Intransigeant* (Sept. 6) that apparently no German might wish to eat a cutlet "without it disappearing immediately in the mouth of a member of the Ligue." Pelletan protested in the *Justice* (Sept. 2) against its presumptuous claim of a monopoly of patriotism. "If a victory which would cause Sedan to be forgotten could be won at the door of a café, it would already have been accomplished. It seems to me . . . that true patriotism has no need of ostentation, that it disdains occasions for brawls and newspaper publicity." [20]

Even the events of 1885, Ferry's fall, the defeat of the colonial policy which meant a renewed emphasis upon Continental affairs, did not immediately assure a friendlier press to the Ligue and to Déroulède's extravagances. The effect of Déroulèdism, according to Rochefort, was "practically that of insanity." [21] The Monarchist *Gazette de France* (March 5, 1885) defined Déroulède "as a dilettante of patriotism. . . . The Déroulèdist defies Europe, a cigar between his

---

[18] Canu, *La Ligue des Patriotes,* p. 4. The market was flooded with patriotic manuals. The old faith seemed about to be replaced by a religious devotion to the fatherland. In some primary schools, altars were erected to the *patrie.* George Goyau, "Patriotisme et Humanitarisme. V. L'Évolution Républicaine, 1882–1900, *"Rev. des Deux Mondes,* 1901, V, 522, 523.

[19] Gooch, *Franco-German Relations,* p. 25. A German historian, however, has estimated the Ligue's membership as 82,000, divided between 500 societies. J. Ziekursch, *Politische Geschichte des Neuen Deutschenreiches,* 3 vols. (Berlin, 1925–1930), II (1927), 183.

[20] When members of the Ligue tore a German flag from the Hotel Continental, and pursued a German into the Ministry of Marine on July 14, 1884, the disapproval of the press was tempered by consideration for patriotic sentiment. *Temps,* July 15. *Figaro,* July 15. *Télégraphe,* July 15. *Intransigeant,* July 16. *XIX Siècle,* July 17.

[21] *Intransigeant,* March 4, 1885.

lips and a cane under his arm. He retakes Metz in a café brawl; and at the head of a school-boy battalion he marches to the conquest of Strassburg." Even the nationalist *Événement* (Aug. 4) admitted that there was a Barnum as well as a patriot in the leader of the Ligue. It was the form, however, rather than the purpose of the Ligue's activities which was objectionable, for little was ever said or done to counteract its campaign of hatred. True patriotism, declared Pelletan, "remains steadfastly regarding the ultimate goal, with the passion but also the patience of fanaticism—the one and only fine fanaticism." [22] The *Figaro* (March 9) held that "one must not be unjust. The Ligue des Patriotes is a sublime work in its purposes, if it is sometimes tactless in its choice of means. I would have everyone a member, but it should be discussed as little as possible. Alone, it is to-day doing for France what Arndt and Kerner, poets like Déroulède, did for Germany." The government steadily ignored the activities of the Ligue, on the ground that it had no power in the premises.[23] Yet, later, when its enterprises not only threatened to create trouble and possibly war with Germany, but even threatened the existence of the Republic, a way was soon found to dissolve it.

An interview in 1883 with General Boulanger, the operatic hero who wished to play the part of a Bonaparte without having genius or audacity, convinced Déroulède that he had " 'at last found a man, I would even say, our man.' " [24] His enthusiasm apparently was caused by Boulanger's opinions as to the weakness of the parliamentary Republic and as to the need of a stronger executive more than by his confidence in the general's military ability. But it was Clemenceau—seeing in him the means of driving the Monarchists from their numerous and high places in the army and perhaps an instrument for a radical revision of the Organic Laws—who secured Boulanger's appointment as Minister of War.[25] His meteoric if brief career owed much to the fact that he was given this place at a time when circumstances and public opinion magnified the importance of the army. Although he had in 1882 reached the exceptionally high rank of a general of division at the comparatively early age of forty-five, his

[22] *Justice,* Sept. 2, 1882.

[23] Déroulède, however, was advised by the government not to speak at the unveiling of a monument to General Chanzy in August, 1885, after the appearance of the *Norddeutsche Allgemeine Zeitung* article of August 3. *Patrie,* Aug. 19. *Gaulois,* Aug. 21.

[24] H. Galli [H. Gallichet] *Paul Déroulède* (Paris, 1910), p. 71.

[25] *Journal des Débats,* Jan. 8, 1886. *Patrie,* July 2, 1886. *Corresp.* O. S., vol. 144, p. 1040.

services in the war of 1870 and in the colonies gave no evidence of particular merit as a strategist. His reputation was, to a large extent, the result of a popular mood.[26] Not only was the army to be concentrated upon the Continent as Freycinet announced at the beginning of his new ministry,[27] but patriotic emotion was to be centered upon it to a degree that had not been equaled since 1871. The annual review of July 14, 1886, the national holiday since 1880, was a dramatic display of military sentiment and of Boulanger's popularity.[28]

"France, the army were loved, acclaimed for themselves," wrote a witness in his diary, "It is clearly a feeling of national pride that has made the popularity of the General. . . . Long live the army, which will permit us to raise our heads . . . Long live the army, which will avenge us against the Prussian and which will render us Metz! That is the significance of the day!"[29]

Beneath this exuberance proceeded a campaign to stimulate confidence in the invincibility of that army. "France has recovered," exulted a member of the Ligue, "and she now looks to the future with confidence, convinced that she is strong enough to secure respect for her *bon droit*."[30] The *France Militaire*, Boulanger's organ, often dwelt upon this theme, and on July 29 declared that the army's selfconfidence had been communicated to the nation. Events were to show, however, that this appearance of confidence was more superficial than real.

Boulanger's sudden popularity was in part the result of careful planning. He made use of every favorable circumstance and occasion to develop it. Comparatively young, vigorous, handsome, and an excellent horseman, he frequently exhibited himself to the public in the rôle of a military hero. His measures as Minister of War were calculated to ingratiate himself with popular opinion: the revision of army rules to permit the wearing of beards, improvement in the soldiers' food, and, above all, his recommendation for the reduction of military service from five to three years won the approval of the mob if not that of conservative opinion. It may be doubted, however, that he would have gone far if certain groups had not decided to organize public opinion in his behalf. Déroulède assured him of the

[26] Georges de Beauregard, *Le Général Boulanger et l'Appel au Peuple* (Paris, 1889), p. 9.

[27] Gooch, *Franco-German Relations*, p. 24.

[28] Newton, *Lyons*, II, 369, 370.

[29] É. Millaud, *Le Journal d'un Parlementaire*, 3 vols. (Paris, 1914–1915), II. Cf. *Figaro*, July 15. *Justice*, July 16. *Patrie*, July 16.

[30] Canu, *Ligue des Patriotes*, pp. 4–7.

support of the Ligue with the suggestion that it could be used, when the moment arrived, for a coup d'état, to rid himself of the Radicals' embarrassing company. The reply was a non-committal, but not discouraging, *"Au Revoir."*[31] For more than a year the radical press urged on the movement of public opinion in his behalf, until in turn the Monarchists took him up. Merchants of publicity reaped a harvest by exploiting, perhaps with the connivance of his friends, the recently developed technic of advertising in his behalf. "This soldier," declared a critic, "has the genius of advertising as much as a manufacturer of chocolate or a mere dentist."[32] A two-penny life of Boulanger, which appeared upon the news-stands the day after the review of July 14, 1886,[33] was the beginning of a deluge of pamphlets, pictures, and songs which continued until the collapse of the Boulanger legend. The moderate and conservative press, without seriously attempting to check it, refused to be swept along by the current. The *Petit Journal,* with the largest circulation of all the Paris newspapers, remained hostile until Boulanger's dismissal from the cabinet in May, 1887. His name itself, according to the *Figaro* (July 1, 1886) would be an insuperable obstacle to the success of his personal ambition. "A very high position can not be attained in France when one's name is Boulanger. . . . If Bonaparte had had that name, he would never have been first consul." But the noisy section of public opinion, that which is too frequently accepted as representing the entire nation, was more influenced by the sensational publications displayed upon the boulevards. "The innocuous *Famille* and the *Journal Illustré,*" wrote a student of public opinion in the spring of 1887, "are replaced by barbarous illustrations. It is a complete stock which the astute publishers have taken from their attics. You again see the *Tambour de Gravelotte, Ils ont fusillé ma mère,* and the *Rubans de l'Alsacienne."*[34]

---

[31] Ducroy, *Déroulède,* pp. 162–164. Boulanger's followers of course denied that he contemplated a coup d'état. *France Militaire,* July 22, 1886. Fernand de Jupilles, *Le Général Boulanger* (Paris, 1887), pp. 90, 91. A. L. A., *Pourquoi Nous Aimons le Général Boulanger* (Paris, 1888).

[32] (Anonymous) "Le Général Boulanger, Ministre de la Guerre," *Corresp.* O. S., 144, p. 1045.

[33] (Anonymous) *La Vie du Général Boulanger* (Paris, 1886). It contains nothing in regard to the *revanche* or to foreign affairs, but he is represented mounted, in full uniform, and in a dashing attitude upon the cover. Cf. G. Grisson, *Le Général Boulanger jugé par Ses Partisans et Ses Adversaires* (Paris, 1888), pp. 171–174.

[34] Léon Goulette, *Avant, Pendant, et Après l'Affaire Schnaebelé, janvier 1887 à . . . ?* (Paris, 1887), p. 95.

The purposes of this propaganda and Boulanger's own views were not as clear as they might seem. A distinction must be drawn between the popular conception of Boulanger's intentions, his own public statements, and his measures as Minister of War. On several occasions he recommended measures to the cabinet which Bismarck almost certainly would have interpreted as provocations. In the spring of 1886, after failing to convince his associates that Germany was planning an offensive for the next year, he proceeded on his own responsibility to increase the production of powder and to build cantonments upon the frontier.[35] This activity is perhaps to be interpreted, however, as misguided zeal rather than as convincing proof of aggressive purposes. His own public statements were studiously prepared to give the impression that he stood for peace and for a strictly defensive policy. "If I desired war, I would be mad," was a pronouncement which was given wide publicity. "If I did not prepare for it, I would be a *misérable.*"[36] A report in September, 1886, that he had recommended an offensive war to a group of army officers was immediately contradicted by an announcement from the semi-official Havas Agency that he had merely urged the adoption of offensive tactics in military training as more in keeping with the temperament of French soldiers.[37] In November, he told a section of the Ligue that preparations were necessary in order to give France the sense of security which was essential to economic and even to intellectual progress.[38] Again he endorsed the ideal of peace in December in an address before the Société Française de la Sauvetage. "You will achieve glory," he said, "saving the lives of your fellow beings, in the midst of that peace which is so necessary that those who have charge of the government must assure it at the price of every sacrifice compatible with the honor and security of the country." [39] The moderating influence of his associates in the ministry is, of course, apparent in these assertions. Nevertheless, it is of some significance that the chief representative of chauvinist sentiment affirmed peaceful purposes.

[35] Bourgeois, *Manuel Historique,* IV, 33.
[36] This statement was printed upon the cover of the cheap life of Boulanger which appeared in 1886. (Anonymous) *La Vie du Général Boulanger* (Paris, 1886).
[37] *Patrie,* Sept. 19, 1886.
[38] *Ibid.,* Nov. 10, 1886.
[39] *Petit Journal,* Dec. 27, 1886. *Patrie,* Dec. 28, 1886. Cf. Charles Chincholle, *Le Général Boulanger* (Paris, 1889), p. 87, for the later period of the agitation. The author was a novelist.

The true character of the chauvinist agitation, which reached a climax in the fall of 1886, is to be found in the press rather than in. Boulanger's speeches. Inferences were drawn from his bearing, and his tone of voice, that were not in accord with his public statements. The *France* (Oct. 17, 1886) insisted that he hoped for a test with Germany in the near future. "It is to be divined in his glance, his attitude, his preoccupations. One senses it. . . . He is the fighter who personifies our aspirations. *Pour quand?* . . . He is ready and so are we. . . . The sooner the better." Peyramont, the editor of the *Revanche*[40] and a second-rate Déroulède, wondered if "you are he whom France awaits?"

". . . The soldier who will march to the conquest of the lost provinces? . . . In any case you are the head of our valiant army, the hope of all, and by a rare stroke of fortune, you have been acclaimed as the personification of the nation's honor. That is sufficient for me." (Oct. 20, 1886.)

In contrast to Boulanger's praise of peace in his speeches, the *France Militaire*[41] (Nov. 11, 1886), accepted as his organ, praised war as an institution, as "the best expression of the divine will," and declared that it was inevitable.[42] In general, however, the chauvinist propaganda aimed at the development of extreme confidence in the army and of a sensitive national pride. "Day after day, week after week," wrote the Paris correspondent of the London *Standard* (Oct. 9, 1886), "the papers are filled with articles boasting of the immense strength of France, and of the perfect state of readiness for action to which her army has been brought." When foreigners criticized the chauvinist agitation, the reply was immediately made that public opinion was peaceful, and interested only in assuring the defense of the nation. Time after time the absence of a demand for an aggressive war was cited as proof of this contention. The argument may have deceived its authors, but it was fundamentally unsound. The

---

[40] More than 130,000 copies of the first number were sold. Not even the Prefect of Police knew the source of its funds. René Goblet, "Mes Souvenirs Politiques: l'Affaire Schnaebelé," *Rev. Pol. et Parl.*, Nov. 10, 1928. Its offices, advertised by a prominent sign, were opposite the Military Club established by Boulanger in the heart of the city at the corner of the Rue de l'Opéra and the Rue de la Paix.

[41] It was credited with only 1,500 subscribers. Mermet, *Annuaire de la Presse Française* (Paris, 1886), p. 92.

[42] One who identified himself as a "patriot" wrote that only war could avert a general state of bankruptcy in Europe due to expenditures for military purposes! C.-H.B., *Réponse d'un Patriote Français aux Défis Continuels de M. de Bismarck* (Paris, 1887).

truth appears in a public letter addressed to Boulanger: "The cry that one hears everywhere, in the press, in books, is not *'À Berlin!'* but, what amounts to the same thing: 'We are ready, ready to the last man, and those who question it are bad citizens.' "[43]

The extravagances of the chauvinist press were suspiciously like the bluster of men who, after years of repression, were enjoying the release of a lively sentiment of national pride and vainglory. They were even prepared to defy England while asserting, at the same time, the nation's ability to defeat Germany. One would expect that their animosity would have been directed exclusively against the latter after the review of July 14. Yet the *France Militaire* (July 15, 16) declared that a Continental league might be formed to break England's habit of regarding the world as her exclusive property. "Let England understand that circumstances may create the occasion for Germany, France, Spain, and Italy to claim Helgoland, the Channel Islands, Gibraltar, and Malta, all without mentioning Egypt where she cannot count upon remaining always." It proceeded, quite calmly, to discuss a settlement which would include an idemnity of *"quelque bons milliards . . .* the tribute that Carthage paid to Rome."[44] The *France* opened its columns quite impartially to the anti-German articles of Lucien Nicot and to Léon Hugonnet's violent attacks upon England. Only the Alsace-Lorraine question separated France from Germany, Hugonnet declared, "while with England it is an incessant conflict in all parts of the globe."[45] "Englishmen," declared the *Petit Journal* (Dec. 31, 1886), at the beginning of a campaign to last more than a generation, "are our worst enemies." Even the moderate *Journal des Débats* (Sept. 11) was irritated by the attempt of the English press to stir up trouble between France and Germany.[46]

The persistence of anti-English sentiment was not accepted in Germany as any assurance of better feeling toward herself.[47] The chauvinist agitation was taken seriously with the result that increasing tension led finally to the crisis of 1887. It was believed that the Ligue, Déroulède, and Boulanger aimed at nothing less than a war for the reconquest of Alsace-Lorraine. Traveling in Germany during

---

[43] Général T. W., *Lettre au Général Boulanger* (Paris, 1886), pp. 8, 9.
[44] *France Militaire,* Nov. 19, 1886.
[45] *France,* Oct. 15, 25.
[46] Cf. *République Française,* Oct. 10. *Cri du Peuple,* Sept. 6 (Socialist).
[47] Herbette, the French Ambassador, pointed it out to Herbert von Bismarck as a promising sign. *G. P.,* VI, 145 (Oct. 18, 1886).

the spring of 1886, Ernest Lavisse, the historian, found that the virulently chauvinist pamphlet *Avant la Bataille,* that had been published with Boulanger's approval, was exhibited in every book-stall.[48] Nevertheless, Déroulède complained in a preface that Gambetta's advice of silence, which he believed had been intended for a limited period, had been transformed into a maxim of state.[49] It was more important that Bismarck had definitely abandoned the policy which he had followed toward France while Ferry had remained in power,[50] insisting that recent events had proved that the majority in France and the government would always yield to the violent minority. The Chancellor found support for his position in the reports of Lieutenant Villaume, the German military attaché in Paris, who sent numerous excerpts from the chauvinist press and the titles of almost all pamphlets of this type, without critical evaluation.[51] Nevertheless, Villaume admitted that these products of ill-balanced minds and the demonstrations of the Ligue were not so significant as the "value, which the government, the political parties, and the army attribute to this product of French patriotism." [52] Bismarck scarcely needed these reports, for his opinion had already been formed.[53] With Russia irritated by her difficulties with Bulgaria, he found it useful to emphasize the chauvinist agitation in order to cool any desire she might develop for an alliance with France. In any event, he covered the more moderate reports of Münster,[54] the ambassador in Paris, with question marks, and when Münster, in alarm, addressed a letter directly to the Emperor,[55] the Chancellor lectured him for this lack

[48] E. Lavisse, "Notes Prises dans une Excursion en Allemagne" (1886), II, 908. Cf. E. Lavisse, *Essais sur l'Allemagne Impériale* (Paris, 1888), p. 267.

[49] *Avant la Bataille,* Preface. The anonymous author of *Pas Encore!* (Paris, 1886—) argued that the time had not yet arrived for war with Germany. A German officer insisted, with some justice, that the two pamphlets differed only as to the timeliness of an attack upon Germany. Lt.-Colonel C. Hoettschau, *La Prochaine Guerre Franco-Allemande* (Paris, 1887), Chapter I.

[50] In 1882, he had given instructions that no attention should be paid to the demonstrations of the Ligue. Fay, *Origins of the World War,* I, 99.

[51] *G. P.,* VI, 127–131; 131–134; 138–143; 146–151. Villaume was recalled in November, 1886, and his successor, Captain von Huhne, was told by the Crown Prince Frederick not to send irritating reports. É. Bourgeois, "L'Allemagne et la France au Printemps de 1887," *Revue des Sciences Politiques,* March, 1924, p. 12.

[52] Villaume's report, Paris, Feb. 28, 1886. *G. P.,* VI, 127, 128.

[53] E. Daudet, *La Mission du Baron de Courcel* (Paris), p. 190.

[54] When he found that the Chancellor refused to accept his point of view, he wrote to Herbert von Bismarck that "war could only come from us." *G. P.,* VI, 159, 160 (Dec. 30, 1886).

[55] Münster to William I, Paris, Dec. 30, 1886. *Ibid.,* VI, 160–162.

of respect for his own authority. When the ambassador insisted that the majority of the French people desired peace, he replied that the same could be said of the masses in every country, but that it was not always true of the leaders. In any case, the decisions of the French government would be determined by the minority, and he pointed out that the moderate press had not warned its readers against the dangers of the chauvinist campaign. Finally, he inquired, what would happen to his proposals for increases in the army if Münster's estimate of French intentions should become known?[56]

The attitude of the French government toward the chauvinist campaign in the press and toward the Ligue des Patriotes apparently justified Bismarck's conclusions. Not until it became a danger to the Republic early in 1889 was the Ligue dissolved. One suit was brought against Peyramont, editor of the *Revanche,* when he published the news of the victory of the protesting candidates in the Alsatian elections of 1887 with the comment, *"Vive la France!"* but he was acquitted.[57] No jury evidently would condemn an editor for endangering the safety of the State if he could say that he had acted from patriotic motives. An explanation of the moderate point of view and of the government's attitude was given by Ernest Lavisse. "It is doubtless not well to provoke these real or assumed alarms [in Germany], but it would be worse to repress by prudence every manifestation of patriotism. Do not let us forget the sound of the *'trumpette guerrière!'* It must be sounded with force to cover the tumult of our parties."[58] Toleration of the chauvinist agitation meant, not a desire of war, but a belief in the need of a strong patriotism in view of possible trouble and as a support for France in her efforts to acquire a larger place in European affairs. The real test would come if Germany went to war with another Power, with Russia for example. "A desire for war in the abstract," wrote Edward Dicey, a friendly critic of public opinion in France, "is quite consistent with an aversion to a particular war at a special time. . . ."[59] With Germany engaged upon her eastern front, the temptation would have been extremely strong. One observer wrote that France would immediately join the country which should first break away from Germany: "until then, let us watch and arm ourselves

---

[56] Bismarck to Münster, Friedrichsruh, Jan. 4, 1887. *G. P.,* VI, 163–166. Cf. Fay, *Origins of the World War,* I, 101, 102.
[57] *Petite Gironde,* March 14, 1887.
[58] *Rev. des Deux Mondes,* 1886, III, 908.
[59] Dicey, "England and Europe," *Nineteenth Century,* 1887, I, 551. The *Temps* (April 5, 1887) thought that his slight acquaintance with public opinion in France weakened his conclusions.

formidably; the time is near." [60] The *Charivari* (Aug. 13, 1886) in its single cartoon relating to Germany during this period of tension represented the German Emperor as abandoned by his two associates in the League of the Three Emperors.

It cannot be said, however, that there was an immediate danger of a French attack. During the summer of 1886, Freycinet had even suggested to Bismarck an arrangement in regard to Egypt, which the Chancellor had rejected, and the French prime minister communicated to him Russia's proposals for an alliance.[61] If the chauvinist press, the *Revanche,* the *France,* and the *France Militaire,* continued and increased its agitation, many newspapers declared for peace. The Monarchist journals made use of the opportunity to attack Boulanger, and even the Republic as representing a war policy. *"Boulanger, c'est la guerre"* they cried as they had against Gambetta.[62] The *Figaro* (Oct. 20, 1886) denied that a war was necessary for the recovery of France's position. "Why war?" it asked. "Cannot an able diplomacy restore France to the rank which is her due?" The Bonapartist *Patrie* (Sept. 2) condemned the "base exploitation of the noblest sentiments. . . . Every means of publicity has been used for this shameless work: pictures, printing, posters, public criers . . ."

One of the most significant features of public opinion was the change of attitude on the part of the Radicals after the October elections of 1885. They no longer gave first place to peace as the necessary condition for the application of reforms. Their argument that reparation would come by the gradual expansion of the ideals of social justice was forgotten. Until Boulanger was forced from the cabinet, he remained their favorite, and in the eyes of the Radical press he could do no wrong. They would not admit a desire for war, but their conception of peace was calculated to cause one. "There are two kinds of peace for a nation," wrote Stephen Pichon, who became Minister of Foreign Affairs in 1906. "The peace which one supplicates and that which one imposes. The latter is the only kind that is suitable for France. . . ." [63]

---

[60] A review of *Pas Encore!* in the *Nouvelle Revue,* vol. 40 (May 1886). The *France Militaire* (Sept. 4, 1886) did not conceal its opinion that France should join Russia if war broke out in the Near East.

[61] G. P., VI, 137, 138, 144, 145, 151, 152. Bourgeois, Pagès, *Origines et Résponsabilités,* pp. 214, 215. Gooch, *Franco-German Relations,* p. 27. J. V. Fuller, *Bismarck's Diplomacy at Its Zenith* (Cambridge, 1922), p. 100.

[62] L. Lavedar [pseud. Philippe Grandlieu] in the *Figaro,* July 25, 1886. Cf. *Gazette de France,* Oct. 20, 1886.

[63] *Justice,* Dec. 23, 1886.

Rochefort anticipated an early attack due to Germany's knowledge that France would have a better rifle in two years.[64] Not even a specific renunciation of the lost provinces, declared Camille Pelletan, would dispose of the danger of an attack, for Germany would not be reassured as to the attitude of future governments. "It is neither our actions, nor our demonstrations, nor our talk, nor our mental reservations which compel her to remain our implacable enemy; it is what she has done to us." [65]

Other leaders of public opinion affirmed France's desire of peace without any reservation, denying that the extremists exerted serious influence. In any event, observed the Bonapartist *Patrie* (Dec. 14, 1886), "our sentiments are pacific at the present time, and that is the essential thing." [66] It was Bismarck, using the chauvinist agitation in France as demonstrating the inevitability of war in order to impress upon a reluctant public opinion the need of increases in the army, who precipitated the first of the two crises of 1887 by his address to the Reichstag of January 11, 1887. After a passing reference to the historic rivalry between the two countries, he turned to the existing situation. No minister and no party, he declared, had ever renounced Alsace-Lorraine; war therefore was certain to come in ten days or in ten years. Although the present government and the masses were peaceful, Germany had no guarantee that a leader, like Napoleon III, would not seek a diversion from troubles at home in a foreign war.

"You who know your French history," he declared, "will agree with me that France's decisions . . . are determined in difficult moments by energetic minorities. In the meantime, they are duly desirous of beginning war with the maximum strength. Their purpose is to maintain '*le feu sacré de la revanche,*' the aim which Gambetta defined as: '*Ne parlez jamais de la guerre, mais pensez-y toujours.*' [*sic*] People do not speak of it directly, but only of being attacked by Germany. There is no foundation for this fear, and those who speak of it in France know that what they say is not true. We will not attack France." [67]

[64] *Intransigeant,* Dec. 19.

[65] *Justice,* Dec. 19.

[66] Cf. *Journal des Débats,* Dec. 26. *Matin,* Dec. 24. *Petit Journal,* Dec. 28.

[67] *Die Reden des . . . Reichskanzlers, Fürsten von Bismarck,* XII, 188. The French press, until this speech, had attributed much of the existing tension to the exaggerated reports of French chauvinism in the London newspapers. *Matin,* Dec. 16, 1886. Jan. 6, 1887. *Patrie,* Dec. 21, 1886. *Instransigeant,* Dec. 23, 1886. *Siècle,* Dec. 23, 1866. *Lyon Républicain,* Jan. 1, 1887. *Petit Journal,* Jan. 2, 1887. *Daily Telegraph* (London) Jan. 8, 1887.

The importance of Bismarck's speech was immediately understood in France.[68] Nevertheless, the press at first chose to emphasize his assurance that Germany would not attack. The *Temps* (Jan. 13), the *Journal des Débats* (Jan. 13), the *Justice* (Jan. 13, 14), and the *Lyon Républicain* (Jan. 13) all agreed that its general tone was reassuring. The Paris correspondent of the London *Daily News* (Jan. 13) wrote that it had been "favorably received, the most anti-German papers sheathing their swords for the occasion." [69] If the Monarchist *Gazette de France* (Jan. 13) criticized the French government, it was on the ground that its attitude constituted the only danger. The *Éclair* of Montpellier (Jan. 15), a Monarchist journal, called for a formal statement "without equivocation" to be addressed to Germany:

"Neither the government, nor the nation, as you have acknowledged, dreams of attacking the victor of 1871. We are resigned to the treaty of Frankfort; but we retain the hope that in the future, which is free, its terms which have mutilated us, may be changed, perhaps without war by means of compensations and by circumstances, in such a way as to return our brothers to us. We are arming to the extent of our resources, following your example, but it is for the defense and not for the attack!"

This moderate first impression was soon abandoned when the chauvinists characterized the speech as "brutal" and as a "provocation." [70] The *Revanche* (Jan. 14) hoped that Russia would attack Austria so that France could throw her sword into the balance. John Lemoinne, an influential publicist, wrote in the *Matin* (Jan. 12) that the "account opened in 1870 will not be settled while the German flag continues to wave at Strassburg and Metz." It was this reaffirmation of loyalty to the lost provinces that chiefly impressed German observers of the reaction in France to Bismarck's speech.[71] Yet many had declared that the treaty of 1871 was recognized, even if hope for the future was not abandoned. It was a question of conscience, in the opinion of the *Petite Gironde* of Bordeaux (Feb. 16). "Must we speak with a light heart of the invasion, of our defeats and of the lost provinces? *Cela jamais.* Our conscience is inviolate. . . ." Who

[68] See the description of Bismarck's menacing manner, when he dealt with France, in the report of the London *Daily News* (Jan. 12, 1887), Berlin correspondent.
[69] Cf. *Times*, Jan. 13, 1887.
[70] *Daily Telegraph* (London), Jan. 14.
[71] *Kölnische Zeitung*, Jan. 15. *Berliner Post*, Jan. 14.

has ever claimed, asked the Bonapartist *Patrie* (Jan. 14), "to destroy the soul of a nation with a scrap of paper (*chiffon de papier*) ?"

When the Reichstag passed the government's army bill for a period of three instead of seven years, Bismarck dissolved it and ordered new elections for February 21. The conservative party in Germany, and at least a part of the press, represented the issue to be war or peace: because a majority hostile to the septennate would encourage France to attack.[72] The more influential of the Paris newspapers attempted to prevent a panic by attributing Germany's apparently threatening attitude to the need of influencing the result of the election. Public opinion was advised to maintain the sobriety and reserve of its first reaction to Bismarck's speech.[73] Again, as in 1875, rumors appeared in Germany of large orders by the French war ministry for acids, wood, and horses,[74] and Bismarck informed the German military attaché in Paris that he was thinking of calling France's attention to the seriousness of these measures. If not contradicted, they would mislead public opinion, he wrote, as to the intentions of the two governments.[75] Misrepresented by the press, this suggestion, which apparently was not carried out, created an impression in certain quarters that Bismarck intended to address a demand for disarmament to France.

The first hint appeared in a brief note published by the London *Daily News* (Jan. 24), representing Her Majesty's ministers as disturbed by the situation. Confidence was expressed in the French government's desire to avoid a war "whilst the peaceful views of the German Emperor are well-known. Nevertheless, circumstances are rapidly tending toward a crisis. The first movement will probably be on the part of Germany, which, it is reported, will on an early date ask France what is the meaning of recent military movements toward the frontier." [76] The measure of the prevailing nervous tension, and, incidentally, the influence of the press, appeared in the panic caused by this note in all of the European financial markets, and especially in that of Paris. Its effect in the French capital was

---

[72] *Kölnische Zeitung,* Jan. 31. *Berliner Post,* Jan. 20.

[73] *Temps,* Jan. 16.

[74] *Kölnische Zeitung,* Jan. 21. *Times* (London), Jan. 21.

[75] Bismarck to van Leyden, Berlin, Jan. 22, 1887. *G. P.,* VI, 166, 167. Fuller, *Bismarck's Diplomacy,* pp. 136, 137.

[76] The Foreign Office at once contradicted this note. *Temps,* Jan. 26. The *Norddeutsche Allgemeine Zeitung* (Jan. 25) and the *Intransigeant* (Jan. 26) likewise reported their governments as refusing to credit it.

somewhat neutralized, however, because, bad as it was, the semi-official Havas Agency was detected in a clear misrepresentation of its contents. The *Temps* (Jan. 26) observed that the qualifying "probably" had been omitted and that Germany was represented as about to present her observations " 'in somewhat peremptory terms.' " Some thought that it was a stock-jobbing maneuver, and others demanded that those who were responsible should be punished.[77]

For a moment it seemed possible that this incident would revive in more intense form the animosity against England,[78] when the *Berliner Post*'s "On the Razor Edge" (*Auf des Messers Schneide*) article of February 1 turned attention back to Germany. It declared that "the peace-loving, or more accurately, the war-hating masses" had been aroused in France by a prolonged campaign of hatred. It was perhaps not a coincidence that this alarmist article followed an appeal by the *Justice* (Jan. 26) that the government should make an official statement "proclaiming France's pacific intentions." The government of course took no action, and the moderate *Temps* (Jan. 27) advised against it. "Europe knows," it declared, "that peace or war in no sense depends upon our country. The issue is in the hands of Alexander III and William I." Another panic upon the Bourse followed the *Post*'s article,[79] but the press, even in these difficult circumstances, managed to retain a reasonable balance with much satisfaction to itself. A comparison with the violent articles in the German press, observed the Bonapartist *Patrie* (Feb. 6), had "caused us to look at ourselves in a mirror and to inform the universe: 'How beautiful we are!' . . . But, in truth, this time we have reason to be proud: we are clean, we are beautiful!"[80] One reward that was much appreciated was the recognition and approval of this moderate attitude by the London press, which had formerly condemned the chauvinist agitation.[81] Yet the results of the elections in Alsace, where the pro-

[77] *Justice*, Jan. 27. *Intransigeant*, Jan. 29. *Patrie*, Jan. 31. Cyon, *Histoire de L'Entente Franco-Russe*, pp. 217, 218.

[78] A few days later, the *Standard* (London) printed a report from Berlin that Bismarck intended to ask France to promise neutrality if war should break out in the Near East. A refusal would be considered as a *casus belli. Patrie*, Jan. 26. *Petit Journal*, Jan. 27. *France*, Jan. 27. *Daily Telegraph*, Jan. 26.

[79] The 3 per cent *rente* fell from 79.5 to 76 between February 1 and February 4. *République Française*, Jan. 29 to Feb. 4.

[80] The *Post*'s article was interpreted as a maneuver intended to influence the elections. *Temps*, Feb. 3. *France Militaire*, Feb. 4. The *Figaro* (Feb. 6) protested that public opinion should not be hypnotized by Alsace-Lorraine, for it enabled Bismarck to increase the German army.

[81] *Temps*, Feb. 6, 8, 11. *Journal des Débats*, Feb. 8.

testing candidates were all returned to the Reichstag, inspired a new expression of extremist opinion. The *Revanche* identified the protesting candidates as those of France, and it concluded with a *Vive la France!*[82] This impressive demonstration of Alsace's loyalty made it more difficult than ever to discuss the problem in a reasonable spirit. "France does not have the right to renounce Alsace-Lorraine," declared the liberal *Lyon Républicain* (Feb. 23), "for Alsace-Lorraine has not renounced her."[83]

Bismarck thought, it seems, of using diplomatic pressure to secure Boulanger's removal from the cabinet.[84] If this measure was suggested as desirable, it was not, however, presented as an ultimatum.[85] The French government itself had not been inactive. On February 8, parliament voted an extra military credit of eighty millions without discussion, and Flourens, the Minister of Foreign Affairs, took the most definitely aggressive step during the crisis in demanding of the German ambassador "categorical explanations" as to the meaning of the mobilization of reserves in Alsace.[86] Surely, if Bismarck had been seeking an excuse for war, this rash demand would have furnished it. Boulanger attempted unsuccessfully to secure the ministry's approval for counter-measures, but the public was assured that his views were moderate. His opposition to war was affirmed in a report of the correspondent of the London *Daily Telegraph* (Jan. 25) : "Of one thing we may be perfectly sure, namely, that General Boulanger will never advocate an attack upon Germany. On this point he speaks in the most decided and unequivocal language." He was even reported as threatening his resignation if the other ministers were in favor of war. The *France Militaire* (Feb. 28, Mar. 1) considered the possibility of the peaceful return of Alsace-Lorraine, adding the threat, however, that only in that way could Germany's accomplishments be assured against the fatal consequences of new diplomatic arrangements. This menacing attitude by no means reflected the general reaction of public opinion. The reserve which had been observed by the press since Bismarck's speech of January 11 was manifestly due to the fear of furnishing an occasion for trouble. Even this moder-

---

[82] *Intransigeant*, March 14.

[83] Cf. *France Militaire*, Feb. 27. *Patrie*, March 2.

[84] The formation of a Boulanger cabinet or his election as President would, he warned Herbette, mean war. Bourgeois, Pagès, *Origines et Résponsabilités*, pp.. 225, 226.

[85] Fuller, *Bismarck's Diplomacy*, pp. 143, 144.

[86] Bourgeois, Pagès, *Origines et Résponsabilités*, p. 224.

ation did not correctly interpret, wrote the correspondent of the *Daily Telegraph* (Feb. 21, 1887), the general desire for peace. "It is no less true that the anxiety which one hears expressed on all sides in private life that the trade and commerce of the country should have full time for development undisturbed by rumors of war, is not expressed by the press with sufficiently passionate earnestness." The attitude of the press, as well as the more intangible body of public opinion, showed that the loudly proclaimed confidence in the army had been vastly overrated. A few months had brought a notable change, and the cause was clearly a fear of war.

Had the crises of 1887 ended with Bismarck's success in securing a favorable majority in the election of February 21 and in the passage of the septennate, there probably would have been no very serious or permanent change in public opinion. The press had given repeated assurances that Bismarck's actions were intended for political effect. In March, the press was able to discuss Ferdinand de Lesseps's unofficial mission to Berlin in the interests of peace without excessive bitterness.[87] Nor did Pope Leo XIII's proposed intervention arouse the storm of indignant protest which would certainly have followed it a year earlier. The idea was first mentioned by "Diplomaticus" in the *Figaro* (Feb. 27) as possibly leading to general disarmament. On March 12, the same journal—for the topic did not receive general attention in the press [88]—described Leo's plan as the possible formation of a buffer state between France and Germany to include Switzerland, Alsace-Lorraine, Luxemburg, and Holland. Probably hostile as she had been from the first, the mention of Alsace-Lorraine meant Germany's refusal. The Pope was informed, March 9, that Germany was not prepared to purchase peace by the return of Alsace-Lorraine,[89] and the Paris correspondent of the *Kölnische Zeitung* (April 12) wrote that it was high time for France to realize that "Alsace was German, is German, and will remain German so long as the German Empire exists." Neither of these attempts to solve the Franco-German problem had any chance of success, but the fact that they could be discussed at all indicated that public opinion had remained relatively calm.

Moreover, Déroulède resigned from the presidency of the Ligue des Patriotes in disgust at the turn of events. His complaint addressed to Gaston Calmette of the *Figaro* (April 21) was primarily

---

[87] *Figaro,* March 10. *Petit Journal,* March 11, 15, 17.
[88] The *Matin* (April 22) refused to give serious consideration to the scheme.
[89] *G. P.,* VI, 178, 179.

against the government's inaction.[90] He protested that his agitation
had been for the purpose of preparing France for the day when Germany would attack her. "And the time at last had come. Our people
had the strength and courage to face a danger for which they were
not responsible." France could count upon Russia, and even Italy
had hesitated. "The occasion had never been more brilliant for us.
. . . Our long years of prudence in the face of menaces and insults
had clearly proved to Europe on which side was the provocation, on
which was justice. In spite of all, the government yielded. . . . What
has decided me to resign are the actions of the president of the council, all of the actions of all of the politicians of to-day. I have lost
heart, in fact, from what I see, and the future of my country seems
very dark." If France waited for three or four more years, all would
be lost, he concluded, for a new generation without a personal experience of the war and without a full knowledge of the bitterness of
defeat would be entering the army. What appeared to Déroulède as
timidity, approaching cowardice, was more accurately a failure to accept his ideas as to France's immediate policy. Then and later, the
government and public opinion accorded him much respect for his
devotion to a patriotic ideal, but at the same time they refused to
follow his leadership into dangerous paths.

On April 21, the sudden arrest of Schnaebelé, a frontier police
official of Alsatian birth who had opted for France, precipitated a
crisis which had a more serious effect upon public opinion than the
earlier tension of January and February. His activities in the secret
service taking him to Metz and Strassburg,[91] he was tried *in absentia*
by a German court in Leipzig and condemned to a term of imprisonment. Gautsch, a German police commissioner, having business with
him, arranged a meeting at the frontier village of Pagny-sur-Moselle.
Schnaebelé, however, was met by other police officials, seized, and
hurried off to Metz. In Paris, parliament was not in session and a
number of the ministers were absent in Algeria when news arrived of
this apparently brutal demonstration of German methods.[92] Three
men, Grèvy, the President, Goblet, the Prime Minister, and Flourens,
the Minister of Foreign Affairs, were chiefly concerned with the de-

[90] The limited influence of his articles in the *Drapeau* in favor of an alliance
with Russia after his trip there in the summer of 1886 was cited by the *Matin*
(April 22) as an explanation for his resignation.

[91] This work had recently been placed under the direction of the Ministry of
War, hence that of Boulanger, René Goblet, "Mes Souvenirs Politiques: L'Affaire
Schnaebelé," *Rev. Pol. et Parl.*, Nov. 10, 1928, p. 180.

[92] *Matin*, April 22. *Temps*, April 23. *Journal des Débats*, April 23.

termination of France's policy during the ensuing crisis. Grèvy, reported as having been found reading Horace in the original during the crisis, was convinced that the government's first and exclusive concern should be the maintenance of peace. "My friend," he told Goblet, "I receive many people; no one desires war, neither the chamber nor the country." The Prime Minister protested his own desire of peace, but he was also determined that his country should not suffer a humiliation.[93] It was Goblet, in the main, who decided that France should take a strong position in demanding Schnaebelé's release. Boulanger was even more aggressive,[94] although his organ, the *France Militaire,* remained distinctly moderate until the end of the crisis, while Flourens stood midway between his chief and the President.

Given Goblet's decision, it was necessary of course to assure himself of the support of public opinion. The first reaction of the press was not promising. Camille Pelletan immediately characterized the arrest as a trap prepared by Bismarck in the hope that France would be led into some ill-considered action,[95] but the general impression seemed to be that the incident was of little importance. The *Berliner Post's* correspondent, writing from Paris on the evening of April 21, declared that the press mostly refrained from comments or advised against thinking of the incident as a provocation until an official explanation appeared. The London *Standard* (April 22) was informed that the arrest "has, on the whole, caused less excitement than might have been expected." At the same time, the German banker, von Donnersmarck, appeared in Paris, and on the evening of Schnaebelé's arrest, assured Joseph Reinach, of the *République Française,* of Bismarck's peaceful intentions. Reinach at once reported this conversation to Goblet,[96] but the Premier proceeded to sanction a semi-official statement to the press which represented the incident in the worst possible light. " 'It is considered for the present,' " announced the note as issued by the Havas Agency, " 'that he (Schnaebelé) has been the victim of a trap,' " and it denied that the arrest had any connection with his activities in Alsace.[97] Like the War-Scare of 1875, the Schnaebelé Affair became one of the chief indictments

---

[93] Goblet, "Mes Souvenirs Politiques," *Rev. Pol. et Parl.,* Nov. 10, 1928, p. 190.
[94] Freycinet, *Souvenirs,* pp. 371, 372.
[95] *Justice,* April 22.
[96] J. Reinach, "Gambetta et Bismarck, L'Affaire Schnaebelé," *Rev. de Paris,* 1917, IV, 761–763. Reinach was confident of von Donnersmarck's sincerity.
[97] Alexandre Zévaès, *Histoire de la Troisième République* (Paris, 1926), p. 206.

against Bismarck's policy. It is now fairly well established that the Chancellor was not involved in the events which led to Schnaebelé's arrest,[98] and it is possible that Gautsch was acting in good faith when he invited the Frenchman to the frontier.[99] But Goblet was naturally more concerned with the effect which the incident would have upon France's prestige. He was determined to make of it an occasion for showing France's ability and determination to secure respect for her rights. The Havas note was evidently intended to mobilize public opinion for this purpose.

It had the desired effect. The *Standard* was informed (April 23) that the first moderate impression had been "short-lived, and panic and excitement now prevail." It was generally assumed that Bismarck was attempting to provoke France. Yet the press, following its policy of January and February, advised public opinion to be patient.[100] It was apparently not the purpose of those who were responsible for the direction of public opinion to inspire a dangerous explosion of chauvinism. They were content to confirm the fear that Bismarck was seeking a cause of war. Later, the *Temps* (April 30) and the *Journal des Débats* (April 30) explained their relatively brief comments during the crisis by a refusal to excite opinion. The *Intransigeant* (April 28) replied to the report of chauvinist demonstrations in Paris which had appeared in the German press: "If silence is a demonstration, it is true. . . . It is an expression of disdain." Of the extremist press only the *France* (April 23) advised a dangerous policy before the end of the crisis. If the arrest should prove to be a provocation, it declared that France should reply in kind. "When they make a move, let us do likewise; when they change the location of a cannon, let us follow their example. An eye for an eye, a tooth for a tooth." Rochefort called for the rigid ostracism of all Germans in France.[101] It is evident that the reserve maintained with some difficulty by a large section of the press was partly inspired by

---

[98] Fay, *Origins of the World War*, I, 103, 104 (note).

[99] Gautsch affirmed this on oath to a correspondent of the *Daily News* (April 29). He explained that he had mentioned his engagement with Schnaebelé to a detective, without attaching any importance to the latter's inquiry. Gautsch also claimed that he had protested against the arrest and that he, himself, had been placed under temporary arrest.

[100] *Temps*, April 23. *Journal des Débats*, April 23.

[101] *Intransigeant*, April 27. The next day, he declared "We know, at this moment, that a bird of prey is watching us, and waits only for the smallest pretext . . . to fall upon us and to feed from our flesh." The correspondent of the *Kölnische Zeitung* (April 25) called such articles as this, "echoes from a madhouse."

the desire to create a favorable impression in those countries whose aid would be necessary in the event of war. The *Lyon Républicain* (April 27) believed that "nothing should be permitted to change this favorable impression." "Knowing by unhappy experience the power of public opinion," wrote a pamphleteer, "France desires the sympathy of other peoples." [102]

When difficulties arose in the attempt to prove that Schnaebelé had been arrested upon French soil, a more effective argument for his release was found in the discovery of the letters in which Gautsch had invited him to the rendezvous on the frontier. Bismarck at once recognized that they amounted to a safe conduct, for the practical reason that if the arrest were maintained, it would be impossible in the future to transact any business under similar circumstances.[103] Nevertheless, his delay in releasing Schnaebelé, although necessary perhaps, added to the exasperation of the French. At length, April 28, Schnaebelé was permitted to return to France. His release was announced in a communication which did little to improve the temper of the authorities in France, for it gave much attention to Schnaebelé's activities in Alsace and it failed to express a frank acknowledgment that Germany had been in the wrong. Flourens, accepting the settlement in excellent spirit, immediately instructed Herbette on his own initiative to present to Count Bismarck the felicitations of the French government on a solution "as much in keeping with the principles of international law as with the relations of *bon voisinage* which should exist between two great nations, and to add that the conduct of France would always be guided by the same principles." Goblet and the majority of the ministry thought this action was too friendly, and later, on the same day, Flourens was directed to cancel his earlier instructions in favor of a mere acknowledgment of Bismarck's communication.[104]

The Schnaebelé Affair was more than a diplomatic crisis, it was a turning-point in public opinion. The comparatively moderate point of view of the preceding winter was replaced by a feeling of intense bitterness. It was not, however, expressed by a demand for an aggressive war, but by an anticipation of continued provocations by Germany. On April 29, Rochefort declared in the *Intransigeant* that the solution of the crisis settled nothing. "The chancellor's plan is

[102] A. Rouyer, *Aura-t-on la Guerre?* (Paris, 1887), p. 18.

[103] Bismarck's marginal note, H. von Bismarck's Memorandum, Berlin, April 25, 1887. *G. P.*, VI, 185.

[104] Goblet, "Mes Souvenirs Politiques," *Rev. Pol. et Parl.*, Nov. 10, 1928, p. 192.

self-evident; he uses every means to exasperate us, in order to be able to say that the rabbit acted first." War was inevitable, affirmed the *France* (April 29), "because the Germans desire it and because the French do not fear it." The *Lyon Républicain* (April 30), anticipated that Schnaebelé's arrest "was only the beginning of a policy of vexation and insults." Mme. Adam thought that provocations were becoming a habit with Bismarck,[105] and a pamphleteer declared that "we must be prepared before two months to defy an aggression for which Germany seems to be seeking a pretext. We must be able to defeat, to crush finally and for always this rival nation if it forces us into war." [106]

The relation between the chauvinist campaign, the government, and moderate opinion became more critical and significant than ever. Were extremists to be permitted to misrepresent France's purposes? The *Daily News* (April 25) thought that the time had come for a specific disavowal of the extremists. The French should

"Ask themselves what they mean by what they love to call a patriotic agitation. . . . The whole body of the nation does not actively connive in these sterile agitations, but it acquiesces in them, and that, in itself, at the present juncture is both a folly and a crime. These new *agents provocateurs* of noisy patriotism should be pitilessly suppressed, whenever their demonstrations constitute an offense against French law."

Once the immediate danger had disappeared, Boulanger's organ, the *France Militaire,* assumed an attitude of provocation. After affirming, April 30, that France would never assume the aggressive, it declared, May 1, that "Germany provokes and threatens us. We face her, ready for the answering thrust, hand upon the hilt of our sword. That means war to-morrow, or day after to-morrow, in six months or a year, one day or another." Four days later, drawing its inspiration from the events of July, 1870, it asserted:

"We are to-day at the third act of the Schnaebelé affair. Injured and outraged in the person of one of her officials, France has the right and the obligation to demand 'guarantees,' or an apology. If satisfaction is refused her, France should notify Europe, leaving it to public opinion to decide on which side there was justice and moderation, provocation and violence."

It concluded in black-faced type: "Whatever happens, we will not declare war."

A few days later, Boulanger was omitted from the new Rouvier

---

[105] *Nouvelle Revue,* vol. 46, p. 172.
[106] E. Bricard, *Alerte Patriotes!* (Paris, 1887), Preface.

ministry. His elimination meant that the government had repudiated the dangerous policy which was attributed to him. Yet for more than a year, strengthened by the feeling that he had been dismissed at Germany's command, his popularity continued to be dangerous. When he was about to proceed to Clermont-Ferrand, where he was to assume command of the 18th Corps, men threw themselves upon the rails to prevent the departure of his train.

Ferry's defeat had more serious consequences than a temporary reversal for the policy of colonial expansion. Tunis and Tonkin no longer occupied the attention of the sensational press, and as the army and Continental affairs took their place, Alsace and Germany played a larger part, with unfortunate results, in the formation of public opinion. These changes gave a powerful impetus to the *revanche* sentiment, to Déroulède's agitation, and to the Ligue des Patriotes. Hitherto concerned primarily with their program of reforms, the Radicals developed an extreme nationalism. They gave their support to Boulanger and contributed to a superficial confidence in the army and to an inflated national pride. The more extremely chauvinist newspapers should not be interpreted, however, as reflecting public opinion in general, or as influencing the great majority of the nation. Even the *Revanche,* which was the most widely circulated of them, appealed to a class which had little contact with the commonplace life of the nation. No newspaper which was read by those who were a part of it would have printed an article (Nov. 24, 1886) by Maurice Talmeyr, the novelist, which denied the right of the peasant to be called a man. "His work and his life cuts him off from the really human part of the population. . . . The peasant in reality is a sort of a medium between the monkey and man. He belongs to the land, not to humanity." Even Déroulède, with the advantage of his admittedly disinterested patriotism, failed to win the confidence of the nation and to influence the government. The limited significance of the *revanche* movement, nevertheless, did not make it less dangerous in view of Bismarck's insistence that it would be the determining factor in a crisis. It was his speech of January 11, inspired by a desire to secure the enactment of the septennate, that led to the long period of tension. The presence of immediate danger, however, revealed the superficial character of the chauvinist agitation, and if it had not been for the accident of Schnaebelé's arrest, it is possible that relations with Germany might gradually have become better. But that incident was represented by a government which was determined not to give way, and by the press, as a calculated provocation. Boulanger's dismissal meant the official repudiation of the *revanche,* but the press insisted that a period of successive provocations was beginning. It was then that public opinion turned in favor of an alliance with Russia.

CHAPTER VII

The Franco-Russian Alliance

Chaque jour, chaque heure nous approche du massacre inévitable. Toutes les forces conscients et inconscients de l'humanité nous y poussent invinciblement. . . . Une main s'offre, voici la nôtre. C'est ainsi que j'analyse le sentiment de beaucoup, je crois qu'on peut dire de tous.

Georges Clemenceau, *Justice*, October 15, 1893.

Bismarck's masterly diplomacy is generally credited with delaying the inevitable union between France and Russia for a generation after the war of 1870. His purposes were facilitated, it is admitted, by Russia's disapproval of French republicanism. It has not usually been thought necessary, however, to give much attention to France's attitude, for she has been represented as merely waiting for a favorable opportunity. A closer examination shows that this generalization is not entirely accurate. Contrary to the general impression, it was Bismarck's own actions after Ferry's defeat, aided by Russian propaganda, that first turned her definitely in the direction of the alliance with Russia.

During their period of power from 1873 to 1877, Broglie and Decazes made use of every opportunity to approach her,[1] for the Monarchists had no scruples as to an association with autocratic Russia. It was indicated by a long tradition of alliances with an Eastern Power, and by a more immediate diplomatic need. Russia enjoyed much popularity in Paris after the War-Scare of 1875, as was evident in the success of *Les Danicheffs*, a play produced at the Odéon. Large audiences applauded the rescue of a Frenchman, attacked by a wild beast, by the play's Russian hero, and its author, Dumas *fils*, is said to have remarked that he had sown the seeds of an alliance.[2] "Russia was astonishingly popular," wrote a contemporary, "she was praised in books, attempts were made to interpret her in novels; she was applauded at the theater . . ."[3] Gratitude for Russia's aid in

[1] Cyon, *Histoire de l'Entente Franco-Russe*, p. 27.
[2] Charmes, *Politique Extérieure et Coloniale*, p. 26.
[3] *Gaulois*, Aug. 4, 1912.

1875 and of hope for further assistance in the future did not, however, create a general demand for an alliance.

It was not one of the aims of the opportunist foreign policy. Persuaded that France needed a long period of peace, the opportunist Republicans refused to provoke Bismarck by seeking an alliance with any Continental Power, Russia least of all.[4] Gambetta and others preferred an entente with England, and they condemned Decazes as more truly a Russian than a French minister, claiming that he had followed a policy of *"les Danicheffs."* [5] In 1879, Waddington rejected Russia's advances and informed Bismarck of them. The assassination of Alexander II in 1881 furnished an occasion for an expression of opinion in regard to Russia. Parliament adjourned as a mark of respect,[6] and Gambetta promised the coöperation of the French police in hunting down nihilists in 1882,[7] but these tactful measures merely meant that the possibility of Russia's friendship at some future time was to be held in reserve. The Radicals, however, denounced the Russian autocracy in unmeasured terms. Camille Pelletan described it as a régime of police, whips, and torture, and he declared that the assassination was not the most tragic episode in the conflict between the Russian people and its barbarous government.[8] France, because of this criticism, refused to participate in a European conference which Russia desired for the discussion of measures against revolutionary movements.[9]

Until fear of France's security was aroused by Bismarck's attitude and by the misrepresentations of the press, the propaganda for an alliance with Russia was addressed to a comparatively unresponsive public. In 1879, Mme. Adam established the *Nouvelle Revue* to combat the opportunist point of view and to prepare for a union with Russia as a necessary condition of the *revanche*.[10] Ferry's defeat and its result in renewed emphasis upon Continental affairs encouraged the Russian propaganda in France. Élie de Cyon was apparently the most active of its agents. A Russian Jew, he was naturalized in

---

[4] Cyon wrote that Russia had no more bitter enemies to contend with. Élie de Cyon, *La France et la Russie* (Paris, 1890), p. 13. Under Ferry, the permanent officials of the Quai d'Orsay were said to be unfriendly. Galli, *Les Dessous Diplomatiques*, p. 17.

[5] *Journal des Débats*, Aug. 26, 1880.

[6] *République Française*, March 15, 1881.

[7] Jules Hansen, *L'Alliance Franco-Russe* (Paris, 1897), pp. 7–9.

[8] *Justice*, March 16, 1881.

[9] Daudet, *Mission du Comte de Saint-Vallier*, pp. 233–240.

[10] Mme. Adam, *Après l'Abandon de la Revanche*, pp. 379, 380.

France, and in 1881 he had served for a time as the editor of the Bonapartist and reactionary *Gaulois*.[11] His connections in Russia were with Katkof, the powerful editor of the anti-German and Pan-Slavic *Moskovskija Vedomosti,* (Moscow), rather than with de Giers, the Minister of Foreign Affairs, who preferred friendship with Germany. In April, 1886, Cyon was instructed by Katkof to begin a campaign for an alliance in his letters from Paris, and in July Katkof endorsed the idea in an article that attracted the attention of Europe. Mme. Adam was persuaded to yield the control of the *Nouvelle Revue* to the Cyon-Katkof combination as a more effective means for influencing public opinion in France.[12]

Not much effort was required to convince public opinion of the merits of an alliance as a general proposition. "Public opinion," wrote a Monarchist in the *Matin* (Dec. 13, 1886), "dashes immediately in pursuit of this mirage." But its reaction to an immediate alliance was cool. Déroulède's articles in the *Drapeau* in its behalf after his trip to Russia in the summer of 1886 had little effect. Cyon admitted later that his propaganda at this time only had the support of the Monarchist *Soleil* and the Bonapartist *Patrie* except for that of the *revanche* element.[13] Some feared that an association with Russia might involve France in a war which would be exclusively concerned with her own interests. "So long as Russia does not abandon her Pan-Slavic dream," wrote Léon Hugonnet in the *France* (July 12, 1886), "she will be a danger for Europe and for civilization, and she will risk continued isolation." She could gain, he added, the alliance of Turkey and Austria, as well as that of France, by reassuring them as to her intentions. "Until then we cannot forget Cavour's prophecy that Russia will one day seize control of Europe." The radical *Justice* was perhaps more definitely hostile than any other newspaper. On September 16, 1886, it protested against the union "of the Republic and the gallows." "In order that a permanent alliance may be established between two countries," it declared (Sept. 21), "there must not be too great a divergence between their morals, their political institutions

---

[11] George Michon, *L'Alliance Franco-Russe* (Paris, 1927), p. 5.

[12] Cyon, *Entente Franco-Russe*, pp. 184, 153, 154, 163. For the beginnings of Slavic studies in France, see Valentin de Gorlov, *Origines et Bases de l'Alliance Franco-Russe* (Paris, 1913), pp. 422, 423. This volume, however, was clearly intended as propaganda in the interests of Russia's ambitions in the Balkans and in the Straits.

[13] Cyon, *Entente Franco-Russe*, p. 134.

and the general level of their civilization." Whereas the moderate and chauvinist press was distinctly partial to Russia in the Bulgarian controversy,[14] the Radical publicists championed the cause of the Bulgarian people. They were only guilty, affirmed Pelletan, of desiring independence,[15] and Rochefort condemned Russia's efforts to crush them.[16] In any event, Russia was not yet ready for an alliance with France, and, although Cyon made it a point to flatter Boulanger,[17] her aversion to the Minister of War was almost as strong as Germany's. Russia at no time had any intention of aiding France to recover Alsace-Lorraine. Far from yielding to the propaganda for an alliance, Freycinet tried to arrange an agreement with Bismarck in regard to Egypt.[18]

The period of tension inaugurated by Bismarck's speech of January 11, 1887, did not at once lead to a definite pronouncement by public opinion in favor of union with Russia. It would be incompatible, it was thought, with the studied moderation which was the rule at this time. Nor was the government prepared to solicit Russia's aid too openly, and Grévy and Flourens prevented Boulanger from sending a personal appeal to the Tsar.[19] Russia was unwilling to join France, but she was not prepared to permit her elimination as a great power. The Tsar would not coöperate "with the Clemenceaus against his uncle [William I]," [20] but on January 10, Bismarck sought in vain to secure Russia's promise of friendly neutrality in return for a free hand in the Straits question and for diplomatic support in Bulgaria.[21] De Giers replied to an inquiry as to Russia's attitude in the event of an attack upon France; "Schouvalov

[14] *Patrie*, Nov. 2, 3, 1886. *République Française*, Dec. 23, 1886. *France*, Dec. 24. The *Journal des Débats* (Jan. 10, 1887) approved the government's discouraging reception of the Bulgarian deputies who came to Paris in search of aid. They were advised to arrange their differences with Russia.

[15] *Justice*, Aug. 26, 1886.

[16] *Intransigeant*, Nov. 3, 1886.

[17] Cyon, *Entente Franco-Russe*, p. 142.

[18] Münster reported rumors that the French cabinet in August had refused an alliance with Russia and also her support in Egypt. Münster to Bismarck, Paris, Oct. 1, 1886. *G. P.*, VI, 93, 94. Later Bismarck refused a request for diplomatic support there. *Ibid.*, VI, 144, 145, 151.

[19] (Anonymous), *La Vérité sur le Boulangisme, par un ancien Diplomate* (Paris, 1889), pp. 32, 33.

[20] Von Bülow to Bismarck, St. Petersburg, Jan. 1, 1887. *G. P.*, VI, 108.

[21] *G. P.*, V, 214, 215. This was the beginning of the negotiations leading to the Reinsurance Treaty. Bismarck is said to have repeated the offer on February 6. Jules Hansen, *Ambassade à Paris du Baron de Mohrenheim (1884–1898)* (Paris, 1907), p. 30.

will reply." [22] Such information as to Russia's attitude as was available to public opinion was limited to an article in the *Nord* (Feb. 19) of Brussels, a newspaper which was said to be in close touch with the Russian foreign office. Russia, it declared, had an interest in the balance of power, and for that reason she did not wish to see a war between France and Germany, but there could be no question of an alliance. It was perhaps this discouraging statement which explains the slight attention given by the French press to the *Nord* article.[23]

After the conclusion of the first crisis, the press began to talk of the debt of gratitude which France owed Russia for her aid. Russia alone had prevented war, according to the Bonapartist *Gaulois* (April 1) and to the independent *Matin*.[24] "The French must know," declared the *Patrie* (April 16), "what they owe to Russia and to her Emperor." During the Schnaebelé Affair (April 23), it asserted that three hundred thousand cavalry were ready for action upon Germany's eastern frontier. During March and April, the *Figaro* printed a series of articles from a special correspondent in Russia representing France as extremely popular, England and Germany as hated.[25] On May 21, the *Figaro* joined those who were urging the need of gratitude to Russia by printing a series of unpublished letters which Decazes and Le Flô had exchanged during the War-Scare of 1875.[26] It was this appeal to gratitude for Russia's aid which was instrumental in winning over some who had formerly been critical of an association with her. According to Cyon's account, Rochefort of the *Intransigeant* was converted at a dinner, August 21, 1887, with himself, Déroulède, and Lucien Millevoye, when he was told that Alexander III had saved France during the Schnaebelé Affair.[27] The fact of Rochefort's conversion is certain, but it is probable that his hatred of Germany was as effective an argument as that of gratitude. In March, he had condemned an alliance with Russia as a betrayal of France's sympathies for oppressed peoples,[28] but on August 22, the day after his dinner with Cyon, he wrote that it was to France's

[22] É.-L. Flourens, *Alexandre III. Sa Vie, son Oeuvre* (Paris, 1894), pp. 312, 313.

[23] On February 27, France was informed that the moment had not arrived for an alliance. Hansen, *Mohrenheim,* p. 34.

[24] *Berliner Post,* April 8, 1887.

[25] The uhlan, not the cossack, who after all was a peaceable fellow at home, wrote the *Figaro,* Feb. 12, 1887, was the chief danger to Europe.

[26] These documents are printed in *Archives Diplomatiques. Receuil Mensuel International de Diplomatie et d'Histoire,* 2d Series, XXII (1887), pp. 351–368.

[27] Cyon, *Entente Franco-Russe,* p. 287.

[28] *Intransigeant,* March 17, 1887.

interest to support Russia in the Balkans. "It was the Tsar in person who protested against the odious trap prepared for France and which the implacable Bismarck hoped would give him a *casus belli*. The Russian Emperor, we guarantee it, wrote a letter to Emperor William . . . which contained this sentence: 'It would be unworthy of you and the German people to create complications of this kind in order to induce France to declare war against you.'" From this date, Rochefort forgot his former attachment to liberalism in an ardent support of an alliance. Clemenceau and the *Justice*, however, remained cold until the formation of the entente in 1891.

Public opinion in the summer of 1887 was fully prepared. Anatole Leroy-Beaulieu, a leading authority upon Russia and perhaps, for this reason, a critic of hasty measures, wrote that Germany's menaces had caused public opinion to declare itself "impetuously for the alliance." [29] Some found it necessary, in view of Russia's evident coolness, to advise restraint, with the warning that Russia was chiefly concerned with her own interests.[30] Even the *France Militaire* (May 27) had admitted that Russia's aid in a Franco-German war would probably be restricted to a friendly neutrality. The *Temps* throughout this period used its great influence against the popular movement. As early as March 1, it had declared that Russia would "abandon France if she attempted any adventures," and on August 28, it asserted that "Russia has her own policy in which we should not participate." A year later, it affirmed that a close association was impossible between two countries so completely separated by their institutions.[31] Anatole Leroy-Beaulieu argued that Russia's ambitions threatened the interests of France in the Near East, especially her protectorate of the Roman Catholics, and the maintenance of Austria-Hungary as a great Power. "The day," he declared, "which sees the disappearance of Austria-Hungary, will bring the end of French power," because it would mean a union between the German Empire and the German part of Austria. To the popular hysteria for the Russian alliance, he replied, "I was not aware that the Russian regimental bands had played the Marseillaise at Moscow." [32]

[29] Anatole Leroy-Beaulieu, *La France, la Russie, et l'Europe* (Paris, 1888). The essential parts of this volume were published by the *Rev. des Deux Mondes*, 1888, I, 896–928. Michon, *Alliance Franco-Russe*, pp. 9–11.

[30] *République Française*, May 22, 1887.

[31] *Temps*, July 6, 1888.

[32] A. Leroy-Beaulieu, *La France, la Russie et l'Europe*, pp. 59, 60, 72–79. An advocate of the *revanche* admitted that Russia was exploiting the possibility of

In the meantime, Russian propaganda was helping to prepare public opinion for an alliance if Russia should desire it at some future time. The *Nouvelle Revue* was supplemented by interviews with Russian statesmen, grand-dukes, and generals who chanced to be in Paris. With Lucien Millevoye's assistance Cyon distributed his material through the news-agency, the *Correspondance Française,* to sixty provincial newspapers,[33] but he, like other professional manipulators of public opinion, exaggerated the effectiveness of his work.[34] It was probably most effective in supplementing other factors such as those which have been indicated above as turning public opinion toward Russia. In the main, the purposes of the Russian propaganda were to convince public opinion that the interests of the two countries were identical, to confirm and strengthen its suspicions of Germany's intentions, and to secure French support if it should be needed against England. The *Figaro* (March 9, 1887) quoted an anonymous Russian diplomat as saying that France had no reason to fear Germany "so long as she is on her guard against Germany's amiabilities. Be certain that the first concession Bismarck has the appearance of making will be the signal for a prompt war." In reply to a plea for better relations with Germany, Cyon wrote that the enterprise would lead to war. A Franco-German entente in his opinion was impossible: a sound enough conclusion, but it came with bad grace from a Russian agent! Peace, he declared, could be most firmly assured by a formal alliance with Russia, for Europe would then be certain that France would never become "the accomplice or the vassal of Germany." As for Russia's desire to open the Straits, it was

"a vital interest for France, and let us say courageously, a more important interest than the possession of Alsace-Lorraine. Already menaced by England's control of Gibraltar, Malta, Cyprus, and Egypt, France's position in the Mediterranean would suffer the final blow in the building of an Italian fleet. Hypnotized by the loss of Metz and Strassburg, France does not see clearly enough that her future is involved. Certainly Germany is a terrible enemy for France. But Germany's hegemony is only a passing accident . . . A far more serious and implacable adversary is and always has been the Englishman! At each step of her national life, France has had to sustain a life-and-death struggle against him." [35]

an alliance with France to secure the revision of the Treaty of Berlin. Rouyer, *Aura-t-on la Guerre?* p. 10.

[33] Cyon, *Entente Franco-Russe,* p. 222.

[34] Rochefort and Millevoye continued for some time to be the chief advocates of Russian alliance outside the ranks of the Monarchist and Bonapartist parties. Hansen, *Mohrenheim,* p. 165.

[35] E. de Cyon, *La France et la Russie* (Paris, 1890), pp. 2, 3, 37, 51, 52.

It is evident that a significant change in French public opinion had taken place since 1887 if the most active Russian propagandist found it advisable to argue against friendly relations between France and Germany. The dangerous possibilities of the Boulangist agitation, after his retirement from the cabinet in May, 1887, had not materialized. His popularity seemed, it is true, greater than ever. Forty thousand votes were given him, although the *brav' Général* was ineligible, in the Paris elections of May 22. In July, well supplied with articles from chauvinist newspapers, Herbert von Bismarck asked Herbette if he seriously expected Germany to be satisfied by Boulanger's departure from the cabinet.[36] Even Grèvy's assurance that France would not attack while he was President was not sufficient to quiet Germany's fears as to France's action if war came in the Near East.[37] The Reinsurance Treaty with Russia, June 18, 1887, reassured Bismarck, and events soon showed that emphasis had changed in France from foreign to domestic affairs, even among the Boulangists. Scandal followed scandal, the decorations affair leading to Grèvy's resignation and the election of the moderate Republican, Sadi Carnot. Boulanger was elected in May, 1888, to the Chamber of Deputies from the Dordogne by a substantial, and from the Nord, by an overwhelming majority, but his success was due to a combination of all groups who hoped to change the existing régime. The Monarchists had replaced the Radicals as his chief backers, and it was from them that the large sums came which financed his campaign. A part of the Radicals continued to support him because of the failure of the ministries since 1885 to secure the enactment of promised reforms.[38]

The final act of the Boulangist melodrama was to be played in Paris.[39] Déroulède and the Ligue des Patriotes threw themselves into the preparations for the election of January, 1889, for it was intended that the capital should declare for or against a change in the government. " 'For the revision of the Treaty of Frankfort,' " wrote a

---

[36] Herbert Bismarck's Memorandum, Berlin, July 5, 1887. *G. P.,* VI, 198, 199.

[37] Münster to Bismarck, Paris, June 16, 1887. *Ibid.,* VI, 197.

[38] *Nouvelle Revue,* vol. 51, p. 558. Cf. *Journal des Débats,* April 14, 1887. A. Leroy-Beaulieu wrote that in so far as relations with Germany were involved, those who voted for Boulanger in the Nord believed that he would ensure France's security. Leroy-Beaulieu, *La France, la Russie et l'Europe,* p. 121 (note).

[39] The sensational newspapers of Paris, having lost ground in the South as the result of the growth of such local journals as the *Dépêche* of Toulouse, capitalized Boulanger's popularity in the department of the Nord. The sale of the *Petit Journal* in Lille is said to have reached three thousand each day during the elections. (Conversation with Professor Émile Bourgeois.)

member of the Ligue, " 'has been substituted the revision of the constitution.' " [40] With the two exceptions of the *Gazette de France* and
the *Correspondant,* the entire conservative and reactionary press, with
the sensational newspapers like the *Petit Journal* and some of the
radical journals, supported Boulanger.[41] France's relations with Germany or with Russia were not directly involved, although a coup
d'état would be certain to affect them. Boulanger received the news
of his decisive victory at the Restaurant Durand, surrounded by the
chiefs of the Ligue des Patriotes, with thousands of followers massed
in the neighboring streets, a few blocks from the presidential palace.
Déroulède advised immediate action, but Boulanger, perhaps fright-
ened by the importance of the decisive or, as he claimed, desirous to
keep within the law, whipped up his horses at a convenient corner
to escape from the mob which was ready to install him in the Élysée.
On the following day, his followers waited in vain to escort him in
force to the chamber.[42] This marked the turn of the tide. His ephem-
eral popularity subsided even more quickly than it had risen. The disgruntled politicians who had hoped to use him as their tool rapidly
abandoned him, for the movement had never been able to enlist the
support of the solid leaders of the nation.[43] Hitherto the government
had never dared, if it had so desired, to take effective measures against
either the Ligue or Boulanger. It now proceeded to dispose of both.
Boulanger was condemned on the charge of conspiring against the
State, and after escaping to Belgium, he committed suicide in 1890.
In March, 1889, the Ligue's executive committee protested against the
government's forceful methods in dealing with the Cossack adventurer, Atchinov, at Sagallo, from which place he had intended to extend his influence into Abyssinia. The government, according to this
statement, had not feared " 'to shed Russian blood by French
hands.' " [44] Thereupon, the police raided the Ligue's headquarters, and
the society itself was declared illegal.[45]

With the temporary elimination of the Ligue and the collapse of
the Boulanger legend, Germany's attitude toward France became

[40] *Temps,* May 4, 1888.

[41] *Ibid.,* Jan. 11, 1889.

[42] Ducroy, *Paul Déroulède,* p. 170. Cf. Raymond Recouly, *La Troisième République* (Paris, 1927), pp. 165, 166.

[43] Gabriel Monod, the editor of the *Revue Historique,* characterized the leaders
of the Boulangist movement as adventurers. *Temps,* Jan. 27, 1889.

[44] *Temps,* March 2, 1889.

[45] *Corresp.,* O. S., 154, p. 991.

more moderate. Bismarck had refrained from exploiting the activities of the Ligue during the election of January, 1889,[46] and Herbert wrote to Hohenlohe, the Stattholder of Alsace-Lorraine, that the success of the French government in emancipating itself from the influence of the street "suggests that we should refrain from creating difficulties for the cabinet and from disturbing the peaceful development of the situation." [47] In France, the accession of Frederick III to the German throne in 1888, although ill health threatened his early death, was well received. A good hater of Germany, like Paul de Cassagnac, the Bonapartist leader of the chamber and editor of the *Autorité*, interpreted the event as an augury of peace, and he even thought that it might lead to a reconciliation between the two peoples.[48] The reaction to William II was quite different. Cassagnac had referred to Frederick as a Marcus Aurelius; he now added that the Roman emperor had a son, Commodus. "Henceforth," he declared, "nothing protects us against the perspective of a supreme conflict." [49] William's instability of character and his emphasis upon the army increased the uncertainty of the future.[50] Yet public opinion, in spite of a demonstration against a group of German students in Belfort which Bismarck used to justify his refusal to approve Germany's participation in the Paris Exposition of 1889,[51] had chosen the less dramatic but safer counsel of moderate leaders. In October, 1889, the moderate Republican groups won a decisive majority in the Chamber of Deputies.[52] Primarily a triumph for the Republic, the verdict also meant a return to a more moderate policy in regard to Germany.

The fear that the young Emperor's restless character would soon lead to new crises was not justified by the events of the first two years of his reign. Like his hero Frederick the Great, he admired French civilization, and he soon began to seek France's friendship. His methods, unfortunately, showed little understanding of French psychology. "To bring about this reconciliation," writes Theodor Wolff, the Paris correspondent of the *Berliner Tageblatt* between

---

[46] *Ibid.*, O. S., 154, pp. 602–604.
[47] H. Bismarck to Hohenlohe, Berlin, March 7, 1889. *G. P.*, VI, 220.
[48] Cf. *Nouvelle Revue*, vol. 49, p. 667.
[49] *Autorité*, June 17, 1888.
[50] The *Temps* (June 18, 1888) believed that the situation required national solidarity.
[51] Herbert von Bismarck's Memorandum, Berlin, May 1, 1888. *G. P.*, VI, 210–214.
[52] *Corresp.*, O. S., 157, pp. 179, 180.

1893 and 1906 and then its editor, "he borrowed his methods from the florist rather than from the politician." [53] In March, 1889, the Emperor and Empress dined at the French embassy for the first time in six years, and a little later William sent his felicitations to President Carnot after his escape from assassination, and a more accommodating spirit appeared in the administration of Alsace.[54] Public opinion in France was not permitted to know much of William's advances, for the press, perhaps anticipating that the chauvinists would renew their agitation, did not for some time give any considerable attention to them.

Nevertheless, a certain number of pamphlets expressed at this time a desire for a peaceful arrangement of the historical differences between the two countries. In 1888, one that was unsigned urged the government, in the interest of peace, to ask Germany what sacrifices she would require for the return of Alsace-Lorraine.[55] This problem was given more attention two years later. Auguste Lalance, the Alsatian engineer, chose the frequently quoted text, *L'Alsace n'est pas un glâcis, c'est un pont,* as his theme. The desires of the Alsatian people, he declared, were misrepresented in Germany for the purpose of justifying her repressive measures and in France as in favor of *les imprudences des impatients.* The truth was that Alsace aspired to the rôle for which her past and her geographical position intended her, "that of a mediator between two great peoples." [56] His assumption that the desires of the Alsatian people constituted the chief question at issue between France and Germany was erroneous, for the recovery of the lost provinces was closely associated with France's return to the place in European affairs which she had lost in 1871.

Colonel Stoffel, in a widely read pamphlet, based his plea for improved relations with Germany upon a better understanding of the motives which influenced French policy. Although he believed that a

[53] Theodor Wolff, *Das Vorspiel* (Munich, 1924), pp. 109, 110. Cf. the French translation, *Le Prélude* (Paris, 1926). Fearing the reaction in England and Italy, the German ministers opposed this policy. W. L. Langer, *The Franco-Russian Alliance* (Cambridge, 1929), p. 140 (note).

[54] Pierre Albin, *L'Allemagne et la France en Europe, 1885–1894* (Paris, 1913), p. 213.

[55] *La Question Allemande* (Paris, 1888), p. 40. A scheme for the neutralization of Alsace-Lorraine had been presented to the "International League for Peace and Liberty" in 1884 and was later published as a pamphlet. Camille Desmoulins, *Neutralization de l'Alsace et la Lorraine* (Paris, 1887).

[56] *L'Alliance Franco-Allemande, par un Alsacien* (A. Lalance) (Nancy, 1888), pp. 1–3.

the Alsace-Lorraine problem was a necessary condition
ation, he opposed an alliance with Russia, for that Power,
l, was a greater menace than Germany. He was ready to
offensive and defensive alliance with Germany if she of-
turn the two provinces.[57] These opinions at once elicited
alliance with Russia, because of her enormous power and
)cratic institutions, Colonel Villot admitted, would not be
iger. But Germany would never voluntarily return Alsace
ie, and to secure them, it would be necessary to have Rus-
rance's long championship of liberal ideas, he wrote, had
ugh no fault of her own. "*'La force prime le droit.'* May
refore have only one thought, self-preservation, for the
mpire will not permit her to live, even diminished as she
is to-day." [58] The nationalist and Boulangist deputy, Camille Dreyfus,
condemned the hope of the recovery of the two provinces by peaceful
means as a delusion, for France and Germany were separated, in his
opinion, by an inevitable conflict. *"C'est la lutte du pays de la bière
avec le pays du champagne."* The moment had arrived, he declared, to
precipitate war,[59] but E. Langlois at once questioned the motives
which had inspired this chauvinist publication at a time when public
opinion was decidedly moderate.[60]

The reaction to Stoffel's pamphlet indicated that the chauvinists
were ready, as they always had been, to denounce any movement toward friendly relations with Germany. For this reason, the Kaiser's
methods in courting France were untimely. His attempt to secure her
participation in the Labor Conference at Berlin in 1890 aroused a bitter
protest in the chamber and the first interpellation upon foreign affairs
since 1885. Francis Laur protested that the proposal to limit the hours
of labor in coal mines threatened the security of France because her
coal reserve was not sufficient for her military needs in the event of
war! Déroulède, Camille Dreyfus, Cassagnac, and Laur, intoxicated by
passion, almost demanded war. But the government maintained its
acceptance, and although no speaker rose to defend the cause of

[57] Colonel C. Stoffel, *De la Possibilité d'une Future Alliance Franco-Allemande*
(Paris, 1890), pp. 30, 32, 35.
[58] Colonel Villot, *L'Alliance Russe. Réponse à M. le Colonel Stoffel* (Paris,
1890), pp. 37–39.
[59] Camille Dreyfus, *La Guerre Nécessaire. Réponse d'un Français à M. de
Bismarck* (Paris, 1890), pp. 14, 15.
[60] E. Langlois, *La Guerre Inutile. Réponse à la Guerre Nécessaire de M. de
Dreyfus* (Paris, 1890), pp. 40–42.

moderation and to denounce the extravagances of these men, it was sustained by a large majority.[61] The French delegation, led by Jules Simon, was well received in Berlin and by the Kaiser,[62] but William and his advisers failed to understand the significance of this outburst in the chamber. It should have warned them that the former Boulangists only needed a favorable opportunity to resume their activities and that moderate public opinion would not have the moral courage to react vigorously against them. Impatient for results, the Kaiser made the mistake of playing into the chauvinists's hands by forcing a public discussion of an entente.

He had sent his condolences to the president of the Académie Française on the death of Jean Meissonier (Jan. 21, 1891), an artist whose reputation was based in part upon his paintings of scenes and soldiers of the Napoleonic wars, but the *Kölnische Zeitung* (Feb. 16, 1891) observed that most of the Paris newspapers paid no attention to his message, and that the few who did buried it without comment in obscure corners. "The Imperial demonstration will doubtless have a favorable effect," it wrote, "upon the majority of the French people who desire to remain at peace with Germany, but the fact that not a single sheet voices this sentiment should be a cause for reflection." Undiscouraged, William had authorized an invitation to the French artists to participate in an exposition of modern art in Berlin. The occasion seemed favorable. Münster reported, February 19, that great progress had been accomplished in the development of a more moderate attitude toward Germany,[63] and on the same day, the Paris press announced the arrival in Paris of the Empress Frederick, the Kaiser's mother.[64] No one, of course, was seriously impressed by the official explanation that she wished to purchase furniture for her Kronberg residence, or that her mission was merely to persuade as many artists as possible to participate in the exposition. It was generally assumed that her visit was a part of her son's campaign for an entente with France. At any rate, he had done nothing to prevent the visit,[65] and once decided, the German press represented it as a step toward an understanding. Its results, unfortunately, provided an ideal opportunity

---

[61] *Annales,* 1890, I, 557–586.

[62] J. Simon, "L'Empereur Guillaume II," *Rev. de Paris,* 1894, IV, 449–465.

[63] Münster to Caprivi, Paris, Feb. 19, 1891. *G. P.,* VII, 271–274.

[64] Herbette warned his government that the slightest misadventure might have serious consequences. Gooch, *Franco-German Relations,* p. 33.

[65] *Letters of the Empress Frederick,* The Right Honourable Sir Frederick Ponsonby, ed. (London, 1929), pp. 422, 423.

for the revival of the chauvinist agitation and for its leaders to regain their lost influence.

At first, Jean Detaille, the president of the Society of French Artists, and a pupil of Meissonier, declared his intention of maintaining the original acceptance of the invitation.[66] The Empress's arrival, however, was soon followed by a storm of protest. Münster reported later that the signal had been given by an article in the *Matin* which he attributed to Russian influences.[67] While there is nothing improbable in the claim that Russian agents contributed to the agitation, it is not an entirely satisfactory explanation. The *Vossische Zeitung* had insured an explosion of patriotic sentiment by asserting that the time had arrived for the desire of revenge to be expelled from the minds of the French people.[68] Moreover, the *Matin*'s first comments did not appear until February 22, while other newspapers had already commenced a campaign. On February 20, the moderate republican *Paix* declared that the visit meant the translation into action of the Kaiser's desire for an entente, and the next day, it added that *"on vient nous chercher,"* as if it were feared that Germany's invitation would not be accepted with sufficient promptness. It observed that Germany had not shown so much interest in art when she bombarded the Strassburg Cathedral. The *Matin* (Feb. 22), however, was the first to emphasize the attitude of Russia, in the article mentioned by the German ambassador.

"Russia's friendship," it affirmed, "assures our absolute security. . . . If it were necessary to be suspicious of the Greeks even when they came bringing gifts, with what circumspection must we not view the advances which are not accompanied by any presents, except a little incense, that is to say, smoke."

The first attack was concentrated upon the artists who had agreed to exhibit at Berlin. A few withdrew at a meeting, February 20, and on the next day, the *Petit Journal* protested that artists and sculptors should contribute most to the "memories of unforgettable disasters." Cassagnac wondered how they could "hang their canvases upon Berlin

---

[66] *Temps,* Feb. 19, 1891. For a detailed account of the Empress Frederick's visit, see Gaston Routier, *Une Page d'Histoire Contemporaine* (Paris, 1901). Albin, *Allemagne et la France en Europe,* pp. 287–310. Langer, *Franco-Russian Alliance,* pp. 141–144. None of these writers have made an extensive study of the press or of public opinion in Paris.

[67] Münster to Caprivi, Paris, Feb. 28, 1891. *G. P.,* VII, 281.

[68] Gooch, *Franco-German Relations,* pp. 33, 34.

walls without thinking of Alsace-Lorraine." [69] He confessed that his patriotic indignation was inspired by a cold calculation.

"We are perhaps chauvinist to an exaggerated degree, but we insist upon it, especially at this time, when skepticism cheapens everything, religious beliefs as well as national hatreds. Too many people are forgetting in France. Here, it is a conversion to the Republic. There, it is a hand held out to Germany." [70]

The signal for a movement of opinion to be directed more definitely against friendlier relations with Germany was given at a meeting of some fifteen hundred former members of the Ligue on the evening of February 21. Francis Laur denounced the recent events culminating in the Empress Frederick's visit. Filled with passion "to the great satisfaction of the audience," he concluded "with a formidable cry of *'À bas l'Allemagne.'*" Déroulède spoke so swiftly that much of what he said was lost, but he was understood as explaining that a committee had just placed a wreath upon the bust of Henri Regnault, the artist who had been killed in the war of 1870, in the courtyard of the École des Beaux Arts. Flags had also been placed upon the statue of Strassburg so that the Empress would see that they "protest against her presence within our walls." Resolutions were adopted acknowledging the obligation of courtesy to the imperial guest but condemning the visit as a move toward a *rapprochement* between the two countries. Other charges, moreover, were added to this which had already appeared in the press. The visit was said to be a preparation for "William II's impending trip to France, a step toward a demand 'for disarmament, for a commercial treaty and for the abandonment of the Russian alliance." After the meeting, Déroulède attempted to lead a demonstration to the statue of Strassburg, but for once the police interfered.[71]

It would serve no useful purpose to quote at length from the inflammatory articles that filled a large section of the press after this meeting. The moderate press made little or no effort to counter-act their effect. The arguments used by the chauvinists agreed for the most part with those stated in the resolutions adopted by the Ligue des Patriotes's meeting. It is sometimes said that the Empress's tactless visits to Versailles and St. Cloud were largely responsible for the agitation. However, she followed the advice of 'the police in going

[69] *Autorité*, Feb. 21.
[70] *Ibid.*, Feb. 22.
[71] *Petit Journal,* Feb. 22.

to the palace of Louis XIV on a Monday when there were no crowds present, and it is at least doubtful that she actually entered the park of St. Cloud.[72] Although the fire was already well under way, these reports added fuel to the flames. It is sufficient, in order to show their effect, to quote an open letter in the *Matin* (Feb. 27) addressed to the Empress on the day of her departure: "You, whose name is associated with memories of incendiary fires and of blood! . . . you started out one morning with your suite composed of a venerable ambassador and of certain attachés, some of whom had worn the helmets of your officers. You visited St. Cloud, filled with ruins, and Versailles filled with the miseries of France. . . . That seemed natural to you, Madam, to us it has seemed monstrous." Hearing that his wreath had been removed from the bust of Henri Regnault, Déroulède and Dreyfus at once assumed that the government had done this at the behest of the German Embassy. They hastened to the chamber, where it required the influence of members of the ministry to dissuade them from interpellating the government.[73]

The government's position with reference to the chauvinist campaign was extremely delicate. It was imperative that the safety of the Empress should be assured, but it was also thought necessary to avoid offense to Russia by seeming to yield in any way to Germany's advances. The action of the police in breaking up Déroulède's demonstration on the night of February 21 showed that it could restrain the chauvinists if it so desired. However, in addition to the press campaign, at least two large public meetings were held by members of the Ligue, with speeches of the most violent character, without any interference. The government's neutral attitude was shared by the moderate press. It was not until the Empress had left that the *Journal des Débats* (Feb. 28) replied to foreign criticism by claiming that the extremist newspapers did not represent public opinion. At no time during her visit was there a courageous protest against those whom Blowitz called the "whirling dervishes" of patriotism. It was not until a month later that Freycinet expressed regrets to Münster for the attitude of the chauvinist press, and the Kaiser with considerable discernment noted in the margin of Münster's report: "Yes, in private conversation, but why not openly in his

---

[72] Münster did not report this visit (G. P., VII, 275, 282, 287–289), and he denied it in a communication to the French Press. *Lyon Républicain*, Feb. 28.

[73] *Paix*, Feb. 26.

press." [74] The failure to condemn this outburst of passion cannot be explained away as a refusal to yield to the comminatory attitude of the *Kölnische Zeitung* (Feb. 26) and as a response to its description of the chauvinists as the "dregs of human society," for this article appeared too late to have any material bearing upon the situation in Paris. The rumor that the Kaiser had said that evening that " '*Si on siffle au moment du départ de l'Empératrice Frédéric, c'est la guerre*' " [75] was not published until later. Once it was clear that her visit would not lead to an entente with Germany, Déroulède advised his followers to permit her departure in peace.[76] By advancing it some hours, the possibility of an unfortunate accident happening at the last moment was avoided.[77]

"To how many deceptions," observed the *Journal de Rouen* (Feb. 27), "one is exposed in going too fast and too far in a work of reconciliation." The withdrawal of the French artists from the Berlin exposition was a relatively minor result in comparison with the effect of this dramatic incident upon public opinion. After its conclusion, regret was sometimes expressed that the moderate press had not condemned the extremist element, and it was even denied that this discreet reserve which had also characterized the attitude of the government meant their complicity with the chauvinists.[78] But the violence of the *revanche* element continued. Rochefort claimed that the incident, like Schnaebelé's arrest, had been intended as a trap,[79] and Cassagnac declared that France had only one reply to make to every attempt to induce France to abandon "that patriotic citadel in which we are enclosed with our *saintes haines,* with our rage, with our implacable hopes." In Germany, the conclusion was drawn that neither the government nor public opinion could resist the pressure of the chauvinist minority.[80] "Germany has made advances to France," wrote the *Berliner Tageblatt.* "She has chosen to remain on guard; there is nothing that we can do. The Germany who won the battles of Worth, Gravelotte, and Sedan has no cause for alarm." [81] It was

---

[74] Münster to Caprini, Paris, March 23, 1891. *G. P.,* VII, 286–290.

[75] *Figaro,* March 3. It is unlikely that a tentative order of mobilization had been given in Berlin. Langer, *Franco-Russian Alliance,* p. 143.

[76] *Autorité,* Feb. 27.

[77] Münster to Caprivi, Paris, Feb. 28, 1891. *G. P.,* VII, 280.

[78] *Temps,* March 1. *Petit Journal,* March 1.

[79] *Intransigeant,* March 1.

[80] *Autorité,* Feb. 27.

[81] *Journal des Débats,* Feb. 27.

not understood in Germany that the incident would bring France and Russia more closely together.

In 1887, France, in the first of a long series of loans, opened her purse to Russia, and, about the same time, a Russian order for half a million rifles was accepted on the condition that they would never be fired against Frenchmen. By 1890, after Bismarck's dismissal and the non-renewal of the Reinsurance Treaty, a tacit understanding had developed between the two governments that they were united by common enmities. Russia's distrust of France had been partially removed by her repudiation of Boulanger and by the dissolution of the Ligue des Patriotes. Since the immediate purpose of the agitation during the visit of the Empress Frederick was to prevent an entente with Germany rather than war, Russia had no cause for complaint.[82] She was informed as to the course of events in Paris, and after the Empress's departure, de Giers spoke warmly of an entente as " 'necessary in order to maintain in Europe a just balance of power.' " He said that the purpose of the visit had been easy to divine, and he described the conduct of the French government as "exceedingly correct and courteous." [83]

Strengthened by the Kaiser's visit to London in July, 1891,[84] France's desire for a public manifestation of Russia's friendship was satisfied by an invitation to send a naval squadron to Kronstadt.[85] Late in July, the French flag was flying there, and the Tsar was listening to the "Marseillaise" with bared head upon the deck of the French flag-ship. Reported in great detail by all French newspapers, the reception created an immense enthusiasm. It was even necessary to warn public opinion that no formal alliance existed.[86] In conformity with France's instinctive reaction to those countries with whom she had close relations, the two peoples were represented as united by bonds of sentiment.[87] Even the *Temps* (July 25) referred to the

[82] W. L. Langer, "The Franco-Russian Alliance," I. *Slavonic Review*, III, 564.

[83] Ribot to Laboulaye, Paris, March 9, 1891. *Livre Jaune: L'Alliance Franco-Russe* (Paris, 1918), pp. 2, 3.

[84] Gaston Routier, *Guillaume II à Londres et l'Union Franco-Russe* (Paris, 1894), pp. 125, 126.

[85] Michon, *Alliance Franco-Russe*, p. 16. Nevertheless, when France asked Russia for a definite assurance of support, she received a discouraging reply. Langer, *Franco-Russian Alliance*, pp. 147, 148.

[86] *Temps*, July 15. *Petite Gironde* (Bordeaux), Aug. 6.

[87] The Belgian ambassador to Russia wrote that the French press entirely misrepresented the spirit of these celebrations, which had differed in no respect

"*élan* of sympathy with which we are profoundly touched." The *Radical* (July 30) wrote that there was "an affinity of soul" between the two peoples. The contrast between their institutions was forgotten or explained away as of no significance. "It is not the resemblance of their social organization," affirmed the *Journal des Débats* (July 27), "nor the similarity of governments which bring nations together. Reasons of State are the sole international bonds . . . Nothing separates us . . . except distance." Irritated by the satirical comments in the London press, the *Temps* (July 28) declared that the incompatibility of French and Russian institutions was "purely one of appearance." There could be no antagonism, it continued, between governments which were separated by so great a distance. It is no wonder that Russia became immensely popular in France, in view of the prevailing ignorance of conditions in Russia and of the joy at finding a friend. The *Lyon Républicain* (Aug. 15, 1891) thought that Russia's vogue was excessive. "It is no longer an alliance; it is a passion. It is no longer friendship; it is love. It is no longer joy; it is delirium." In Paris, the Grand Duke Alexis was serenaded by fanfares and organs playing the "Marseillaise," the Russian national hymn, and the "Père de la Victoire." Boulangists and leaders of the Ligue appeared in the Place de la Concorde "gesticulating and orating before the statue of Strassburg." Even the Russians felt that this hysteria had gone too far, and the *Nord* of Brussels suggested that it would be desirable if the Russian anthem were not played too frequently.[88]

If anything is clear in regard to Russia's point of view in her relations with France, it is her refusal to give either military or diplomatic support to France's claims to Alsace-Lorraine. Yet Russian propagandists pretended that the recovery of the lost provinces would follow a formal alliance. It was described by Notovich, the editor of the *Novosti* of St. Petersburg, as the beginning of a new diplomatic group whose superior power would lead to the fulfilment of France's aspirations. In spite of the antagonism between England and Russia in the Far East, he believed it possible to win England as an associate by a compromise of the Egyptian question. "Once England is drawn into the new group, the Triple Alliance will find itself enclosed in an iron circle and finally constrained to reconcile its

from those given a Dutch squadron only a year before. *Die Belgischen Dokumente zur Vorgeschichte des Weltkrieges*, B. Schwertfeger, ed. 8 vols. (Berlin, 1925), I, 349. (Sept. 21, 1891.)

[88] *Progrès de la Côte d'Ôr* (Dijon), Aug. 19.

interests with those of other countries." [89] Notovich, it is to be noted, did not suggest that Russia would aid France to recover Alsace-Lorraine by force of arms, nor did Cyon. The latter also thought that a new grouping of the Powers might lead to a peaceful revision of the Treaty of Frankfort. France, he alleged, could do much toward a peaceful solution by convincing Germany that her unity was definitely recognized. Yet he ventured to affirm that "the basis of their (France and Russia) alliance is the reciprocal guarantee of their possessions, and the *abolition* of the existing territorial divisions, in so far as they constitute a violation of the interests and honor of the two contracting parties." [90] It is certain that the chauvinists, at least, counted upon France's association with Russia to secure the return of Alsace-Lorraine,[91] for as the years passed without the realization of their hopes, they became embittered and extremely critical of the Russian alliance. In 1891, however, discretion forbade the open expression of this point of view. The moderate *Paix* (Aug. 31) thought it necessary that public opinion should be told not to anticipate the revision of the Treaty of Frankfort. "Diplomaticus" wrote, however, that unforeseen events might enable the Franco-Russian entente to accomplish this result.[92]

Joy that the period of isolation had come to an end was by all odds the dominant reaction of public opinion. It was expressed by Rouvier, Ferry, and Freycinet, who was then the President of the Council, in public addresses.[93] "What joy after this night of twenty years!" exclaimed the *Lyon Républicain* (Aug. 20, 1891). "At last, the horrible nightmare has vanished; at last, we are no longer the beaten and almost disdained nation which the insolent victor attempted to place in quarantine in the middle of Europe." Peace, according to the *Paix* (Aug. 8), would no longer depend upon Germany alone, for the balance of power had been restored.[94] The *Temps* (Sept. 13) welcomed the new period in which France's voice would have more weight in the affairs of Europe. "The time of monologues has

---

[89] This appeared simultaneously in the *Justice* (Aug. 15), and in the *Figaro* (Aug. 15). Cf. *Journal des Débats* (Aug. 18), which discounted the prospects of including England. In fact, England's relations with the recently renewed Triple Alliance aroused much speculation.

[90] *Figaro*, Aug. 23.

[91] Public opinion, wrote the *Radical*, Aug. 11, "is not far from seeing in the new attitude of the Russian government an encouragement for France's claims."·

[92] *Lyon Républicain*, Aug. 15.

[93] Hansen, *Alliance Franco-Russe*, pp. 70, 71.

[94] "Kronstadt," it exclaimed, "*c'est la paix!*"

passed," it declared, "and that of dialogues has commenced." Clemenceau, consistently critical of an association with Russia until 1891, refused to accept the claim that it was based upon a sentimental attachment between the two peoples. "It belongs to the category of historical facts over which no one has any control." He still had his doubts, for he wondered what the product would be of the union of the two countries. "Will the child be Cossack or Republican?" What concerned him most immediately was the danger of a new chauvinist outburst, and he would have it carefully guarded against.[95]

A minority warned public opinion of the need to fix certain limits to France's support of Russia. The Paris correspondent of the *Lyon Républicain* (Aug. 1, 1891) advised against a formal alliance which would include reciprocal promises of armed support. The balance, in his opinion, would always favor Russia, for normally the danger of war would be greater in the Near East than in Western Europe. France should reserve her freedom of action "to be able, at her discretion, to seize a favorable occasion, and in order never to be involved against our will, because in a word it is better to remain isolated and master of the time, place, and arms." Ernest Judet, at the beginning of a long and troubled career as a publicist, urged the need of a careful study of the international situation for the purpose of avoiding the sacrifice of France's interests for those of Russia.[96] Among the conservatives, some would give France's support without reservation as the only certain way of retaining Russia's friendship. She would never say, as the Marquis de Castellane wrote in the *Figaro* (Aug. 30.), *"Belle France, vos beaux yeux me font mourir d'amour."* Only by way of the Russian alliance could Metz and Strassburg be recovered, "if not by the bayonet, at least for a consideration. *La paix! la vrai paix, voilà! Mais ne nous dissimulons pas: tout cela n'est possible que donnant, donnant . . ."* But these subtle considerations as to the future implications of an alliance with Russia were of little effect upon a public opinion which was in the midst of a joyous celebration of the end of France's isolation.

The government shared with public opinion its new feeling of self-confidence. In September, 1891, the army maneuvers were held at Nancy, nearer the eastern frontier than ever before. Stimulated by the renewal of the Triple Alliance, and by rumors of England's

[95] *Justice,* Aug. 3. Barthélemy Saint-Hilaire was one of the few who still opposed the alliance. *Paix,* July 18.

[96] *Petit Journal,* Aug. 30.

association with it,[97] France urged on the conversations with Russia. She was, however, unable to secure anything more than a promise of immediate conversations in the event that peace should be threatened or that either Power should be in danger of an aggression from a third Power.[98] What France desired especially was an immediate mobilization without any preliminary conversations,[99] and it was to this end that her diplomats continued to work. They encountered discouraging obstacles in the Tsar's reluctance to commit himself, in his long absences from St. Petersburg, and in de Giers's illness. There is little evidence in the *Yellow Book* that the French ministers made any serious effort during these protracted negotiations to prevent their country from being involved in a war for Russia's special interests in the Balkans.[100] Primarily concerned with cementing the relations between the two countries, they were unwilling to risk the success of their chief purpose. Nevertheless, Russia gave an assurance, for what it was worth, that she wished to maintain the *status quo,* and it was agreed that the two Powers would strengthen the Sultan against the efforts of the Triple Alliance to bend him to its will. An arrangement was reached in regard to the Holy Places, and in return for certain assurances in regard to Egypt, France agreed to support Russia in Bulgaria.[101] No embarrasing questions were asked, however, as to Russia's ambitions in regard to the Straits or as to her rivalry with Austria.

Russia, it seems, thought of her relations with France as a source of possible aid against England. In 1890, Cyon had written that France might recover Egypt with the assistance of Russia's Black Sea fleet.[102] France, however, was not prepared to risk a definite break with England. "Russia," Ribot wrote to Freycinet, President of the Council, August 6, 1891, "is evidently desirous of securing our eventual support even against England . . . That is the obstacle which we foresaw."[103] The same squadron that visited Kronstadt stopped at Portsmouth on its way home. With the approval of at least

---

[97] *Livre Jaune: L'Alliance Franco-Russe,* pp. 3, 4, 6, 16.
[98] *Ibid.,* p. 4.
[99] Ribot to Carnot, Aug. 11, 1891. *Ibid.,* p. 14.
[100] The alliance "was made without conditions on the part of France." Margaine, *Rapport fait sur le* Livre Jaune *relatif à l'Alliance Franco-Russe* (Chambre des Députés, No. 6636). (Paris, 1919), p. 9.
[101] Ribot's résumé of a conversation with de Giers. *Ibid.,* pp. 19–22.
[102] Cyon, *La France et la Russie,* pp. 38–40.
[103] *Livre Jaune: L'Alliance Franco-Russe,* pp. 10, 11.

a part of the moderate press,[104] Laur and Millevoye told a meeting of former members of the Ligue des Patriotes that England "who extends her hand to us, conceals a dagger in her sleeve." [105] Rochefort wrote that in the event of a French victory, Germany would only lose two provinces. "To what dangers, on the contrary, would England be exposed?—to Russia's immediate march upon India, for we have no interest in preventing her from going there. The evacuation of Egypt would then be the fatal complement of the fall of England's Indian Empire." [106] Resentment against England increased as a result of Anglo-French friction over Siam in 1893. After the murder of one of her nationals, France presented an ultimatum to Siam, but on the excuse of protecting her interests, England forthwith dispatched a gunboat to Bangkok. France stood by her guns with the solid support of parliament and of public opinion,[107] until she secured a satisfactory reply to her ultimatum,—an indemnity, and a commercial treaty. The measure of hostile sentiment against England was dramatically revealed by Déroulède's and Millevoye's grotesque indictment of Clemenceau in the chamber as a paid agent of England,[108] and its failure did not save Clemenceau from defeat in the elections of that fall.

Since 1891, the Russian government had considered the possibility of naval coöperation with France in the Mediterranean. It was first suggested as a reply to recent demonstrations by British and Italian ships in Turkish water.[109] In July, 1893, a report reached the Paris press that Russia had ordered the establishment of a permanent squadron in the Mediterranean,[110] and Toulon was chosen rather than an Atlantic port for the return visit of Russian naval vessels in October.[111] The choice of this port was probably intended to impress England, but this second and open manifestation of Franco-Russian understanding was also intended as a reply to the recent

[104] *Paix,* Aug. 19, 1891.

[105] *Progrès de la Côte d'Or* (Dijon), Aug. 19, 1891.

[106] *Intransigeant,* Aug. 3.

[107] *Temps,* July 20, 1893.

[108] *Annales,* 1893, III, 693 (June 19), IV. 727–734 (June 22).

[109] De Giers to Nélidoff, St. Petersburg, Dec. 14, 1891. *Livre Jaune: l'Alliance Franco-Russe,* p. 31.

[110] *Intransigeant,* July 26, 1893.

[111] Montebello to Develle, St. Petersburg, Aug. 10, 1893. *Livre Jaune: L'Alliance Franco-Russe,* p. 31. Certain ships were to winter in the Mediterranean.

German army maneuvers in Alsace, where the Prince of Naples had been a guest.[112] The popular imagination saw in the visit of the Russian naval officers to Paris a new proof of solidarity between the two countries against Germany.[113] Measures were taken by the government, however, to prevent an open attack upon Germany in the press, and all phases of the celebration were carefully supervised. Nevertheless, the statue of Joan of Arc was decorated with wreaths from the Alsace-Lorraine society and by others marked with the names of Metz and Strassburg.[114] It is difficult to distinguish between the current of opinion which celebrated the event as a promise that the delay in the satisfaction of France's hopes would be shortened,[115] and the more moderate point of view which attributed the prevailing joy to the increased confidence in the nation's security and in peace.[116] Both were present, and it would depend largely upon future events which one would prevail. It is of some significance that Lord Dufferin, the British ambassador, considered the possibility that public opinion, whose attitude toward England he described as one "of unmitigated and bitter dislike," might be turned in favor of a war with England.[117]

The ceremonies and street demonstrations were scarcely over when Cyon reminded France that after surrendering her *dot* and herself, it was high time that the marriage was consummated.[118] A difference of opinion as to the conditions which should lead to the joint mobilization of the two Powers had delayed the arrangement of a formal alliance. Each naturally had sought to establish such necessary conditions as would best serve its own interests: Russia insisted that both should act after the mobilization of any member of the Triple

[112] *Temps*, Sept. 4, 1893. Yet Flourens emphasized the anti-English implication of the Toulon visit in his volume. Flourens, *Alexandre III*, pp. 340, 341.

[113] Five socialist members of the Paris municipal council refused to vote for an appropriation to meet the expenses of the reception to the Russian naval officers. *Radical*, Sept. 21, 1893. The socialist newspapers, insisting that Germany had no intention of attacking France, argued that there was no need of an alliance with Russia. *Parti Ouvrier*, Sept. 18, 19, 1893. *Petite République*, March 14, June 11, 1894.

[114] *Petite Gironde* (Bordeaux), Oct. 26, 1893.

[115] *Justice*, Sept. 21.

[116] *Temps*, Sept. 19.

[117] Dufferin to Rosebery, Paris, Nov. 3, 1893. *British Documents on the Origins of the War, 1898–1914*, G. P. Gooch, Harold Temperley, eds. (London). II, 287. This series will henceforth be referred to as *Brit. War Docs*. He attributed much influence in the formation of anti-English opinion to the editorials of the *Petit Journal*.

[118] *Événement*, No. 4, 1893, quoted by Cyon, *Entente Franco-Russe*, p. 462.

Alliance, and France, after attempting for some time to limit her own obligation to a mobilization by Germany,[119] finally yielded. In explaining his reasons to Freycinet, Ribot wrote, August 12, 1892, that neither Germany nor France would be able to remain neutral if Russia and Austria should go to war or even mobilize their armies, "and I add that as for us we would have no interest in doing so." [120] In January, 1894, the military alliance at last received the Tsar's approval. Like almost all of the alliances and accords which eventually divided Europe into two armed camps, it was essentially defensive. It provided for mutual aid if Russia were attacked by Germany alone, or by Austria with Germany's support, or if France were attacked by Germany alone or by Italy with Germany's support. Nevertheless, in specifying a simultaneous mobilization in reply to a like action by the Triple Alliance or by any one of its members, it might lead in certain eventualities to a French attack upon Germany prior to the latter's declaration of war.[121] If Austria mobilized even without Germany, France was thereby obliged to mobilize, and it was the understanding of the French and Russian generals who participated in the negotiations that mobilization meant war. This concession to Russia was the one provision of the alliance which was not in accord with public opinion. None but the chauvinist minority believed that France should assume the responsibility for the declaration of war. Freycinet evidently gave some consideration to this point, for he wrote that Germany's action would inevitably follow that of Austria.

The terms of the alliance, due in part to the insistence of Russia, remained scrupulously secret. Only the ministers of foreign affairs and the Presidents of the Republic knew them, for Ribot in June, 1895, merely affirmed the existence of the alliance in a general way.[122] The chamber never insisted that its terms should be communicated to it, and if the press occasionally ventured a desire for their publication, this display of independence was usually limited to the socialist newspapers. Without precise knowledge of its terms, the alliance became an article of faith among almost all groups. Public opinion from 1891 was profoundly influenced by it, for its preservation was

[119] *Livre Jaune: L'Alliance Franco-Russe,* p. 37.
[120] *Ibid.,* p. 86.
[121] *Ibid.,* pp. 56, 95, 96. Cf. Fay, *Origins of the World War,* I, 120. Langer, *Franco-Russian Alliance,* pp. 261, 262. Professor Langer thinks that the French were prepared to evade this obligation, just as Russia would refuse to act against Italy if she were to mobilize.
[122] *Annales,* 1895, III, 322,

placed above every other consideration. In order to prevent criticism and because of its wilful blindness, the moderate press either ignored the evidence of Russia's military and social weakness or consistently misrepresented conditions there.[123] This blind attachment to the alliance was not a positive proof that it was most esteemed as an instrument of the *revanche,* for the value placed upon it was largely due to its usefulness in assuring France's security and in enhancing her prestige and influence. It strengthened France's hand in current diplomatic questions, and the *Temps* (May 26, 1896) doubtless expressed the hope of many in anticipating that the display of military power, with the development of social justice, might in the end realize France's hopes without war.

The desire of revenge, in fact, had been only one of several factors in arousing public opinion in favor of an alliance with Russia. Those who were most devoted to the *revanche* were of course its uncompromising advocates. But it was Ferry's defeat, with the consequent change in Bismarck's policy toward France, that increased the effectiveness of Russian propaganda and turned moderate opinion in favor of the alliance. Even this change was not decisive. The repudiation of Boulanger and the dissolution of the Ligue des Patriotes reassured Russia, but these events also meant at least the temporary success of the moderate point of view in France. In 1889 and 1890, public opinion became somewhat less eager than it had been. It was William II's clumsy efforts to bring about an entente with France that gave the chauvinists an opportunity to resume their campaign. During the Empress Frederick's visit, they dominated the scene, and imposed their point of view upon the intimidated or tolerant moderate groups and upon a willing government. To each step in the formation of the eventual alliance, the characteristic reaction was one of joy that France was no longer isolated, that her security was more firmly assured, and that her word would count for more in international affairs.

---

[123] Michon's *Alliance Franco-Russe* has removed any doubt as to this effect of the alliance. A socialist predicted that the alliance would have a reactionary effect upon French politics. Maurice Charnay, *L'Alsace-Lorraine Vingt Ans Après* (Paris, 1892), p. 46. This topic probably merits further investigation.

CHAPTER VIII

ENGLAND OR GERMANY?

Nous suivons une politique continentale qui nous commande de rester toujours l'arme au bras contre l'Allemagne; pouvons nous suivre dans le monde entier une politique coloniale qui nous met en perpétuel conflit avec l'Angleterre, contre laquelle nous sommes désarmé sans l'Allemagne?
Correspondant, O. S., 193 (Nov. 8, 1898).

If the Russian alliance could not be used for the immediate reconquest of Alsace-Lorraine, and events soon showed that the hopes of the *revanche* element were ill-founded, it increased the weight of France's influence in foreign affairs and added to her feeling of security. These intangible satisfactions caused a distinct decline in the nervous tension which for years had characterized public opinion. Russia's dislike of the chauvinist agitation, as containing the possibility of a war which would not be concerned with her own interests, doubtless encouraged the government to resist its pressure. Moderate public opinion likewise refused to be stampeded by the extremists, and in 1893, Déroulède and Millevoye were discredited by their naïve acceptance of the obviously forged Norton papers which purported to show that Clemenceau had accepted money from the British government.

Russia, in fact, used her influence to improve the relations between France and Germany. When Germany first invited France in 1895 to send naval vessels to the celebration at the opening of the Kiel Canal, the reaction of the ministry was favorable. Not only was Hanotaux, the President of the Council, well disposed, but the Minister of Marine and President Faure regretted that their duties would not permit them to attend in person.[1] Nevertheless, after a week had passed without a formal reply, Münster finally was told that opposition had developed within the cabinet.[2] His suspicion that the

[1] Münster to Hohenlohe, Paris, Feb. 21, 1895. *G. P.*, IX, 399, 400. See, however, Bourgeois, Pagès, *Origines et Résponsabilités*, p. 253, where Hanotaux is represented as intending at first to refuse. According to Poincaré the entire cabinet was against going to Kiel. R. Poincaré, *Les Origines de la Guerre* (Paris, 1921), p. 64.

[2] Münster to Hohenlohe, Paris, March 4, 1895. *G. P.*, IX, 401, 402, Münster to Hohenlohe, Paris, March 9, 1895. *Ibid.*, IX, 404.

French government had consulted Russia was correct, and the final acceptance of the invitation was in part due to her advice. Certain conditions were apparently made, however, in order to avoid offense to patriotic sentiment in France, among others, that the French ships should not be shown any special consideration, that no political significance should be attributed to her participation, and that no German vessels named after the battles of the war of 1870 would be present.[3] The fact that the French flag was to fly in honor of a German achievement was sufficient to arouse the more excitable patriots.[4] Radicals and Monarchists united once more in protest against the government's alleged disloyalty to patriotic memories. The *Radical* (March 11) declared that participation would mean the abandonment of Alsace-Lorraine, and the *Lanterne* (March 4) suggested that Germany might propose a return visit by her own warships to a French port or a visit of the Kaiser to the Paris Exposition of 1900. Under the headline "Metz-Sedan-Kiel," the *Intransigeant* (March 7) insisted that French sentiment had never been so bitterly offended. Cassagnac spoke of "the national shame."[5] In contrast to its attitude during the Empress Frederick's visit in 1891, the moderate press refused to yield to this agitation. The *Temps* (June 19) and the *Matin* (June 18) defended the government's decision as another demonstration of the union with Russia rather than as necessary to correct international relations. But the *République Française* (June 10) did not hesitate to condemn the attempt to stir up old memories, and the government was able to carry out its promise in spite of the wild denunciation of its critics. The extremists had clearly lost much ground since 1891.

The government's action was the more creditable because its coöperation with Germany and Russia after the Sino-Japanese war had increased the bitterness of the attack. Preceding the Kiel celebration by some weeks, this new evidence of coöperation with Germany was interpreted as additional proof that the Russian alliance was forcing France to forget her grievances against Germany. It was said that France was pulling Russia's chestnuts out of the fire without any profit to herself, that she was within *"deux doigts"* of war against

---

[3] Pagès, Bourgeois, *Origines et Résponsabilités*, pp. 254, 255. These conditions do not appear in the reports of the German ambassador.

[4] Cf. the monarchist *Gazette de France*, March 12, 1895. Clemenceau claimed that public opinion alone had prevented the government from agreeing to have the French ships fly the German flag. *Justice*, May 7, 1895. Public meetings were held for the purpose of arousing public opinion, but without success. *Revue Blanche*, IX (1895), 37, 38.

[5] *Autorité*, June 12, 1895.

Japan in company with her national enemy,[6] that she was facilitating a *rapprochement* between Germany and Russia.[7] The moderate press again supported the government's action as in accord with the interests of France,[8] but François Deloncle, a leader of the colonial party, was one of the few to endorse the principle of a permanent entente between the three Continental Powers against England.[9] However reluctantly,[10] Hanotaux continued to act with Russia and Germany until the Treaty of Shimonoseki had been revised.

Doubtful of the tendencies of the government's foreign policy, Alexandre Millerand interpellated it on June 12. A socialist in domestic politics, he yielded to none in his attachment to the memories of Alsace-Lorraine, although he believed that these provinces would eventually be recovered as a result of the general development of liberty and of social justice. The union of the extreme parties in the chamber failed to prevent a vote of confidence in the government's policy.[11] Nevertheless, Ribot, the President of the Council, thought it wise to reassure public opinion by affirming the existence of an alliance. This assurance was far from satisfactory to those who had condemned the presence of French warships at Kiel and France's coöperation with Germany in the Far East. France might be the ally of Russia, wrote the *Justice* (June 21), but was Russia the ally of France? "To the present moment," declared Cassagnac, "we see very clearly what we have done for Russia, but we do not see at all what she has done for us." [12] As for the Russian alliance being a guarantee against a German attack, the monarchist Delafosse was confident that "it was directed against an eventual danger which will not develop." [13] The monarchist *Gazette de France* (June 12) and the independent *Matin* (June 23) believed that the alliance had reaffirmed the Treaty of Frankfort. It would be a mistake to think that these criticisms meant a desire to dissolve the alliance, for they were in part the normal reaction of the opposition parties, and even more of extremists

[6] J. B. Eustis, "The Franco-Russian Alliance," *North American Review,* CLXV, 112. Eustis was a former ambassador of the United States to France. Cf. *Figaro,* May 20, 1895.

[7] *Petit Journal,* April 30.

[8] *Temps,* April 18, 20, 26. *Journal des Débats,* April 21, May 10. *République Française,* May 8.

[9] *Matin,* May 10.

[10] Münster to Hohenlohe, Paris, April 30, 1895. *G. P.,* IX, 408.

[11] The vote was 362 to 105. *Annales,* 1895, III, 325.

[12] *Autorité,* June 13.

[13] *Figaro,* May 20.

who were disappointed by the failure of the alliance to achieve immediate results. Nor were the attacks upon the sending of French ships to Kiel and upon France's coöperation with Germany in the Far East effective in arousing public opinion. Édouard Drumont, the nationalist and anti-Semitic leader, who presumably was a good judge of effective propaganda, confessed "that if these violent protests honor those who make them, they merely emphasize more clearly than before the profound indifference of the masses." [14] Having retired to the country, Déroulède was not on hand to organize street demonstrations, and, as Francis Charmes observed, there was a more general recognition of the need to observe the usual amenities of international intercourse.[15] Even in the midst of the excitement aroused by the Kiel question, French artists were able to exhibit at a Berlin exposition without outraging patriotic sentiment.[16]

Because it had never been under the illusion that the alliance could be used immediately to achieve the *revanche,* and because it had no desire for a prompt war with Germany, the government did not share the bitter disappointment produced among certain sections of public opinion by the meager returns of the alliance. Léon Bourgeois, the Minister of Foreign Affairs, is reported to have told an Italian agent, in refusing an accord in regard to African questions while Italy remained a member of the Triple Alliance, that "events will return Alsace-Lorraine to us," and for that reason "all our foreign affairs must be subordinated to that end." [17] The Russian alliance for this reason, as well as for its more general utility in current questions, remained the fundamental element of French foreign policy under every ministry. Measures were taken to preserve as much as possible of the original enthusiasm. The coronation of Nicholas II in May, 1896, was observed as a holiday,[18] and in October of the same year the Tsar's visit to Paris was an occasion for another brilliant celebration.[19] A

---

[14] *Libre Parole,* June 15.

[15] *Rev. des Deux Mondes,* 1895, III, 477, 478. For several years, Charmes had been the chief permanent official of the Quai d'Orsay, and at this time, he was beginning his long service as the political editor of this important review.

[16] *Journal des Débats,* March 10. *Matin,* May 2.

[17] Bülow to Hohenlohe, Rome, Feb. 5, 1896. *G. P.,* XI, 89. Bülow to Hohenlohe, Rome, Feb. 9, 1896. *Ibid.,* XI, 288.

[18] Münster regarded these ceremonies with a jaundiced eye. He wrote that Paris celebrated the event as if Nicholas had likewise "been crowned Emperor of France." Münster to Hohenlohe, Paris, May 26, 1896. *Ibid.,* XI, 348.

[19] The German ambassador, however, noted the criticisms of the radical and conservative newspapers. Münster to Hohenlohe, Paris, Oct. 3, 1896. *Ibid.,* XI, 348.

year later, the heads of the two states emphasized the existence of the alliance in the exchange of toasts on the deck of a French warship at Kronstadt.[20]

If the union with Russia was maintained especially with a view to France's Continental interests, leaders of public opinion and certain politicians turned their attention again to the policy of colonial expansion. "A notable change of opinion," wrote the *Temps* (Oct. 1, 1894), "has occurred in regard to colonial enterprises. From an indifference which approached hostility it has passed to an open sympathy." This claim was exaggerated[21] by 1894 there was, however, a small but active group of colonial enthusiasts in the chamber.[22] In spite of the opposition of the two extreme groups, supplies were granted regularly for enterprises in Dahomey, Madagascar, Central Africa, and elsewhere. Even the Egyptian question, whose place in the national consciousness resembled more closely that of Alsace-Lorraine because of its historic associations than the other colonial interests, was revived. Unwilling to brave the dangers that would follow a direct challenge of the British occupation, it was proposed that the question should be reopened indirectly by establishing French influence in the Bahr-el-Gazel, a district of the Egyptian Soudan that controlled the access to the Nile from Central Africa. This plan was threatened for a moment by the Anglo-Congo treaty of 1894 which gave to the King of Belgium, the sovereign of the Congo Free State, a life lease to this area in return for the lease of a long strip along the western bank of Lake Tanganyika. Resentment developed in France, for it was felt that England had disposed of territory to which it had no legal claim, since it belonged to Egypt, and since England had withdrawn her forces from the Sudan after the defeat of General Gordon at Khartoum in 1885.[23] Machinery was at once set in motion to remove this obstacle to France's plans. In June, 1894, credits were voted for the consolidation of her control of the Upper Ubanghi, the approach to the Bahr-el-Gazel.[24]

Friction between France and England over Egypt had on earlier

[20] Michon, *L'Alliance Franco-Russe*, p. 77.

[21] "The Colonial group is very noisy," wrote Monson in August, 1898, "and has very able exponents in the press . . . but I do not believe that the country at large either cares much about such matters or knows anything about them." *Brit. War Docs.*, I, 161.

[22] Al. Isaac, "L'Orientation de la Politique Coloniale et le Ministre des Colonies," *Rev. Pol. et Parl.*, 1894, II, 2.

[23] *Rev. des Deux Mondes*, 1894, V, 236.

[24] *Temps*, June 11, 1894.

occasions suggested coöperation with Germany. Germany, whose East African colony was affected by the Anglo-Congo treaty, initiated negotiations for this purpose, and it was finally agreed that the two Powers, while acting independently, would consult each other as to the progress accomplished.[25] On June 17, England yielded to Germany's threat of a conference for the settlement of the Egyptian and Congo questions by canceling that part which had aroused her criticism.[26] Germany had not observed the spirit of her tacit agreement with France, but two months later France was able to secure from the King of Belgium the abrogation of the proposed lease of the Bahr-el-Gazel.[27] The way was thereby prepared for an advance to the Nile, but no appreciable progress had been made in securing an assurance of Germany's support, although it was essential if France proposed to precipitate a crisis with England.

It was therefore without adequate diplomatic preparation that France took the preliminary steps in entering her claim to the Upper Nile. In September, 1894, local authorities in the Ubanghi were instructed to occupy the Bahr-el-Gazel, and Colonel Monteil left France on a similar mission only to be diverted later to other purposes. Rumors of French activity and indiscretions of leaders of the colonial party in the chamber,[28] led to a formal warning by Edward Grey, then the Under Secretary of State for Foreign Affairs, in the House of Commons, March 28, 1895. An attempt by France to establish her influence in any part of the valley of the Upper Nile, he declared, "would be an unfriendly act and would be so viewed by England." [29] Its attention concentrated upon the Kiel affair, the French press failed to attribute to this pronouncement the importance it deserved. Few newspapers printed a verbatim report of it,[30] and none conceded that it was the expression of a rightful claim. The *République Française* (March 30, 1895) voiced the general reaction of those who gave any attention to the matter, if in somewhat forceful terms, in referring to Grey's statement as "an impertinence which it is the

---

[25] Marschall's Memorandum, Berlin, June 13, 1894. *G. P.*, VIII, 450, 451. Bourgeois et Pagès, *Origines et Résponsabilités*, p. 245.

[26] Marschall to Hatzfeldt, Berlin, June 15, 1894. *G. P.*, VIII, 454.

[27] *Rev. des Deux Mondes*, 1894, V, 236. No *Yellow Book* was published for these negotiations.

[28] T. W. Riker, "A Survey of British Policy in the Fashoda Crisis," *Polit. Sci. Quarterly*, XLIV, 56, 57.

[29] *Parliamentary Debates*, 4th series, vol. 32, pp. 405, 406.

[30] It was not printed by the *Temps, Journal des Débats, Petite République Française, Petit Journal,* or *Matin.*

duty of the government to meet with dignity." [31] It cannot be said that public opinion was thoroughly aroused, but such as existed endorsed Hanotaux's reply in the Senate, April 6, 1895, when he defended the French thesis that England's withdrawal from the Egyptian Sudan had left that region as *res nullius* or at most under the exclusive sovereignty of Egypt.

Neither the government, nor the press, nor public opinion was prepared to arrange a satisfactory basis of coöperation with Germany, although her aid was obviously essential to the success of France's purposes. Until the latter's traditional attitude toward Alsace-Lorraine should be changed, Germany could not afford to risk the dangerous clash with England which would follow the support of France in any part of Egypt. France, for her part, doubted the possibility of an arrangement under existing circumstances, and she held herself ready to profit by any differences between Germany and England in order to advance her own interests in Egypt. This interplay of interests and aversions developed after the Kaiser's telegram to President Kruger, January 1, 1896, congratulating him on the repulse of the Jamieson raid. The mysterious Baron Holstein had just drawn up a plan for a Continental league to be directed against England,[32] and it would seem that the telegram may be interpreted as the beginning of a campaign to achieve this purpose. Profiting by President Faure's remark that public opinion in France in regard to Germany had greatly improved, Hohenlohe, the Chancellor, had already suggested that the time was ripe for coöperation in specific questions "without committing the political future of either Power." [33] The Kruger telegram first found a sympathetic audience in France,[34] but the bad feeling it caused in England offered a tempting prospect for the advancement of French interests in the Upper Nile. Germany's silence as to Egypt disposed of the one inducement which might have persuaded France [35]; the latter's failure to respond to Germany's limited advances can only be explained, therefore, by the hope that the Anglo-German difference might be exploited for her own profit. England's hostility, wrote Münster, had pleased the French. "The

[31] The *Figaro* (April 6) discounted Grey's statement as a parliamentary maneuver to strengthen a weak cabinet.

[32] He proposed to attract France by granting her concessions in the Congo. *G. P.*, XIII, 67, 68. (Dec. 30, 1895.)

[33] Münster to Hohenlohe, Paris, Dec. 25, 1895. *Ibid.*, IX, 425.

[34] *Temps*, Jan. 5, 1896.

[35] Bourgeois, Pagès, *Origines et Résponsabilités*, p. 264. A. Mévil, *De la Paix de Francfort*, pp. 8–11.

press here adopts an attitude of observation and awaits the reaction of the English press." [36] The *Temps* (Jan. 6), sensing possible developments, had protested against "unnatural alliances," and declared that France did not "intend to fall in step with the German emperor, to diverge the least bit from her policy. . . ." [37] But the hope that England would make an attractive offer was disappointed by her announcement of an Anglo-Egyptian expedition to Dongola. It was explained as a move to save the Italians from the Abyssinians and to prevent the extension of unrest to Egypt, but the *Temps* (March 19, 1896) assumed that its real purpose was the restoration of England's control throughout the Upper Nile. An attempt was then made to prevent England's use of Egyptian money for this purpose, but this maneuver only led to England's assumption of the financial burden.

The Marchand expedition was France's reply. The explorer was instructed to proceed through Central Africa to the Nile. His purpose, sometimes described as exclusively military and even as in the common interest of civilization, was essentially political. Little progress had been made in securing the support of other Powers, for it is by no means clear that Russia's aid was assured, in the event of a crisis following the raising of the French flag upon the Upper Nile. Nevertheless, on November 21, 1896, Hanotaux, the foreign minister, told the chamber that France did not stand alone in the Egyptian question: "we are glad to believe that a cause which concerns all of the Powers will gradually secure the support of those who are the most reluctant." [38] Germany had been approached indirectly without effective results. During the summer, the French ambassador in London had urged the need of an understanding to his German colleague, [39] and about the date of Marchand's departure from France a former correspondent of the *Matin* appeared in Berlin on a mission to sound the ground for a limited accord to be directed against England in Egypt. He was told that Germany could not consider this suggestion unless it were proposed by responsible officials. [40]

Nevertheless, the German Foreign Office sanctioned a conversation

[36] Münster to Hohenlohe, Paris, Jan. 16, 1896. *G. P.*, XI, 80.

[37] France's enthusiasm, observed Hohenlohe, had lasted only twenty-four hours when it was pointed out that sympathy for the Transvaal should not supersede France's obligations to Alsace-Lorraine. Hohenlohe to William II, Berlin, Jan. 7, 1896. *Ibid.*, XI, 38.

[38] *Annales*, 1896, III, 459.

[39] Hatzfeldt to Hohenlohe, London, May 22, 1896. *G. P.*, XI, 195–198; June 18, *Ibid.*, XI, pp. 204, 205; July 24, *Ibid.*, XI, p. 323.

[40] Huhn's Memorandum, Berlin, June 22, 23, *Ibid.*, XI, 317-322.

between Jules Hansen, a secret agent of the Quai d'Orsay, and von Huhn, the Berlin correspondent of the *Kölnische Zeitung*, at Copenhagen on the condition that it should be unofficial. Hansen's remarks were not without interest for a study of French public opinion. In view of the peaceful character of the Russian alliance, and of the impossibility of isolating Germany, France and the chief of her ministry, Hanotaux, were said to be convinced that an understanding was preferable to a policy which would lead to war. "It may be assumed," he declared, "that about three thousand men were in a position to exert a determining influence upon France's fate. All the rest are the 'mob.' Of these three thousand, a third had been won over to the new policy and it seems possible to change this minority into a majority." Hansen proposed that Germany should send an agent to Paris for a thorough discussion of the question, and he promised that Hanotaux would receive this agent.[41] There is no evidence, at present, that this suggestion was adopted, nor did it apparently become known to the press, although journalists had figured largely in these unofficial discussions. Hohenlohe refused to make any advances on the ground that his offer after the Kruger telegram had elicited no reply and that Germany's aid in the Franco-Chinese treaty of 1885 had not had a permanent influence upon the attitude of the French government.[42] Germany's reluctance to risk a final break with England by backing France in Egypt, as well as France's refusal to forget 1871, continued to be a barrier to an understanding. Yet France proceeded to challenge England as if she were amply prepared to deal with her alone.

By the spring of 1898, Kitchener's expedition and that of Marchand were slowly converging upon the Upper Nile. Occasional hints had appeared in the French press that Kitchener would arrive too late for England to settle the question alone.[43] The government failed to take public opinion into its confidence, and its own policy was either foolhardy or confused as to its purposes. The beginnings of an understanding with Germany on the occasion of the Kruger telegram had led to no positive results, the later conversations were nothing more than feelers, and Russia's attitude during the Fashoda crisis suggests that she had at least not been enthusiastic. Another opportunity to ap-

---

[41] Huhn's Memorandum, Berlin, Sept. 19, 1896. *G. P.*, XI, 324–331.
[42] Later, the Kaiser described Hanotaux as France's most dangerous man because he had the confidence of England and Russia. See his annotation of Münster's letter to Hohenlohe, Paris, June 30, 1898. *Ibid.*, XIII, 238–242.
[43] *Temps*, Jan. 13, 1898.

proach Germany was sacrificed when Delcassé, on succeeding Hanotaux as Minister of Foreign Affairs, took no action upon her suggestion of an understanding in regard to Portuguese finances and to the
future of her colonies.[44]

Delcassé's intentions at the beginning of his seven years' tenure
in control of France's foreign policy are to-day almost as mysterious
as they were to his contemporaries. He is variously represented as
determined from the first to encircle Germany [45] and as prepared to
listen to any serious proposals which she might màke.[46] So far as one
may judge from his public statements, consistency was not one of his
virtues. Since his opinions apparently changed to a certain degree with
circumstances, the conclusion seems to be warranted that he was
more of an opportunist than has been supposed. In 1892, he said, quite
frankly, in discounting the discussion of a peaceful solution of the
Alsace-Lorraine question, that it could only be settled by war,[47] but
his support of France's claims in the Upper Nile was certainly not
calculated to hasten the issue. As to the colonial policy, in 1895 he expressed the opinion that France had acquired about all of the territory
she needed,[48] while on February 8, 1898, he told the chamber that it
was not his fault "if the French flag had not already been taken to the
banks of the Nile where it was expected." [49] The British,[50] as well
as the German ambassador,[51] anticipated that he would follow a strong
policy against their respective governments. It is of some significance that he had first entered political life as a Gambettist and as
a member of the staff of the *République Française,* the leading opportunist newspaper.[52]

[44] Mévil, *De la Paix de Francfort,* pp. 16–18. Bourgeois, Pagès, *Origines et
Résponsabilités,* p. 275. Bourgeois, *Manuel Politique,* IV, p. 372. A contemporary study of Delcassé's policy, reputed to have been inspired by Hanotaux,
represents the latter as having been prepared to act upon Germany's suggestion. (Anonymous) "Quatre Ans de la Politique Extérieure," *Rev. Pol. et Parl.,*
vol. 34, pp. 9, 10. This article with few changes was incorporated as the first
chapter of René Millet, *Notre Politique Extérieure de 1898 à 1905* (Paris, 1905).
Both the article and the book are exceedingly critical of Delcassé's policy.
[45] Georges Reynauld, *L'Oeuvre de M. Delcassé* (Paris, 1915), p. 5.
[46] Bourgeois, *Manuel Politique,* IV, 443, 444.
[47] An interview in the *Petit Champenois* of Rheims. X (A. Lalance), *La
France veut-elle la Guerre avec l'Allemagne?* (Brussels, 1892), p. 26.
[48] *Annales,* 1895, II, 837. Yet he was present when President Carnot gave
the final instructions to Monteil. Monteil's statement in the *Matin,* June 21, 1905.
[49] *Annales,* 1898, I, 631.
[50] Monson to Salisbury, Paris, July 1, 1898. *Brit. War Docs.,* I, 158.
[51] Münster to Hohenlohe, Paris, July 9, 1898. *G. P.,* XIII, 241 (note).
[52] It was essentially the opportunist point of view which he stated to the

When the presence of white troops at Fashoda was first reported in Paris, indicating that Marchand had reached his goal, Delcassé at once acted to assure for himself the control of the situation. On September 8, he assured Monson, the British ambassador, that Marchand was " 'only an emissary of civilization,' " that he had no authority " 'to assume the decision of questions of right which appertain exclusively to the competence of the British and French governments,' " adding that the ministry, as well as himself, was confident of a satisfactory solution.[53] The appointment of Paul Cambon as the French ambassador to England was also cited as a proof of France's desire for a peaceful arrangement.[54] Nevertheless, this temperate beginning did not change England's immediate conclusion, especially as the report of Marchand's presence on the Nile followed Kitchener's crushing defeat of the Dervishes at Omdurman, that her claim to the Upper Nile was challenged and that the entire Egyptian question was involved. There was no doubt as to the position of the government and of public opinion in England. With a unanimity rarely equaled, both the government and public opinion insisted that Marchand must be withdrawn prior to any negotiations.[55] Blowitz attempted to convince French opinion of the need to yield by emphasizing the importance which England attached to the question. "Of what value is Fashoda to France," he wrote in the *Matin* (Oct. 22), "in comparison to the price which England places upon it?"

It was England's grim determination expressed without any consideration for French sensibility, however, which, to a large extent, stimulated resistance in France. Just at this time, the protracted Dreyfus Affair had reached a crisis in the granting of a new trial.[56] The streets, it is said, were dominated by the anti-Dreyfusard agitators,[57] and another question had appeared in the strike of the building

---

Giornale d'Italia in explaining his policy in negotiating the entente with Italy. After the commercial treaty of 1898, he had only followed the course of events " '. . . I had only to follow what was certain to happen. Do not seek to discover a carefully worked-out plan, subtleties or diplomatic combinations. *La force de ce qui est arrivé, c'est que cela devait arriver.*' " *Temps,* Jan. 5, 1902.

[53] Monson to Salisbury, Paris, Sept. 8, 1898. *Brit. War Docs.,* I, 163.

[54] Monson to Salisbury, Paris, Sept. 18, 1898. *Ibid.,* I, 165.

[55] Riker, "Fashoda Crisis," *Polit. Sci. Quarterly,* XLIV, 65, 66.

[56] Colonel Henry's forgeries were revealed on the eve of the crisis.

[57] A. Zévaès, *Histoire de la Troisième République,* pp. 395–400. Relations with Germany played a surprisingly small part in the agitation either for or against Dreyfus, and the best indication of this is the tendency of the most virulent of the anti-Dreyfus newspapers to favor an entente with Germany against England. See below, p. 176 f.

trades to divert attention from the situation upon the Upper Nile.[58] ⟨
The London *Times* (Sept. 29) admitted that the majority of the Paris
newspapers were moderate. The first signs of resentment appeared in
connection with the campaign being waged in the British press for
Marchand's unconditional withdrawal. Since Omdurman, declared the
moderate *Journal des Débats* (Sept. 20), "the French press had maintained an attitude towards England of perfect courtesy. . . . It has
been answered from the other side of the channel by an explosion of
rage and of hate." The Bonapartist and nationalist *Autorité* (Sept.
23) observed that the campaign in the British press had begun while
France was absorbed by the Dreyfus Affair. "They must have a
pitiful idea in London of our government if they suppose that it is
capable of cowardice in the face of such pretensions." The normally
even temper of the *Temps* was ruffled. The British government, it
declared (Oct. 6), "cannot but see that in following the lead of
the chief English newspapers it will necessarily cause a complete
change in the conciliatory attitude which public opinion has manifested to the present." Francis Charmes observed that "we have
not been accustomed to hearing ourselves talked about in this way,"
and he added that even in Bismarck's worst mood Germany had been
more restrained.[59]

Eager to resist any slight to France's interests or prestige, whether
it came from Germany or England, nationalists insisted that Marchand's exploits had given France a legitimate claim to the Upper
Nile. "Major Marchand," wrote Mme. Adam, "is the complete expression of our race, he is our standard-bearer." [60] Moderate opinion
was of course prepared at the beginning of the crisis to defend
France's rights, but it was also prepared to negotiate for compensations elsewhere. Delcassé expressed the moderate point of view in
telling Monson, September 28, that a break would only come if
England refused to negotiate.[61] " 'Do not ask me for the impossible,' "
he pleaded, " 'do not drive me into a corner!' " [62] Early in October,
Cambon suggested that Marchand might be withdrawn if a public
announcement were made that negotiations were in progress for

[58] *Rev. des Deux Mondes*, 1898, V, 945.
[59] *Rev. des Deux Mondes*, 1898, V, 952.
[60] *Nouvelle Revue*, vol. 114, p. 718.
[61] Monson to Salisbury, Paris, Sept. 27, 1898. *Brit. War Docs.*, I, 169, 170.
Delcassé anticipated an attack as the author of a national humiliation if he
yielded. Cf. *Autorité*, Sept. 24.
[62] Monson to Salisbury, London, Oct. 6, 1898, *Brit. War Docs.*, I, 173–175.

the delimitation of French and British interests in Africa.[63] But the sudden appearance of a *Blue Book,* showing that the Foreign Office was in accord with the press in demanding Marchand's unconditional withdrawal, eliminated this hope of a graceful retreat for France. Nevertheless, the *Yellow Book,* which soon followed the British official publication, attempted to create the impression, inaccurately it is true, that Salisbury had promised to consider France's desire for an outlet to the Nile through the Bahr-el-Gazel.[64] England's unbending attitude excited the chauvinists perhaps more intensely than any incident since 1871. Cassagnac declared that the question was more serious for France than the Hohenzollern candidature had been.[65] Delcassé was showing himself to be a "foreign" minister of French affairs, exclaimed Déroulède who had just reorganized the Ligue des Patriotes, rather than a French Minister of Foreign Affairs.[66] Rochefort thought that it was the Dreyfusard party which would have France yield,[67] and the nationalist and clerical *Echo de Paris* (Oct. 22) asserted that the entire Egyptian question should be referred to a conference.

The newspapers which were understood to be close to the government soon began to prepare opinion for the eventual evacuation of Façhoda. A despatch from London in the *Matin* (Oct. 19) described Façhoda as a "marshy and unhealthy village," while insisting that France, under no circumstances, could yield her claim to the control of confluence of the Bahr-el-Gazel and the White Nile.[68] The *Temps* (Oct. 25) wrote that France should state clearly her intention to withdraw provided that "courtesy was observed toward her and that the question was not arbitrarily isolated from others." There was no reason, according to the *Journal des Débats* (Oct. 29), why Marchand should not be withdrawn "if we are paid for it." Clemenceau declared that "the brutal fact is that France cannot think of throwing herself into a war for the possession of some African marshes, when the German is camped at Metz and Strassburg." [69] Even the

[63] Salisbury to Monson, London, Oct. 6, 1898. *Ibid.,* I, 173–175.

[64] *Livre Jaune: Affaires du Haut Nil et du Bahr-el-Gazel.* p. 25. Cf. *Rev. des Deux Mondes,* 1898, VI, 237.

[65] *Autorité,* Oct. 16. He wrote later: "Yes, England has spoken to us as one would not speak to a dog. . . ." *Ibid.,* Oct. 25.

[66] *Patrie,* Oct. 17.

[67] *Intransigeant,* Oct. 22.

[68] Monson suspected that this communication had been written in Paris. *Brit. War Docs.,* I, 176, 177.

[69] *Aurore,* Oct. 25. The Paris municipal council adopted a resolution urging every effort, without neglecting the material and moral interests of the country,

extremists admitted that the negro village of Fashoda was not worth a war,[70] but it was as generally agreed that England should concede something in return. She was in no mood, however, to build a golden bridge for France's retreat, and despite Monson's apprehension that Russia would side with France, it seems clear that she advised moderation. Aside from the question of Delcassé's original intention as to an entente with England, and her apparent readiness to resort to arms, it was the reluctance of public opinion in France for war that explains Delcassé's decision, November 4, to evacuate Fashoda without a definite assurance of compensation.[71]

For the first time since 1871, France had suffered humiliation and defeat in an important crisis by a Power other than Germany. "The feeling of rage and wild desire for vengeance to which the French press now gives expression," wrote the correspondent of the *Daily Telegraph* (Nov. 3), "exceeds in degree the outburst of hatred which the loss of Alsace-Lorraine provoked against Germany a generation ago." The attitude of the extremists justified even this strong report. "England treats us with such complete hostility and insolence," declared Cassagnac, "that we will be obliged at one time or another to go to war with her." [72] Lucien Millevoye, Déroulède's associate, declared on the eve of France's surrender that "henceforth England has France as her irreconcilable enemy. *Le duel sans merci est commencé.*" [73] Of the moderate section of the press, the *Matin* (Nov. 4) urged that "the national honor is never at stake in colonial enterprises. These only represent a business policy." [74] It was, however, England's refusal to grant any compensations which offended the more responsible newspapers. The *Temps* (Nov. 6) regretted that England had not made use of an exceptional opportunity for a "general accord in regard to questions in Africa and elsewhere." The vital

to avoid a grave conflict with England. *Journal de Rouen,* Oct. 22. This moderate journal wrote "No one desires war *à propos* of Fashoda."

[70] *Autorité,* Nov. 9. *Écho de Paris,* Nov. 5. *Petit Journal,* Nov. 10, 11. Cf. *Temps,* Nov. 3. *Journal des Débats,* Nov. 5. For what is known as to Russia's attitude, see M. B. Giffen, *Fashoda. The Incident and its Diplomatic Setting,* (Chicago, 1930), pp. 159–185.

[71] Delcassé confided this decision to Münster two days before it was announced publicly. Münster to the Foreign Office, Paris, Nov. 2, 1898. *G. P.,* XIV, 384.

[72] *Autorité,* Oct. 25: "Fashoda" he added (Nov. 9), "is going to become more atrocious in our history than Crécy, Agincourt, or Sedan."

[73] *Patrie,* Nov. 4. This newspaper had become the organ of the reorganized Ligue des Patriotes.

[74] The *Figaro's* comments, however, were scarcely less extreme than those of the *Autorité, Journal de Rouen,* Nov. 6.

question, declared the *Journal des Débats* (Nov. 5) had not been the evacuation of Fashoda but its conditions. "The good relations of the two countries have received a permanent injury." Jaurès, the Socialist leader, blamed the government of France rather than England, for it had assured parliament in asking for funds that the Marchand expedition contained no danger of international complications. "We were given peaceful assurances," he wrote, "and we remained silent." He even thought that the occasion was favorable for the dissolution of the Russian alliance and for an entente with England.[75]

Resentment against England revived the project for an understanding with Germany. It received more attention than at any time since 1884, but there was a significant reversal of the groups which supported it. The majority of those who found that it had merit in 1898 had done everything in their power to prevent it on the earlier occasion. Cassagnac wrote that an invasion of England in company with Germany would be the "greatest joy of my life as an ardent patriot. If Germany is hated, it is because of one fact which can be remedied. With the cause, the effect would disappear. Neighborly relations, an accord, a frank alliance would follow the acute situation created by Alsace-Lorraine." [76] The nationalist and Catholic *Écho de Paris* (Nov. 3) declared that "Germany is an accidental adversary, while England is the eternal enemy." [77] The thoughts of more moderate leaders were evidently turned in the same direction. The *Temps* (Nov. 10) and the *Journal des Débats* (Nov. 10) observed that the Kaiser's obvious avoidance of Egypt on his return from the Near East showed that Germany would not support England there. As early as October 23, the moderate *Journal de Rouen* wrote that the Fashoda affair was persuading public opinion that "France's most dangerous adversaries are not always those against whom she is in the habit of remaining armed and upon the defensive." The Paris correspondent of the *Kölnische Zeitung* (Nov. 7) was much impressed by this tendency of the press. He reported that the hatred formerly concentrated upon Germany had been diverted against England, and that "we only need to bring up the diplomatic question of Egypt with the Sultan and France as one man would support us. We would also be on the way to becoming France's ally."

If this discussion had been limited to a few newspapers, it would

---

[75] *Petite République,* Nov. 13.
[76] *Auiorité,* Nov. 10.
[77] The *Journal de Rouen* (Nov. 5) noted this statement with the comment: "The way things are going, how many Frenchmen will think like M. Fouquier?"

be chiefly interesting as a passing expression of wounded pride. But Delcassé's references in his conversations with Monson to a possible entente with Germany were not merely a bluff. On December 9, Monson reported him as giving a solemn warning "that if France had to go to war with England, she would not consider it enough to have the support of Russia alone, but that she would seek for and obtain that of Germany also. He had frequently told me, he said, of the overtures indirectly made by Germany to the French government." [78] In the meantime, in the spring of 1898 Germany had rejected Joseph Chamberlain's suggestion of an alliance with England, in part to avoid offense to Russia,[79] and the treaty arranged with her in August in regard to the Portuguese colonies did not end her unpopularity in Germany. Reports of the unusually friendly attitude of public opinion in France were therefore received with some satisfaction. The *Berliner Tageblatt* (Dec. 11) observed that Germany was enjoying the rare experience of being courted by England and France at the same time.

Although she was not disposed to commit herself to either, Germany was quite willing to encourage each to a certain extent. A few days before Delcassé's warning to the British ambassador, the same unofficial agent of the German foreign office, von Huhn, who had acted in a similar capacity in 1896, appeared in Paris. Hansen entertained him at a breakfast with certain subordinate officials of the Quai d'Orsay and with Jules Valfrey, the historian and former diplomat, who was a frequent contributor to the *Figaro* under the pseudonym of "Whist." The german agent was given the same assurances as two years earlier in regard to public opinion, with the further comment that the Russian alliance had been a disappointment in its failure to aid France during the Fashoda crisis. To remedy a situation which only benefited England, it was necessary, he was told, that sensible folk in France and Germany should prepare for a *rapprochement*. According to von Huhn, the suggestion was made that the Kaiser should visit a French port, with the assurance that Déroulède and his revived Ligue des Patriotes would not be permitted to organize a hostile demonstration. Later, during a conversation with Delcassé, the French Minister spoke in general terms of an understanding, and when von Huhn objected that no French minister would ever risk his political future by defending an accord with Germany in parliament, Delcassé

---

[78] Monson to Salisbury, Paris, Dec. 9, 1898. *Brit. War Docs.*, I, 196, 197.
[79] Friedrich Meinecke, *Geschichte des Deutsch-Englischen Bündnisproblems, 1890–1901* (Munich, 1927), p. 103.

declared: " *'J'y irai demain, si vous voulez.'* " The old question of Alsace-Lorraine and Germany's reluctance to support France in Egypt, however, prevented any definite results from these conversations.[80]

The press continued the discussion of an accord with Germany into February, 1899. The exchange of a French colony for Alsace-Lorraine, according to Lalance, would lead to a new Triple Alliance between Russia, Germany, and France. "It is said," he wrote, "that the Emperor William desires to come to Paris in 1900; it only depends upon him to come here with the Tsar and to receive the most enthusiastic reception ever accorded a sovereign." [81] Jules Lemaître, a member of the Académie Française and the first president of the Ligue de la Patrie Française, suggested that the Alsace-Lorraine question should be referred to a European conference.[82] Cassagnac went so far as to consider the liquidation of the old grievance against Germany without a return of the lost provinces. "People are beginning," he wrote, "to weigh deliberately the two hatreds; that of the German, a little cooled with time; that of the English suddenly revived and burning. Would it not be better to resign oneself to the cruel mutilation of France thirty years ago than to share Spain's horrible fate?" [83] The more temperate *Correspondant* warned against an obstinate attachment to unchanging ideas. "One must not say 'never' to an idea, nor accept it too quickly." [84] Observers in Germany continued to follow this development with interest. "The masses," wrote the *Kölnische Zeitung* (Dec. 9), "seem to reply to flag-waving: 'My God, leave us in peace with those old stories, we know them, and they are beginning to bore us.' " The Paris correspondent of the *Berliner Tageblatt* (Dec. 23) wrote that the popular songs and rimes were now directed against England rather than against Germany. It was Valfrey, after his conversation with von Huhn in Paris, who was the first to make a somewhat definite suggestion. Writing as "Whist" in the *Figaro* (Jan. 14, 1899), he declared that in his opinion an alliance would outrage those who had a personal experience with the war of 1870: "but a colonial understanding between the

[80] Huhn's Memorandum, Berlin, Dec. 5, 1898. *G. P.*, XIII, 247–254. For a discussion of this incident, see Giffen, *Fashoda, pp.* 105, 106.

[81] A. Lalance, "La Nouvelle Triplice," *Grande Revue*, Dec. 1, 1898. Cf. comments in *Journal de Rouen*, Dec. 3, 1898. *Kölnische Zeitung*, Dec. 3, 1898.

[82] *Écho de Paris*, Dec. 5, 1898.

[83] *Autorité*, Dec. 10, 1898.

[84] O. S., 193, p. 1295.

belligerents of twenty-eight years ago would raise neither the same repugnance nor the same prejudices." Léon Daudet admitted that the idea of an alliance with Germany had aroused no protest in France, but in view of the probability that England would attack France if she were to seek one, he concluded that "we must wait for Germany to make a proposal." [85]

So far as the press in both countries was concerned, the discussion finally culminated in a brief exchange of articles between the *Kölnische Zeitung* and the *Figaro*. On January 28, the German newspaper considered the question of Franco-German relations at considerable length. The German press, it wrote, had shown little enthusiasm for the suggestion of an entente because of France's attitude during the past twenty-five years. Bismarck's conclusions as to the dominant influence exerted by the chauvinist minority in a crisis had been correct. Its purposes had been attained by exploiting sensational catchwords, "the man-eating Bismarck," "the Prussian clock-thieves," etc. But at present, according to the *Kölnische Zeitung*, another point of view was struggling into existence, for the French had decided that their first impressions were mistaken. The Emperor's courtesy, and even more Germany's industrial development, had contributed to this new and saner impression. Moreover, better relations with France would improve Germany's contacts with Russia, and the article concluded with a suggestion to "Whist" that he should develop his idea of an entente. Valfrey's reply, proposing that France would open certain regions such as Siam to German capital in return for support in minor questions pertaining to Egypt,[86] was certainly not too ambitious, but before his article could have reached Cologne or Berlin, the *Kölnische Zeitung* announced the *"Schlusse der Debatte."* Although the project had been received in Germany with reserve from the first, the French press, it declared, was now representing it as more necessary to Germany than to France and as if Germany were disposed to change or moderate the self-evident conditions for such a *rapprochement*. "Scarcely had a few newspapers expressed themselves as in favor of the renunciation of Alsace-Lorraine when they immediately changed their position by proposing an exchange of a colony for the lost provinces. Ink has flowed uselessly, all the press discussion has been in vain; we are at least richer by one more lesson and we can conveniently close the discussion

[85] *Gaulois*, Jan. 17.
[86] *Figaro*, Feb. 4.

of the Franco-German *rapprochement* until further notice." There could be no discussion of an exchange or sale, France must renounce Alsace-Lorraine. However, in Valfrey's opinion, the explanation of this sudden change of attitude was to be found in the statement in an important morning newspaper (the *Matin?*) that the discussion had been started by Germany. This, he thought, had offended the Kaiser.[87] In any event, England's position added to the underlying difficulties of an understanding by assuring her open hostility to that country which assumed the responsibility for the formation of an unfriendly combination.[88] It may be noted that Chamberlain chose the first days after the French government had ordered Marchand's withdrawal to renew his proposal of an alliance with Germany.[89]

It was, of course, the bitter resentment aroused by England's policy during the Fashoda crisis which had persuaded those who had been among the most active chauvinists to flirt with the idea of an accord with Germany. The idea had originated with the *Autorité,* the *Écho de Paris,* the *Gaulois,* and the *Liberté.* If the same resentment had been as deeply felt by the groups which either already had or were about to entrench themselves in power, something definite might have been accomplished.[90] Valfrey, in fact, was one of the few more moderate leaders of public opinion who favored an arrangement against England. The moderate press, for the most part, maintained complete silence. In view of its reputed connection with Delcassé, the *Matin's* failure to take part in the discussion was significant. Past events had frequently found the Radicals acting with the Conservatives, but in this instance the leaders of the parties of the left had nothing good to say of an entente with Germany. Clemenceau's new journal, the *Aurore,* founded in connection with his efforts in behalf of Dreyfus, identified the project with the reactionary anti-Dreyfus party and as the result of Russia's suggestion.[91] The friends

[87] *Kölnische Zeitung,* Feb. 4. *Figaro,* Feb. 5.

[88] London newspapers, following the trend of comment in the Paris press, referred with emphasis to the impossibility of a Franco-German arrangement. *Times,* Dec. 12. Cf. *Matin,* Dec. 13. Their Berlin correspondents were careful to report such editorial opinions against France as appeared. *Times,* Nov. 11. *Daily Telegraph,* Dec. 2. *Morning Post,* Nov. 19, Dec. 8, 1898.

[89] See his speech before the Conservative Club of Manchester, *Times,* Nov. 17. Also his Wakefield speech, *Times,* Dec. 9.

[90] Erich Brandenburg, *Von Bismarck zum Weltkrieg,* 2d ed. (Berlin, 1925), p. 105.

[91] *Aurore,* Dec. 7, 18.

of democracy would rejoice, according to the *Aurore,* if the chauvinists abandoned their campaign for a war with Germany, but it believed that Cassagnac had advised the renunciation of Alsace-Lorraine merely in order to "excite hatred of England, to work for war with her, and to throw France into colonial conquests." In 1884, Francis Charmes had favored a limited coöperation with Germany, but in December, 1898, he urged an understanding with England.[92] It was not until March 2, 1899, when a discussion arose of a Continental league against England, that the *Temps* broke its silence with a firm repudiation of any policy that would imply a renunciation of the lost provinces. "France," it wrote, "has not yet reached the point of repudiating the fundamental principles of her public law by passing off to the account of profit and loss the sacrilegious mutilation which has taken from her the flesh of her flesh and the purest of her blood." The failure of the Fashoda crisis to bring France and Germany together, even in the restricted coöperation of Ferry's time, or to arouse an effective movement of public opinion for this purpose, was due in part to the character of the leaders who championed this policy. They were neither sufficiently numerous, nor did they have sufficient influence with the directing classes or with the masses to manage a successful campaign.[93]

It was soon evident that the tide had turned. On January 16, Delcassé informed Monson that he would place himself at Salisbury's disposal for the discussion of any question which he might wish to consider.[94] The same point of view was clearly implicit in the debate, January 23, upon the Fashoda Affair. Delcassé affirmed in a long exposition of his policy that every question separating France and England could be settled amicably. Other speakers, who were not under the restraining influences of the Minister of Foreign Affairs, condemned the idea of an entente with Germany. Even the pacifist d'Estournelles de Constant believed it "full of risk and danger," while Denys Cochin, a leader of the Monarchists, preferred an entente

---

[92] *Rev. des Deux Mondes,* 1898, VI, 953.

[93] The *Kölnische Zeitung* (Dec. 13, 1898) suspected that France did not know her own mind. But Germany's insistence through her press (*Kölnische Zeitung,* Dec. 3, 9; *Berliner Tageblatt,* Dec. 11) that a definite renunciation of Alsace-Lorraine would be an essential condition to an understanding was an insuperable obstacle. It is clear, however, that these statements were made after the idea of an exchange of a colony for the two provinces had been suggested in the French press. On December 21, the Kaiser assured Lascelles, the British ambassador, that France would not receive aid from any other Power in the event of an Anglo-French War. *Brit. War Docs.,* I, 103.

[94] Monson to Salisbury, Paris, Jan. 16, 1899. *Brit. War Docs.,* I, 199.

with England to one with Germany. "It was possible for a moment to ask oneself," said another Monarchist, "if France's Continental policy might accompany her colonial policy. To-day that question is not involved. Time has disposed of it." [95] Valfrey, who had been the most practical of the advocates of a new orientation of French policy, characterized the Anglo-French accord of March, 1899, which defined the claims of the two Powers in the Upper Nile, as unexpectedly generous. [96] "Do not speak any more of the past: a new future is opening for England and France . . . Everything points to the resumption of the friendly relations of other times between the two countries." The anti-English agitation was continued by a few of the nationalist newspapers, [97] but the choice of moderate public opinion had been made in favor of friendship with England. [98] Neither the influence of Russia nor England's high-handed treatment of her aspirations in the Upper Nile had succeeded in bringing about a *rapprochement* between France and Germany.

[95] *Annales,* 1899, I, 132–150.
[96] *Figaro,* March 23, 1899.
[97] See the comments in regard to the Anglo-French accord in the *Écho de Paris,* March 24. *Libre Parole,* March 23, 1899.
[98] *Journal des Débats,* Jan. 25, Feb. 21, 1899.

CHAPTER IX

THE PARTING OF THE WAYS, 1899–1904

En ce moment, le mode est à la.paix dans un certain monde. Avec leur vivacité héréditaire, des Français se sont jetés sur le nouveau refrain et ils vous le chantent.

Écho de Paris, August 2, 1903.

Nous ne voulons pas qu'on puisse croire au dehors que la France renonce à son devoir et prononce elle-même la déchéance de ses légitimes révendications. Nous ne voulons pas leurer de faux espoirs notre jeunesse de demain et amollir les courages auxquels, à une heure quelconque, nous pourrons avoir à faire appel.

Georges Leygues, *Annales de la Chambre des Députés,* Nov. 23, 1903.

It was not an outburst of *revanche* sentiment as in 1884 that prevented a Franco-German entente after the Fashoda crisis. The possibility of making terms with Germany had been chiefly considered by those who had always preached hatred against her. They could not, however, bring themselves to accept the sacrifice of their attachment to the lost provinces, and Germany, insisting that the hope of recovering them must be renounced, closed the discussion when an exchange of Alsace-Lorraine for a French colony was suggested. Nevertheless, it seemed possible at the close of the nineteenth and at the beginning of the twentieth century that the relations between the French and German peoples might become more tolerable and that suspicion of Germany's intentions might become a less potent factor in the development of public opinion in France. Independent of any specific event, a more reasonable point of view was expressed from time to time by those who did not feel themselves, either because of their official status or their position in the public eye, to be the interpreters of French traditions. This evidence does not prove the existence of a well-defined and effective current of opinion, but it does indicate the possibility of such a movement if effective leadership had been available.

The Russian alliance had created a welcome feeling of security; it had increased France's influence in foreign affairs without permanently encouraging the advocates of the *revanche.* On the contrary, it was generally understood that Russia desired better relations between

France and Germany. The Tsar's call for a conference in August, 1898, without consulting France,[1] for the discussion of disarmament was interpreted as another proof of her slight consideration for France's interests. The reaction of the most important newspapers showed at once that the press could not be expected to furnish the necessary leadership for the mostly inarticulate elements which insensibly were developing a saner point of view in regard to France's relations with Germany. As one of the Powers who were not satisfied with the *status quo,* France, it was said, could not accept a limitation of armaments based upon the relative strength of existing armies. Even the moderate *Temps* (Aug. 30) declared that France could not endorse the Tsar's aims "until her existence had been safeguarded and the reparation of the past and the *redressement* of the future had been assured." France, it was conceded, would have to participate in order to avoid the charge of being responsible for the failure of the conference, but this concession was grudgingly made with the understanding that Alsace-Lorraine should not be mentioned.[2]

Allusions to the *plaie saignant,* to the *blessure toujours douloureuse* continued to appear in the press and in the speeches of politicians in search of office. The *revanche* was still the theme of café and vaudeville entertainers. Nevertheless, the old appeal was not as effective as it had been. An engineer, who wrote frequently upon technical questions, expressed an extremely low opinion of those who were influenced by it.

> "The theme has not changed for twenty-five years," he declared, "it is the same ridiculous phrases. It is always a question of retaking Alsace-Lorraine. . . . These platitudes are effective with us, with fools, that is to say. For them, an evening *au concert* without a *revanche* air is not a pleasant evening. One drinks a beer, smokes a cigar, and while the bass-drum and the trombone rage, one has the illusion of entering Berlin as a conqueror. . . . The people who spend their time in these sterile manifestations make us ridiculous." [3]

In practice, it was possible for the two peoples to have contacts without outraging patriotic sentiment, as had happened as recently as 1891. In 1895 and again in 1899 French artists exhibited paintings in Berlin without exciting much comment in the Paris press. "What

---

[1] *Aurore,* Aug. 30. *Temps,* Aug. 31. *Autorité,* Sept. 1.

[2] *Temps,* Aug. 31, Sept. 3.

[3] Léon Laffitte, *Une Opinion sur la Question Alsace d'Alsace-Lorraine* . . . (Paris, 1897), p. 51.

seemed abominable in 1891," wrote a contemporary, "seemed entirely natural in 1899." [4] The *Journal des Débats* (March 10, 1895) admitted that a more accurate understanding of Germany was displacing the biased opinions which had been current for twenty years. Germans visited the Paris Exposition of 1900 in numbers that were said to have exceeded those of any other nation, while the German building, "half castle and half beer-garden," with its exhibition of French paintings from Potsdam, is said to have overshadowed the unimpressive structure that England had built.[5] Chauvinists sometimes regarded public opinion with alarm. "The moment that one dares to speak of the lost provinces," one complained, "you are regarded with as much anger as astonishment. What does this troublemaker want, is the cry." [6] As late as May 24, 1908, the *Patrie*, the organ of the Ligue des Patriotes, confessed that "the dismemberment is an event as distant as the Seven Years' War for the new generations." Theodor Wolff, whose service as the Paris correspondent of the *Berliner Tageblatt* covered the period of this chapter, is convinced that the attitude of the French public contained a promise of better relations. No one would tolerate the thought of renunciation among the republican circles to which he was admitted, but he was able to form not only courteous but warm social relationships.[7]

Serious efforts were sometimes made to study public opinion in the two countries as to the issues which divided them. The *Figaro* (March 5, 1892) printed several letters from leading politicians and men of letters in Germany presenting their opinions. They were unanimous in insisting that there could be no question of the return of Alsace-Lorraine, but they also agreed in affirming Germany's desire for peace. Ernest Lavisse agreed, for in his opinion nothing could have prevented the defeat of France if Germany had desired war.[8] Auguste Lalance discovered from an examination of editorial opinion in seventy-three French newspapers upon these letters that

---

[4] Routier, *Un Point d'Histoire Contemporaine*, p. 163. In 1894, Routier had been greatly incensed by the Empress Frederick's visit. Routier, *Guillaume II à Londres*, pp. 146, 147.

[5] Wolff, *Das Vorspiel*, I, 13, 14. Cf. *G. P.*, XVII (2), pp. 767–769. Pierre de Coubertin later referred to Germany as "the queen of the Exposition." *Figaro*, April 21, 1905.

[6] Jules Gleize, "La France peut-elle avoir Deux Politiques," *Nouvelle Revue*, N. S., Vol. 22, p. 57.

[7] Wolff, *Das Vorspiel*, I, 114, 115. Léon Daudet complained that the German soldiers who appeared in Adam Beyerlein's [a German dramatist] play, *La Retraite*, had aroused no indignation. *Gaulois*, Feb. 20. 1905.

[8] *Figaro*, March 14, 1892.

only nineteen "considered that the Alsace-Lorraine Question could not be settled except by war." [9] Three years later, the *Mercure de France,* an organ of the younger generation of writers, published the results of a questionnaire addressed to men of letters in France as to the value of intellectual and social relations between the two countries. Charles Gide, then on the faculty of the University of Montpellier, suggested an exchange of students as a supplement for the inadequate instruction of the German language in the lycées. [10] The famous chemist and former Minister of Foreign Affairs, Marcellin Berthelot, was in favor of the suggestion, but in view of his association with government circles it is significant that he was more concerned that Germany should cease to claim an intellectual supremacy and that she should permit the people of Alsace-Lorraine to hold a plebiscite. [11] The press maintained an almost complete silence in regard to this enterprise. Only the chauvinist *Intransigeant* (March 23, 1895) mentioned it, and then in a spirit of bitter protest. From every point of view, it declared, France was superior to Germany; she therefore had nothing to gain and much to lose by such relationships. [12]

In December, 1897, the *Mercure de France* gave its readers more than 130 replies to an inquiry as to public opinion in regard to the *revanche.* They showed, according to the German ambassador, the opposition between the older generation, which continued to hope for revenge, and the youth for whom the Treaty of Frankfort had become an historical event. [13] While this was true, Münster failed to see the more subtle differences between those who claimed to speak in the name of French traditions and those who spoke only for themselves. The first group included members of the Chamber of Deputies, notably Joseph Reinach, the academicians Jules Claretie and Henry Houssaye (the historian of Napoleon), the historian Vandel, and the composer Saint-Saëns. The deputy Henry Maret's reaction was that of a disillusioned nationalist. "At the present moment," he complained, "I no longer believe in anything or anyone. There is feebleness everywhere. Cowardice is universal. A government, whose pusillanimity equals its imbecility, is obeyed by a soft nation. No-

[9] X (A. Lalance), *La France veut-elle la Guerre avec l'Allemagne?* p. 13.

[10] *Mercure de France,* XIV, 19, 20 (March, 1895).

[11] *Ibid.,* XIV, 8, 9.

[12] The republican deputy, Édouard Lockroy, was profoundly impressed and considerably alarmed by the evidence of Germany's progress during a visit to Germany. *Temps,* Sept. 9, 1900.

[13] Münster to Hohenlohe, Paris, Dec. 10, 1897. *G. P.,* XIII, 108, 109.

where is there a trace of passion. This therefore is my answer: for the immense majority Alsace-Lorraine is a source of embarassment."[14] The point of view expressed by Reinach agreed with that which was always maintained by the moderate press and by politicians. France, he wrote, would remain mutilated in body and spirit until the recovery of the last provinces; nevertheless, "the average opinion of the country is what it always has been, everywhere, at all times, hostile to war."[15] But Henry Houssaye, of the Académie, believed that the recovery of Alsace-Lorraine would not be entirely satisfactory to veterans of 1870, that it would not efface the memory of the "greatest military collapse recorded by history."[16]

One of the few women consulted by the *Mercure*, Mme. Jane de la Vaudière, replied that "a war would find *la jeunesse* disillusioned or skeptical."[17] The *fin de siècle* mood, which has attracted much attention from the psychologists who have written upon these questions, permeated the opinions of the younger correspondents of the *Mercure*. One observed that the war of 1870 and its results were too distant to merit the concern of those who were then attaining their majority. "These things do not interest me," he concluded.[18] Another, twenty-four years of age, flippantly remarked that it was the first time he had heard of the Treaty of Frankfort. "I do not think that this question interests the youth of to-day or the country, nor does it interest me . . ."[19] The novelists, Paul and Victor Marguerite, sons of a general who had been killed at the head of a cavalry charge during the Franco-Prussian War, had received too many letters in protest against the realistic picture they had drawn of France in 1870 in the *Désastre* to believe that a permanent peace was possible until the last survivors of the war had died.[20] This youthful cynicism was something of a pose, yet it was also something more. The old values were being examined in a critical spirit, and some were reaching the conclusion that new values were in order. One observer, of Alsatian birth, who hoped for the reunion of his native province with France, confessed that the question was kept alive by a small minority.

[14] *Mercure de France*, XXIV, 655, 656.
[15] *Ibid.*, XXIV, 654, 655.
[16] *Ibid.*, XXIV, 742.
[17] *Ibid.*, XXIV, 743.
[18] *Ibid.*, XXIV, 652.
[19] *Ibid.*, XXIV, 653.
[20] *Ibid.*, XXIV, 634.

"The general public gives less and less attention to Alsace-Lorraine, and then vaguely, on special occasions such as Christmas or July 14, when the press solicits its interest. . . . It must not be forgotten, however, that the Alsace-Lorraine question preoccupies the superior minds, the historians, thinkers, politicians: they are few in number, but it is the *élite.*" [21]

The solicitude with which events in Alsace had been watched and conditions there had been studied during the first years after 1871 was followed by a régime of almost complete silence. The Ligue des Patriotes had then attempted, without great success, to revive the passionate desire of revenge with which the Treaty of Frankfort had been received. More moderate leaders of public opinion, like Ernest Lavisse in 1891, urged the resumption of the discussion, not in order to stimulate the passion of revenge, but to convince Europe that France's claims were based upon principle rather than hatred.[22] It was Fernand de Dartein, an Alsatian who wrote under the pseudonym of Jean Heimweh, who urged most strongly the need of reopening the question. In view of the current discussion in England, Spain, Italy, and even by the Austrian and German socialists, and in order to show the Alsatian people that they were not forgotten,[23] he urged the use of every instrument of propaganda for this purpose.[24] There was no real response, however, to his plea for systematic propaganda, in the daily press, because the theory of an imprescriptible right encouraged silence. Even the liberals did not think it necessary to keep in touch with the development of public opinion in Alsace. They were not prepared to admit that the improbable acceptance of German rule would affect France's right, for it was founded once and for all upon the violence done to the principle of the self-determination of peoples in 1871.[25] The press, therefore, did not usually inform public opinion in France as to the progress of the autonomist movement in Alsace. In 1887, for the last time Alsace elected a solid group of protesting candidates under the influence of a rumor that France under Boulanger was going to attempt the reconquest of the lost provinces. Then followed Boulanger's repudiation by the government, the dissolution of the Ligue

[21] Y, "En Alsace-Lorraine," *Revue Bleue,* 4th series, XII, 833.

[22] Ernest Lavisse, *La Question d'Alsace dans une Ame d'Alsacien* (Paris, 1891), p. 3. This is a reprint from the *Revue de Famille.*

[23] Jean Heimweh, *Pensons-y et parlons-en* (Paris), pp. 4, 5.

[24] *Ibid.,* p. 13.

[25] Such, for example, was Clemenceau's point of view. "I take my position," he wrote, "upon the first violation of right . . . Neither Jaurès nor I can change it." *Aurore,* July 10, 1905.

des Patriotes, events which proved that France had no intention of precipitating a war. Alsatian opinion thenceforth gave its support to those who were seeking to protect local institutions and interests by securing the status of a member State in the German Empire.[26] The few newspapers that occasionally referred to this movement represented it as another form of the old protest and as in no sense implying a weakened attachment to France.

The Alsace-Lorraine question was discussed in rather numerous pamphlets, which, in almost every instance, favored a peaceful solution. Not a few recognized that even a successful war would not be a permanent settlement, for Germany would then, in her turn, prepare for a revenge.[27] Alsace, it was said, was intended by geography and history to serve as a bridge over which the best in the two civilizations might be exchanged. *"L'Alsace allemande est un mur: L'Alsace française était un pont."* [28] Definite solutions were suggested. In 1893, Édouard Waldteuffel, a journalist of Alsatian origins, proposed the purchase of the two provinces, but even Bebel, the German socialist leader, replied that his party could not endanger its standing by supporting this project.[29] The exchange of a French colony, Tonkin or Madagascar, was a favorite theme of the pamphleteers.[30] Much was written of a neutralized Alsace-Lorraine, either alone or in union with Switzerland or Holland.[31] Those in France who thought of the ques-

[26] Very few in 1902, writes the best historian of Alsace, were hopeful of a return to France either by peaceful means or by war. A. Reuss, *Histoire d'Alsace*, 14th ed. (Paris, 1918), p. 430. Cf. X, "La Question d'Alsace-Lorraine," *Revue Bleue*, 4th series, XII, 65–69. The traditional view of Alsatian sentiment, however, was endorsed by one whose doubts had been aroused by the socialist campaign. René Martial, *Enquête en Alsace-Lorraine* (Paris, 1905), p. 3.

[27] X. (A. Lalance), *La France veut-elle la Guerre avec Allemagne?* p. 8. (Anonymous), *L'Alsace-Lorraine et la Paix Européenne* (Niort, 1905), p. 10. René Viviani in the *Petit Provençal* (Marseilles), Feb. 22, 1905.

[28] *Europe Nouvelle,* June, 1908. This little-read weekly was a pacifist publication.

[29] E. Waldteuffel, *Mémoire pour la Rétrocession de l'Alsace-Lorraine adressé à S. M. l'Empereur et Roi Guillaume II* (Paris, 1893), pp. 3–6. Lalance, however, found numerous protests in the press that the plan was incompatible with the nation's military honor. Lalance, *La France veut-elle la Guerre*, pp. 20, 21. For a similar project, see H. Marini, *Le Question d'Alsace-Lorraine Résolue* (Paris, 1897), p. 21.

[30] Henry Denbourg, *L'Alsace-Lorraine et Madagascar* (Paris, 1896), p. 5. Lalance, *La France veut-elle la Guerre,* p. 23.

[31] E. Bricard de Card, "L'Alsace et la Lorraine et le Projet de Neutralization," *Rev. Pol. et Parl.,* 1895, IV, 38–54. J. Heimweh, *L'Alsace-Lorraine et la Paix* (Paris, 1894), pp. 75, 76. Cf. the letter from Bishop Freppel to Emilio Castilar, *Revue Catholique des Institutions et du Droit,* 1888, p. 288.

tion as a moral issue were not prepared to accept a compromise, but the prospects seemed brighter for a favorable reaction to the suggestion of a plebiscite.[32] It was often said, of course, that the question must be settled in accordance with the desires of the Alsatians, yet it was generally assumed that their wishes had been expressed for all time in 1871. Conservatives were not in favor of even the principle involved. For them, the question was essentially one of territory. In 1895, a certain number of distinguished men had endorsed the idea of a plebiscite, but the Monarchist *Gazette de France* (April 2) protested against the "principle that a citizen of a State belongs only to the nation of his choice, that he has no duties except toward his favorite people. It is the extreme negation of obligatory patriotism." The *Écho de Paris* (Sept. 14, 1898) doubtless expressed the opinion of a larger group in rejecting a plebiscite on the ground that its result would be determined by the authority which controlled the urns. Because no important party or group in France, except the Socialists, participated in it, the discussion of means by which it might be solved peacefully was of limited significance. Heimweh's pamphlets were highly esteemed, because he held that no other solution than the unconditional return of the two provinces was practicable.[33] Concern for France's security, endangered by the presence of German troops within twelve days' march of Paris,[34] also discouraged the consideration of any solution short of the recovery of Alsace-Lorraine. In any event, Germany did not intend to abandon her conquests for a money payment or for a French colony, or to sanction a plebiscite.[35] The significance of these pamphlets is not in the practical value of the

[32] *L'Alliance Franco-Allemand,* par un Alsacien (Lalance), p. 5. Maurice Charnay, *L'Alsace–Lorraine Vingt Ans Après* (Paris, 1892), pp. 26–28. Gaston Moch, *Alsace-Lorraine. Réponse à un Pamphlet Allemand* (Paris, 1895). This was a reply to Franz Wirth, "L'Alsace-Lorraine" in the *Revue Libérale Internationale.*

[33] J. Heimweh, *Allemagne, France, Alsace-Lorraine* (Paris, 1899), p. 29. Heimweh, *L'Alsace et la Dépêche d'Ems* (Paris, 1894). Heimweh, *Triple Alliance et Alsace-Lorraine* (Paris, 1892). Heimweh, *L'Alsace-Lorraine et la Paix* (Paris, 1894). Heimweh, *La Question d'Alsace* (Paris, 1889). In 1895, he found that a large majority of Parisian and provincial newspapers approved his scheme for the demilitarization of Alsace and Lorraine after their return to France. Heimweh, *Lösung der Elsassisch—Lothringischen Frage. Antwort auf die Schrift des F. Wirth* (Basel, 1895).

[34] Stoffel, *De la Possibilité d'une Future Alliance Franco-Allemande.*

[35] Otto Arendt, *Ein Deutsch-Französisches Bündniss?* (Berlin, 1892). Heinrich Molenaar, however, organized a Franco-German committee in Munich, 1903, whose platform included the return of Metz and French-speaking Lorraine to France. See Molenaar's letter to Professor A. Aulard, *Dépêche* (Toulouse), April 5, 1904. Adolphe Aderer, *Vers la Fin d'une Haine* (Paris, 1907),

suggestions which they contained but in the point of view of their authors.

The balance of political power in France turned definitely to the left during the Dreyfus Affair. The differences between the Republican groups, which had weakened them since 1881, were arranged in view of the efforts of the Monarchists and clericals to exploit the Dreyfus Affair. With the Waldeck-Rousseau cabinet of 1899, the liberal thesis in France's political and social problems received the endorsement of public opinion. Although Millerand was expelled from the party after his acceptance of a place in the ministry, the Socialists gave their support to the anti-clerical program of the Republican *bloc*. Unfortunately, these changes were of little significance in regard to questions of foreign affairs, and especially as to relations with Germany; [36] otherwise, the question of leadership for the scattered elements which were tentatively weighing the traditional ideals of French nationalism would have been solved. Old traditions in domestic problems were broken, and it seemed that the leaders who blazed new trails in this respect, might also break with the past in foreign affairs. Something, in fact, was accomplished. Since the Dreyfus Affair had revealed the extent of the Monarchist and clerical influences in the army, militarism was attacked, and in 1905 the period of service was reduced from three to two years.[37] More clearly than before, the army was regarded as serving defensive purposes, since more reliance was placed upon the reserves than upon the first-line troops.

A new nationalist movement was dealt with courageously and defeated. In opposition to the humanitarian Ligue des Droits de l'Homme, which united a large number of intellectuals in defense of Dreyfus, appeared militant nationalist societies. Chief among them was the Ligue de la Patrie Française, which at once enrolled an imposing list of members. The names of twenty-three members of the Académie Française [38] among others were proudly cited as evidence that the intellectual élite was not entirely won over to the cause of the liberal Republic. The new Ligue existed, according to Article 3

[36] A nation could not be guilty of a greater folly, wrote the *Journal des Débats,* May 2, 1904, than "to make the principles of its domestic policy those of its foreign policy. . . .Abroad, there is only the interest of State."

[37] Urbain Gohier was one of the most active anti-militarist propagandists. See his *L'Armée contre la Nation* (Paris, 1898) ; *L'Armée Nouvelle* (Paris, 1897) ; *A Bas la Caserne* (Paris, 1902).

[38] They included the historian Albert Sorel and Ferdinand Brunétière, the critic and editor of the *Rev. des Deux Mondes.*

of its statutes, "to maintain and strengthen the love of country and respect for the French army, to enlighten opinion in regard to the great interests of the country and to watch and combat foreign interference." [39] There is no better indication of its ideals than a statement by Maurice Barrès, who had developed from intellectual anarchism to philosophic nationalism. While in his novels he was coöperating with René Bazin in establishing the impression of a sorrowful Alsace,[40] he preached the need to Frenchmen of an absolute national unity and discipline. "Our nation is disrupted and unbalanced," he wrote, "that is to say it does not coördinate its strength and it lacks direction. Happy are those nations whose every movement, whose every effort are in accord as if a plan had been made by one superior mind!" [41] Moderate Republicans, Monarchists, the advocates of a dictatorship were all welcome if they agreed upon the essential tenets of nationalism, and if they opposed the radical tendencies of the times. In Dreyfus, these men did not see a victim of criminal officials, but a danger to the fundamental institutions of the country, just as the liberals saw in him a symbol of their cause. There was no doubt as to the potential strength of this movement. It was able to make use of all the catchwords that in the past had stirred the nation. A zealous ally was found in Déroulède, who left his retirement to reorganize the Ligue des Patriotes in September, 1898, and to resume his career as a popular agitator.[42] In May, 1900, the nationalists gained control of the municipal council of Paris,[43] but already Déroulède had been exiled for ten years after the failure of his melodramatic attempt to lead the troops parading in the funeral of President Faure against the Élysée. The control of the Paris council was soon recovered, and in the parliamentary election of 1906 the Republicans won decisive majorities.[44] The government and public opinion had again successfully

[39] Maurice Barrès, *La Terre et les Morts* (Paris, 1899). This is a lecture delivered before the Ligue de la Patrie Française, March 10, 1899.

[40] A direct investigation of conditions in Alsace sometimes convinced observers that they were not correctly represented in such novels as Bazin's *Les Oberlé*. Charles Fischer, *Essai de Psychologie Alsacienne* (Paris, 1904), p. 319.

[41] M. Barrès, *Scènes et Doctrines du Nationalisme* (Paris, 1902), pp. 65–80.

[42] *Journal des Débats,* Sept. 27, 1898. He again urged the need of revising the Organic Laws of 1875. *Patrie,* Oct. 26, 1898. The strength of the nationalist movement, wrote a critic, was due to its claim, advanced by Barrès, Brunetière, Paul Bourget and Jules Lemaître, to represent the traditions and interests of the race. Henry Bérenger, "Le Génie de la France d'après ses Origines," *La Revue et Revue des Revues,* vol. 86 pp. 2, 3 (Jan., 1901).

[43] *Temps,* May 15, 19, 1900.

[44] *Ibid.,* May 11, 1906. *Patrie,* May 11, 1906,

resisted the pressure of the extremists. In 1905, the Monarchists tacitly admitted the bankruptcy of the Ligue de la Patrie Française by organizing a separate society, the Action Française.[45]

As in the earlier test of strength with Boulanger and the Ligue des Patriotes, the resistance of the republican parties was strengthened by the knowledge that the success of the nationalist movement would mean not only the failure of their program of reforms but also, in all probability, the end of republican institutions. The issue was by no means clearly identified with a definite point of view in foreign affairs. The great majority of Republicans would doubtless have been content with quiet relations with Germany. The chief hope for the gradual acceptance of the *status quo,* as the basis of a permanent peace, was exactly in this passive attitude. Experience had shown that nothing good could result from the discussion of an understanding with Germany. Nor would it have been desirable, in the interest of international understanding, had it been accomplished either in 1884 or in 1898, for it would have been directed against England. Neither the numerous suggestions of a peaceful settlement of the Alsace-Lorraine question nor the attack upon militarism had been inspired by animosity against England, but by a desire for a more tolerable basis for international relations. It was this point of view that most needed the direction of leaders who could organize an effective movement of opinion in its behalf. Men like d'Estournelles de Constant and Frédéric Passy, the leaders in France for international conciliation, could not supply this need, for they were not closely identified with a large political group which they could enlist in support of this cause. The need was not only for leaders who already and for other reasons had an important following, but also for those who had a feeling for what was practicable.

Such leadership as was available came from the Socialists, a fact which partly explains the failure of this point of view to become a more important factor. The Socialists, it was true, formed a considerable party, but the greater their strength the more active was the opposition they aroused among the moderate middle classes. Moreover, men like Jaurès, Francis de Pressensé, and others, courageous and admirable as was their support of an unpopular thesis, were too combative. Experienced in the rough-and-tumble tactics of socialist propaganda, they sought to take the shortest road to their goal, with the result that they missed it entirely. In spite of Taine's

[45] *Ibid.,* March 13, 1905.

pronouncement in 1871 that French Socialism had been buried in the grounds of Père Lachaise for at least fifty years,[46] the parliamentary elections of 1893 returned more than forty Socialist members to the Chamber. Their leaders at once forced themselves upon the attention of parliament and of the nation.[47] Always hostile to extreme nationalism and unsympathetic toward the usual forms of patriotism, Socialism, however, did not for some years concern itself seriously with questions relating to foreign affairs. Its propaganda in parliament and in the press—its chief organ until 1904 was the *Petite République*—remained chiefly concerned with social and economic questions within France. Acceptance of the *patrie* as a unit of the ideal international society was frequently affirmed.[48] In part, this was intended as a defense against the charge that its members were "men without a country," but if their conception of the fatherland differed from that of others, their love of France was in its own way at least as real as that of the Monarchists, the nationalists or the moderate Republicans. Many Socialists, in fact, were strongly influenced by the same passions that had led the Radicals in September, 1870, to insist upon the continuation of war.[49]

In 1894, Juarès's point of view in regard to the Alsace-Lorraine question did not differ materially from that of all liberals. "We do not forget," he declared, "the deep wound which the country has received, because it was also inflicted upon the universal right of peoples." [50] He did not, of course, approve the sentiment of hatred against Germany. *"Ni haine, ni renonciation,"* [51] characterized the Socialist position at this time. Then and later, Juarès and his party remained the

---

[46] Alexandre Zévaès, *Le Socialisme en France depuis 1871* (Paris, 1908), pp. 10, 11.

[47] Georges Weill, *Histoire du Mouvement Social en France, 1852–1924* (Paris, 1924), p. 294.

[48] Declaration of the Executive Council of the Workingmen's Party, June, 1894. Zévaès, *Socialisme en France,* pp. 328–331. Cf. Annales, 1897, I, 599.

[49] Radicals were convinced that internationalism was one of France's traditions. Pierre Mielle, "Patriotisme et Internationalisme," *Revue des Revues,* XXXIII, 560.

[50] *Annales,* 1894, I, 318.

[51] Like the Radicals in 1880, the Socialists believed that the Alsace-Lorraine question would be solved by the progress of social justice. *Annales,* 1895, III, 309–312. Cf. Millerand's introduction to Dr. Anton Nyström, *L'Alsace-Lorraine* (Paris, 1903). The most serious danger of war, in Jaurès opinion, was in the contest for power implicit in middle-class philosophy. *Patriotisme et Internationalisme. Discour de Jean Jaurès* (Lille, 1895), pp. 8–16. The left wing of the Socialist party of course thought of patriotism as a luxury of the rich. Maurice Charnay, *L'Alsace-Lorraine Vingt Ans Après* (Paris, 1892).

most consistent and determined opponents of the Russian alliance, a consideration which further limited their effectiveness as the leaders of the peace movement. So far their activities in regard to foreign affairs had received little attention or had been regarded with tolerant indifference. A marked change took place in the first years of the twentieth century. Juarès had been defeated for reëlection to the chamber in 1898, but his party and his own pen as a contributor to the *Petite République* and the *Dépêche* of Toulouse continued to support the Republican bloc in its anti-clerical campaign. Socialism was becoming a more serious danger to French traditions than it had been merely as represented by a party. Textbooks continued to inculcate hatred of Germany and the fear of a new German attack, but the numerous pedagogical journals had been converted almost without exception to the ideals of internationalism.[52] Many feared that the education of youth was in dangerous hands. Moreover, the coöperation of the Socialists, while useful in the anti-clerical campaign, was most embarrassing to the right wing of the Republican bloc, and it is possible that only an excuse was needed for this alliance to be broken.

Jaurès returned to the chamber in 1902 and was selected, in recognition of his support of the Combes ministry, as one of its four vice-presidents. He was now prepared to begin the peace campaign in and out of parliament which was to last until his assassination on the eve of the World War. In a sense, he personified the vague aspirations that had been struggling for expression, but his methods unfortunately contributed to their failure. Experience should have convinced him that no good could come from a brusque attempt to force public opinion to renounce the values which for thirty years had been represented as fundamental. Nevertheless, he declared that the time had come when France must identify herself officially and definitively with the cause of peace. She must, he said, "get rid of her reticence, her hypocrisy and double meaning."[53] In September, 1902, he identified the Triple Alliance in a letter to Andrea Costa, the president of the Italian Socialist party, as the "necessary counterbalance to our chau-

[52] The following reviews were named by the *République Française* (Oct. 4, 1902) as expressing this point of view. *Revue de l'Enseignement Primaire, Volume, École Läique, Manuel Général, École Nouvelle, Bulletin des Instituteurs.* The most convenient source of information in regard to this development in the schools is in the nationalist pamphlet, Émile Bocquillon, *La Crise du Patriotisme à l'École* (Paris, 1905) (introduction by René Goblet). Gustave Hervé, the extremist leader of this movement, was sentenced to four years' imprisonment. *Humanité,* Jan. 1, 1906.

[53] *Annales,* 1902, III, 113–119.

vinism and to the Franco-Russian fantasies." Its preservation, he believed, was necessary to peace, for otherwise Russia would be tempted to achieve her ambitions in the Balkans, and France to recover Alsace-Lorraine.[54] This letter, which might have passed unnoticed five years earlier, aroused a storm of protest.[55] If the Triple Alliance was pacific, it was due, so it was asserted, to the restraining influence of the Franco-Russian alliance. Jaurès's proposal for simultaneous disarmament was likewise condemned and even entirely misrepresented. The *Temps* (Sept. 25, 1902) insisted that the reason for armaments had no relation to the Alsace-Lorraine question. Its solution "would not hasten disarmament by a single hour, nor would it remove a single motive for suspicion. . . ." And, according to the *Petit Journal* (Oct. 1, 1902), Jaurès had proposed submission to Germany and that France should immediately scrap her armaments!

An able ally for the Socialist campaign was found in Francis de Pressensé. Since 1887, he had been the foreign editor of the *Temps*. He had become a Socialist as a result of the Dreyfus Affair when he had labored in defense of that victim of injustice,[56] and after his election to the chamber in 1902 he soon became their leading technical expert and the *reporteur* of the committee upon foreign affairs. At no time did he have a liking for Germany's policy, but, like Jaurès, he was convinced that France should identify herself with a policy of international conciliation. He would not have Alsace-Lorraine renounced, but he was certain that France "should not remain hypnotized as she had been for too many years by a prospective *revanche* which no one desires and which no one has ever desired." Jaurès and the other Socialist leaders had not infrequently advised a specific renunciation of the *revanche* in the press, but never before had a deputy, and especially one who held an important parliamentary office, said as much on the floor of the chamber. The reaction to Pressensé's bold assertion demonstrated the weakness of the Socialist methods. The Paris delegation at once protested, and the president of the foreign affairs commission declared that Pressensé had only spoken for himself.[57] The Socialist orator, wrote Clemenceau, was mistaken in thinking that the people of France did not desire the *revanche*. The Socialists, affirmed the *Temps* (Nov. 25, 1903), "do

[54] *Petite République*, Sept. 23, 1902.
[55] *Figaro*, Sept. 18. *Journal des Débats*, Sept. 20, 30. *Temps*, Sept. 21. Alcide Ebray in *Rev. Pol. et Parl.*, XXXIV, 203.
[56] *Temps*, Jan. 21, 1914. André Tardieu succeeded him on the *Temps* in 1904.
[57] *Annales*, 1903, IV, 653.

not think, do not feel, nor do they desire what the rest of France thinks, feels or desires . . . nothing can be done with them." The republican groups joined with the conservatives to defeat a motion inviting the government to initiate negotiations for simultaneous disarmament.

There was much rejoicing in the press on this reply to Pressensé's repudiation of the *revanche*. It had, according to the *Journal des Débats* (Nov. 25) confounded "the insolence of the Socialists. . . . The Chamber . . . has recovered its good sense and its firmness." "For the first time in two years," wrote Gaston Calmette in the *Figaro* (Nov. 25), "the Chamber has had the courage to repudiate the internationalist and anti-militarist doctrines which form the program of M. Juarès and his friends." "Pertinax," the nationalist contributor to the *Écho de Paris* (Nov. 25), praised the chamber's decision as the first triumph of the nationalist sentiment since the Dreyfus Affair. "It satisfies the national conscience," exclaimed the chauvinist *Patrie* (Nov. 25), "the representatives of the nation have executed the *sans-patrie* with crushing contempt." Jaurès explained the vote as the result of the defection of the Radicals, or right wing, of the republican *bloc*. Disarmament had been included in the platform of this group, but Pressensé's pronouncement on the *revanche* had aroused its indignation.[58] A little later, Jaurès was himself defeated for reëlection as a vice-president of the chamber.[59] These reverses by no means discouraged the Socialists. In Parliament and in the *Humanité*, founded by Jaurès in 1904, the unequal struggle continued, but events had shown the disadvantages of this leadership for the peace movement. Its tactless procedure furnished an exceptional opportunity for the revival of the chauvinist agitation and for those who desired to purge the republican parties of their compromising association with the Socialists. In the absence of other leaders, the unorganized sentiment in favor of peace without reservations could not develop. It remained at the mercy of events over which it had no control.

In the meantime, the foreign policy of France progressed without special regard for the vague aspirations for more solid guarantees of peace. Delcassé controlled its destinies for seven years unhampered by any effective criticism. "Those who should have spoken in the Chamber," wrote an opponent, "remained silent due to their feeling of futility. As for the Senate, not a single serious debate upon

---

[58] *Petite République*, Nov. 26, 1903.
[59] André Daniel, *L'Année Politique, 1904* (Paris, 1905), p. 3 (Jan. 12, 1904).

foreign affairs for four years has been thought necessary." [60] Chiefly concerned with questions of domestic politics, for it was upon them that their influence depended, the radical Republican newspapers did not develop a distinctive point of view in foreign affairs. In August, 1899, Delcassé negotiated a significant change in the Russian alliance which had no relation whatever to public opinion. Whereas the alliance with Russia had originally been co-terminous with the life of the Triple Alliance—hence with that of the Dual Monarchy—he arranged with Russia that the alliance should exist for the maintenance of the equilibrium as well as for the preservation of peace, its original purpose. "The significance of the arrangement of 1891," he wrote to President Loubet, "has been singularly extended; while the two governments declared themselves in 1891 as only concerned with the maintenance of peace, my project implies that they are concerned quite as much with the maintenance of the equilibrium between the European forces." [61] This arrangement, which has been characterized by a reputable French historian as implying a bargain by which France gained Russia's support for her aspirations as to Alsace-Lorraine in return for aid in the Balkans,[62] had no effect upon public opinion because it was unknown until 1918.

Nevertheless, it seems clear that Delcassé, perhaps under Russian influences, was receptive to any suggestion that might come from Germany for an anti-English understanding. French public opinion, like that of almost all of the Continental Powers, was bitterly hostile to England during the Boer War. Its expression varied from the *Temps*'s (Sept. 13, 1899) comparatively mild disapproval to the wild extravagances of Paul de Cassagnac in the *Autorité,* of Lucien Millevoye in the *Patrie,* and of Mme. Adam in the *Nouvelle Revue.* The cartoons that filled the *Rire* and other humorous periodicals reflected a hatred of everything English that had never been surpassed in the moments of bitterest resentment against Germany. The nationalist André Mévil wrote after a trip through Germany, Holland, and Belgium that the universal sentiment against England should lead to dip-

[60] R. Millet, *Notre Politique Extérieure,* p. 2. "The Quai d'Orsay," wrote another critic, "resembled a mysterious house, which M. Delcassé might not leave except to pronounce oracles or to command silence in parliament." *Corresp.,* O. S., 219, p. 1236.

[61] Delcassé to Loubet, Paris, Aug. 12, 1899. *Livre Jaune: Alliance Franco-Russe,* p. 132.

[62] Michon, *L'Alliance Franco-Russe,* pp. 55–84, quoting Professor Albert Mathiez. This, of course, was an exaggerated interpretation.

lomatic action.[63] Robert de Caix, the *Journal des Débats*'s expert in foreign affairs, regretted that Germany's earlier experiences would probably discourage her.[64] During the summer of 1899, before the beginning of hostilities in South Africa, the Kaiser visited the French training ship *Iphigenia* at Bergen, two German warships put in at an Algerian port, and when the war began, Bülow spoke of the common interests in Africa between France and Germany.[65] In reply, Delcassé complained that this opinion had never led to the slightest proposition of a concrete nature from Germany since he had taken office as Minister of Foreign Affairs. Nevertheless, he believed that the idea merited examination "in concert with our ally, Russia." [66] He had forgotten, of course, the suggestion of an agreement in regard to the Portuguese colonies which he had left unanswered in 1898. Perhaps he had in mind a definite proposition in regard to Morocco, for he was turning in that direction in order to complete France's North African empire. As England was at this time making a series of agreements with Germany in regard to the Samoan Islands and a trans-African railway, and even suggesting an agreement in regard to Morocco,[67] it was manifestly wise not to reject brusquely a suggestion of a Continental league.

Delcassé therefore agreed with Russia's proposal, February 28, 1900, to invite Germany to intervene with Russia and France in the South African War. He is said, however, to have suggested that Germany should take the initiative.[68] Naturally suspecting a maneuver to embroil her with England, Germany informed that country of Russia's proposal,[69] and proceeded to kill whatever prospects there might have been for a combination of the Continental Powers by requiring a preliminary guarantee, for a long period, of existing fron-

[63] A. Mévil, "L'Europe et la Guerre Sud-Africaine," *Nouvelle Revue,* New Series, III, 126, 127. He wrote later that France's criticism of England during the Boer War had been due alone to humanitarian motives. Mévil, *De la Paix de Francfort*, p. 70.

[64] *Journal des Débats*, Oct. 27, 1899.

[65] Bourgeois, Pagès, *Origines et Résponsabilités*, pp. 278–281. The editors of the *Grosse Politik* report that the German Archives contain no evidence as to this conversation between Bülow and the French ambassador. *G. P.*, XV, 406, 407 (note).

[66] Bourgeois, Pagès, *Origines et Résponsabilités*, p. 281.

[67] Hatzfeldt to Foreign Office, London, Nov. 3, 1899. *G. P.*, XVII, 297. Negotiations leading to the *entente cordiale* did not begin until three years later. *Brit. War Docs.*, II, ch. 14.

[68] Bourgeois, Pagès, *Origines et Résponsabilités*, p. 286.

[69] Prince Edward to William, Marlborough House, March 7, 1900. *G. P.*, XV, 523.

tiers.[70] In rejecting this condition, Delcassé undoubtedly acted in accordance with the desires of the articulate leaders of moderate opinion, although not necessarily with the more intangible current of opinion. The *Temps* (March 2, 1900), for example, had no sympathy for a move which would prevent an understanding with England. When President Kruger visited France, it insisted (Nov. 20, 1900) that the sympathy with which he was received had no political significance.

During the next two years, while no definite progress had as yet been made toward an arrangement with England, Delcassé was distinctly encouraging to the unofficial agents or third persons who interested themselves in a Franco-German *rapprochement*.[71] These incidents followed the arrival of Prince Radolin in 1900 as the German ambassador. He had won, according to the *Figaro* (July 24, 1902), the good-will of Parisian society. The Minister assured Léon y Castillo, the Spanish ambassador, in June, 1901, that he desired nothing better than a discussion of specific questions, even that he was "very desirous of an entente." Again it may be suggested that Morocco was in his mind, but it is evident that he did not intend to make any advances. " 'As the representative of the defeated Power,' " he told Castelar, " 'the initiative of a discussion must come from the German Ambassador.' " It was in this haughty aloofness that Delcassé differed from even moderate opinion, as became clear in June, 1905, when the press unanimously turned against him. Radolin was urged "to strike while the iron was hot," [72] but nothing was done. In October, 1901, Jules Hansen told the German ambassador that Delcassé was anxious for a personal interview with Bülow, the new Chancellor. " 'It is difficult for me to take the first step,' " Delcassé is reported to have said, "it would be misunderstood. After all, Count Bülow is the victor, he should extend a hand to us. The first occasion, however, must be used." He disposed of the approaching conference at Brussels, which was to deal with tariff questions relating to sugar, as not sufficiently

[70] Bülow to Radolin, Berlin, March 3, 1900. *G. P.*, XV, 516, 517. Cf. F. Meinecke, *Geschichte des Deutsch-Englischen Bündnisproblems, 1898–1901*, p. 161.

[71] The silence of the recently published French diplomatic documents for the year 1901 in regard to these incidents is merely proof that they did not lead to official negotiations. *Documents Diplomatiques Français* (1871–1914), 2d series, vol. I.

[72] Radolin to Bülow, Paris, June 15, 1901. *G. P.*, XVIII (2), pp. 775, 776. Bülow's annotation of this document shows that he recognized the moderate tendencies of public opinion in France.

important to warrant the Chancellor's presence, and he suggested that Bülow might visit Paris incognito.[73] Bülow, it is interesting to note, took these suggestions seriously. He recognized the favorable development of public opinion in France, but he felt that the ground should be more carefully prepared.[74]

As in 1898, the prospects of improved relations with England may explain Germany's hesitation. Three days after Bülow's letter, an official of the British Foreign Office wrote that the German Emperor and Government were more insistent than they had been in their offers of an alliance, for "otherwise we shall be too late as they have other offers." [75] When Castelar again broached the subject in May, 1902, he found that Delcassé was perceptibly cooler after his entente with Italy, and in October the minister was even more discouraging.[76] If Holstein's understanding was correct, this change was to be explained by Germany's decision to push her interests in Morocco and to claim the protectorate of German Catholics in Palestine.[77] Henceforth, Delcassé had little to say to the German ambassador,[78] and during the negotiations with England in December, Paul Cambon openly affirmed France's desire to exclude Germany from Morocco.[79] Germany's insistence upon a definite guarantee of her western frontier, her failure voluntarily to recognize France's desires as to Mo-

---

[73] Pallain, the Governor of the Bank of France, repeated the substance of Hansen's remarks. Radolin to Bülow, Paris, Oct. 27, 1901. *G. P.*, XVIII (2), pp. 782–784. Two days later Radolin recommended the idea of an interview. *Ibid.*, XVIII (2), p. 784 (note).

[74] Bülow to Radolin, Berlin, Nov. 6, 1901. *Ibid.*, XVIII (2), p. 785 E. N. Anderson, *The First Moroccan Crisis, 1904–1906* (Chicago, 1930), pp. 41–51.

[75] Bertie's Memorandum, London, Nov. 9, 1901. *Brit. War Docs.*, II, 73.

[76] Delcassé told Radolin that in 1898 he had instructed the French ambassador in Berlin, with the approval of the ministry and of the President, to arrange an understanding upon specific questions. Radolin to Bülow, Paris, Oct. 15, 1902. *G. P.*, XVIII (2), p. 798. There is no supporting evidence for this assertion in the German documents, while it is clear that Delcassé had left unanswered Germany's suggestion of an understanding in regard to the Portuguese colonies. Holstein later prepared a memorandum for the Kaiser showing that France had rejected Germany's overtures on four different occasions. *G. P.*, XVIII (2), 802, 803 (April, 1903). E. D. Morel's hint of a possible understanding between France and Germany in 1902 during Delcassé's abortive negotiations with Spain for a partition of Morocco is not supported by the German documents. E. D. Morel, *Morocco in Diplomacy* (London, 1912), pp. 57–64.

[77] Holstein's Memorandum, Berlin, April, 1903. *G. P.*, XVIII (2), 805.

[78] He was reported as refusing to give Radolin more than a few moments of his time after December, 1902. Klehmet's Memorandum, Berlin, April 19, 1903. *G. P.*, XVIII (2), 801, 802.

[79] Landsdowne to Monson, Foreign Office, Dec. 31, 1902. *Brit. War Docs.*, II, 274, 275.

rocco, her refusal of England's offer of an understanding in the place of an alliance,[80] Delcassé's refusal to initiate direct conversations, and England's accommodating attitude toward France all contributed to the failure of a Franco-German *rapprochement*. Bülow agreed with Holstein in a watch-and-wait policy.

Not even the Socialists had any objection to Delcassé's system of diplomatic understandings in so far as they were intended to remove causes of friction. They favored a union with Italy and England as a substitute for the Russian alliance until it could be extended to all countries. The best-informed opinion held that the understanding with Italy announced in 1901 should not be interpreted as dividing the Triple Alliance. "Her presence in the Triple Alliance," wrote André Tardieu, "that is, in a combination which in itself is not a danger to the peace of Europe, loses the troublous significance it formerly had." [81] In 1902, unknown to the public, a change was made in the entente which assured Italy's neutrality even if France, under slight provocation, should be the aggressor.[82] Since 1898 there had been a great deal of bitterness against England. Popular newspapers, like the *Petit Journal* with the editorials of Ernest Judet, had fanned its flames. The moderate *Temps* and *Journal des Débats,* however, had been preparing the way for an understanding much more systematically than that part of the press which occasionally preferred an arrangement with Germany. The newspapers which were regarded as reflecting Delcassé's point of view had almost always been silent when a *rapprochement* with Germany was suggested. Nevertheless, both the *Temps* and the *Figaro* in July, 1901, indicated Morocco as furnishing Germany a specific occasion for a demonstration of her friendship.[83] Not all of the chauvinists participated in the anti-English campaign. The organ of the Ligue des Patriotes, the *Patrie,* printed the anti-English effusions of Lucien Millevoye in one column, while in another appeared articles from Déroulède in St. Sebastian in favor of an entente.[84]

The work of the friendly press in France was paralleled by propagandists and newspapers in England. The activities of Thomas Bar-

---

[80] Lansdowne to Lascelles, Foreign Office, Dec. 19, 1901. *Ibid.,* II, 82.

[81] *Nouvelle Revue,* N. S., X, 288. It was natural that the press should exult at this evidence of weakness within the Triple Alliance. *Temps,* June 19, 1902. *Journal des Débats,* July 2, 1902.

[82] Fay, *Origins of the World War,* I, 147, 148.

[83] Richthofen to Hatzfeldt, Berlin, July 5, 1901. *G. P.,* XVIII (2), p. 781.

[84] The nationalists feared that an entente with England was about to be negotiated at the expense of the Russian alliance. *Journal des Débats,* April 29, 1903.

clay, the president of the British Chamber of Commerce in Paris,[85] need only be mentioned here. They doubtless helped to overcome the atmosphere of suspicion and dislike between certain sections of the two peoples. King Edward was able to visit Paris in the summer of 1902 without any untoward results. Soon President Loubet and Delcassé were in London, and presently the negotiations were under way which led to the *entente cordiale*. Its conclusion was due chiefly to England's recognition of France's supremacy in Morocco. The terms, as published in April, 1904, provided for this, with the understanding that France withdrew her claim that England should set a date for the evacuation of Egypt, while secret provisions envisaged a future partition of Morocco between France and Spain. Although England's economic and strategic interests in Morocco were safeguarded, she had sacrificed more than France. Her commerce was superior to that of any other Power in Morocco, and earlier she had affirmed that she would never permit the establishment of the exclusive influence of one country.[86] Since Fashoda, few in France had any illusions as to the possibility of forcing a settlement of the Egyptian question in accordance with her interests. The reaction in France to the settlement in general was therefore favorable. Details were criticized, and some like Judet never abandoned their hostility to England, but her friendship was welcomed alike by chauvinists and by those who were eager for a permanent peace.

"Never was there an idea . . . ," wrote Barclay, "of a joining of forces against another Power. The *rapprochement* had the exclusive object of counteracting hostile tendencies between Great Britain and France." [87] Public opinion in France was informed to this effect by the newspapers which spoke with the greatest authority. The *Journal des Débats* (May 11, 1904) mentioned the new relations with Italy and England as merely additional assurances of peace. If, instead of acknowledging the peaceful character of the *entente cordiale,* Bülow had condemned it, observed the *Temps* (April 16), it would have been a confession of hostile intentions against France. But it was quite futile to pretend that the understanding was limited to the specific

---

[85] He had secured Delcassé's approval before arranging the meeting of the British Chambers of Commerce in Paris during the exposition of 1900. Sir Thomas Barclay, *Thirty Years. Anglo-French Reminiscences, 1876–1906* (Boston, 1914), p. 214.

[86] Memorandum for Kaïd Sir H. Maclean, Foreign Office, Oct. 24, 1902. *Brit. War Docs.,* II, 272, 273.

[87] Barclay, *Thirty Years,* p. 214.

settlement of colonial questions. Men like Déroulède and Clemenceau had long favored a policy of friendship with England in order to strengthen France. Whether it would be dangerous to Germany depended upon her understanding of its implications. Bülow told the Reichstag there was no reason for alarm, but a year earlier, in April, 1903, he had defined his attitude more closely. "Delcassé's coquetry with England," he wrote to the Foreign Office, "would become serious for us if the Foreign Minister succeeded in bringing about a *rapprochement* between England and Russia." [88] It was evident in the reaction to the entente in France that the moderate and conservative leaders hoped that Russia would be added. Étienne, who was the reporter of the commission in the chamber to which the entente had been referred, believed that it would not be limited in its results to its specific stipulations, and he hoped "that our country will one day be persuasive and perhaps strong enough to bring about an entente between England and Russia." [89] Jaurès, of course, condemned this suggestion,[90] but the Monarchist Delafosse thought that nothing divided them. "If this Triple Alliance could be realized, it would give its members the *empire du monde.*" [91] The defeat of Bismarck's diplomacy, wrote the *République Française* (May 13, 1904), would not be finally assured until England and Russia had composed their differences in Asia. "It is in this direction that we must work, without haste, but without interruption." The *Figaro* (April 15) endorsed this policy, and the *Temps* (Dec. 8, 14) recommended it in the interest of peace. It was quite obvious to well-informed observers that the *entente cordiale* meant the diplomatic coöperation of France and England in the future. The *Journal des Débats* (April 10) spoke of it as the beginning of a new era in international relations, and the *Temps* (May 9), still insisting upon the pacific character of the new ties France had formed, described them as "a turning-point in continental history."

Germany's refusal to reopen the Alsace-Lorraine question made it impossible for the peace movement in France to secure the services of leaders who could gain the confidence of the nation. By 1904, the Socialists had clearly failed. They had played into the hands of the extremists by attempting to force a definite and official stand for peace upon the basis of the *status quo*. The failure to find satis-

[88] Bülow to Foreign Office, Sorrento, April 3, 1903. *G. P.,* XVIII, (2) 839.
[89] *Annales,* 1904, V, 351.
[90] *Ibid.,* 1904, V, 398.
[91] *Ibid.,* 1904, V, 339.

factory leadership would not in itself have been fatal without the succession of international crises which began in 1905. They were prepared by Delcassé who, without the restraining influences of an organized public opinion, introduced significant changes in the Russian alliance and established new diplomatic understandings with Italy and England which were at least potentially directed against Germany. These diplomatic arrangements, in so far as they were published, were of course represented as assuring peace. They were valued most highly for their usefulness in the struggle for security and prestige, but in general public opinion did not attribute to them a definitely anti-German significance until Germany's policy in Morocco was interpreted as an attempt to destroy them.

CHAPTER X

Morocco and the Balance of Power, 1905–1908

L'immense majorité de la nation n'avait vu dans l'accord avec l'Angleterre qu'un accord liquidant des questions coloniales et n'impliquant aucun effet fâcheux pour les relations franco-allemandes. Cette conception auraient certainement persisté et se serait trouvée consolidée d'une manière définitive, si la diplomatie allemande s'était prêtée à un réglement de la question marocaine après la crise de mai-juin 1905 . . . il fallait se résigner à subir son hostilité systematique ou accepter de marcher complètement a sa remorque.

Journal des Débats, January 27, 1908.

Comparatively little interest was shown in regard to Morocco before the end of the nineteenth century,[1] for the new development of the colonial propaganda had emphasized other parts of Africa. Since its appearance in 1891, the *Bulletin de l'Afrique Française,* the official organ of the colonial group, had scarcely mentioned Morocco. The campaign to arouse interest in that direction accompanied, if it was not inspired by, Delcassé's Moroccan policy. At first, it had to contend with the determined resistance of the nationalist press, of Clemenceau's group,[2] and of the Socialists, as well as of such moderate newspapers as the *République Française* and the *Siècle.* "The most serious resistance to our policy in Morocco," wrote the *Bulletin* (Aug., 1903), "would undoubtedly come from public opinion in France." [3]

To satisfy opinion at home and to quiet suspicions abroad, assurances were given in the press and parliament that the government would respect all of its engagements and that it would only act in cooperation with the Powers having a legitimate interest in Morocco. France, it was said, would be satisfied if no other Power established its political influence there.[4] These assertions were of doubtful sincerity if they were intended to express Delcassé's purposes, but they did not more correctly reflect the real views of propagandists. The foreign minister was clearly determined sooner or later to add

[1] *Journal des Débats,* Jan. 25, 1899.
[2] *Aurore,* June 29, 1904.
[3] *Bulletin du Comité de l'Afrique Française,* Aug., 1903, p. 261. In November, it still urged the need of arousing public opinion. *Ibid.,* Nov., 1903, p. 333.
[4] *Rev. des Deux Mondes,* 1901, III, 954, 955.

Morocco to France's North African empire. Publicists almost always identified this result as a national interest, although they usually repudiated the use of force. Repeated violations of the Algerian frontier gave plausibility to the argument that French control was a necessary measure of self-defense, and they inevitably suggested the need of extending to Morocco the benefits of civilization. Considerations of general policy influenced those who were most concerned for the future strength and influence of France. In one of its earliest editorials upon the Moroccan question, the *Temps* (July 9, 1901) declared that the acquisition of its resources alone would enable France to keep pace with the expansion of the great colonial Powers and more especially with Germany's rapidly increasing population.

In the absence of an offer from Germany between 1900 and 1902, Delcassé had studiously omitted her from his diplomatic arrangements with Italy, England, and Spain. Nor had the press given more serious consideration to her possible objections. It is of some interest that the most active colonial propagandists were also those who most clearly recognized the need of satisfying her. In October, 1903, Robert de Caix urged in the *Bulletin* the need of assuring the open door to her commerce.[5] "England's recent cordiality," he wrote after the publication of the Anglo-French accord, "should not cause our colonial group to forget the constant good-will with which its aspirations have been received by the German Empire."[6] Prior to the negotiation of the *entente cordiale*, it was England's opposition rather than Germany's which was feared most. Eugène Étienne, the leader of the colonial group and vice-president of the chamber, even recommended a formal and official statement, on the model of Grey's declaration of March, 1895, warning other Powers to keep out.[7] The press failed to enlighten public opinion as to Germany's probable attitude, but it was of course Delcassé who actually prepared for future trouble not only by neglecting to secure her disinterestedness but also by his failure to communicate the Anglo-French accord to her in due form.[8]

[5] *Bulletin*, Oct., 1903, p. 301.
[6] *Ibid.*, Nov., 1904, p. 333.
[7] E. Étienne, "L'Accord Franco-Italien et le Maroc," *Questions Diplomatiques et Coloniales*, vol. 13, p. 71 (Jan., 1902). He repeated, without success, this suggestion in the chamber. *Temps*, Jan. 23, 1902. *Annales*, 1902, I, 124 (June 21).
[8] The Monarchist Delafosse later remarked that no one in the chamber had thought that it should be communicated to Germany. *Annales*, 1905, II (April 19). Earl Cromer was one of the few in either France or England who anticipated that she would object. Cromer to Lansdowne, Cairo, March 14, 1904. *Brit. War Docs.*, II, 355.

Differences of opinion among Germany's leaders at first weakened her power of decision. William continued to hope for a Continental league, while Bülow and Holstein wavered between conciliatory methods and intimidation.[9] Unsuccessful efforts in 1904 to detach Russia from France and to bring about a meeting between the Emperor and President Loubet during the latter's visit to Rome persuaded William against his better judgment to use the Moroccan question as a means of reviving Germany's influence and of attacking Delcassé. Holstein and Bülow, it was evident, had elected to follow a policy of intimidation. Considerations of general policy were chiefly responsible for this decision, but the prospect that France would gradually secure complete control of Morocco by means of "peaceful penetration" was of considerable influence. William agreed to visit Tangier during his spring cruise in 1905, and by this means to serve notice of Germany's claim to be heard. Without much interest in the affair, he hesitated even at the last moment before landing on March 31.[10]

A significant division of opinion appeared in the press comments upon the Tangier incident. These in the main agreed with the divergent views which had already developed as to Delcassé's Moroccan policy. The *Matin* (March 23), generally accepted as inspired by the Quai d'Orsay, had already taken the position that William's action "changes nothing. France's policy will be the same in Morocco, and the legitimate influence which she exercises there will also continue." [11] Germany, according to the *Temps* (March 22), had no reason for complaint since she had in effect been informed as to the Anglo-French entente.[12] But the main tendencies of opinion were clearly favorable to a change of policy in order to repair Delcassé's mistakes. A communication in the official *Norddeutsche Allgemeine Zeitung* (March 21, 26) had declared that Germany's policy was exclusively concerned with her economic interests in Morocco. With this assurance that the demonstration at Tangier was not intended as an attack upon France's more fundamental interests, the critics of an active Moroccan policy main-

---

[9] R. J. Sontag, "German Foreign Policy, 1904–1906," *Amer. Hist. Rev.*, XXXIII, 280, 281.

[10] Bülow had written that a change of plans would give Delcassé a chance to claim a diplomatic victory. Bülow to William, Berlin, March 20, 1905. *G. P.*, XX (1), p. 264.

[11] See also *Matin*, April 5. *Journal des Débats*, April 2. *Temps*, April 4.

[12] Privately Tardieu confessed to Radolin his inability to understand Delcassé's failure to communicate the accord according to diplomatic usage. Radolin to Holstein, March 25, 1905. *G. P.*, XX (1), p. 266 (note). Delcassé had only spoken of it to Radolin at a dinner in reply to a direct question.

tained that negotiations should be inaugurated immediately. The Berlin correspondent of the nationalist *Liberté* (March 24) had advised an arrangement with Germany if "her conditions are acceptable." "France should negotiate with Germany," declared the chauvinist *Patrie* (March 31), "in order to secure freedom of action." The moderate *Siècle* thought that she was within her rights, while the *République Française* (April 2) urged that courteous relations should not be interrupted.[13] Nothing had happened at Tangier, according to the radical *Petit Provençal* of Marseilles (April 2), "of a disquieting or disobliging character." Clemenceau urged the immediate inauguration of negotiations. "We would be mad to persist in this *jeu de chiens de faïence.* . . . We have certain explanations to ask of Germany. Nothing simpler than to ask for them since we are certain in advance that the conversation will be most courteous and that an understanding is inevitable." The responsibility, it was said, was largely Delcassé's because he had failed to provide for Germany's probable action,[14] and this point of view, as the correspondent of the *Berliner Tageblatt* (April 1) observed, moderated the natural resentment inspired by the Kaiser's *coup de théâtre.* Public opinion was prepared to approve an initiative on the part of French diplomacy for the purpose of satisfying Germany.

Delcassé yielded to the extent of informing certain of Germany's representatives that he was prepared to consider such definite suggestions as she might wish to make. In reply to an interpellation by Jaurès on April 7, he assured the chamber that the government was "ready to clear up every misunderstanding if, in spite of its formal declarations, any still existed." [15] Bihourd, the French ambassador in Berlin,[16] was in favor of an arrangement, and Jules Hedeman, then the London correspondent of the *Matin,* undertook an unofficial mission to prepare for negotiations. He desired a friendly word to take back to Paris, and a chance remark by Hammann, the director of the press bureau of the German Foreign Office, expressing regret for the newspaper attack upon Delcassé was at once welcomed as satisfactory if it could be described as coming from Bülow. Delcassé, according to Hedeman, was willing to take the first step if he could be cer-

---

[13] Jules Méline was now its editor.

[14] Clemenceau in the *Aurore,* March 25. *Patrie,* March 30. Jaurès in the *Humanité,* March 24.

[15] *Annales,* 1905, II, 1561.

[16] Bihourd to Delcassé, Berlin, March 23, 1905. *Livre Jaune: Affaires du Maroc, 1901–1905,* Pt. I, 204.

tain that it would be favorably received.[17] A week later, the French minister spoke to Radolin with some emotion of his desire for an understanding. " 'I am ready to say to you in formal terms,' " he said, " 'that if there is any misunderstanding whatever in spite of all the declarations I have made in the Chamber and which I have always made, I am ready to dissipate it. I beg you to inform the Imperial Government to this effect.' " [18] Nevertheless, there was no indication that Delcassé was prepared to acknowledge a fault. Everything he said implied that his real intentions had been stated with complete frankness, and that if Germany had taken offense it was due to a misunderstanding.

Having maintained a policy of sphinx-like silence since the Tangier incident, Bülow had no intention of making a definite statement of Germany's wishes.[19] He believed that public opinion in France might turn against Delcassé if it had to choose between a diplomatic defeat and a Moroccan war, a choice which would be necessary if the Sultan could be persuaded to refuse the reforms which France had demanded.[20] Radolin felt that an understanding in response to Delcassé's plea would have a salutary effect upon the international situation, but, on instructions from Berlin, he gave Delcassé no satisfaction.[21] On April 19, Bülow's policy nearly succeeded, for Delcassé was then only saved from defeat in the Chamber by the intervention of Rouvier, the President of the Council. Jaurès had insisted that Germany should be asked to state the guarantees which she desired for her economic interests in Morocco, but the foreign minister evaded the question by replying that he had already stated his readiness to explain any misunderstanding. Rouvier evidently did not consider Delcassé's explanation to be entirely satisfactory, for he added that France had taken the initiative and that "we are waiting for the answer." [22]

No reply from Germany was forthcoming. She continued to seek Delcassé's elimination as the author of the objectionable diplomatic arrangements. Rouvier, it was known, believed that his foreign minister's aims were dangerous in view of the slight aid England could

---

[17] Hammann's Memorandum, April 7, 1905. *G. P.*, XX (1), pp. 310–313. Bülow noted in the margin of this document that Delcassé should have chosen a more responsible agent.

[18] Radolin to Foreign Office, Paris, April 14, 1905. *Ibid.*, XX (1), p. 239.

[19] *Ibid.*, XX (1), pp. 267, 268.

[20] Bülow to Tattenbach, Berlin, March 29, 1905. *G. P.*, XX (1), p. 280. Cf. *Ibid.*, XX (1), pp. 287, 288.

[21] Radolin to Bülow, Paris, April 14, 1905. *G. P.*, XX (1), pp. 331, 332.

[22] *Annales,* 1905, II, 1928, 1932, 1935.

give in the event of war with Germany.[23] As this division within the. French cabinet could be used to serve Germany's purposes, only an expression of general satisfaction was therefore given in reply to Rouvier's plea for an understanding and to his assertion that only a small minority desired a war of revenge.[24] It is highly improbable that Germany, as it was asserted in the famous communication to the *Gaulois* (June 17), presented a direct demand through von Donnersmarck for Delcassé's dismissal,[25] yet she left Rouvier in no doubt that an improvement in Franco-German relations was impossible while he remained in charge of France's foreign policy.[26] Rouvier was prepared to rid himself of an embarrassing colleague, but as he told Bülow's agent, he would never be forgiven if he appeared to yield to a menace from Germany.[27] A week later, on June 5, he won the approval of the cabinet and of President Loubet, in a test of strength with Delcassé, although the latter claimed that Germany was bluffing while France could count upon England's military aid.[28] The next day brought the announcement of Delcassé's resignation. Instead of arousing patriotic indignation and denunciation of Germany, this event received the virtually unanimous approval of the press.

In time, this event became associated with the War-Scare of 1875 and the Schnaebelé affair as an example of Germany's alleged brutal methods chiefly because the *Gaulois*'s (June 17) article was accepted as authentic. Delcassé's friends, although recognizing that it would be impossible for him to continue in power, naturally represented him as a martyr, but Ernest Judet in the *Éclair* (June 6), Lucien Millevoye in

[23] The British fleet, he said, could not travel on wheels. Radolin to Foreign Office, Paris, April 27, 1905. *G. P.*, XX (2), p. 345.

[24] Bülow to Radolin, Berlin, April 28, 1905. *Ibid.*, XX (2); p. 346.

[25] According to the editors of the *Grosse Politik* [XX (2), p. 390 (note)],, von Donnersmarck's name only appears in Radolin's communication of June 17 in regard to the *Gaulois*'s article. Fay, *Origins of the World War*, I, 187 (note). E. N. Anderson, *The First Moroccan Crisis, 1904–1906* (Chicago, 1930), p. 225 (note).

[26] Holstein's memorandum of a conversation with Rouvier's friend Betzold, Berlin, May 2, 1905. *Ibid.*, XX (2), p. 370. On May 30, Bülow announced to Radolin the despatch of a special agent who would warn Rouvier of the dangerous character of Delcassé's policy. *Ibid.*, XX (2), pp. 389, 390.

[27] Miquel's memorandum of conversations with Rouvier, May 30, May 31. *Ibid.*, XX (2), pp. 393–398.

[28] *The Brit. War Docs.* contain no evidence that military aid was promised. Diplomatic support was assured to France in the event Germany should demand a Moroccan port. Draft by Sir F. Bertie, Paris, April 24, 1905. *Brit. War Docs.*, II, 73, 74. Later it was agreed to exchange opinions if a danger of more general complications arose. Lansdowne to Bertie, London, May 31, 1905. *Brit. War Docs.*, II, 77.

the *Patrie* (June 10), the nationalist *Liberté* (June 7), and the Social-ist *Petite République* (June 10), all critics of his policy, denied that Germany had any connection with his fall. He had been kept in office since the Tangier affair, wrote the radical *France de Bordeaux et du Sud-Ouest* (June 7), to avoid the impression of yielding to her pres-sure, but public opinion had finally repudiated his policy of limited and exclusive understandings in regard to Morocco. Nor did the *Gaulois's* alleged revelations convince public opinion or the press at the time that his dismissal had been decided at Germany's demand.[29] There is no doubt that she had sought Delcassé's elimination, but this purpose does not entirely explain either Rouvier's decision or its ap-proval by public opinion.[30]

Like Ferry, Rouvier believed that France could best serve her in-terests by coöperation with Germany, and already in 1887 he had been instrumental in getting rid of Boulanger. As for the press, suf-ficient reasons were found for his repudiation regardless of pressure from Germany. Newspapers, whose attachment to the *revanche* was not open to question, took the position that France was not prepared to accept the war which was implied in his policy. "It was perhaps in the tradition of Richelieu," wrote the *Liberté* (June 7), "to seek Germany's isolation, but that policy requires a Richelieu and also the France of Richelieu's time: a great statesman and a nation stronger than its rival." "He would have us follow him into the unknown," de-clared Millevoye in the *Patrie* (June 10), "we had to choose between dismissing him and following him perhaps to defeat. The public con-science chose the former course." Equally firm in testifying to France's desire of peace and in his belief that a future conflict was inevitable, Clemenceau protested that Morocco should not be the occasion for war.[31] Even the *Matin* (June 7), perhaps Delcassé's most consistent ally in the press, admitted that his policy had been in advance of public opinion. While his diplomacy, it was said, was leading France into war, his colleagues, General André in the Ministry of War and Camille Pelletan in the Marine had dangerously weakened France.[32] But more

[29] It is not mentioned in A. Tardieu, *La Conférence d'Algésiras*, 2d ed. (Paris, 1908), p. 9.
[30] Nor is it to be entirely explained as the result of fear as in G. H. Stuart, *French Foreign Policy. From Fashoda to Sarajevo* (New York, 1921), p. 186.
[31] *Aurore*, June 8. Cf. *Patrie*, June 8. É. Flourens, *La France Conquise* (Paris, 1896), pp. 94, 95.
[32] *Liberté*, June 7. *République Française*, June 12. *Journal de Rouen*, June 25. Charles Maurras, *Kiel et Tanger, 1895–1905* (Paris, 1921), p. 133.

important than these disgruntled nationalists, most of whom were hostile to anything connected with the radical ministries, was that important section of public opinion, which included the Socialists but which was by no means limited to them, that had hoped for a more solid foundation of peace. The Tangier incident had suddenly awakened it to a realization of the dangerous course into which France had been led. Delcassé was condemned for his failure to enlighten parliament and the nation. Even the *Gaulois* (April 20), which was later to attribute his dismissal to a demand from Germany, had declared that "the kind of diplomatic dictatorship which he had exercised could only be justified, under a government of discussion, by striking successes." [33]

It was generally hoped that Delcassé's fall would be followed by a change in the direction of France's foreign policy. The *République Française* (June 8) advised an arrangement with Germany, and the *Temps* (June 8) urged that Delcassé's mistakes should be remedied. On June 7, the *Matin* asserted that a new beginning could be made, as he had been the unique cause of misunderstanding. The *Gaulois* (June 7) anticipated a *détente* in France's relations with Germany, for "M. Rouvier will understand that he must change the orientation of our foreign policy." It was therefore possible to secure the approval of the press and of public opinion for a settlement of the Moroccan question that would satisfy Germany, and perhaps for a more general understanding. Clemenceau was careful, however, to sound a warning that, "Our friends remain our friends . . . and the others . . . remain the others." [34]

It is a great pity that Bülow did not welcome this opportunity to dispose once and for all of the Moroccan question as a source of friction between the two countries. Rouvier went so far as to suggest a comprehensive settlement of colonial questions upon the model of the Anglo-French entente.[35] Although the German Chancellor agreed

---

[33] See also *Corresp.*, O. S., 219, p. 1236.

[34] *Aurore*, June 8.

[35] For Rouvier's point of view see Flotow to Foreign Office, Paris, June 6, 1905. *G. P.*, XX (2), p. 404. Radolin to Bülow, Paris, June 11, 1905. *Ibid.*, XX (2), pp. 407–409. The offer noted from unpublished documents by Professor Brandenburg was not communicated to William until 1907, when he declared that it should have been accepted. E. Brandenburg, *From Bismarck to the World War* . . . (London, 1927), pp. 224, 250. The *Berliner Tageblatt* (June 16) thought the "ground had been prepared for a policy of *rapprochement* and of reconciliation."

that the critical phase of the question had ended with Delcassé's dismissal,[36] the hope of weakening the *entente cordiale* and perhaps of securing a part of Morocco persuaded him to ignore these friendly overtures. On the same day that sealed Delcassé's fate, Bülow definitely committed his country to an international conference by accepting the Sultan of Morocco's invitation of May 27, which he had himself inspired.[37] The argument that it was Delcassé's policy rather than his person to which Germany objected, and that she could not be certain that it would be changed, may well have influenced his point of view. It at least had the desirable result of restraining unwise exultation in the German press. In Paris Radolin continued the policy of silence. As Germany persisted in demanding a conference, opinion in Paris began to change, for it was felt that she would concede nothing.[38]

Neither Morocco nor Germany's insistence upon a conference adequately explains the gradual change of temper on the part of public opinion during the early summer of 1905. The efforts of propagandists had never quite succeeded in creating a general interest in Morocco, and to a considerable degree that which existed had been due to Germany's intervention. The reaction, however, was immediate and intense to the various suggestions that her real purpose was to break the *entente cordiale*.[39] German leaders again betrayed a fatal misunderstanding of French psychology in permitting this idea to gain currency. Many in France had insisted that the issue was not between hostility and coöperation, but between hostility and subordination to Germany. Professor Schiemann, who was understood to be a confidant of the Emperor, wrote in the *Kreuzzeitung* (June 14)[40] that in the event of a war with England, "Germany could only wage it in France," and he told the correspondent of the *Temps* (June 21) that France, having rejected Germany's friendly overtures, would have to choose between Germany and England if war broke out between these countries. The "hostage theory" exerted a deep and permanent

---

[36] Bülow to Tattenbach, Berlin, June 7, 1905. *G. P.*, XX (2), p. 418.

[37] Bülow to Tattenbach, June 5, 1905. *Ibid.*, XX (2), p. 413.

[38] Tardieu, writing in the *Temps* under the pseudonym of George Villiers, at first (June 9) noted Radolin's moderation with approval, but Germany's persistence in demanding a conference persuaded him that there was no hope for an agreement (June 13, 19). His position was like that of Rouvier at this time as reported by Radolin. *G. P.*, XX (2), pp. 452, 453 (June 21).

[39] Pierre de Coubertin in the *Figaro*, April 23. *Aurore*, June 26.

[40] Theodor Schiemann, *Deutschland und die Grosse Politik, 1905* (Berlin, 1906), V, 171.

effect upon the French press and through it upon public opinion. It aroused uinversal indignation. "We are duly warned," declared the radical *Petit Provençal* of Marseilles (June 24). "Germany intends to use France as a screen (*paravent*) against England." The moderate Republican *Journal de Rouen* (June 22) wrote that this question would survive the probable settlement of the Moroccan crisis. Although it had earlier been among those who favored an arrangement, the nationalist *Liberté* (June 14–31) published a series of articles dealing with the military situation on the frontier in a spirit of hostility and suspicion.[41] Jaurès shared the general resentment. France, he wrote, was willing to accept a conference, but Germany was in serious error if she thought "that France will accept the direction of German policy and that she will renounce England's sympathetic coöperation in the settlement of diplomatic questions." [42]

Nevertheless, the two governments were able, July 8, to arrange a preliminary agreement which assured to France her special interests in the policing of the Algerian frontier in return for her acceptance of a conference.[43] News of this arrangement was received without enthusiasm. Earlier indifferent to Morocco, the nationalist *Liberté* (July 11) declared that France had suffered a diplomatic defeat, while the *Figaro* (July 21) predicted that Germany would yield nothing. Clemenceau, however, joined the *Matin* (July 9) in approving the arrangement on the ground that France's position in the conference would be the stronger.[44] It was the *République Française* (July 11) that expressed the dominant impression in observing that neither country had been defeated nor had either been victorious. The explanation of this mediocre reception of a fairly satisfactory compromise is to be found in the persistent suspicion that Germany was attempting to dissolve the *entente cordiale*. According to the *Journal des Débats* (July 10), this pretension "had profoundly wounded the conscience of every Frenchman without exception." Clemenceau was convinced

---

[41] Déroulède, writing from St. Sebastian, argued that the aid of the British fleet would insure Germany's defeat. *Patrie*, June 23. Millevoye, however, believed that France should not become too closely associated with either England nor Germany. "*Ni l'un, ni l'autre.*" *Ibid.*, June 27.

[42] *Humanité*, June 17.

[43] Bülow and Holstein foresaw the ultimate breakdown of any form of international control which might be set up in Morocco, and planned then to make an understanding with France. Bülow's Memorandum, Berlin (July, 1905), *G. P.*, XX (2), pp. 497, 498. Holstein to Radolin, Berlin, July 2, 1905. *Ibid.*, XX (2), pp. 502, 503.

[44] *Aurore*, June 19.

that Germany's real purpose had been a realignment of the Powers, and he was pleased to note that the princely honors conferred upon Bülow had not been earned by the dissolution of the entente.[45] No one was more zealous in defense of the friendship with England than Jaurès. In a speech to be delivered before the Socialist party in Berlin, which was canceled on the request of the German embassy, but which was printed by his newspaper, he affirmed that "we will resist to the last breath an attempt to break it," but he was of course equally hostile to a policy that would give an anti-German significance to the understanding with England.[46] Delcassé chose to emphasize the value of England's friendship in an interview that appeared in the *Gaulois* (July 12) by attributing Germany's failure to attack France to her fear of the British navy. Nevertheless, a section of the nationalist press continued its criticism of a close union with England on the ground that it might involve France in a war which would not be of her own choosing.[47]

Late in July, the meeting of the German Emperor and the Russian Tsar at Björkö added to the alarm inspired by the hostage theory. It is known to-day, as was only suspected then, that the "little agreement" which William had induced his weak-willed cousin to sign was a defensive alliance. Later, France was to be invited to become a member.[48] Clemenceau wrote from Carlsbad, where he was taking the cure, that William was planning to join France in aiding the recovery of Russia from the effects of the Russo-Japanese War "as a preliminary step to a political alliance. Thus, France would be subordinated as if she were an annexed province, and England would be isolated." [49] The *Matin* (July 26) claimed on alleged official authority that France had been fully informed as to the plans for the interview and as to its purposes, but this gesture had little effect in reassuring a nervous public opinion. Germany's apparent intimacy with Russia failed to arouse a desire for compensatory relations with Germany.[50] On the con-

---

[45] *Aurore*, July 11.

[46] *Humanité*, July 7. See the *Temps*, July 8.

[47] *Patrie*, July 8. *Libre Parole*, July 8, 9. Ernest Judet in the *Éclair*, July 21, 23. See his *Ma Politique, 1905 à 1917* (Paris, 1923), p. 18. This is a volume of excerpts from his editorial comments.

[48] Fay, *Origins of the World War*, I, 171–177.

[49] *Aurore*, July 28.

[50] Some consoled themselves with the thought that existing international relations would make a Russo-German understanding impossible. *Temps*, July 25, 27. *République Française*, July 26. *Presse*, July 27.

trary, even the *Journal des Débats* (July 24), usually hostile to any measure that might offend Russia, hinted very strongly that Russia must remain a loyal member of the alliance if she hoped to secure further loans from France. The *Temps* (July 25) invited Count Witte, the Russian finance minister who was then in Paris, to observe the disposition of the French government "to fulfil in spirit and letter its obligations as an ally." Jaurès was one of the few who approved the Björkö meeting as a demonstration of the futility of attempting, as Delcassé had done, to isolate Germany.[51] For almost every one in France to mention an accord with Germany at this moment, even in Russia's company, was to condemn it. "Many people were formerly disposed to consider it," wrote the nationalist *Presse* (July 29). "They hoped for reciprocal concessions, but Germany's brutality . . . has awakened us from a deceitful dream. William has yielded none of his pretensions. Nor have we." Not the least important result of Germany's failure to make use of Delcassé's fall for an arrangement was this change of position by the nationalist press.

The opinion became firmly entrenched during the summer of 1905 that it was hopeless to think any more of a Franco-German entente. It seemed to the *Figaro* (July 31) that Germany was seeking a thousand concessions in Morocco while yielding nothing in return. "We were told, 'Advance a step. Change your minister of foreign affairs.' We were then told, 'Take another step. Change your policy toward us.' Again we yielded, but again without result." The irritation caused by Germany's methods gradually inspired a spirit of resistance. Two months of fruitless negotiations concerning Morocco, wrote the *République Française* (Aug. 4), had reawakened the national spirit and had caused partisan differences to disappear. The attempt to break the *entente cordiale,* declared the *Journal des Débats* (Aug. 6), "had gradually revealed a broader significance in an understanding (*entente cordiale*) which at first had only meant the liquidation of colonial differences." These tendencies were strengthened by Germany's maneuvers in Morocco, which resulted in a loan for her bankers and concessions for her industrialists. The critics of an active Moroccan policy, aroused by Germany's intransigeance, joined its advocates in a vigorous protest. Clemenceau called upon the government to speak *"haut et ferme,"* [52] and the nationalist *Presse* (Sept. 4) hoped for energetic

[51] *Humanité,* July 24.
[52] *Aurore,* Aug. 5.

action. Too late to be judged fairly upon its merits, the agreement of September 25 finally fixed the agenda of the conference which had been agreed upon three months earlier.

Nevertheless, that understanding assured France's essential interest in the policing of the Algerian frontier.[53] Rouvier was satisfied, for he suggested to Dr. Rosen, the German representative, an accord of a more general character "like those we have made with other countries." For the first time since Ferry, specific questions, the Cameroon and Bagdad railways, were mentioned by a responsible French minister as the basis for an understanding.[54] Rosen advised a favorable reply, and Bülow agreed in principle, although he thought that Germany should act "without conspicuous haste." [55] It was probably no coincidence that the two newspapers which Delcassé had used most frequently for the expression of his opinions chose this moment for the publication of fresh evidence that Germany was seeking to separate France and England. An anonymous German diplomat was reported by the *Gaulois* (Sept. 30) as explaining that Morocco was an object of secondary interest to Germany that her chief desire was a *rapprochement* with France and Russia.[56] A similar statement, identified as from a person in close relations with the Emperor, appeared in the *Matin* (Oct. 1). These reports anticipated and insured a hostile public to Bülow's interviews which appeared in the *Petit Parisien* (Oct. 2) and in the *Temps* (Oct. 3).[57] They were obviously intended to improve the relations between France and Germany, but the nationalist *Presse* (Oct. 7) described them as a new and brutal attack upon the *entente cordiale*.

There shortly appeared Stéphane Lauzanne's sensational revelations in the *Matin* (Oct. 6, 7, 8) in regard to England's supposed promise in June to land one hundred thousand men in Schleswig in the event of war.[58] After giving this material illustration of the potential

[53] *Rev. des Deux Mondes,* 1905, V, 708.

[54] Radolin to Foreign Office, Paris, Sept. 29, 1905. *G. P.,* XX (2), p. 593.

[55] Bülow to Foreign Office, Baden-Baden, Sept. 30, 1905. *Ibid.,* XX (2), p. 595.

[56] It also called attention to Déroulède's article in the *National Review* in which the entente was represented as the means of destroying Prussia's hegemony in Europe.

[57] On October 9, Tardieu affirmed in the *Temps* the maintenance of France's existing diplomatic arrangements as her true policy.

[58] Lauzanne did not deny that Delcassé had inspired these articles (*Matin,* Oct. 11), and the former minister was himself equally indefinite. *Figaro,* Oct. 12.

strength of the *entente cordiale*, he quoted Delcassé as saying that the fundamental issue in the Moroccan question was neither economic nor personal. " 'The problem is more serious; it is a question of breaking the friendships which we have contracted and of becoming the allies of Germany . . . I will never agree. An alliance with Germany means France's ratification of her dismemberment . . .' " [59] Whatever the motives were that had inspired these publications, Rouvier promptly reversed his position in regard to an understanding. He ignored his earlier statements when, on October 18, Rosen asked him if he were still ready to consider a general arrangement. This idea had been advanced, replied Rouvier, at a time when he had hoped that the Moroccan affair could be settled between the two countries without a conference.[60] With the approval of a public opinion which was convinced that Germany was trying to force an alliance upon France,[61] France turned to her allies and friends to accomplish her purposes through the conference which had been forced upon her. Speaking for the important radical groups, Maurice Sarraut, a frequent contributor to the *Dépêche* of Toulouse and after 1912 its editor, refused to join the war-dance of the *Presse*, the *Libre Parole*, and the *Patrie*, but he too believed that Germany was making the Moroccan question a test of national existence.[62]

Rouvier had discountenanced Delcassé's methods; nevertheless he was equally determined to solve the Moroccan question in accordance with the interests of France. The firm position of French diplomacy throughout the prolonged Algeciras Conference (Jan.–March, 1906) was effectively supported by the section of the press which had greatest influence in the formation of public opinion. It was a clear test of strength with Germany, and the *Temps*, the *Journal des Débats*, and Clemenceau's *Aurore* were in no mood to tolerate any weakness.[63] Their attitude led Jaurès to demand of the government a specific repudiation of their policy, but he spoke only for the Socialists.[64] Nor did a public meeting, addressed by Jaurès, Anatole

[59] *Matin*, Oct. 6.

[60] Radolin to Foreign Office, Paris, Oct. 18, 1905. *G. P.*, XX (2), pp. 596, 597.

[61] The *Frankfurter Zeitung* had revived the subject by affirming Germany's right to know what France's action would be in an Anglo-German war. France would decide according to circumstances, was the reply. *Temps*, Oct. 21. *République Française*, Oct. 22. *Journal des Débats*, Oct. 22. *Presse*, Oct. 22.

[62] *Humanité*, Oct. 22.

[63] Tardieu, *La Conférence d'Algéciras* (Paris, 1908), p. 94.

[64] *Annales*, 1905.

France, and Professor Charles Seignobos, against secret diplomacy have any general effect.[65] For a moment, de Lanessan's articles in favor of a completely international control of the policing of Morocco caused rejoicing in Germany as an endorsement of her policy,[66] but they were promptly disavowed by the more influential newspapers in France.[67] The long delay in reaching a decision, however, allowed the public's attention to be diverted to the incidents of the conflict between the State and the Church. On March 8, the Sarrien cabinet was formed on the anti-clerical issue with Clemenceau taking office, for the first time in his long career, as Minister of the Interior.

The change of government had no bearing upon the direction of French diplomacy at Algeciras or upon the attitude of public opinion. Only a few days before taking office, Clemenceau again identified Germany's desire to break the *entente cordiale* as the chief reason for resistance.[68] It was, however, the diplomatic support which France received from other Powers that explains the success of her policy. Russia's weakness made her assistance of doubtful value, and England's backing was perhaps the principal factor. The Campbell-Bannerman liberal cabinet and Edward Grey, as its foreign minister, had chosen to continue the policy of its conservative predecessor in a close coöperation with France. While no definite promise of military aid was given in reply to a plea from Paris at a time when rumors of war were current, Grey did say that British public opinion would not tolerate a policy of neutrality in the event of hostilities,[69] and he permitted conversations to begin between the general staffs of France, England, and Belgium in preparation for eventual operations upon the Continent.[70] These technical negotiations remained a secret, of course, so far as public opinion was concerned. The Socialists's warning that the entente was being given a definite point against Germany was ignored or denied, for it was an article of faith that the entente, like

[65] *Aurore,* Jan. 20, 1906.

[66] *Siècle,* Jan. 24. *Patrie,* Feb. 2. *Figaro,* Feb. 6. *Journal des Débats,* Feb. 6.

[67] *Matin,* Feb. 9. *Temps,* Feb. 9, 11. In spite of the *Matin's* consistently anti-German attitude, its owner, Philippe Bunau-Varilla, offered his support to Radolin for a Franco-German understanding. Radolin to Bülow, Paris, Jan. 16, 1906. G. P., XX (2), pp. 697, 698.

[68] *Aurore,* March 4.

[69] Grey to Lascelles, Foreign Office, Jan. 9, 1906. *Brit. War Docs.,* III, 209–211.

[70] Grey to Bertie, Foreign Office, Jan. 10, 1906. *Ibid.,* III, 170, 171. *Ibid.,* III, 72–88.

all of France's diplomatic arrangements, was defensive. "Our foreign relations," wrote Tardieu during the conference, "whether they take the form of alliances, ententes or sympathies, will never have, unless under compulsion, a point against any one." [71] England's aid was a bulwark of strength at Algeciras, and when Italy and Austria declared for a compromise, France secured the substance of her Moroccan policy, control of the police on the Algerian frontier, and a division of this authority with Spain in the eight chief ports under a somewhat innocuous international supervision. Above all, no serious obstacle was raised to the development of France's policy of peaceful penetration.

The crisis had lasted for nearly a year. Germany had refused an unusually favorable moment for a definitive solution in June, 1905, and instead she had given the impression that she was seeking to dictate France's friendships in addition to obstructing her policy in Morocco. It was only the unfavorable international situation caused by Russia's defeat in the war with Japan which had compelled her to accept a conference. These circumstances pointed to a period of intense hostility on the part of public opinion in France. "Pacifism was dead," writes Hammann, then the chief of the press bureau in the German Foreign Office, "and the *revanche* was in preparation." [72] This analysis is inaccurate. A contemporary witness, whose position as the German *chargé d'affaires* in Paris was an adequate defense against a charge of partiality, wrote at the time that a fear of war had been more general than was apparent: "the immediate effect of the conclusion of the crisis is a sigh of relief and of satisfaction that more serious complications had been avoided." [73] The general condemnation of Gustave Hervé's extreme pacifism and the unfavorable reaction of Jaurès's more moderate agitation was far from an endorsement of the chauvinist point of view. Although the *République Française* had urged a strong defense of France's interests during the conference, it admitted (April 1) that public opinion had been oppressed by "the nightmare of a Franco-German War," and it advised silence in regard to old grievances. [74]

The consciousness that a notable victory had been won was not

[71] *Temps*, Feb. 7.
[72] Otto Hammann, *Deutsches Weltpolitik, 1890–1912* (Berlin, 1925), p. 149.
[73] Flotow to Bülow, Paris, April 23, 1906. *G. P.*, XXI (1), pp. 348–350.
[74] Baron Holstein's dismissal in 1906 was accepted in France with satisfaction and as a possible indication of a more conciliatory policy on Germany's part. *Journal des Débats*, April 20. *Temps*, April 22. *Figaro*, April 30.

without effect. "The conference and its results," declared the *Aurore* (April 15), "leave us nothing but satisfaction." "France returns from Algeciras," wrote the *Figaro* (April 2), "without disappointment and without bitterness." Ferdinand Buisson, who had been working against the teaching of an exaggerated nationalism in the schools, likewise believed that France had no reason for complaint. "She returns with neither disappointment, nor humiliation, nor irritation," [75] Some, however, were disposed to exult at Germany's expense. For the nationalist *Patrie* (April 9), events had proved that the Triple Alliance existed only in name, and Tardieu thought that Germany could no longer hope to change the diplomatic map of Europe. She was advised to accept the "Franco-Russian alliance, the Anglo-French, Franco-Italian, Franco-Spanish and Anglo-Russian friendships." [76] The moderate *Siècle* (April 3) felt that the conference had shown France, Russia, England, and Italy were united "like the fingers of a hand." There was no longer any talk of a comprehensive Franco-German understanding. "If certain politicians envisaged a *rapprochement* as desirable only a short time ago," wrote the Belgian ambassador, "there is no one to-day who would dare to formulate such a project." [77]

The favorable results of the conference of course strengthened the attachment of public opinion to the diplomatic ties which had been established with England, Russia, and Italy. By the same token, French diplomacy aided at every turn the development of the Anglo-Russian *rapprochement* of August, 1907.[78] Tardieu had already begun his systematic campaign in the *Temps* in behalf of the equilibrium. In innumerable editorials he urged the need of close coöperation between the three Powers, and this point of view was gradually communicated to the press as a whole, always with the exception of the socialist newspapers. Public opinion, perhaps incapable of forming a precise view of a complicated policy, could easily appreciate the theory of a perfect balance of power as the most effective guarantee

[75] The *Patrie* (April 9) declared that the conference had been "a painful sacrifice of our self-esteem."

[76] *Temps*, April 6, 1906.

[77] Schwertfeger, *Zur Europäischer Politik*, II, 72. (This is the first German publication of the Belgian diplomatic correspondence.) By January, 1908, Delcassé was able to defend his policy on the floor of the chamber with the approval of the majority and of the press. *Annales*, 1908, I, 128 ff. (Jan. 21). *Journal des Débats*, Jan. 26, 27. *Figaro*, Jan. 28. *Temps*, Jan. 26. *Liberté*, Jan. 26. *Patrie*, Jan. 26. *Dépêche* (Toulouse), Jan. 27, 29.

[78] *Brit. War Docs.*, IV, 235, 245, 267, 274, 275, 282, 283.

of peace and of France's diplomatic influence. It was as an instrument of peace that the Triple Entente was presented to the French people and of course Tardieu never ventured openly to acknowledge any other point of view. The aims of French diplomacy, he wrote on numerous occasions, were peaceful, but the peace which France desired differed from that which Germany had maintained since 1871. "Germany," he declared, "has given the *pax germanica* to the world. We must definitely refuse our approval to that conception of peace. . . . It is the kind of peace which gave us the menaces of 1875, the Schnaebelé affair, the blackmail of 1905. We are acquainted with it and we do not desire it. We desire a peace founded upon equality, not upon the hegemony of one Power." [79] Germany, he declared, should accept the Triple Entente as a necessary factor in the balance of power, for there was no justification for her haunting fear of encirclement. "These fears," he wrote, "must be renounced if she desires a peaceful Europe. She must agree that the equilibrium is based upon two systems of alliances. . . . Otherwise, there will be trouble." [80] Accustomed to predominant power in Europe as she was, he agreed that Germany would have to experience a moral crisis before accepting the new situation, but this change was imperative.[81] Continued talk of encirclement in Germany irritated him to the point of addressing a scarcely veiled threat against her. "The Germans," he wrote, "are complaining that they are being 'encircled'! But is it not a daily occurrence with them as with us that people with such illusions are confined? The alienist sees in them a symptom of a mania of persecution which may become dangerous." [82]

Tardieu's idea of the balance of power often seemed perilously close to an hegemony by the Triple Entente under the direction of France. Public opinion was not prepared to follow him in this respect, although a noticeable increase of self-confidence had followed the Algeciras Conference. The army became more popular with the middle classes,[83] and it would obviously be many years before another Delcassé would be repudiated. Nevertheless, the great majority

[79] *Temps*, Aug. 6, 1908.

[80] *Ibid.*, May 4, 1907.

[81] *Ibid.*, Aug. 8, 1908.

[82] *Ibid.*, June 22, 1908. See the *Siècle* (July 29, 1908) for a similar statement. Tardieu's conception of Franco-German relations was fatalistic. A. Tardieu, *La France et les Alliances. La Lutte pour l'Équilibre* (Paris, 1909), pp. 343, 344.

[83] Henri Jouvenel wrote in the *Matin* on the anniversary of the battles of Jena and Auerstadt that the strength of the German army should not be exaggerated. Flotow to Bülow, Paris, Oct. 18, 1906. *G. P.*, XXI (2), pp. 543–546.

desired peace, and it was generally assumed that peace could be maintained for an indefinite period. Even the press refused to follow Tardieu's lead in May, 1908, when in "total ignorance of English public opinion,"[84] he urged the formation of a military alliance to supplement the *entente cordiale,* on the occasion of President Fallières's reception at Buckingham Palace by Edward VII.[85] While some thought it untimely,[86] others opposed it on the ground that Germany would be certain to interpret it as a menace.[87] The discouraging reaction of the British press to his advice that England should adopt a system of universal military service apparently surprised him. He would, he wrote, remain loyal to the entente, but France, unable to count upon effective aid from England, would retain her freedom of action in the event of war between England and Germany.[88]

Domestic politics gave France in October, 1906, a government, that of Clemenceau, which failed to represent adequately the essentially moderate tendencies of public opinion. Few had done more than he to keep alive the feeling of hostility toward Germany and the traditional attachment to the memory of Alsace-Lorraine. He had never shared the opportunist point of view in foreign affairs which implied, in the long run, the acceptance of the *status quo.* In 1885, he had been instrumental in defeating Ferry's moderate policy and in launching Boulanger's political career. He had often denied that he desired war, but he was nevertheless convinced that a war with Germany was inevitable. "I have always thought," he wrote in June, 1905, "that an implacable fatality from which we cannot escape will force some day the military weapon forged by the founding of the German Empire upon the battlefield."[89] For him, at least for journalistic purposes, the German people were still barbarous hordes forced by their *"fureur dévastatrice"* toward the Atlantic and the Mediterranean.[90]

[84] *République Française,* May 31, 1908. Cf. *Times,* May 28. J. A. Farrar, *England under Edward VII* (London, 1922), p. 216.

[85] He would have England become "a second Russia" as a source of military strength for France by adopting a system of universal military service. *Temps,* May 27, 1908. Cf. *Liberté,* May 30, 1908.

[86] *Patrie,* May 20, 1908.

[87] *Siècle,* May 27, 1908. *République Française,* May 31, 1908. *Humanité,* June 1, 1908.

[88] *Temps,* May 31, 1908.

[89] *Aurore,* June 18, 1905.

[90] *Ibid.,* June 21, 1905.

The responsibility of power changed his attitude in some respects. Instead of his cool and even critical attitude toward the Russian alliance, he continued the traditional policy of loyalty to it as the corner-stone of France's foreign policy.[91] He was much more definite in recognizing the tragedy of a war with Germany in his private conversations with the German ambassador than he had ever been in the press.[92] But he continued to believe, as he told Georges Louis (July 28, 1908), that war was inevitable. " 'I have even written as much— which was perhaps unnecessary. We will do nothing, we must do nothing to provoke it, but we must be ready to wage it. . . . In any event, it will be a life and death struggle.' " [93] The prospect of a ministry under Clemenceau alarmed Germany. No one seemed certain of what he would do.[94] He was reported as intending to seduce Austria-Hungary from the Triple Alliance,[95] and it was suspected that he might seek a diversion in foreign affairs for difficulties at home.[96] Jules Cambon, who had been accepted in Berlin as the French Ambassador in spite of the Kaiser's judgment that "he is, next to his brother, our worst enemy," [97] was in fact instructed from Paris to present his credentials to certain South German courts, indicating some thought of a return to the old policy of seeking their friendship as against Prussia. The lame explanation that this measure was believed to be in accordance with precedent, in spite of the constitutional provision that the Imperial Government should have exclusive control of foreign affairs, naturally failed to convince Bülow.[98] Clemenceau, it is clear, was giving a definitely anti-German direction to

---

[91] Michon, *L'Alliance Franco-Russe*, p. 139. For the statement of his policy, see *Annales*, 1906, V, 5.

[92] Radolin to Bulow, Paris, Jan. 13, 1907. *G. P.*, XXI (2), 556.

[93] *Les Carnets de Georges Louis*, 2 vols. (Paris, 1926), I, 21. The nationalist press, it is to be supposed because of its opposition to his anti-clerical policy, represented him as a danger to peace. *Patrie*, May 17, 1906. Radolin to Bülow, Paris, Oct. 31, 1906. *G. P.*, XXI (2), p. 550. He was later reported as on friendly terms with Déroulède who had been permitted to return to France. Radolin to Bülow, Paris, Feb. 22, 1907. *Ibid.*, XXI (2), p. 559.

[94] Flotow to Bülow, Paris, Oct. 18, 1906. *G. P.*, XXI (2), pp. 544, 545.

[95] Flotow to Bülow, Paris, Oct. 25, 1906. *Ibid.*, XXI (2), p. 547. He was in close relations with certain newspaper editors in Vienna. *Diplomatische Aktenstücke des Österreichisch-Ungarischen Ministerium des Aussern*, 8 vols. (Vienna, 1930), I, 603. This work will henceforth be referred to as *Ö.-U. A.*

[96] Radolin to Bülow, Paris, Feb. 22, 1907. *Ö.-U. A.* XXI (2), p. 559.

[97] William's note, Bülow to William, Berlin, Dec. 31, 1906. *Ibid.*, XXI (2), p. 552.

[98] *Ibid.*, XXI (2), pp. 585, 591, 594, 595.

French policy that was in accord only with the chauvinist section of public opinion.

The Casablanca affair of September 25, 1908, occasioned by the arrest of three German nationals among six deserters from the French Foreign Legion while they were under the protection of the German consul, gave the press an opportunity to appeal to public opinion with some success for a firmer attitude. At first, neither country showed any desire to magnify the incident, for each acted to moderate the comments of its press.[99] The *Kölnische Zeitung* (Sept. 30) urged a prompt and friendly solution, and the *Temps* (Sept. 30) noted the unexpected reserve of the German press with approval. "The self-esteem of certain persons," wrote the *Journal des Débats* (Sept. 30), "might be involved, but not the honor of States."[100] Nationalist newspapers like the *Écho du Nord* of Lille (Oct. 7) insisted, of course, that the incident proved the impossibility of friendly relations. The questions eventually came to be one of prestige and national pride, and for these reasons the more serious, rather than of material interest in Morocco. The difficulties arising from the recognition of Mulai Hafid after his successful revolt against the rule of his brother, Abdul Aziz, were about arranged before the Casablanca incident.[101] Germany finally had shown a disposition to agree that France should have a guarantee of the pretender's good faith in regard to the Act of Algeciras prior to his recognition.

For more than two weeks, each of the two governments waited for the other to propose a solution of the incident, without any excessive agitation in the press. On October 15, Germany was the first to make a definite suggestion. Without presenting a formal demand, Radolin proposed that France should discipline her officers who had mistreated Germany's consular official and that the three German deserters should be released while Germany would agree to stop the activities of Lüderitz, her consul, in encouraging desertions from the Foreign Legion.[102] Four days later, Schoen proposed that France and Germany should each express regrets, and that the legal questions should be referred to arbitration. France at once took the position that both the law and the facts involved should be arbitrated, and no reply was made to the suggestion of reciprocal regrets. She intended to wait for

[99] Bülow's Memorandum, Berlin, Sept. 28, 1908. Steinrich's Memorandum, Berlin, Sept. 29, 1908. *G. P.*, XXIV, 346, 347.
[100] Cf. *Temps*, Sept. 29, 30, 1908.
[101] *Figaro*, Sept. 25, 29, 30, 1908.
[102] Schoen to Radolin, Berlin, Oct. 15, 1908. *G. P.*, XXIV, 346, 347.

a full report of the incident from her representatives at Casablanca before further action.[103]

The question then ceased to concern either the diplomats or the press [104] until after the Kaiser's famous interview in the London *Daily Telegraph,* October 28. His cool repudiation of German public opinion in the claim that he had favored England's success during the Boer War aroused a storm of protest in Germany. It threatened to precipitate an unprecedented attack upon the government during the approaching session of the Reichstag. The interview also stiffened France's attitude in regard to the Casablanca incident, for the Kaiser had attempted in it to discredit her with England by asserting that she had initated negotiations for a Continental league for the purpose of intervening in the Boer War. In search, apparently, of a diversion for the impending crisis at home, Bülow proceeded to revive the Casablanca incident in an exaggerated form. On October 30, he instructed Radolin, in view of France's failure to reply to Germany's friendly overtures and to communicate the results of her investigation at Casablanca, to demand satisfaction for the mistreatment of the German consular official, and the unconditional release of the three deserters. The future development of the Moroccan question and of the relations between France and Germany would, he wrote, depend upon the reply.[105] The response was a firm negative.[106]

The stage was set for a crisis of the first order. Nothing quite like it had occurred since 1870, when Gramont had sought a diplomatic victory at Prussia's expense. But before the French press began its campaign on November 4, Germany, on second thought, had virtually withdrawn her demands. Schoen, who was then confined to his bed, at first considered the sending of a warship to Casablanca,[107] but the next day, November 2, he accepted Cambon's suggestion of reciprocal regrets, of the arbitration of both the legal and factual aspects of the question, and he agreed that the deserters should remain in the custody of France until the decision had been rendered.[108] It only remained to agree upon the form to be used in the expression of regrets. Cambon, who wished to have the negotiations restricted either

---

[103] Bülow to Radolin, Berlin, Oct. 19, 1908. *Ibid.,* XXIV, 351, 352.
[104] The Bosnian crisis absorbed the attention of the press.
[105] Bülow to Radolin, Berlin, Oct. 30, 1908. *G. P.,* XXIV, 354-356.
[106] Radolin to Foreign Office, Paris, Oct. 31, 1908. *Ibid.,* XXIV, 356-357.
[107] Schoen's annotation of Flotow's memorandum. Berlin, Nov. 1, 1908. *Ibid.,* XXIV, 357, 358.
[108] Schoen to Cambon, Berlin, Nov. 2, 1908. *Ibid.,* XXIV, 358.

to Berlin or to Paris,[109] was more accommodating than the Quai d'Orsay, for Pichon at first refused to accept any formula which would imply a repudiation of the French officers until the arbitration had been completed.[110] Whereas the press knew nothing of the agreement reached between Schoen and Cambon in Berlin, it was informed as to the demands of October 30. At first, they were interpreted as a maneuver to distract the attention of public opinion in Germany from the *Daily Telegraph* interview.[111]

In 1887 Bismarck's speech had been given the same interpretation, but public opinion had then been advised to remain quiet. In November, 1908, it was called upon to defend the national honor. "It is not M. Clemenceau," wrote the correspondent of the *Times* (Nov. 7), "it is hardly even M. Pichon, or M. Cambon . . . who is conducting the affair. It is the whole French government backed by the whole French nation." While this sweeping generalization was more accurate for the press than for the nation, it was approximately true of public opinion for a moment. "French opinion must see the situation as it is, without panic and without weakness," wrote Tardieu, "with the consciousness of our rights and of our resources and also with the conviction that a firm attitude will arrange everything." [112] "A prouder attitude," declared the *Gaulois* (Nov. 5), "is the logical consequence of the foreign policy which we have adopted." The *Figaro* (Nov. 6) warned its readers that if Germany did not change her methods France would be led by "one demand to another until she would have to call upon all her forces or disappear forever. Such is the lesson of these last few days, and that is the idea which henceforth will haunt our souls." On the same day, November 10, that a formula was accepted by the two governments,[113] the *République Française* declared that "the

---

[109] Schoen's memorandum, Berlin, Nov. 4, 1908, *G. P.,* XXIV, 361.

[110] Radolin to Foreign Office, Paris, Nov. 3, 1908. *Ibid.,* XXIV, 360.

[111] *Figaro,* Nov. 4, 5. *République Française,* Nov. 5. *Gaulois,* Nov. 5. *Lyon Républican,* Nov. 6. *Temps,* Nov. 6. This was the *Temps's* first leading article dealing with the Casablanca question since October 14. A despatch from Berlin in the same issue quoted an anonymous German diplomat as declaring that Germany's honor was involved. Bülow later denied that he had shared this point of view. Bülow to William II, Berlin, Dec. 29, 1908. *G. P.,* XXIV, 464, 465.

[112] *Temps,* Nov. 6.

[113] Kiderlen-Waechter to Radolin, Berlin, Nov. 10, 1908. *G. P.,* XXIV, 370. Bülow immediately acknowledged, when it was finally communicated to him, that the report of the French police commissioner upon the Casablanca incident put the conduct of the German consular officials "in a very serious light." Bülow to Jenisch, Berlin, Nov. 7, 1908. *Ibid.,* XXIV, 367. William thought that "when one is in the wrong, it should be honorably recognized." See his comments upon the above communication. In response to urgent advice from Khevenhüller, the

prospect of war must be accepted in a virile spirit." The press had obviously been misinformed as to Germany's position. Its excitement was inspired by the belief that she required a unilateral expression of regret, whereas this demand had only been maintained for a day or so after October 30. Yet the radical *Dépêche* of Toulouse (Nov. 7) insisted that Germany was seeking "to inflict a moral humiliation upon our country." The *Journal des Débats* (Nov. 9) refused to admit that even a mutual expression of regrets would be satisfactory, since it would imply a disavowal of France's soldiers.

The *Petit Parisien* (Nov. 8), a newspaper which had the largest circulation, thought that the affair had been exaggerated: "but it is not serious in reality, and it does not merit so long a controversy." On November 5, Pichon assured Radolin that he would use what influence he had with the press to moderate its comments, but there is little evidence that he fulfilled his promise. His friend, Eugène Lautier, even defended the attitude of the press in the *Figaro* (Nov. 10).

"Aside from the immediate question at issue," he wrote, "there were never more powerful reasons for resistance. It is the capacity for reaction which proves that one is alive. By constantly yielding, in spite of the justice of our cause, we would have ceased to exist. Every one understood in France that it would be better to plunge into the holocaust since the other decision would threaten our existence."

Jaurès was almost alone in retaining a sober judgment of the situation. "It is amazing," he declared, "that an aggressive and arrogant reply is given to demands whose character and extent are unknown in France." [114] He denied, as had been reported, that a personal apology had been required of France's officers at Casablanca or that Germany expected an expression of regrets without equivalent action on her part. "I will simply ask this question: how many among the thousands of Frenchmen who are being excited by appeals to the national honor have the slightest idea of what happened at Casablanca?" [115] He was mistaken, of course, if he thought that the real issue was concerned with the degree of violence done to Germany's consular official or

Austrian-Hungarian ambassador in Paris (*Ö.-U. A.*, I, 382, 385, Nov. 4, 5, 1908), Aehrenthal was instrumental in persuading the Emperor Francis Joseph to speak to William II in favor of a peaceful solution (*Ö.-U. A.*, I, 407, Nov. 7). Khevenhüller thought this service to France would be helpful in the Bosnian crisis.

[114] *Humanité*, Nov. 5.
[115] *Ibid.*, Nov. 6.

with Lüderitz's encouragement of desertion. It was the consciousness that a test of strength and of prestige was involved which in the main explained the attitude of the press.[116] It is by no means certain that public opinion had been completely aroused. "The concern caused by Germany's demands," wrote the Paris correspondent of the *Lyon Républicain* (Nov. 7), "had now entirely disappeared, and it is only in search of reassuring news that the bulletin boards are watched."

The press at least had been almost unanimous. Not a false note, declared the *Aurore* (Nov. 11), had been sounded. "It is a good sign. Let us retain the coolness which accompanies our new self-confidence, and then it will not be too much to anticipate that France is entering upon a new era which will not be without glory." When on November 10, a formula for the announcement of the arbitration was arranged, some of the nationalists claimed a diplomatic victory. "Germany has yielded," exulted the *Écho du Nord* of Lille (Nov. 12). "For the first time since the terrible year, Germany has found in a united France, a nation firmly resolved to resist her haughty pretensions." But this reaction was exceptional. In most instances, the firmness of the press was noted with satisfaction, and the prediction was sometimes ventured that France would benefit in her future contacts with Germany by her new attitude.

Germany's failure to profit by the exceptionally favorable opportunity which had presented itself after Delcassé's fall for an understanding had fatal consequences. Formerly indifferent to Morocco, public opinion was thereby persuaded to accept it as a national question. Both Clemenceau and the nationalists abandoned their earlier opposition. It was generally believed that Germany's real purpose was to force the dissolution of the *entente cordiale* and to compel France to accept her alliance. There could be only one answer. Morocco henceforth was added to Alsace-Lorraine as a source of bitterness and friction between the two countries. It was this latent tension which explains the brief but ominous Casablanca crisis, and the concerted appeal then made to the nationalist sentiment.

[116] The *Petit Parisien* (Nov. 5) was distinctly moderate but it supported a policy "*à la fois pacifique et ferme.*"

CHAPTER XI

THE FRANCO-GERMAN ACCORD OF 1909 AND THE AGADIR CRISIS, 1911

Les événements ont, une fois de plus, fait échec à l'opinion facile, qu'il sera nécessaire un jour, que la France et l'Allemagne en viennent aux prises.
Lyon Républicain, November 9, 1911.

The tension of public opinion in France at the close of 1908 again became an important factor in her relations with Germany. It was offered as a decisive argument in favor of an understanding which would, as Caillaux hoped, remove Morocco as a source of friction.[1] Clemenceau declared that the nation's desire for peace did not weaken its readiness to accept any sacrifice to prevent a humiliation by Germany.[2] Radolin believed that the situation was critical. Aroused by Germany's policy during the Casablanca crisis, "the politicians, the intellectuals and business men," who, according to the German ambassador, had made no secret of their desire for better relations with her, were now asking themselves if war were not preferable to a perpetual state of uncertainty.[3] Bülow was certain of a French attack if the Bosnian question should lead to war, but he agreed with Radolin that an understanding in regard to Morocco should be made as soon as possible.[4]

It is probable that Austria used her influence with Germany for this purpose. She had always been cool toward her ally's Moroccan policy, and presumably she was prepared to facilitate a satisfactory arrangement. Jaurès protested during the Casablanca crisis against what he suspected was a bargain with Austria to secure her support in Morocco in return for France's neutrality in the Bosnian crisis.[5] According to Crozier, the French ambassador to Austria, Pichon had been forewarned that Austria intended to annex Bosnia-Herzegovina

---

[1] Van der Lancken to Bülow, Paris, Dec. 14, 1908. *G. P.*, XXIV, 461.
[2] Radolin to Bülow, Paris, Jan. 9, 1909. *Ibid.*, XXIV, 482, 483.
[3] Radolin to Bülow, Paris, Dec. 24, 1909. *Ibid.*, XXIV, 462–464.
[4] Bülow to William, Berlin, Dec. 29, 1908. *Ibid.*, XXIV, 464, 465.
[5] *Humanité*, Nov. 4, 1908. Cf. *Journal des Débats*, Nov. 28, 1908.

although he did not communicate this information to Russia.[6] The French press was sharply divided in its reaction to this measure. The *Journal des Débats* (Oct. 11, 1908) condemned Austria's violation of the Treaty of Berlin and her hostility to Serbia's aspirations. It was even more incensed by the apparently tolerant attitude of the French government. Tardieu, however, had occasionally called attention to the advantages of an understanding with Austria since the first Moroccan crisis,[7] and her sudden seizure of the two provinces elicited a somewhat more definite statement. "If Austria," he wrote, "finds it possible during the next months to profit by circumstances to dispose of the Moroccan danger, not by vague assurances but by a definite understanding . . . it is clear that we would find in it a new reason for being agreeable to her." [8] Early in November, during the Casablanca crisis, Francis Joseph, acting upon a hint from Paris, spoke to William in the interest of moderation.[9]

The fear of further complications was, however, of greater influence than Austria's problematical good-will. Jaurès only expressed in extreme form what many were thinking in his eloquent plea, January 18, 1909, for a Franco-German reconciliation.[10] When negotiations were commenced, it was wisely agreed that they should be kept secret until a solution had been found.[11] The Franco-German Accord of February 8, 1909, provided that France would respect the independence and territorial integrity of Morocco and the open door in return for an assurance that Germany would not obstruct her

[6] See his letter to the *Petit Comtois* of Besançon in the *Siècle*, Sept. 7, 1912. According to the recently published Austrian diplomatic documents, Pichon was informed of the impending action on Oct. 3. *Ö.-U. A.*, I, 129. Cf. R. Poincaré, *Le Lendemain d'Agadir* (Paris, 1926), pp. 236–281, for France's relations with Austria after the treaty of November 4, 1911 and for Crozier's recall. Russia had protested against opening the Paris financial market to Austria-Hungary and de Selves had decided against these loans before Poincaré became Minister of Foreign Affairs in January, 1912. *Documents Diplomatiques Français*, 3d series, I, 242, 320, 373. Neither in his memoirs nor in the *Éclair* (June 13, 1921) does Poincaré question Crozier's statement that Austria desired an understanding after the Casablanca crisis. Philippe Crozier, "L'Autriche et l'Avant-Guerre," *Rev. de France*, June 1, 1921, pp. 615–617.

[7] *Temps*, Nov. 1, 1908.

[8] *Ibid.*, Oct. 10, 1908. He later attributed the accord of 1909 almost entirely to Austria's influence. *Temps*, July 2, 1909. He was given a "scoop" of the first news relating to the annexation of Bosnia-Herzegovina. *Ö.-U. A.*, I, 126 (Oct. 3, 1909).

[9] Tschirschky to Foreign Office, Vienna, Nov. 7, 1908. *Ibid.*, XXIV, 366, 367. Cf. Janisch to Foreign Office, Nov. 7, 1908. *Ibid.*, XXIV, 367 (note).

[10] *Annales*, 1909, I, 37–46.

[11] Radolin to Foreign Office, Paris, Jan. 20, 1909. *G. P.*, XXIV, 484.

political interests. Neither government would seek special economic privileges for its nationals, and it was agreed that the coöperation of their merchants and industrialists would be encouraged. In a secret exchange of letters, Germany promised that her nationals would accept no position in the service of the Moroccan government and that the superiority of France's interests would, if possible, be considered in any attempt at economic coöperation.[12] Each government apparently used its influence to prevent an exaggerated estimate in the press of the merits of the accord. Already, Bülow had indicated that its negative significance (*"keine Reibereien, keine Nadelslichen"*) should be emphasized.[13]

In France, the accord was not interpreted as changing the Act of Algeciras in any essential respect, nor was it thought that Germany had made any new promises.[14] Nevertheless, it was accepted with satisfaction by all except the chauvinists. Its chief value, according to many, was in its bearing upon the future relations between France and Germany. Tardieu, who was to become an advocate of economic coöperation, welcomed the agreement as meaning perhaps the end of the struggle for the equilibrium. "This conclusion of the Moroccan question," he wrote, "may be a decisive date in the history of Europe." [15] It should mean, he thought, the end of Germany's fear of encirclement.[16] The independent and widely circulated *Petit Parisien* (Feb. 10) welcomed it "as one of the decisive factors in the pacification of Europe: its moral value infinitely exceeds its specific terms." It seemed to the *Journal* (Feb. 10), another informational newspaper, a turning-point in history: "The shadows of the past are disappearing and the future is clearing up." Jaurès was enthusiastic. "The Franco-German accord," he wrote, "is especially valuable as a sign of *détente,* as a first promise of the *rapprochement* which is the absolute condition of peace. In this respect, it is a great joy for us." [17] The moderate *Siècle* (Feb. 10) and the *République Française* (Feb. 10) even expressed the hope that the economic coöperation pledged in

[12] *G. P.,* XXIV, 490, 491. It is said that an alliance between the Schneider and Krupp interests, the great French and German munition firms, was behind this agreement. Élie Halévy, *The World Crisis of 1914–1918, An Interpretation* (Oxford, 1930), p. 24.
[13] Radolin to Foreign Office, Paris, Feb. 5, 1909. *Ibid.,* XXIV, 487 (Bülow's annotation). Cf. *Kölnische Zeitung,* Feb. 9, 1909. *Kreuzzeitung,* Feb. 10, 1909.
[14] *Radical,* Feb. 10. *Figaro,* Feb. 11. *Gaulois,* Feb. 12.
[15] *Temps,* Feb. 10. Cf. A. Tardieu, *Le Mystère d'Agadir* (Paris, 1912), p. 11.
[16] *Temps,* Feb. 11.
[17] *Humanité,* Feb. 11.

the accord would be extended to other regions than Morocco. Only the chauvinists were openly hostile. "In principle" declared the *Patrie* (Feb. 12), "the joining of these two words, France and Germany, embarrasses and shocks me. Frenchmen and Germans can not be in 'accord' so long as the question of Alsace-Lorraine is not solved. The recognition of France's rights in Morocco do not return Metz and Strassburg to us." There was, however, no general attempt to discredit the accord by playing upon patriotic sentiment. The danger came instead from the divergent interpretations of the agreement in the two countries, for if Germany counted most upon the provision for economic coöperation, French opinion neglected that feature in favor of the prospect that Germany would abandon the obstructive methods which she had used since 1905.

Clouded from the first by this emphasis upon national interests, the prospects were unfavorable for either the application or the development of the accord. Moreover, individuals in both countries who hoped to benefit financially from enterprises in Morocco were not as seriously impressed by the need of fair dealing as the diplomats who negotiated the accord. The prevailing point of view in France in regard to Morocco did not promise well for economic coöperation with Germany. French supremacy in Morocco was regarded by the leaders of public opinion as a part of the natural order of things, so that any concessions to Germany came from France's good-will and were not essentially rights which she could claim. During the two years that followed the accord, none of the various attempts to provide for economic coöperation were successful. A proposal for a comprehensive agreement in which French financial interests would predominate was rejected by Pichon in October, 1909, as too closely resembling a condominium.[18] The quarrel between the French-controlled Union des Mines and the Mannesmann brothers for mining privileges in Morocco was not arranged before the crisis of 1911.[19] Likewise, the efforts to provide for coöperation in the building of railroads there, or between the French Congo and Cameroons and in the N'goko-Sangha enterprise, in which Tardieu was interested, came to nothing.[20] Auguste Gauvain, the expert on foreign affairs of the *Journal des Débats*, later expressed the opinion of many at this time: "As regards the Accord of 1909," he wrote

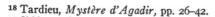

[18] Tardieu, *Mystère d'Agadir*, pp. 26–42.
[19] *Ibid.*, p. 58.
[20] *Ibid.*, pp. 288–359.

(Nov. 14, 1912), "Germany should have waited until France had begun to realize a profit before asking something for herself."

But, not unnaturally, it was feared in Germany that it would then be too late, for the policy of peaceful penetration merited and was given much respect. From time to time, France had found it necessary to occupy certain parts of Morocco, including Casablanca, and there was little indication of an early evacuation. In December, 1910, a French crusier landed forces at the open port of Agadir in order to put an end to the smuggling of arms. Under these circumstances, France's reiterated assurances of her loyalty to the Act of Algeciras inspired little confidence.[21] Nor did negotiations in regard to other questions have more satisfactory results. France showed no inclination to admit German securities to the Paris Bourse.[22] By the spring of 1911, it was clear that the attempt to revive the policy of colonial coöperation had failed.

The progress of French influence in Morocco caused unrest and suspicion among the natives as well as in Germany. What France thought of as pacification, they regarded as subjugation, as natives will the world over. The execution of the two Moroccan deserters on the order of the French military mission at Fez suddenly brought this discontent to a head. It is by no means clear that the subsequent uprisings were as serious as they were represented by a part of the Paris press. In addition to the well-known testimony to the contrary by the Russian agent, and the Belgian consul at Tangier,[23] some of the Paris newspapers which had never been entirely won over to an active Moroccan policy questioned the seriousness of the situation. The *Radical* (March 9), the official organ of the Radical-Socialists, warned against *"des nouvelles fausses"* and against the dangers of a Moroccan expedition. The chauvinist *Patrie* (March 10) asserted that the government would not reveal its motives for they were *"inavouables,"* and even Tardieu believed that observers in Paris were more pessimistic than those who were on the scene in Morocco. Ac-

[21] F. Hartung, *Die Marokkokrise des Jahres* 1911 (Berlin, 1927), pp. 9, 10.
[22] French banks, it is said, had acquired 30 per cent of the Bagdad Railway bonds, although they were not admitted to the Bourse. When on July 4, the president of the Deutsche Bank, von Gwinner, asked Caillaux to permit them to be listed or to sell them in Germany, the French minister refused the first suggestion without condition. Mermeix (Gabriel Terrail), *La Chronique de l'An 1911* . . . (Paris, 1912), pp. 232, 233.
[23] B. Schwertfeger, *Die Belgische Dokumente,* IV, 311–315, 363–365 (May 2, 1911 and July 12, 1911). Cf. Schoen to von Bethmann-Hollweg, Paris, April 28, 1911. *G. P.,* XXIX, 98, 99.

cording to his own sources of information the Sultan, he wrote, was holding his own.[24]

The news that the French military mission in Fez was in danger furnished the means of a more effective appeal to public opinion. The dispatch of a relief expedition was at once represented as a question of life or death for all foreigners in the Moroccan capital,[25] although the Paris press was rather more concerned for the fate of the men who wore the French uniform.[26] On April 17, Cruppi, the foreign minister in the Monis cabinet, with his colleague of the war ministry, decided to send an expedition, but it was not until April 23 that the cabinet's sanction was secured.[27] The question as to its possible effect upon France's international relations, and especially those with Germany at once arose. Already on March 16, Isvolski (since December, 1910, the Russian ambassador in Paris) had asked Cruppi if his Moroccan plans would not lead to trouble with Germany.[28] The same question arising when the ministry considered the sending of an expedition to Fez, Cruppi read a part of Jules Cambon's report of a conversation with von Bethmann-Hollweg, the German Chancellor, to show that Germany had no objection. " 'I do not say no, because I do not wish to assume responsibility for your fellow-citizens.' "[29] This was essentially a misrepresentation of Germany's attitude, although Cambon believed that she only questioned the timeliness of an expedition.[30] On April 5, Kiderlen-Wächter indicated a willingness to dispose of the entire question but upon the condition that Germany should be compensated.[31] The Chancellor, on April 19, wrote that he had strongly advised against a military expedition on the ground that it would excite public opinion in Germany and possibly lead to a holy war in Morocco.[32] Cruppi may have told the cabinet on April 23 that Germany did not object, but he did not neglect the necessary diplomatic precautions in view of possible trouble. It seems clear that a week earlier, on April 16, he had ad-

[24] Temps, March 21, 1911.
[25] Livre Jaune: Affaires du Maroc, VI (1910–1912), pp. 180, 189, 190, 192, 193.
[26] Temps, April 21. République Française, May 8.
[27] J. Caillaux, Agadir. Ma Politique Extérieure (Paris, 1919), pp. 93, 94.
[28] Un Livre Noir: Diplomatie d'avant Guerre d'après les Documents des Archives Russes, 1910–1914, R. Marchand, ed., 2 vols. (Paris, 1922, 1923), I, 56.
[29] Caillaux, Agadir, pp. 93, 94.
[30] Cambon to de Selves, Berlin, April 8, 1911. Livre Jaune: Affaires du Maroc, VI (1910–1912), p. 185.
[31] Cambon to de Selves, Berlin, April 5, 1911. Ibid., VI (1910–1912), p. 191.
[32] Bethmann-Hollweg to Schoen, Berlin, April 19, 1911. G. P., XXIX, 85, 86.

dressed the same question to England that had been asked on the eve of the Algeciras Conference: could France count upon her armed aid?[33] In any event, preparations were made and the expedition was ordered to proceed to Fez as if Germany's approval was certain.

Public opinion was informed by the press that no complications would arise with Germany. Since the relief expedition was for the purpose of protecting foreigners in Fez, it was represented as justified by international practice without reference to the Act of Algeciras. Germany, therefore, could not object, nor could she claim any compensation in view of France's promises to respect her engagements.[34] Raymond Recouly had already rejected the suggestion that Germany might give France a free hand in Morocco in return for the admission of her industrial values to the Paris Bourse: "I do not see that there is, for the moment, any connection between the two questions. Do not insist upon creating imaginary dangers."[35] France, according to Albert de Mun, the Catholic leader and an advocate of a vigorous Moroccan policy, should proceed regardless of Germany. "Let no one speak this time of foreign complications, let no one make use of the German specter which has already made us commit so many serious faults. Neither Germany nor Europe will say anything because they can say nothing."[36] Germany would not forget, declared André Mévil, "the treaties which she has signed, she does not dream of questioning our formal and indisputable rights."[37] He added two days later that "the diplomatic situation is what it should be. There is no need at the present moment of seeking an arrangement of any kind. We are acting in perfect harmony with Russia and England, who are ready to support our efforts with all necessary energy." In his *Mystère d'Agadir,* written somewhat later, Tardieu was distinctly of the opinion that more could have been done to facilitate Franco-German economic coöperation, but he wrote in the *Temps* (April 27) that Germany had actually secured more advantages under the Accord of 1909 than she had any right to expect. He therefore argued that she could claim no additional concessions for her approval of the necessary changes in Morocco. "The exchange of

[33] Grey to Asquith, April 16, 1911. Grey, *Twenty-Five Years,* I, 91, 92. Cf. Hartung, *Die Morokkokrise des Jahres* 1911, p. 13.

[34] *Temps,* April 9.

[35] *Figaro,* March 15.

[36] *Gaulois,* April 22.

[37] *Écho de Paris,* April 21.

views which has taken place in Berlin," affirmed the *Petit Parisien* (April 29), which was understood to be in close relations with the Quai d'Orsay,[38] ". . . is of a nature to clear up any doubts which the Pan-German press would like to propagate.

Even the warning note in the *Norddeutsche Allgemeine Zeitung* (May 1) to the effect that any violence to the Sultan's independence would give complete freedom of action to the signatory Powers of the Act of Algeciras failed to change the tone of the Paris press. Tardieu immediately replied that "the article . . . contains nothing which should alarm us," [39] and two weeks later, he declared that "the international horizon is clearer than it has ever been in similar instances." [40] "Our action is approved," affirmed the *République Française,* "by every government, for responsible statesmen *all know* how indispensable it is." The *Journal des Débats* (April 11) was one of the few who warned against the advice of those who were demanding an expedition, for once French troops were in Fez they would probably find it impossible to withdraw. "According to certain articles . . . one would really believe that the French flag is identical with his Moroccan Majesty's umbrella and that French honor is at stake in Fez." Jaurès, of course, protested against a policy which might make of Morocco the occasion of a new crisis or of war, and he refused to admit that Fez was in serious danger. [41] Among the extreme nationalists, Charles Maurras declared that "the solution of the Moroccan crisis is not to be found at Fez, but among the pines of the Vosges. What is afoot in Morocco makes sense if we are prepared to fight in the Vosges." [42] The *Patrie* was unable to follow a consistent policy. Rochefort, a frequent contributor, declared that public opinion had been misled as to the situation in Fez, while Millevoye, in the same edition, approved the expedition and asserted that Germany's attitude need not be taken into consideration.[43] She might object, André Mévil conceded, but she would have to count "this time with a better instructed and fore-warned public opinion." [44]

Once the expedition had reached Fez, after an uneventful march, the press lost something of its confidence that there would be no international complications. It was agreed that the Act of Algeciras

[38] Schoen to Bethmann-Hollweg, Paris, June 10, 1911. *G. P.,* XXIX, 141.
[39] *Temps,* May 2.
[40] *Ibid.,* May 17.
[41] *Humanité,* April 22, 26, 27. Cf. Tardieu, *Le Mystère d'Agadir,* pp. 395, 396.
[42] *Action Française,* May 5.
[43] *Patrie,* April 26.
[44] *Écho de Paris,* May 3.

should be scrupulously respected and that the period of occupation should be as brief as possible.[45] The possibility that events might require France to remain had been admitted by the *Radical* (May 10),[46] but this could not, it was said, be included in the government's official policy. Tardieu noted a suggestion in the German press of a new understanding. "The tempter," he wrote, "would lead us to the mountain-top: if the view inspired us with vast designs, the Evil One would soon be the master of our souls." France would prefer to remain "in the valley." [47] "It depends upon our government," wrote the *Journal des Débats* (June 5), "to defeat these projects by a strict observance of its official statements." Tardieu's position was not one to justify confidence in France's intentions, for he recommended the reënforcement of the expedition as the best means to secure its early withdrawal.[48] When he declared that France was observing the Act of Algeciras with a "refinement of loyalty," the *Berliner Tageblatt* (May 30) replied: "while we will not question this loyalty, a little less 'refinement' would have been better."

The press, having taken the position that the troops would be withdrawn when the situation justified it, gave no sign that an arrangement was desired. The *Matin* (May 14) alone suggested a permanent settlement which would secure to France a protectorate in Morocco in return for the cession of a part of the Congo. Nor was the government more favorable even when Spain, anxious to be assured her part as provided in the accord of October, 1904, increased the danger of Germany's intervention by occupying Larache.[49] In the meantime, Germany's policy had been outlined on May 3. Kiderlen-Wächter had then decided to await events. It was his plan to withhold any complaint until the French had established themselves in Fez, when, after a friendly question as to the date of its evacuation, warships would be sent to one or two Moroccan ports on the pretext of protecting German interests.[50] An offer of tangible concessions from Paris might have prevented the carrying out of this

[45] *Petit Parisien,* May 24. *République Française,* May 25. *Action Française,* May 25. *Temps,* May 25. *Journal des Débats,* May 25, June 5. *Siècle,* May 29.

[46] An army officer predicted in the *République Française* (May 8) that destiny would keep the French troops at Fez just as had happened in Tunis. Mulai Hafid, according to the *Matin,* desired a permanent garrison of fifty thousand. *Rappel,* May 30.

[47] *Temps,* June 1.

[48] *Ibid.,* May 25.

[49] Schön to Bethmann-Hollweg, Paris, June 10, 1911. *G. P.,* XXIX, 141.

[50] Kiderlen's Memorandum, Berlin, May 3, 1911. *G. P.,* XXIX, 101–108. Cf. Fay, *Origins of the World War,* I, 281, 282.

policy, but none was forthcoming. Kiderlen at length, a month after the occupation of Fez, closed his conversations with Jules Cambon at Kissengen (June 20-21) with the invitation to bring something back with him from Paris, although the ambassador had been the first to suggest the idea of compensations.[51] What happened to this suggestion in Paris remains a mystery. It was perhaps overlooked during the confusion resulting from the fall of the Monis and the formation of the Caillaux ministry. Mouis, the retiring President of the Council, later declared that it was not brought to his attention,[52] and Caillaux claims that he assumed power without an accurate understanding of the seriousness of the international situation. Germany's attitude, he writes, had never been adequately explained to the preceding cabinet of which he had been a member.[53] In any event, Cambon failed to mention the subject for several days after his return to Berlin. It was this silence which convinced Kiderlen of the need of action. On June 26, Kiderlen's message, "Ships granted," from the imperial yacht gave the necessary authority.[54]

At noon on July 1, von Schoen presented himself at the Quai d'Orsay with the announcement that the gunboat *Panther* had been sent to Agadir. This measure was necessary, he explained in a carefully prepared statement, for the protection of German merchants, but the ship would be withdrawn as soon as the danger was past.[55] Whatever its intentions were in Morocco, the French government evidently had no desire for a crisis, for steps were taken to moderate the effect of Germany's decision. On official inspiration, an explanation of German policy was added to the report of Schoen's statement in the majority of newspapers.[56] "M. de Schoen added," according to the *Journal des Débats* (July 3), "that the French government must not see in it a change of Germany's Moroccan policy, that French opinion should not find in it à cause of concern, and that Germany has no intention of abandoning the Act of Algeciras and the Franco-German Accord of 1909."[57] A special edition of the nationalist *Liberté*

[51] *Livre Jaune: Affaires du Maroc,* VI (1910–1912), pp. 372–374.
[52] *Rev. des Deux Mondes,* 1912, I, 471.
[53] *Ibid.,* pp. 100–105. Neither the *Grosse Politik* nor the *Livre Jaune* throw any light upon the reaction to Kiderlen's hint.
[54] Kiderlen to Foreign Office, On Board the *Hohenzollern,* June 26, 1911. *G. P.,* XXIX, 152.
[55] Kiderlen to Schoen, Berlin, June 30, 1911. *Ibid.,* XXIX, 153–155.
[56] Schoen to Bethmann-Hollweg, Paris, July 2, 1911. *Ibid.,* XXIX, 159.
[57] P. Albin, *Le Coup d'Agadir* (Paris, 1912), p. 4. *Petit Parisien,* July 2. *Gaulois,* July 2. *Figaro,* July 2. *Matin,* July 2. According to Schoen, this report

promptly announced a "German Intervention in Morocco" in flaring headlines, and others referred to a "grave incident" and to "German menaces." Nevertheless, the general tendency of editorial comment was moderate. The impression, wrote the correspondent of the *Berliner Tageblatt* (July 3) was one of surprise rather than of "worry or alarm." Raymond Recouly was not at all disposed to exaggerate the extent of moderate opinion, but he admitted that the general public, just at the beginning of its summer holiday season, did not wish to be disturbed.[58] "Public opinion," he wrote, "is undecided, wavering. It does not understand very well what it is all about." "No one desires war," wrote Albert de Mun in the *Figaro* (July 7), "and no one anticipates it." Nevertheless, he regretted that Caillaux had not made a formal protest. Every one understood that Germany's action signified her desire for negotiations. It was merely her way, according to the *Patrie* (July 3), of asking for her share of the Moroccan *gateau*. "And she proceeds to take a seat at the table without being invited." The *Radical* (July 3) advised moderation and confidence in the government, but it also interpreted the *Panther*'s mission as a reminder that Germany was to be reckoned with. "The Chancellor has struck a blow, on the *tapis vert* of the diplomatic table. *C'est le coup d'Agadir.*"

It was not to be expected that the nationalists and the advocates of an aggressive Moroccan policy would share this moderate point of view. Were they "about to leap into the saddle," asked the *Journal des Débats* (July 3). "The moment is favorable. The spirit of Émile Ollivier is watching you." Tardieu continued to insist that France had respected her promises in the Accord of 1909, and if Germany evaded those which she had made, France would conclude that it would be impossible to maintain normal relations with her.[59] Clemenceau, he declared, had given a tone to public opinion which still persisted.[60] The *Patrie* (July 3) at once insisted that Germany intended to establish herself permanently in Morocco, a decision which should

---

did not seriously misrepresent what he had said. Schoen to Bethmann-Hollweg, Paris, July 3, 1911. *G. P.*, XXIX, 160, 161.

[58] The Paris correspondent of the *Kölnische Zeitung* (July 6) reported that the majority of the Paris newspapers acknowledged that compensations should be given to Germany. This point of view, however, was implied rather than stated in so many words. Pierre Baudin, a senator and a member of a Franco-German committee for the encouragement of commerce, referred to the question as essentially one of bargaining. *Matin*, July 4.

[59] *Temps*, July 3.

[60] *Ibid.*, July 4.

convince public opinion that all pacifists were insane. The government, declared the nationalist *Liberté* (July 3), should be inspired in its reply by what it described as offended national sentiment.[61] Germany should make the first move, according to the *Matin* (July 7), but if she continued her recent attitude, she would discover that France could apply certain measures which might not please her. Some advised the dispatch of a warship to Agadir, alone or in company with one from England. The idea commended itself to Recouly, in spite of his recognition of the moderate tone of public opinion.[62] Public opinion, it is clear, did not rally to this dangerous proposal. The suggestion of a new conference as a means of avoiding separate negotiations with Germany in which it was feared that France would be at a disadvantage secured a more general approval.[63] Nevertheless, there was no clear agreement upon a single point of view. The future development of public opinion would depend upon events and official influence.

Caillaux's first reaction was unfavorable to negotiations with Germany without the coöperation of England and Russia,[64] but this policy was soon abandoned. Germany had no intention of repeating her experience at Algeciras, where she had been dangerously isolated, and she therefore refused to consider the idea of a conference. Grey's suggestion that the conference should provide for the complete return to the *status quo ante* by the evacuation of all points in Morocco by France and Spain as well as by Germany cooled Caillaux's interest in it.[65] Russia's evident reluctance to go very far in her support of French interests in Morocco was perhaps of some influence in turning the French Prime Minister toward separate negotiations with Germany,[66] although he of course was more favorably disposed to direct conversations than any other leader in France. For a few days, each of the two countries waited for the other to make a definite proposal. On July 9, Cambon and Kiderlen both sought to avoid the initiative, and each attributed to the other, in his official report, the suggestion that the Kissengen conversation should be continued.

[61] France, declared Rochefort, was in danger of "a disaster or of shame." *Patrie*, July 4.

[62] *Figaro*, July 2.

[63] *Patrie*, July 5. *Petit Parisien*, July 6. *Radical*, July 9. *Siècle*, July 21.

[64] Caillaux to Cambon, Paris, July 4, 1911. *Livre Jaune: Affaires du Maroc*, VI (1910–1912), pp. 390, 391.

[65] Caillaux, *Agadir*, pp. 114, 115.

[66] Kiderlen's Memorandum, Berlin, July 5, 1911. *G. P.*, XXIX.

Cambon's first tangible proposition of economic coöperation in Turkey was rejected as insufficient.[67]

Germany's desires were at length stated, July 15, with forceful directness when Kiderlen indicated all of the French Congo as a satisfactory compensation for the recognition of France's freedom of action in Morocco. He offered Togoland, however, to make his demand more acceptable. Highly indignant, Cambon replied that public opinion in France would never approve the cession of an entire colony.[68] Germany intended that her demand should be kept secret, but a leak occurred in Paris. On July 19, the *Matin* published it in a sensational article covering the greater part of its first page. Germany, it declared, was requiring "nothing less than the entire coast of the Congo, including Libreville." It believed, however, that she had made this demand in order to establish an effective trading position: she was asking for *"un bœuf pour avoir un œuf."* Her offer of Togoland was not mentioned.[69] This article, it is certain, was intended to arouse public opinion against the cession of the Congo. It was successful, so far as the press was concerned. "The cession of a magnificent colony," wrote Tardieu, "would be an unacceptable blow to France's dignity. . . . The suggestion does not even merit consideration." Germany had offended French sentiment, he added, by her exorbitant demands.[70] The successful completion of the negotiations which, according to the *République Française* (July 20), had commenced in a conciliatory spirit, was endangered, and Millevoye called for a unanimous expression of national spirit as the only proper reply.[71] Not until the *Matin's* article had exerted its effect did the Quai d'Orsay issue an official communication to the press declaring that the story had no foundation.[72]

In order to create confidence in the nation's ability to resist Germany's demands, the press exaggerated the extent to which the aid

[67] Kiderlen's Memorandum, Berlin, July 9, 1911. *Ibid.,* XXIX, 173–176. Cambon to de Selves, Berlin, July 10, 1911. *Livre Jaune: Affaires du Maroc,* VI (1910–1912), pp. 403, 404.
[68] Cambon to de Selves, Berlin, July 15, 1911. *Ibid.,* VI (1910–1912), p. 413. Cf. Bethmann-Hollweg to William, Hofenfinaw, July 15, 1911. *G. P.,* XXIX, 184–186.
[69] Mermeix, *Chronique de l'An 1911,* pp. 114, 115. The *Écho de Paris* (July 20) referred to Kiderlen's demands as *ballons d'essais. Ibid.,* pp. 116, 117.
[70] *Temps,* July 20.
[71] *Patrie,* July 22.
[72] *Petit Parisien,* July 22.

of England and Russia could be counted upon. This confidence had some justification in regard to England.[73] Since Germany had not reassured her as to the purpose of the demonstration at Agadir, England was determined to leave no doubt as to her intention of preventing the establishment there of a German naval base. On July 21, Lloyd George, the Chancellor of the Treasury, declared in his Mansion House speech that England must be considered in the settlement of the question.[74] Except for the anti-English element among the nationalists in France who suspected that England was working for a war upon her own account,[75] this assurance of support was accepted without a close scrutiny of its motives.[76] It was even given a broader interpretation than was justified, for British diplomacy not only opposed a dangerous move such as the dispatch of a ship to Agadir, but it approved an arrangement which would give Germany compensation elsewhere than in Morocco. After England's suspicions had at length been quieted,[77] Asquith reaffirmed her support of France in a statement, July 27, to the House of Commons, but he also left no doubt as to her readiness to accept a bargain that would not injure her own interests.[78] The French press, for the most part, omitted any reference to this latter point of view, and it continued to represent England as opposed to any compromise. "If France was weak enough," declared the Monarchist Delafosse, "to yield on the question of compensations to Germany, England would not agree. . . . Therefore, neither Morocco nor Congo." [79] It was likewise assumed without sufficient evidence that Russia was giving France her effective support. In reality, she was distinctly lukewarm.[80] Isvolski had little liking for a policy which might endanger peace on account of the Moroccan question, and he urged Caillaux to profit by the occasion to acquire a protectorate in Morocco in return for a *pourboire*. Russia, he said, was not prepared, and she had no

[73] Grey told the German ambassador, Metternich, that British public opinion would side with France in the event of trouble. He discouraged, however, the idea of sending a ship to Agadir. Grey, *Twenty-five Years*, I, pp. 211, 212.

[74] *Ibid.*, I, 216, 217.

[75] The *Patrie* (July 23) was tempted to remark, *"Tirez les premiers, messieurs les Anglais!"* See Ernest Judet's comments in the *Éclair*, Aug. 2. Judet, *Ma Politique*, p. 241.

[76] *République Française*, July 22. *Temps*, July 23.

[77] Kiderlen to Metternich, Berlin, July 23, 1911. *G. P.*, XXIX, 203.

[78] *Parliamentary Debates*, XXVIII (5th series), 1829.

[79] *Gaulois*, Aug. 4. Cf. *Liberté*, July 29. *Patrie*, July 29. *Radical*, Aug. 28.

[80] *Livre Jaune: Affaires du Maroc*, VI (1910–1912), pp. 389, 390, 399, 403.

desire to risk a European war for the sake of the Congo.[81] Far from desiring to antagonize Germany, she chose to make an understanding, August 19, with her in regard to the Bagdad railway.[82] Public opinion was clearly misled as to the support France could expect in a policy of extreme resistance.

Differences of opinion as to the proper policy within each government contributed to the long delay in reaching a solution. Until July 19, Kiderlen was prepared to insist upon Germany's extreme demands regardless of the danger of war, and de Selves, the French Foreign Minister, whose inexperience in diplomacy, it is said, led him to accept the direction of the permanent officials of the Quai d'Orsay,[83] was prepared to risk the consequences of a sharp defiance of Germany.[84] The German minister, however, by July 20 was persuaded by Bethmann-Hollweg to moderate his policy, and in August, Caillaux, alarmed by de Selves's attitude, placed the conduct of negotiations under the ministry's control.[85] Neither this difference of policy nor Caillaux's use of a secret agent in negotiating with Germany were known at the time, although they were later used with effect in discrediting the Prime Minister. It did not matter who had control of French policy, in so far as the demand for the entire Congo was concerned, for even Caillaux, anxious as he was for a peaceful solution, could not brave the storm of denunciation that was certain to follow a surrender upon this point. Cambon therefore maintained an unyielding resistance with the united support of his government and of public opinion.

The diplomats and responsible ministers may have appreciated the need of a prompt solution, but they continued through interminable weeks of negotiation to hold public opinion in suspense while they

[81] Caillaux, *Agadir*, pp. 142, 143. He even urged the need of a prompt solution of the economic difficulties in Morocco. *Livre Noir*, I, 133 (Sept. 14, 1911). When it seemed probable that a peaceful solution of the crisis would be found, he wished to trade Russia's approval for France's support for her ambitions in the Straits question. *Ibid.*, I, 140, 141 (Sept. 22, 1911).

[82] Russia made no serious effort to intervene in behalf of France. Fay. *Origins of the World War*, I, 292.

[83] Mermeix, *Chronique de l'An 1911*, p. 114.

[84] Caillaux, *Agadir*, p. 156.

[85] *Ibid.*, p. 159. For the German side, see von Bethmann-Hollweg to William II, Berlin, July 20, 1911. *G. P.*, XXIX, 191–193. Bethmann warned the Kaiser that insistence upon Kiderlen's demand for all of the French Congo might compel an eventual demand for the strict execution of the Algeciras Act—and this would involve the evacuation of Casablanca and other places.

maneuvered for a larger or smaller section of Central African swamps and jungles and for such prestige as might be secured. Four months of suspense were at least as important a factor in exciting public opinion as Germany's most extreme demands. The possibility of war began to be given serious consideration.[86] In August and September, the usually moderate *République Française* published a series of technical military articles under the title, "The Eventual War," which ordinarily would have appeared in an army journal. Jules Hedeman declared that the army had never been in better condition,[87] and the temperate *Siècle* (Aug. 21) suggested the retention of the class of 1908 under the colors. Nationalist newspapers, such as the *Liberté* (Aug. 2), represented German policy as directed against the "sovereignty and independence of the French nation" rather than for the possession of colonial territory. The tension which in July had been limited to a restricted public grew until opinion in general became more excited. As usual, it did not take the form of a demand for war, because it was not desired by the nation, but of fear that Germany would force a conflict.[88]

The increase of nationalist sentiment was not entirely due to the protracted negotiations, for it was in part stimulated in order to strengthen the government's policy. This procedure, instead of expediting a satisfactory solution, delayed it, for Cambon used the state of public opinion in France as an argument against accepting excessive sacrifices.[89] He feared that war might result from the Pan-German agitation.[90] It was not until November 4 that the final agreements were signed, although certain terms had been known for some time. In return for a definitive recognition of a French protectorate in Morocco, France conceded the principle of the open door for an indefinite period, and in a separate agreement, she ceded to Germany a large section of the French Congo, receiving in exchange the Bec du Canard (a part of Togoland) to round out her Central African possessions. Those who appreciated the great value to France of a Moroccan protectorate had been prepared from the first to yield something in return for this prize.[91] "France is ready to pay," the Paris correspondent of the *Journal de Génève* (Oct. 30) had written.

[86] Major von Winterfeldt's report, Paris, Aug. 19, 1911. *G. P.,* XXIX, 333.

[87] *Radical,* July 28.

[88] *Matin,* Aug 22.

[89] *Livre Jaune: Affaires du Maroc,* VI (1910–1912), pp. 475, 476, 492.

[90] Cambon to de Selves, Berlin, Aug. 20, 1911. *Ibid.,* VI (1910–1912), pp. 477, 478.

[91] *Journal des Débats,* July 27, Sept. 10. *Figaro,* July 30. *Radical,* Sept. 17. *Temps,* Sept. 19. *Petite Gironde* (Bordeaux), Oct, 13.

"No importance should be credited to the clamoring of certain brag-garts, who exploit patriotic sentiment in declaring that not an inch of the Congo must be ceded." It remained to be seen if the reaction of public opinion to the final accord would justify this conclusion.

The first impression was, in general, favorable. Aroused by four months of obstinate negotiations, and determined to avoid any expression of weakness, the press rarely voiced the relief which many must have felt that the storm had passed without war. The accord was in fact approved, in some instances perhaps as a result of official influence,[92] by a considerable number of important newspapers of divers political opinions. "The mass of Germans and Frenchmen," observed the moderate *Siècle* (Nov. 7), "are satisfied with this peaceful solution." Even the conservative *Gaulois* (Nov. 4) was not extremely critical. France, according to the nationalist *Liberté* (Nov. 5), would not tolerate another Agadir, but it admitted that in signing the accord France "sacrificed no part of her honor" and that the measure of her profit would depend upon her own initiative. The radical *Lyon Ré-publicain* (Oct. 29) characterized the territory France had ceded as impenetrable swamps and forests. For the *Petite Gironde* of Bor-deaux (Nov. 3), the addition of Morocco to France's North African empire more than compensated the sacrifice of territory in Central Africa. "The country in general," it concluded, "is satisfied by the conclusion of differences with Germany which have lasted six years and which threatened the peace of the world." The dissatisfaction manifested by the Pan-Germans seemed to the radical *France de Bordeaux et du Sud-Ouest* (Nov. 5) a reason for the acceptance of the accord in France. "If it is bad for them, it must be good for us." Gaston Doumergue was convinced that public opinion was "content that these interminable negotiations had come to an end."[93]

Any treaty with Germany, as Doumergue pointed out, was bound to arouse criticism. Tardieu recognized the value of the Moroccan pro-tectorate, but he felt that "four months of chicanery had killed any faith in it."[94] Public opinion would have been more favorably impressed, wrote the conservative *Gaulois* (Oct. 19) and the radical *Lyon Républicain* (Oct. 9), if the solution had been found two months earlier. Unlike the *Liberté,* the chauvinist *Patrie* (Oct. 15) forgot what was gained in Morocco in view of the loss of territory in the Congo. "The crime which is being prepared . . . is more perfidious

[92] Schoen to Foreign Office, Paris, Nov. 4, 1911. *G. P.,* XXIX, 427.
[93] *France de Bordeaux et du Sud-Ouest,* Nov. 9.
[94] *Temps,* Nov. 5.

and treasonable than could be imagined." Rochefort had never shown much interest in colonies, but he now wrote of "peace at any price. We do not have Morocco, it is Germany who has us." [95] It was sometimes claimed that the loss of Congo territory was resented as a sacrifice of a part of the nation's patrimony, and as such, an object of "the fervent tenderness which the popular sentiment attaches to the soil of France." [96] Tardieu wrote that the cession of any territory was extremely painful to Frenchmen,[97] but the *Lyon Républicain* (Nov. 7), which believed that Morocco was worth the entire Congo, replied that "the intelligent peasant never hesitates to sacrifice less valuable lands for others which would round out his chief holding."

Raymond Poincaré, who was about to become the dominant personality in French politics, had exacting ideas as to a proper settlement with Germany. Writing in the *Petit Comtois* of Besançon (Oct. 21), he had described a perfectly balanced arrangement as alone acceptable. "If the entente," he wrote, "is established at our expense, complications may be disposed of for the moment, but they will inevitably return more dangerous than ever. There is only one equitable accord, based upon reciprocal and exactly balanced sacrifices which can be acceptable to a great nation. . . ." He did not communicate his immediate impression of the settlement of November 4 to the press, but that he did not consider France's sacrifices to be excessive appeared later in his approval of the accord as the reporter of the senatorial commission.[98]

It is evident therefore that there was a considerable section of public opinion which was prepared to accept the solution as satisfactory—the more so because the accord was highly unpopular among certain groups in Germany. If this point of view prevailed, there was no reason for despairing of a return to better relations with Germany. Those who felt that Germany's concessions were unreal, that the provision for the open door would limit the value of the protectorate,[99] that France had received the "bill" and Germany the "duck" [100] were by no means certain to have the deciding voice in directing public opinion. It was no action of Germany's nor was it a fault of the accord

[95] *Patrie,* Nov. 9.
[96] *Gaulois,* Nov. 5. Cf. Albin, *Le 'Coup' d'Agadir,* p. 297.
[97] *Temps,* Nov. 5.
[98] Poincaré, *Lendemain d'Agadir,* p. 3.
[99] *Journal des Débats,* Nov. 5.
[100] The historian Louis Madelin in the *République Française,* Nov 8. Even Jaurès approved the accord only as a step toward a Franco-German reconciliation. *Humanité,* Nov. 4.

itself that embittered public sentiment most. The unfavorable impression was immensely strengthened when the *Matin* (Nov. 8) published the secret terms of the Franco-Spanish entente of October, 1904,[101] for it was then fully realized for the first time that France was not after all to receive Morocco in its entirety. Spain, it appeared, had a sound claim to a considerable part of the northern coast. Some thought of denying her right,[102] but only for a moment, and then the disappointment, reënforced by older reasons for animosity against Germany, found an outlet in a condemnation of the accord of November 4. "Day before yesterday," wrote Jaurès, "the majority of the Chamber exulted over maps of Morocco. . . . Yesterday, the honey-cake, stale and poisoned, seemed bitter to it." [103] "Opinion was suddenly plunged," wrote the correspondent of the *Lyon Républicain* (Nov. 15), "into the most complete disorder. Nothing was more natural, for the conditions of the accord were already accepted unwillingly simply because they at least had the merit of assuring to us the protectorate over all of Morocco."

Few, other than the chauvinists, were prepared to advise parliament to reject the accord.[104] Its sanction, though necessary, should be given in silence, it was said. Nevertheless, the debate in the chamber continued from December 14 to December 20. The defense was limited to the government and to the socialist leaders, Jaurès and Marcel Sembat, who saw in the accord a step in the direction of a Franco-German reconciliation. As a rule, the Socialist point of view had been left unanswered in parliament, but on this occasion the nationalists abandoned all restraint. One declared that the mention of an accord with Germany was repugnant to him. Another spoke of an inevitable war. A

---

[101] Disclosures of other secret treaties followed in rapid succession. On November 10, the *Figaro* published the Franco-Spanish accord of 1902 which England had blocked. The *Petite République* (Nov. 10) confirmed the existence of the secret terms of the *entente cordiale*, and the *Temps* (Nov. 11) published them. The Franco-Spanish treaty of 1905 was published in full by the *Temps* (Nov. 12), and the *Écho de Paris* (Dec. 11) printed the secret exchange of letters which had accompanied the Franco-German Accord of 1909. Spain's approval of the publication of the Accord of 1902 was asked on the ground that it was desired by members of parliament. De Selves to Geoffray, Paris, Nov. 7, 1911. *Documents Diplomatiques Français,* 3d series, I, 52.

[102] *Matin,* Nov. 10. *Siècle,* Nov. 11. There was some discussion of a plan to secure a modification of the Spanish accord by using the state of public opinion in France as an argument. *Note pour le Ministre,* Paris, Nov. 20, 1911. *Documents Diplomatiques Français,* 3d series, I, pp. 158, 159.

[103] *Humanité,* Nov 9.

[104] *Journal des Débats,* Nov. 7. *Petit Comtois* (Besançon) Dec. 7. *Patrie,* Dec. 16.

more numerous group condemned the accord because it would increase the danger of war instead of assuring peace. Even the eleven republican deputies from the eastern departments who refused to vote in the affirmative because the ratification of the accord would have a distressing effect in "our mutilated Lorraine" explained through their spokesman that they "intended to remain the resolute adversaries of every aggressive measure." De Selves expressed the prevailing point of view in representing ratification as a disagreeable necessity. It was certain from the first that favorable action would be taken, and on December 20 the accord was ratified by a vote of 393 to 36 [105] with more than 150 abstentions.[106] "When the Chamber proceeded to ballot," wrote the correspondent of the *Journal de Génève* (Dec. 23), "a tragic breath passed over it, and the glacial silence with which the result was received was more significant than the most eloquent discourse."

Less than three years had elapsed since the accord of February 8, 1909, had been made under conditions that had promised a radically different result. Public opinion had then approved a policy of friendly relations with Germany; after the Agadir crisis, the chief indictment brought against Caillaux was his adaptation of this policy. The change, as usual, was due to causes for which public opinion was not, in any real sense, responsible. The failure of Pichon and Cruppi to convince Germany of their good-will in providing opportunities for the participation of her nationals in the economic development of Morocco and the steady advance of French influence there almost necessarily resulted, as Isvolski had foreseen, in action by Germany. Public opinion was doubtless at fault in its failure to exert a more effective control upon the government's policy, but this failure was due to the common assumption that Morocco was in the nature of things certain to become French, and to the lack of effective machinery for the control of foreign policy rather than to any desire to challenge Germany. The press failed almost completely to communicate to the public a fair opinion of the situation. Germany's attitude during the expedition to Fez was misrepresented, her demands were presented in the worst possible light, and France's secret arrangements for the partition of Morocco were revealed at the psychological moment to turn opinion definitely against the treaty of November 4. And the solution of the crisis was sometimes used to revive the memories of 1871. "In the light of

[105] *Annales,* 1911, V, pp. 1350–1562.
[106] Fifty had decided to withhold their votes after Jaurès's speech, according to the German ambassador, Schoen to Bethmann-Hollweg, Paris, Dec. 21, 1911. *G. P.,* XXIX, 439.

present grievances," wrote the *Petit Comtois* of Besauçon (Nov. 5), "those of the past reappear. . . . The cession of territory in the Congo almost equal to half of France recalls the loss of Alsace-Lorraine to the hearts of Frenchmen." The day of reckoning with Germany, declared Rochefort, was merely adjourned. "None can be certain of the future. Let us give much iron, a great deal of iron to the government for the defense of France." [107] Those who excited public opinion in this way were not acting under the influence of the Caillaux government, but some of the men then in power and others who were about to acquire it coöperated in the effort to arouse a nationalist spirit. They were determined that France should not suffer another Agadir.

[107] *Patrie,* Dec. 16.

CHAPTER XII

THE NEW NATIONALISM, RUSSIA, AND THE BALKANS

De 'réponse' en 'réponse' où doivent en venir Triple Entente et Triple Alliance. Il n'est que trop facile de la prévoir. Et quant aux imperturbables théoriciens de la politique étrangère du régime qui affirment que le groupement anglo-franco-russe opposé au groupement austro-germano-italien est une guarantie d'équilibre et de la paix, sont-ils bien sûrs de ce qu'ils disent?

J. B. (Jacques Bainville), *Action Française,* September 13, 1912.

Germany's policy after 1905 and the reaction to it in France gave the nationalist movement a significance which it had formerly lacked. Its leaders had not hitherto been able to enlist the active support of the majority of the middle classes, who as moderates or radicals controlled the Third Republic.[1] Their support of a monarchical restoration or a dictatorship had been a fatal handicap in view of the trend of French politics toward the parties of the left. With the growing belief that Germany's policy was one of systematic obstruction to France's legitimate interests in Morocco and that she was seeking to interfere with France's diplomatic arrangements and to humiliate her, the nationalist point of view became a more significant element of public opinion. It attracted more attention during the last two years before the World War than at any time since the Boulanger agitation.

There was nothing new in its emphasis upon the national honor and prestige, upon the army or upon a sensitive national pride. Germany's aggressive purposes and the need of assuring France's security were also familiar themes. It was more significant that the frankly chauvinist press was strengthened, to a certain extent, by the coöperation of the more moderate elements. Politicians, professors, and publicists

---

[1] Maurice Barrès succeeded Déroulède as the president of the Ligue des Patriotes after the latter's death in 1914, but it was predicted that his influence would be slight. *Radical,* July 12, 1914. "The cult of the dead of which he has made himself the high priest," wrote a Republican whose sympathies were with the nationalist movement, "has little influence upon souls who love life." Étienne Rey, *Le Renaissance de l'Orgeuil Française* (Paris, 1912), pp. 162, 163. Cf. M. Poirier, "Trois Directeurs: Jaurès—Léon Bourgeois—Barrès," *Grande Revue,* vol. 85, p. 222.

united in urging the need of a strong national spirit. André Tardieu in the *Temps,* Auguste Gauvain in the *Journal des Débats,* André Mévil in the *Echo de Paris,* and Jules Hedeman in the *Matin* were among those who sounded this characteristic note in the press. Historians helped to confirm the belief that Russia's aid alone had prevented an attack by Germany in 1875 and 1887 and that the conditions which determined the foreign policy of France were independent of individual statesmen and of public opinion.[2] Ernest Lavisse, the director of the École Normale and one of the most distinguished of French historians, did his part to stimulate an exalted patriotism and an anticipation of war. " 'If I did not give to the flag,' " he is said to have declared, " 'a pagan's cult for his idol, I do not know what I would do in this world.' " [3] In October, 1912, when the war clouds were about to break in the Balkans, he chose to talk to the pupils of his native village of Nouvion-en-Thierache and to the nation of the need of mastering fear in order to fulfil the duties of citizenship in time of war. War, he said, had been and would continue to be predicted for the immediate future. "War would be a great and terrible event. France, defeated and suffering from a wound which is still open, knows it well, but she remains tranquil." He regretted the tendency in France toward self-depreciation, for there were many reasons to be proud.

"Her history is great and glorious . . . She feels herself to be noble among the nations. True, the world about her has changed during the last half-century. A people has arisen near us, who reminds us on every occasion and too frequently in a tone of insolent hatred that it also is great and strong. That people is indeed great and strong. But France who threatens no one, fears no one. She knows that she is still France."

Nevertheless, Lavisse insisted that he was opposed to an aggressive policy.[4]

Others, who expressed the same point of view, were not as worthy of confidence. André Mévil was inspired by the three-year service law of 1913 to exalt the military strength of France and of Russia. Their "timorous policy," he wrote, was not in keeping with the conditions

---

[2] René Pinon, "France et Allemagne," *Rev. des Deux Mondes,* 1912, II, 96.

[3] Gustave Dupin (Ermenonville), *Poincaré et ses 'Souvenirs Politiques'* (Paris, 1927), p. 20.

[4] *Temps,* Oct. 7, 1912. In August, 1911, he had spoken under similar circumstances of the Alsace-Lorraine question, when he urged the need of unwavering loyalty to the lost provinces. Alsace, he said, still refused to accept Germany's rule, and therefore no Franco-German understanding was possible, *Ibid.,* Aug. 16, 1911.

which assured Germany's final and complete defeat.[5] He pictured the Poles as rising at Russia's signal, the Danes and Alsatians as revolting against their oppressors in the "next war." [6] War, he insisted, was inevitable because of Germany's "immoderate desire of domination, her incredible pride, and because of that perpetual suspicion, that delirium of persecution which has seized her. . . . Finally, there is a past between Germany and us which cannot be forgotten." [7] But, for the most part, the nationalist leaders were too much concerned with the immediate present, and the Franco-Prussian War was too distant, for them to appeal to the memories of 1871. Déroulède's influence, in fact, had declined.[8] "For the last ten years," wrote the *Journal des Débats* (Jan. 31, 1914) after his death, "he was the object of an ungrateful silence." "He was the last witness who continued to relive the *année terrible*," declared the *Figaro* (Jan. 31, 1914), "it seemed that the tragic memories which he defended were disappearing with him."

Emotional chauvinism was not entirely absent in this new phase of the nationalist sentiment. The anti-German play, *Alsace,* and the *revanche* sentiment which, according to the Belgian ambassador, was a part of every vaudeville program aroused thunderous applause.[9] The boulevards of Paris were not any more representative of France in 1913 than in 1870; nevertheless a feeling of tension existed outside of Paris. It was especially evident near the eastern frontier, where a series of incidents occurred during the spring of 1913. Three German visitors from Metz were handled roughly in Nancy; the forced landing upon French soil of a Zeppelin and an airplane was variously interpreted as evidence of espionage or as a deliberate provocation. In part of spontaneous origin, this nervousness was encouraged by the exaggerations

[5] A. Mévil, *La Paix est Malade* (Paris, 1914), pp. 119, 120; 127, 128. An army officer predicted the break-up of the German Empire. Commandant de Civrieux, *Le Germanisme Encirclé* (Paris, 1913), p. 5.

[6] Mévil, *La Paix est Malade,* pp. 181–194.

[7] *Ibid.,* p. 23. Mévil, according to Jaurès, had served the purposes of the Pan-Germans by describing the German people as a "'horde of babarians'" and by declaring that "'the only reason for the existence of the Franco-Russian Alliance is its anti-German character.'" Jaurès, "Un Exemple," *Rev. de l'Enseignement Primaire,* June 28, 1914. Mévil replied that "we preach only a thoroughly defensive policy." *Écho de Paris,* July 14, 1914.

[8] Speaking to the Ligue des Patriotes on the occasion of this annual pilgrimage to the battle-field of Champigny, he expressed the hope that an occasion for the inevitable conflict with Germany would be found during the Balkan War. *Patrie,* Dec. 10, 1912.

[9] *Ibid.,* Jan. 12, 1913. Schwertfeger, *Die Belgischen Dokumente,* V, 191 (Report from Paris, May 5, 1913).

of a section of the press. A clear example of mercenary motives in stimulating anti-German sentiment had occurred in March, 1911, when the *Journal* announced an aëronautical contest whose itinerary included Berlin. The *Matin,* having organized a similar project within the frontiers of France, compelled its competitor to eliminate Berlin by declaring that the secrets of French aviation were about to be revealed to the enemy.[10]

Instead of discounting the significance of the nationalist movement, as had been done during its earlier phases, the general tendency was to call attention to it as representative of public opinion. France, it was said, was determined not to endure another Agadir. Particular attention was given to the development of nationalist sentiment among the youth of the universities and colleges, as from it would come the future leaders of the nation. The cynical indifference of its elders to patriotism, it was said, had been discarded. Pessimism had given place to a love of action and of positive beliefs. Under the influence of Bergsonian philosophy, the emotions were given precedence over the intellect as the guide of life.[11] And the Abbé Dimnet presented the new spirit to the English-speaking world in his *France Herself Again* (New York, 1914) as representing the dominant tendencies of French spirit. Tangier, he wrote, had been "a flash of lightning, after which the clouds lifted," [12] for France had recovered her national unity by putting her party divisions in their proper place. These writers were not describing an imaginary state of mind, but, themselves nationalists, they naturally found what they wished to find.

It is probable that the extremist element was still a minority. Perhaps the best indication of this is to be found in the attitude of its more moderate allies, who thought of the nationalist spirit principally as a useful moral support for France's foreign policy. The *Siècle* (Sept. 12, 1912) wrote, for example, that her recent diplomatic suc-

[10] *Journal,* March 30, 1911. *Humanité,* March 31, 1911.

[11] Agathon (Henri Massis, Albert de Tarde), *Les Jeunes Gens d'Aujourdhui* (Paris, 1913). This study, which was recognized by the Académie Française, has been used extensively. C. E. Playne, *The Neuroses of the Nations* (New York, 1925), pp. 273–281. F. Gouttenoire de Toury, *Jaurès et le Parti de la Guerre* (Paris, 1922), pp. 61, 62. Cf. Émile Henriot, *A Quoi rêvent les Jeunes Gens* (Paris, 1912). This pamphlet appeared originally in the form of articles in the *Temps.* A. Albert-Petit, "Les Tendances de la Jeunesse," *Journal des Débats,* Jan. 28, 1913. Gaston Riou, *Aux Écoutes de la France qui Viennent* (Paris, 1912). For an affirmation of peaceful sentiment on behalf of the younger generation, see Ph. Laurent, Alex. Mercereau, "La Paix Armée et la Jeunesse Française," *Grande Revue,* vol. 88, p. 391.

[12] Dimnet, *France Herself Again,* p. 151.

cesses were due even more to the impression abroad than "we dispute less and act more" than to her able diplomatic service. The nationalist point of view was sometimes represented as the best means of maintaining peace. "A true policy of peace," wrote the nationalist *Petit Marseillais* (Dec. 10, 1912), "consists in not fearing war and even in appearing to desire it. Be assured then that it will not come and that we will profit diplomatically." With practically no exceptions, France's policy was represented as peaceful, and it was held that Germany's attitude alone required France to be upon the alert.[13] It was this claim which increased the difficulties of an open opposition. He who would question the need of resistance to aggression, it was said, could not be a true Frenchman.

An important body of criticism developed, it will be seen, against a policy which would involve France in a general war having its origins in the Balkans, and it may be supposed that a large group desired a return to more normal relations with Germany. As usual, a public expression of that desire was often rejected as a confession of weakness. Some, however, refused to remain silent. Maurice Ajam, a deputy and the director of the Comité du Commerce Français avec l'Allemagne, urged the development of economic relations.[14] The commercial expert, Charles Aubert, felt that France should take into consideration the importance of Franco-German relations in the maintenance of world peace. Every effort should be made, he wrote, to solve the difficulties between the two countries by arbitration, conversations, and the development of economic relations. Even if these efforts failed to dispose of the Alsace-Lorraine question, Aubert was still in favor of

[13] When the German Chancellor, in April, 1913, spoke to the Reichstag of the chauvinist spirit in France as a legitimate cause of concern for the security of Germany, Professor Aulard replied that even the nationalist press never mentioned an offensive war: ". . . not a single chauvinist newspaper proposes a declaration of war against Germany. The most exalted of Frenchmen speak only of the defense." *Dépêche* (Toulouse), April 16, 1913. This was almost literally true, but in attributing aggressive purposes to Germany, in accepting extraordinary military expenses, and in encouraging a strong nationalist spirit, this defensive attitude was perilously close to provocation.

[14] M. Ajam, *Le Problème Économique Franco-Allemand* (Paris, 1914), p. 6. The greater part of this volume appeared at first in the *France,* (September, 1913). Ajam became an under-secretary in the Ministry of Commerce in the Viviani Cabinet of 1914. The reports of the German ambassador and military attaché (von Schoen and Winterfeldt) in 1913, and on the eve of the war, gave at least due, and perhaps exaggerated, credit to this moderate tendency. " 'The desire for military revenge as it was incorporated in Boulanger and Déroulède, is a stage that is past,' " wrote von Schoen in Feb., 1914. Bernadotte E. Schmitt, *The Coming of the War,* 1914, 2 vols. (New York, 1930), I, 60–68.

peace, and in supporting this position, he showed the great risks which France would incur in a war with Germany.[15] The ideas of the Socialist millionaire, Marcel Sembat, attracted more attention because they were expressed with much spirit in a challenging manner. His book, *Faites un Roi, sinon faites la Paix* (Paris, 1913) reached fourteen editions within a year after its first publication.[16] Its thesis was that France must, as she never had, choose definitely between a policy of peace and one of war.[17] If she chose the latter, she would have to scrap the republican régime, for it was notoriously incapable of conducting a successful war. But, as France was republican in sentiment, she must necessarily elect for a policy of peace upon the basis of the *status quo*. He refused to admit that the policy of the equilibrium was satisfactory. "In my opinion," he wrote, "the present system of Europe and our alliances prepare war and not peace." [18] Sembat's position was essentially that which Juarès and de Pressensé had expressed ten years earlier, and it is of some significance that, if it was not widely approved, it did not occasion the violent denunciations which had been directed against its earlier expression.

The question as to the extent of the nationalist spirit was not as important as its relations with the government. If official circles were not responsible for its origins,[19] they encouraged it as a necessary support of France's foreign policy. That policy, represented to public opinion as the maintenance of peace by means of the balance of power, was at least potentially directed against Germany, and Germany so regarded it. The possibility that war might result from it, therefore, could not safely be ignored, and for this reason it was necessary that public opinion should be prepared. Delcassé had developed a system

---

[15] C. Aubert, *La Folie Franco-Allemande* (Paris, 1914), p. 10, 13.

[16] Its main points were first developed in an article for the *Rev. de l'Enseignement Primaire*, March 28, 1913. See M. Sembat, "La Double Question," *Grande Revue*, vol. 81, pp. 44–49 (Sept., 1913). Aulard, the historian, denied that the foreign policy of France could be determined by a simple question capable of being answered by "yes or no." *Dépêche* (Toulouse), July 14, 1913. For a similar criticism see Georges Renard, "France et Allemagne," *Revue*, vol. 103, pp. 391. The same question, however, had been raised by Dr. Flaissières in the *Petit Provençal* (Marseilles), March 18, 1913. For other comments upon Sembat's book, of diverse character, see *Journal des Débats*, Aug. 4, 1913, *Écho de Paris*, May 29, 1913, *France de Bordeaux et du Sud-Ouest*, July 18, 1913, *Lanterne*, July 21, 1913, *Petit Comtois* (Besançon), July 21, 1913. The reaction of the last three journals, representing the parties of the left, was favorable.

[17] Sembat, *Faites un Roi*, p. 87.

[18] *Ibid.*, p. 75.

[19] Charles Maurras claimed more credit than was its due for the *Action Française*. Maurras, *Kiel et Tanger*, p. 223.

of diplomatic understandings around the Russian alliance without much reference to public opinion, and its reaction to his dismissal in June, 1905, had shown that it was not then prepared to endorse a definitely anti-German policy. By 1912, circumstances of which Germany's policy had been the most important, had defeated Rouvier's and Caillaux's policy of amicable negotiations. Especially since 1907, the *Temps,* followed by many other moderate newspapers, had been campaigning in behalf of the policy of the equilibrium. It was in support of that policy that members of the government appealed to a nationalist spirit during the last two years before the war.

Raymond Poincaré became the man of the hour and of the future on his selection as President of the Council in February, 1912, and on his election as President of the Republic a year later. His policy was that of the equilibrium, interpreted with legal exactness, but it was applied in such a way as to justify the suspicion that he was seeking a distinct superiority for the Triple Entente rather than an equality of strength with the Triple Alliance. His Lorraine birth has been interpreted as evidence of his unchanging will to recover Alsace-Lorraine, and this purpose was perhaps present in his mind. His chief concern was, however, for the security, the influence, and the prestige of France.[20] He believed that they could be advanced by the policy of the equilibrium. To this end, he used his influence to tighten the bonds which united the members of the Triple Entente, to remove the causes of friction between them and to prevent the development of close relations between them and members of the Triple Alliance. A word from Paris helped to prevent the Haldane mission from bringing about a limitation of Anglo-German naval armaments in the spring of 1912.[21] Sir Edward Grey agreed, in the Grey-Cambon letters of November, 1912, to an immediate preparation for common action in the event of a threatened aggression, and for the first time

[20] His election as President was aided by the success of the foreign policy of his cabinet. *Figaro,* Dec. 27, 1912. "France will ask him," wrote the *Est Républicain* (Nancy), Jan. 12, 1913, "to conserve the benefits which he has been able to win for France from the Balkan imbroglio by the authority and influence of his personality, and to increase constantly her prestige. France desires a President who is a guide and a counselor at the same time, the creator at home and the symbol abroad of the renaissance to which she aspires." Poincaré assured Szécsen, the Austrian Ambassador, that his election as President would not change French policy. " '. . . I will see to it that a man is put in my place who will follow my policy. *Ce sera comme si j'étais toujours encore au Quai d'Orsay.'* " *Ö.-U. A.,* V. 493, 494 (Jan. 19, 1913).

[21] He had acted, however, upon Bertie's suggestion. Fay, *Origins of the World War,* I, 317.

he was persuaded to take official cognizance of the military plans which had been worked out in the conferences between the French and British army officers.[22] An understanding was reached which permitted France to concentrate her fleet in the Mediterranean. The Port Baltic interview between the Russian Tsar and the German Emperor [23] was soon followed by the Franco-Russian naval treaty and by the first of Poincaré's diplomatic voyages to St. Petersburg.[24] Georges Louis was eventually recalled from his post as ambassador to Russia on her complaint that he was not in sympathy with her policy. Although Poincaré acted with Germany at the beginning of the Balkan Wars, he was in general unfriendly to the earlier practice of informal conversations. Cambon became more reserved under the Poincaré government,[25] and no encouragement was given to the German Charles René who was working for a Franco-German *rapprochement* to be based upon the granting of autonomy to Alsace-Lorraine within the Empire.[26] In listening to such proposals as those of M. Charles René," wrote Poincaré to Jules Cambon, March 27, 1912, "we would have difficulty with England and with Russia, we would lose the benefit of the policy which France has followed for many years, we would secure only illusory advantages for Alsace, and we would find ourselves isolated . . . ." [27]

The state of public opinion in France aroused the concern of Jules Cambon and the German officials in Berlin,[28] while in France, Poin-

---

[22] Grey to Cambon, Foreign Office, Nov. 22, 1912. Grey, *Twenty-Five Years,* I, 95.

[23] This episode, as indicating an undesirable intimacy, aroused considerable uneasiness in the French press. *Presse,* July 7, 1912. *Journal des Débats,* July 8, 1912.

[24] Marcel Hutin wired from St. Petersburg that a written accord had been made between England, Russia, and France not to negotiate with another Power without consulting the other members of the Triple Entente. *Écho de Paris,* Aug. 6, 1912. A Havas wire dated from London at once denied this. *Journal des Débats,* Aug. 8. *Figaro,* Aug. 8. Cf. Friedrich Stieve, *Der Diplomatische Schriftwechsel Iswolskis, 1911–1914,* 5 vols. (Berlin, 1926), II, 388.

[25] Theobald von Bethmann-Hollweg, *Betrachtungen zum Weltkriege,* 2 vols. (Berlin, 1919), I, 39. See English translation, *Reflections on the World War,* pp. 40, 41.

[26] Poincaré, *Lendemain d'Agadir,* pp. 125–127. *L'Europe sous les Armes* (Paris, 1926), pp. 355–360. The German government, it is true, was equally cool. Poincaré, although pessimistic as to his chances, permitted Sir Thomas Barclay to go to Berlin upon a private mission in the interests of better relations between France and Germany.

[27] Poincaré, *Lendemain d'Agadir,* p. 126.

[28] Jules Cambon refused a decoration from the Emperor on the ground that it would not be well received in France. *Ibid.,* pp. 123–124.

caré helped to confirm the nationalist spirit as a source of strength for his foreign policy. On October 27, 1912, when Austria's menacing attitude toward the victorious Serbs threatened to lead Russia's intervention, Poincaré chose to make a dramatic and unusual appeal to public opinion in a speech at Nantes. "We must," he declared, "maintain all of the patience, all of the energy, all of the pride of a people which does not desire war but which nevertheless does not fear it." It was not only a question, he added, of maintaining a strong army and a powerful navy, but also of "that persevering care of the national conscience, of that unanimous and integral acceptance of patriotic duty, without which the most glorious and prosperous nations are condemned to humiliations and decadence."[29] This part of the speech, according to the *Écho de Paris* (Oct. 28, 1912) was emphasized by gestures and by a grave tone of voice which left no doubt as to its importance.[30] The *Figaro* (Oct. 28) thought that it was addressed to Europe as well as to France, but the *Phare de la Loire* of Nantes (Oct. 28) described it as an appeal for national union as the only means by which France could "impose her *influence dominatrice et pacificatrice.*" The army was given more publicity than usual under the Poincaré government, for Millerand, its Minister of War, revived the annual spring review at Vincennes.[31] The spirit in which the national holiday was celebrated in 1912, with its imposing military maneuvers at Longchamps, resembled Boulanger's triumph in 1886.[32] "If a revival of military spirit has been discussed," Poincaré told a Dutch journalist, "it is because it has been seen that France appreciates her army and because she is profoundly conscious of her national

[29] Poincaré, *Les Balkans en Feu* (Paris, 1926), pp. 278–282. The author is evading the point when he declares that the tone of the speech was not aggressive, for its chief significance was its appeal to a nationalist spirit. "If there is no one in France who cherishes the sacrilegious hope of a European war," he declared at Bar-le-Duc, August 18, 1913, "there is also no one who is not ready to defend France's rank as a Great Power and her independence of action." The *Journal des Débats* (Aug. 20, 1913) observed that this statement spoken near the frontier "assumed a more serious significance."

[30] The *Écho du Nord* (Lille) Oct. 27, 1912, announced before the speech was delivered that it would be an appeal for national union. The correspondent of the *Times* (London), Oct. 29 wrote that it had united "French opinion in a remarkable demonstration of unanimity such as has only been witnessed on one or two occasions in recent years." See Schoen's comments, *G. P.*, XXXIII, 311, 312.

[31] *Livre Noir*, I, 213 (March 14, 1912).

[32] *Journal des Débats*, July 16, 1912. "What enthusiasm," exclaimed Colonel Rousset in the *Gaulois*, July 15, 1912. "I have never seen such crowds, or such a communion of sentiment in the passion of the flag and army."

dignity." [33] Although his whole political career had previously been that of a "man of the left," as Poincaré has frequently described himself, his foreign policy turned him more and more to the parties of the center and right for support. It was largely their votes which elected him President of the Republic.[34]

Public opinion is necessarily concerned for the most part with definite incidents, and it is rarely conscious, though its leaders may be, of a need for a strong resistance apart from the specific occasions for its expression. The years 1912–1914 were crowded with problems and situations which required decisions of the utmost importance. They involved France's relations with Russia and her Balkan ambitions, the Alsace-Lorraine question, and the proper reply to recent increases in the German army. The Balkan wars involved the vital question which had always been implied in the Russian alliance. Would France enter a general war resulting from the Austro-Russian rivalry for the control of the Balkans? A few publicists and perhaps a considerable section of public opinion had protested against this possibility before the formation of the alliance.[35] This contingency had then been thought of as a danger to be avoided, but these doubts were later forgotten in the greater sense of security and the increased influence which resulted from the association with Russia. When it became apparent that she had no intention of aiding France to recover Alsace-Lorraine by force of arms, and when even her diplomatic support in France's difficulties in Morocco and Egypt was given with serious reservations, the alliance lost something of the sentimental interest with which it had been at first invested. Many, perhaps a majority, of liberals were antagonized by the ruthless suppression of the Revolution in 1905,[36] but the alliance survived all tests. Millions of rubles were distributed to the French press in order to maintain confidence in the Russian bonds in which Frenchmen had so liberally invested. It is by no means certain, however, that this was necessary, for the government and the directing classes were determined to maintain the al-

[33] Radical, Aug. 5, 1912.

[34] Gaston Doumergue in the Grande Revue, vol. 77, p. 417 (Jan. 25, 1913).

[35] See above, p. 156.

[36] Nekluduff's despatch, Paris, Dec. 1/14, 1910. Livre Noir, I, 14–16. Clemenceau in the Aurore, Jan. 31, 1905. Petite République, Jan. 25, 1905. Humanité, Jan. 23, 29, Feb. 9, 1905. "The Tsar," wrote René Viviani in the Petit Provençal (Marseille), Jan. 4, 1905, "has just undertaken the assassination of an entire people." In July, 1914, Viviani was (with Poincaré) a guest of the Tsar in St. Petersburg.

liance at any price. The nation's political ideals were not to be permitted to interfere with its foreign policy.[37]

The Austro-Russian understanding of 1897 had put the Balkan question "on ice" for a decade, and it was not until the Bosnian crisis of 1908–1909 that public opinion in France was forced to express itself as to the aid which should be given to Russia in the Balkans. No clear decision was then reached. Uninformed as to the situation there, the immense majority of the nation was certainly cold to the idea of fighting in behalf of Serbia or of Russia's interests. Even the nationalists were divided, for Millevoye insisted that Russia's attention should be concentrated upon the German frontier. He declared that the alliance did not commit France "to complications which would be adventurous for Russia and disastrous for France." [38] The *Figaro* (Oct. 5, 1908) thought that Austria's annexation of Bosnia-Herzegovina was merely a formal change of the existing situation. The *Siècle* (Nov. 2, 1908), the *Journal* (Feb. 25, 1909), and the *Petit Parisien* (Feb. 24, 1909) invited Russia to restrain the Serbs. Coöperation with Germany as well as England was recommended by the *Temps* (Jan. 10, 1909) in the interest of peace. "There are times," it declared, "when there is an obligation to judge things coolly. However deserving of sympathy Serbia may be, she is not worth the risk of a general war." Yet a section of the moderate and conservative press warmly championed the cause of the Serbs, and insisted that France was prepared to fulfil her duties if Russia became involved in war for the defense of Serbia. Nor was it said that such a war must result from an aggression against Russia which Germany supported to warrant France's intervention, although it was assumed that Germany would be certain to act.[39] The first test of public opinion had resulted in no clear conclusion as to the proper policy. Public opinion continued to be misinformed as to conditions in Russia, not perhaps primarily because of the influence of her money, but because those who controlled the press

[37] *Temps,* Jan. 22, 29. Feb. 1, 2, 1905. *Journal des Débats,* Jan. 24, 25, 30, 1905. *République Française,* Jan. 23, 31, 1905. *Gaulois,* Jan. 25, Feb. 7, 1905. *Liberté,* Jan. 27, 1905.

[38] *Patrie,* July 18, 1908.

[39] *Journal des Débats,* Oct. 6, 7, Dec. 26, 1908; Feb. 24, 26, March 4, 5, 1909. *République Française,* Feb. 24, 1909. *Siècle,* Feb. 26, March 3, 10, 15, 1909. *Écho de Paris,* Feb. 19, 24, 25, March 3, 1909. *Gaulois,* Feb. 25, 1909. Khevenhüller wrote from Paris, Oct. 12, 1908: *"Für uns habe ich bisher teils mit, teils ohne geld gesichert:* Éclair, Gaulois, Figaro, Temps, Radical, Petit Parisien *und* Écho de Paris." At that time only the *Journal des Débats, Matin,* and Hanotaux in the *Journal* were hostile. *Ö.-U. A.,* I, 200, 201.

were in principle opposed to anything which would damage the alliance.[40] By 1913, about seventeen billions of francs had been advanced to her in the form of public or private loans.[41] Few, except the Socialists, saw that Russia's superficial appearance of strength concealed weaknesses which greatly increased the dangers of an association with her.

The press could scarcely have been expected to enlighten public opinion as to the war in preparation in the Balkans during the summer of 1912 when diplomats failed to see the seriousness of the situation.[42] In March, Isvolski had concealed from Poincaré the full significance of the offensive and defensive alliance which Serbia and Bulgaria had formed under Russia's patronage.[43] When all of its terms were revealed to him during his visit to St. Petersburg in August, Poincaré characterized it as an "instrument of war," [44] but he did not exert himself seriously to moderate its more dangerous features. He repeatedly urged upon Isvolski the need of a prior understanding with France before undertaking any initiative that was not a reply to an actual or imminent aggression by Germany or by Austria with Germany's support.[45] This intimacy which he sought and which in a measure he secured might have been used, it seems, to restrain Russia's Balkan protégés, but he was unwilling to risk offending her or to interfere with her freedom of action. Nevertheless, he had no desire in 1912 for war in the Balkans. All of the Great Powers, with the possible exception of Russia, were more or less embarrassed when the Balkan States took events into their own hands in October by attacking Turkey. Poincaré's belated efforts to prevent the war and

[40] Michon, *L'Alliance Franco-Russe*, pp. 297–300. Michon has shown conclusively that the principal fault lay with the wilful blindness of those who should have informed public opinion.

[41] *Ibid.*, p. 127.

[42] Élie Halévy is impressed by the failure of French and German diplomats alike to see the significance of the agitation among the Southern Slavs. Élie Halévy, "Documents Diplomatiques Français," *Rev. de Paris*, Sept. 1, 1929, p. 63. This is a review of the first volume of documents to appear in accordance with the decision to publish a large selection of documents dealing with French diplomacy, 1871–1914.

[43] But Poincaré now writes that he was not entirely satisfied with Isvolski's account, and it appears from the diplomatic correspondence that he endeavored to discover the truth. Poincaré, *Les Balkans en Feu*, pp. 31–67.

[44] Poincaré's report of his conversation with Sazonov, the Russian foreign minister. Aug. 1912. *Livre Jaune: Affaires Balkaniques*, I, 38, 39.

[45] Poincaré to Louis, Paris, March 14, 1912. *Ibid.*, I, 12, 13. Isvolski believed it necessary to avoid every occasion of misunderstanding with the French cabinet. Isvolski to Sazonov, Paris, March 1/14, 1912. *Livre Noir*, I, 333.

then to coöperate with the other Powers for the restoration of peace upon the basis of the *status quo,* while maintaining the unity of the Triple Entente, had in general the support of public opinion. They were even appreciated in Germany.[46]

It was at once evident that the Triple Entente faced the Triple Alliance in the Balkans. Even more clearly than in the Bosnian crisis, the possibility of a general European war demanded and secured the attention of the press. "The state of war in the Balkans," wrote the conservative *Gaulois* (Oct. 15), "constitutes a permanent danger to the peace of Europe. A very fragile thread, which the slightest imprudence may break, supports this sword of Damocles." It was quite evident to the Monarchist Jacques Bainville, a keen critic of the policy of the equilibrium, as the quotation which heads this chapter proves, that "the real question is that of knowing whether the Franco-Russian alliance goes into effect if Russia becomes involved." In his judgment, France should keep her interest and sympathies at home.[47] Even more definite protests against a policy which might involve France came from the parties and leaders of the left. The Radical-Socialist congress at Tours was inspired by the immediate danger to show an unusual interest in the international situation. "The fate of France, the greatness and glory of our country," it declared, "depends above all upon the maintenance of peace." [48] Jaurès believed that the Balkan States would not dare to disturb peace unless they felt themselves supported by more powerful friends, and he would have the concert of Europe warn them that the partition of Turkey would not be tolerated.[49] The more influential moderate section of the press, fearing that only the intervention of the Great Powers would save the Balkan League from a disastrous defeat, in general supported Poincaré's policy. Even the *Journal des Débats* (Oct. 2), in spite of its Serbian sympathies, spoke of the "absurdity of a war from the point of view of the Balkan States, even of its folly for some among them." Blame for the war was placed upon them, and Recouly declared that their demand for Macedonia could not be tolerated. Gaston

[46] *Frankfurter Zeitung,* Oct. 16, 1912. Schoen thought that Poincaré's efforts for the maintenance of peace were caused by his fear that the war would become a general conflict. Schoen to Bethmann-Hollweg, Paris, Nov. 10, 1912. *G. P.,* XXXIII, 310. The German ambassador remained convinced that the French government would exert itself to the utmost to prevent a European war. *Ibid.,* XXXIII, 437.

[47] *Action Française,* Oct. 22, 1912.

[48] *Radical,* Oct. 14, 1912.

[49] *Humanité,* Oct. 7, 26.

Calmette wrote that "France has no part at all in the present difficulties of eastern Europe. This must not be forgotten: none of her interests are involved." He noted with satisfaction that France's efforts for peace had "for the first time in forty years brought her into perfect harmony with Germany. . . ."[50] Tardieu somewhat coolly approved France's coöperation with Germany in the interest of peace,[51] but he was noticeably more concerned with condemning the action of the Radical-Socialist Congress and with his admiration for the *"grandeur"* of the war and of the magnificent patriotism of the Balkan peoples.[52]

The prevailing tendency in the press during the first two weeks of the Balkan War was favorable, therefore, to a policy which would restore peace. Nevertheless, some observers expressed a different point of view. France, according to Gabriel Hanotaux, was "necessarily an agent of conciliation and of peace," but it is somewhat surprising to find that she should in this capacity persuade England to accept Russia's thesis as to the opening of the straits! In his opinion the fate of humanity was at the mercy of an inexorable destiny. "Let us be attentive, . . . let us be ready."[53] The moderate *Petit Comtois* of Besançon (Oct. 3), even before the beginning of military operations, had insisted that the Triple Entente should aid the Balkan League against Turkey. Business men and politicians were alarmed, according to the *Patrie* (Oct. 15), but "the real France" was prepared to follow the example of the Balkan peoples if they succeeded in emancipating themselves. Even the strictly limited and temporary association with Germany soon inspired doubts among those who had accepted the thesis that the interests of France could best be served and that the best guarantee of peace was in a close contact with the other members of the Triple Entente. On October 18, Recouly feared that "The actual crisis had somewhat confused the normal play of alliances and of the European understandings. . . . France's rôle, it seems to us, is clearly traced. Absolute fidelity to

---

[50] *Figaro,* Oct. 14. See Cremin to the head of the Russian police in Paris, Oct. 8, 1912, for an identification of Recouly as an agent of the Russian police. *Hinter den Kulissen des Französischen Journalismus,* von einem Pariser Chefredakteur (Berlin, 1925), pp. 97, 98. On Oct. 6, he published an interview with Sazonov in the *Figaro* in which the Russian foreign minister denied that his country was in any way responsible for the actions of the Balkan States.

[51] *Temps,* Oct. 14.

[52] *Ibid.,* Oct. 15.

[53] *Revue Hebdomadaire,* Oct. 12, 1912, in G. Hanotaux, *La Guerre des Balkans et l'Europe, 1912-1913* (Paris, 1914), p. 124.

our allies and friends, such should be . . . the essential rule of our diplomacy." [54]

The Bulgarian victories of Kirk Kilisse, October 23–24, and of Lule Burgas, October 29–31, strengthened this emphasis upon the need of close union within the Triple Entente. It would be fatal, declared the *Journal des Débats* (Oct. 28), "to permit it to be suspected that France was disposed to take an extra dance with a member of the Triple Alliance." "The stronger and more disciplined are the alliances and ententes," wrote Tardieu, " the more assured the maintenance of order in Europe, and also the greater the chances of avoiding the disorder which may come from the Balkans. Europe and peace have no worse enemy than diplomatic anarchy." [55] It was this moment that Poincaré chose for his appeal, October 27, for close relations with England and Russia, and to public opinion in his speech at Nantes. Three days later, he virtually abandoned his former position in favor of the *status quo,* by asking all of the Powers to affirm their disinterestedness.[56] It was thought impossible to deprive the League of its conquests, but it was more important that neither the Russian nor the French government had any interest in such an enterprise. Isvolski had already predicted that the complete success of the League would lead to a clash between the Pan-Slavic and Pan-German movements [57]; nevertheless, moderate and nationalist opinion became more certain that France should aid the Balkan States in retaining their conquests. "More than ever," wrote the *Gaulois* (Nov. 5), "must we defend the cause of these valiant little peoples . . . who . . . are firmly resolved not to betray the interests of the Triple Entente." According to Millevoye, it would be dishonorable for France to abandon the interests of her ally. "Let the Socialists proclaim the puerile power of the proletariat. Follow the work of the chancelleries. *Haut les*

[54] *Figaro,* Oct. 23.

[55] *Temps,* Nov. 1. See Schoen to Bethmann-Hollweg, Paris, Oct. 26, 1912 (*G. P.,* XXXIII, 257) for a report of the effect of the Balkan victories upon French opinion. Much enthusiasm was aroused by the success of French artillery and military methods against the German matériel and training of the Turkish armies.

[56] In other words, he would permit the Balkan States to retain their conquests. Poincaré to Ambassadors at Berlin, Vienna, Rome, Oct. 30, 1912. *Livre Jaune: Affaires des Balkans, 1912–1914,* I, 127. According to Isvolski, this proposal was made in accordance with Sazonov's suggestion. Paris, 25 Oct. 7/Nov., 1912. *Livre Noir,* I, 341. But Poincaré writes rather of an understanding with Grey as to the terms of his note. Poincaré, *Les Balkans en Feu,* p. 289.

[57] *Livre Noir,* I, 333 (Paris, 10/23 Oct., 1912).

cœurs, patriotes de France!" [58] Phrased in more moderate terms, Hanotaux's articles were equally firm in their support of the Balkan States and of Russia's interests. Jean Herbette, a relative of Maurice Herbette, an official of the Quai d'Orsay, insisted that France's own interests were involved in the victories of the League and in the defense of Russia's position. *"Se concerter, se taire et agir,"* was his advice.[59] If Austria attempted directly or indirectly to establish her control over the route to Salonica, he believed that France should declare "without bluster but unequivocally that . . . we will support Serbia with all our strength." [60] A sufficient number of provincial newspapers expressed approximately the same point of view to warrant the conclusion that it represented at least the nationalist element and perhaps a fraction of the more moderate public opinion.[61] It was stated with unusual force and precision by the historian Albert Malet, who had been the tutor in diplomatic history of Prince Alexander, later the King of Serbia. He believed that if Austria should attempt to take from Serbia the fruits of her victories, the intervention of Russia and a general war would be inevitable. "Public opinion," he wrote, "should above all be told to expect this eventuality." It should be persuaded that Serbia is deserving of sympathy and support, for

"a Frenchman is welcomed like a brother by the Serbs; they have a right to our support because their interests are ours . . . because a large Serbia south of Austria-Hungary will be in peace as well as in war a natural ally adding her strength to the strength of Russia and France. . . . If the blood of France's children must flow, be certain that it will be in the service of her own cause. The hour of reparations has sounded in the Balkans; we have been awaiting it for forty-one years; it must also sound from the steeples of Strassburg and of Metz." [62]

Poincaré was more reserved, for he insisted that France's support of Russia would be conditioned upon information as to her plans and

[58] *Patrie,* Nov. 11.

[59] *Siècle,* Nov. 9. The Paris correspondent of the *Kölnische Zeitung,* Nov. 11, named this newspaper with the *Temps, Gaulois, Figaro, Écho de Paris,* and *Petit Parisien* as receiving the inspiration of the Quai d'Orsay.

[60] *Siècle,* Nov. 10.

[61] *Phare de la Loire* (Nantes), Nov. 14. *Petit Comtois* (Besançon), Nov. 21. *Petit Marseillais,* Dec. 8.

[62] A. Malet, "Conflagration Générale," *Parlement et l'Opinion,* Nov. 10, 1912. See also his article in the *Revue du Foyer,* Dec. 15, 1912, quoted in de Toury, *Jaurès et le Parti de la Guerre,* pp. 63–67. Schoen believed that only the conservative and clerical circles were attacking Austria and Germany. Schoen to Bethmann-Hollweg, Paris, Nov. 13, 1912. *G. P.,* XXXIII, 443.

upon the terms of the alliance.[63] Perhaps blinded by his own passion for revenge against Austria for his defeat in the Bosnian crisis, Isvolski reported Poincaré as giving him more definite assurances than the facts warranted. On November 7, after the Bulgarian victory of Lule Burgas (Oct. 29–31), Isvolski wrote that France "seems to recognize now that an acquisition of territory by Austria would involve the general equilibrium of Europe and therefore the special interests of France, whereas she had formerly insisted that her intervention in the Balkans could only be diplomatic." [64] Isvolski ignored Poincaré's letter of November 16, in which the need of an understanding was again emphasized, and he reported the next day that France was prepared to support any initiative which Russia might decide upon.[65]

The Russian ambassador was also concerned with the state of public opinion in France. Fearing that Russia's interests were not approved with sufficient enthusiasm and that less dependable leaders than Poincaré, Millerand, and Delcassé might be in power at the moment when supreme decisions would be required,[66] he had advised his government to renew the subsidies to the French press which had been suspended in 1907.[67] No action was taken until the beginning of the Balkan War in October, 1912. In announcing the arrival in Paris of a special agent, Davidov, who was to conduct these negatiations, Kokovtsev, the President of the Imperial Council and Minister of Finance, wrote Poincaré "that if in your judgment a direct action on Russia's part is indispensable in this matter, I will join in the opinion dictated by your great information and experience of affairs." [68] He feared, however, that the proposed action would have little effect, as experience had proved in 1904–1905, except to stimulate the cupidity of the press.[69] Isvolski did not always report Poincaré accurately, but in this instance his interpretation of the

---

[63] Poincaré to Isvolski, Paris, Nov. 16, 1912. Poincaré, *Les Balkans en Feu,* pp. 336–338. See also his conversation with Isvolski of November 18. *Ibid.,* p. 339.

[64] *Livre Noir,* I, 342. Poincaré, it is to be noted, does not comment upon this statement. Poincaré, *Les Balkans en Feu,* pp. 312–316.

[65] *Livre Noir,* I, 346.

[66] *Ibid.,* I, 364 (22 Nov. /5 Dec., 1912).

[67] *Ibid.,* I, 130 (6/19 Aug., 1911), 148, 149 (29 Sept. /12 Oct., 1911).

[68] Kokovtsev to Poincaré, 4/17 Oct., 1912. *Humanité,* Jan. 9, 1924. Cf. Kokovtsev to Sazonov, St. Petersburg, 3/16 Dec., 1912. Stieve, *Dipomatische Schriftwechsel Iswolskis,* II, 391–636. Although the documents printed by this newspaper were edited without regard for critical standards, their authenticity has not been successfully challenged.

[69] Kokovtsev to Sazonov, 2/15 Dec., 1912. *Ibid.,* Jan. 10, 1924.

latter's decision was substantially correct. "Poincaré," he wrote, "is ready to give us his coöperation in this matter and to indicate the most opportune plan for the division of the subsidies." [70] The French Minister now writes that, opposed in principle, he could only yield in order to secure for his government a check upon the distribution of money which it could not, in the absence of legislation, prevent. His approval, accordingly, was given, and Klotz, the Minister of Finance, was placed in control of the Russian subsidies. [71]

It was agreed, however, that the first instalment of 100,000 francs of the 300,000 originally allotted to this purpose should not be spent immediately. Davidov wrote late in October that it would be kept in reserve "for sudden use if there should be an occasion." [72] Poincaré insists that he secured this delay with the idea that no occasion would arise, [73] but, according to Isvolski, one of Poincaré's arguments for a complete understanding with Russia as to her intentions was the need of time "to prepare public opinion for participation in the war which may arise from the Balkans." [74] The French minister now finds it somewhat difficult to explain this statement. According to his present version, he had intended to provide for the consultation of public opinion if the Russian alliance, in the event Russia became involved in war, should threaten to bring France in. "We did not wish," he writes, "this eventuality to develop without first consulting Russia and submitting the case to the judgment of our public opinion." [75] He unquestionably desired a prior understanding with Russia, for that was an essential factor in his efforts to maintain unity of purpose between the members of the Triple Entente. His concern for public opinion, and his professed desire to consult it upon the vital question of France's participation in a war, were more doubtful. His method of submitting a question to the judgment of public opinion, as was evident in his speech at Nantes, October 27, 1912, was more in the nature of an appeal to it. The disposition of the press-fund, in any event, passed into French hands, for Raffalovitch, the financial agent of the Russian embassy, wrote in December 11, 1912, that "it is escaping us completely," and in February, 1913, that "we

[70] Isvolski to Sazonov, 10/23 Dec., 1912. *Humanité*, Jan. 7, 1924.

[71] Poincaré, *L'Europe sous les Armes*, pp. 97–114.

[72] Davidov to Kokovtsev, 16/29 Oct., 1912. *Humanité*, Jan. 9, 1924.

[73] Poincaré, *L'Europe sous les Armes*, pp. 99, 100. He also asserts that Kokovtsev had warned him of Isvolski's venality.

[74] *Livre Noir*, II, 15 (16/29 Jan., 1913).

[75] Poincaré, *L'Europe Sous les Armes*, pp. 95, 96.

are completely excluded from the control of these subsidies."[76]

It was not long before the distribution began, after Lenoir, the go-between who had served in the same capacity in 1904–1906, had argued that the Radical-Socialist campaign directed against the prospect of a war arising from Austro-Serbian relations required action.[77] On December 12, 1912, instructions from St. Petersburg directed that 25,000 francs should be paid to Lenoir for the advances he had already made and that the remaining 75,000 of the first contingent should be placed at Klotz's disposal.[78] By July, 1913, 300,000 francs had been distributed,[79] and in November, 1913, Raffalovitch accounted for an additional total of 410,000 francs.[80] Not even Poincaré questions the authenticity of almost all of the documents which reveal the corruption of the French press, his own part and that of other French officials in it. It is even said that Austria, Italy, and Turkey had adopted the same practice.[81]

Although these facts are well established, it would be a mistake to attribute the attitude of the press, or even that of the Radical and Radical-Socialist newspapers, entirely to the influence of Russian money. Their irritating criticism had, it is true, been used as an argument for distributing the first subsidies, but in fact this money was diverted to another purpose. Under Klotz's direction, it was distributed with a view to overcoming the opposition to Poincaré in the parliament and in the press and to the three-year service law.[82] It

[76] Raffalovitch to Isvolski, 29 Nov. /11 Dec., 1912. *Humanité*, Jan. 10, 1924. Raffalovitch to Kokovtsev, 31 Jan. /13 Feb., 1913. *Ibid.*, Jan. 11, 1924.

[77] Raffalovitch to Kokovtsev, Nov. 20/Dec. 2, 1913. *Ibid.*, Jan. 8, 1924.

[78] Davidov to Raffalovitch, Nov. 30/Dec. 12, 1912. *Ibid.*, Jan. 9, 1924. Already the general tone of the Paris press had alarmed Berchtold, the Austrian foreign minister. On Dec. 13, 1912, he asked Szécsen in Paris to call Poincaré's attention to the unfortunate impression which it was creating. *Ö.-U. A.*, V, 113, 114. Poincaré told Szécsen that he was attempting to moderate press comment, but Austria's attitude made success difficult. *Ibid.*, V, 122 (Dec. 14, 1912).

[79] Raffalovitch to Kokovtsev, 2/15 July, 1913. *Ibid.*, Jan. 13, 1924.

[80] Raffalovitch's reports of Nov. 7, 19, 1913. *Hinter den Kulissen des Französischen Journalismus*, pp. 107, 108.

[81] Poincaré, *L'Europe sous les Armes*, p. 98. Isvolski to Sazonov, 10/23 Oct., 1912. *Humanité*, Jan. 7, 1924. Sir Francis Bertie, the British ambassador in Paris, told Szécsen that, in his opinion, Isvolski was receiving money from the Pan-Slavic group as well as from the Russian government for distribution to the press. *Ö.-U. A.*, VI, 122 (Apr. 12, 1913).

[82] Kokovtsev to Sazonov, 22 May/4 June, 1913. *Humanité*, Jan. 12, 1924. On December 12, 1912, Schoen reported that the criticism which the radical press had directed against Russia and the dangerous character of her policy had been turned against Austria. He believed that the change was due to Russian rubles. Schoen to Bethmann-Hollweg, Paris, Dec. 12, 1912. *G. P.*, XXXIII, 468,

will be seen later that the Radical and Radical-Socialist newspapers which shared the Russian subsidies continued to oppose a return to the three-year law. When, in June, 1913, Klotz asked for another 100,-000 francs, Sazonov, on advice from the Russian agents in Paris, required as a condition the support of Russia's interests in the Balkans.[83] Evidently, the results of the money already spent had not been satisfactory. Moreover, Isvolski's statements as to his influence upon the press cannot always be trusted. His estimate of the significance of certain newspapers was sometimes inaccurate, for he attributed a small circulation of the *Dépêche* of Toulouse, which was perhaps the most widely read of provincial newspapers.[84] Like other and more professional propagandists, he exaggerated his personal influence in order perhaps to increase his credit in St. Petersburg. Of the three newspapers mentioned in his report of December 18, 1912, as especially under his influence,[85] the *Journal des Débats* and the *Écho de Paris* had been as zealous in their support of Russia and Serbia in 1908–1909 on the occasion of the Bosnian crisis after Russia had withdrawn her subsidies as they were during the Balkan wars.[86] The policy of the *Temps,* the third newspaper mentioned by the Russian ambassador, it is true, changed completely. In 1908, it had declared that Serbia was not worth a general war, whereas it affirmed, December 14, 1912, that the "evident interest of the Triple Entente is that the Balkan Confederation, a new and precious factor in the European equilibrium, should be firmly united and strong." It also approved, January 29, 1913, the union of all Slavs under Russia's direction. "May this solidarity of interest prepare a solidarity of action!" [87] Nevertheless, the interest of France in adding the strength of the Balkan League to that of the Triple Entente probably had more weight in determining the editorial policy of this important news-

469. The Russian documents, and the contents of the newspapers in question, do not entirely substantiate this suspicion. The victories of the Balkan League and the danger that Austria would interfere were apparently the determining factors.

[83] Sazonov to Isvolski, 5/18 June, 1913. Isvolski to Sazonov, 21 June/4 July, 1913. Sazonov to Kokovtsev, 23 June/6 July, 1913. *Humanité,* Jan. 12, 1924.

[84] Isvolski to Sazonov, 8/21 July, 1913. *Hinter den Kulissen des Französischen Journalismus,* p. 105.

[85] *Livre Noir,* I, 371.

[86] See above, p. 262.

[87] Émile Laffon wrote to Davidov that Russian influences had influenced the news section of the *Temps,* and upon one occasion, Raffalovitch found in it a despatch dated from St. Petersburg which Isvolski had dictated in Paris. *Humanité,* Jan. 15, 1924.

paper than Isvolski's influence. Events had shown the hopelessness of its Austrophil policy of 1908–1909. Finally Isvolski acknowledged in a letter to Sazonov that he had no direct influence upon the provincial press, "which however has a great influence upon public opinion." [88]

The Monarchists were critical of the policy of the equilibrium, but their influence was too limited to create an effective opposition. The parties of the left were in a much better position to obstruct a policy which might lead France into war on the ground that the existence of the balance of power was at stake in the Balkans. The Socialists, under the leadership of Jaurès, Marcel, Sembat, and Francis de Pressensé, worked constantly to this end, but their social and economic opinions, their indifference to the usual forms of patriotism placed them under a heavy handicap. In depending upon a proposed general strike to avoid war, they overestimated the discipline of the working classes and their defenses against the appeal of patriotism. Since the Dreyfus Affair, the balance of power in French politics had been held by the Radicals and the Radical-Socialists with such smaller groups as the Republican-Socialists. They had succeeded in separating the State and the Church, in enacting the two-year service law of 1905, and in bringing about other social and economic reforms; so completely successful had the Radicals been, in fact, that their continued existence as a group, except for the purpose of holding offices, was thought to be doubtful.[89] The most promising prospects for a powerful and organized support of a definitely peaceful policy were evidently to be found in these groups, for the moderate parties were converted to Poincaré's interpretation of the balance of power supported by a mobilized national sentiment. The reactionary implications of extreme nationalism in regard to questions at home and the movement for proportional representation tended to unite them in a common opposition.

This unity was not maintained, however, in regard to foreign affairs and especially in regard to the issues involved in the Balkans. If the Radicals turned in the direction of the moderate parties, the Radical-Socialists tended toward the United Socialists. It was the contention of the Radical-Socialist press that the balance of power should be what its name suggested, a perfect balance between the two groups. "The policy of the equilibrium," declared the *Aurore* (Aug.

---

[88] Isvolski to Sazonov. 1/14 Feb., 1913. *Humanité,* Jan. 11, 1924.
[89] See article upon the Radical and Radical-Socialist Congress at Tours, *Frankfurter Zeitung,* Oct. 10, 1912.

15, 1912), "which France pursues, in alliance with Russia and in accord with England, is that of the neutralization of the opposing forces in Europe for the maintenance of peace. It is the Triple Entente exactly counter-balancing the Triple Alliance." Others of the moderate and conservative groups affirmed the same point of view while manifestly meaning something quite different. The *Radical,* Senator Perchot's organ and a leading Radical-Socialist newspaper, protested against the dangerous practice of aligning the two diplomatic groups against each other. "It would be disastrous," it affirmed, July 27, 1912, "if the Triple Entente and the Triple Alliance were to form two compact and exclusive groups." It was this, and other Radical-Socialist newspapers, which most definitely protested against the claim that the friendship of the Balkan League for the Triple Entente should reconcile France to a "holocaust of thousands of human beings." [90] Victor Augagneur, a power in the politics of Lyons, a Republican Socialist who became the Minister of Public Instruction in the Viviani cabinet of 1914, remained a firm opponent of an adventurous policy throughout the Balkan wars. "We Frenchmen," he wrote, "would be without justification if we permitted ourselves under any circumstances to be drawn into this adventure. Not a French soldier, not one, should be risked . . . in the conflict caused by the aggression of the Balkan League." [91] Public opinion in Paris, he thought, was too much under the influence of the nationalists; it should be told again and again that war was impossible. [92] "Public opinion," declared the *Aurore* (Nov. 9, 1912), "fears war and especially it would not understand why we should be drawn into one. The efforts of forty years to assure our defense cannot be used for any other purpose than our own defense. . . . We do not wish to fight for Albania and the Balkans." Reason, declared the *Petite République* (Nov. 12, 1912) refused to admit this even as a possibility.

The attitude of the Radical-Socialists in parliament and in their press in regard to the Balkan situation may have been influenced by their opposition to the Poincaré government. The *Journal des Débats* (Nov. 11, 1912) thought that it was a "kind of parliamentary intrigue," but Gaston Doumergue, a Radical, suggested that Poincaré's foreign policy was itself inspired by a desire to mobilize public opinion against the program of the radical parties.[93] In any event, the first sum of one hundred thousand francs was by February, 1913, distributed among the newspapers whose criticism was feared by Poincaré and Isvolski. The *Aurore,* Millerand's *Lanterne,* the *Événement,* Senator Bérenger's *Action,* the *France,* and the *Rappel* were those which were the first to profit. The same newspapers appear in the lists of November, 1913, reporting the disbursal of 410,000 francs, with the addition of the *Radical,* which received 120,000, and of the *Temps,* the *Figaro,* the *Libre Parole,* the *Gaulois,* and the *Liberté.*[94] The last-mentioned group may be disposed of at once in an attempt to estimate the effect of the Russian subsidies, for its support had usually been accorded to Russia's interests. Even among the newspapers which were the source of particular concern, there were some which had foreseen and approved the possibility that France might be involved in a war arising from the Balkans before they had received any Russian money. The *Action* (Oct. 10, 1912) had urged the need of extensive military preparations before the opening of hostilities in the Balkans. On October 22, 1912, Jean Herbette wrote in the same journal that the Franco-Russian alliance included the Balkans "for the excellent reason that it did not specifically designate any limits. It establishes complete solidarity between the two countries." Early in November, he protested against any move which would irritate or offend the Balkan States.[95] A week later, Bérenger defined the policy of the *Action* in terms which left no doubt as to its meaning. "We must," he wrote, "depend at the same time upon Russia, England, and the Balkan States. It is the Quadruple Entente which must be increasingly the essential formula of our foreign policy. . . . The half million of heroic bayonets of the Balkan League, if it joins the Triple Entente, will form a useful counterweight to the increasing megalomania of the Central Powers." A European war was possible, he declared, if not inevitable, and for this reason, he urged the need of "awakening public opinion." Those who refused to see the importance to France of defending the interests of Serbia demonstrated "an unbelievable ig-

---

[93] *Grande Revue,* vol. 74, p. 865 (Aug. 25, 1912).

[94] These are the newspapers which Poincaré describes as *petites feuilles* and which, according to Poincaré, for the most part had only a limited circulation. No one, he declared, has shown that any one of them ever printed a bellicose article. Poincaré, *L'Europe sous les Armes,* p. 114. This implies, of course, a friendly interpretation of the comments especially of the *Action.*

[95] *Action,* Nov. 3, 1912.

norance of foreign affairs. Let us stand prepared, let us not forget that the frontiers of our allies are also ours." [96] Since it was not until December 16 that even the first step was taken in advancing money to any part of the French press, the explanation of Berenger's attitude must be found elsewhere.[97] It was doubtless inspired by an appreciation of the supposed interest of his country.

Of the other newspapers which shared the Russian subsidies, the *Aurore* and the *Événement* rarely commented upon foreign affairs, but when they did, they did not actively participate in the effort to prepare public opinion for a war.[98] The *Lanterne*, Millerand's organ, wrote December 18, 1912,—the date of Isvolski's letter in which he congratulated himself upon his success in enlisting the support of the press,—that the responsibility of a general war would be Russia's, "for if she remains quiet the conflict will be limited to the Serbians and Austrians. . . . Our diplomacy must more than ever be prudent." [99] As late as May, 1913, it refused to admit the possibility of a general war in connection with the tension over the question of Scutari.[100] With the settlement of this crisis and the conclusion of the Balkan wars, there was no immediate occasion for the further expression of opinion in regard to Russia's interests in the Balkans.[101]

[96] *Action*, Nov. 13, 1912.

[97] Provincial newspapers, which did not receive Russian subsidies, expressed the same point of view. *France de Bordeaux et du Sud-Ouest*, Oct. 28, Nov. 24, Dec. 18, 1912. *Petit Comtois* (Besançon), Nov. 2, 21, Dec. 5, 1912, March 21, 1913. Correspondents in Paris of Radical-Socialist newspapers in the provinces frequently expressed a more friendly attitude toward the interests of the Balkan States than appeared in their editorials. *Dépêche* (Toulouse), Nov. 14, 28, 1912. *Lyon Républicain*, April 1, 9, June 8, 13, 1913.

[98] See moderate comments, *Aurore*, Oct. 19, 21, Nov. 9, 1912, *Événement*, Nov. 22.

[99] Lenoir, according to Raffalovitch, had already advanced money to the *Lanterne* as well as to the *Aurore*. It was doubtless included in the 25,000 francs which were later returned to him. Raffalovitch to Kokovtsev, 20 Nov./2 Dec., 1912. *Humanité*, Jan. 8, 1924.

[100] *Lanterne*, May 1, 1913. *Est Républicain* (Nancy), April 25, 1913. The zeal of the *Temps* (April 3, 5, 7, 1913), and of the *Matin* aroused even Isvolski's concern. *Livre Noir*, II (March 27/April 9, 1913). The *Temps's* (April 26) chief interest was in the ability of the Triple Entente to resist Austria's dictation.

[101] The *Temps* (April 3, 5, 1913) protested against the decision of the London Conference for an international naval demonstration to compel Montenegro to evacuate Scutari. Its zeal displeased even Isvolski, who was moved to advise moderation. *Livre Noir*, II, 67, 68. (27 March/9 April, 1913). In regard to the Greco-Bulgarian dispute (July-Aug., 1913) concerning the port of Kavalla, the French government and press supported the claims of Greece against Russia's desires. *Ibid.*, II, 122, 123 (30 July/12 Aug., 1913).

Interest then became more concerned with direct relations with Germany and with political questions at home. Events had strengthened the prevailing confidence in the unity of the Triple Entente as an essential factor in the balance of power, and even in the value of a favorable situation in the Balkans. But Russian influences were not primarily responsible for this tendency, nor did they succeed in entirely overcoming the opposition of the Radical-Socialists to a general war originating in the Balkans. Seriously disturbed by the tendencies of French policy, Victor Augagneur in August, 1913, called upon the republican parties to show a more consistent interest in foreign affairs. Circumstances, he said, required that the usual feeling that these questions should be left to the professional diplomats should be abandoned. "The peace of Europe and of the world, the preservation of independence abroad, and of the victory or defeat of the republican ideal at home are involved. I say that our present foreign policy may lead us one day to a catastrophe, and in the meantime it is causing a halt in the evolution of the Republic whose consequences may be reaction or revolution." [102] Like Sembat, he would have France assure a permanent peace by making an entente with Germany upon the basis of the *status quo,* for he believed it to be the only permanent guarantee against war. Moreover, Alsace, in his opinion, was now content with the program of autonomy within the German Empire.[103]

This appeal was received with the same silence that had been the unfailing answer to the Socialists' argument that France must choose once and for all between a policy of peace and one of war. So far as the radical republican parties were concerned, their reaction was not entirely determined by their refusal to approve a specific renunciation of Alsace-Lorraine, for their first thoughts were always for the political situation in France. There were of course many even in this group for whom any connection with Prussian militarism seemed a betrayal of their liberal principles. The failure of Augagneur's appeal did not prove the existence of a desire for war, nor had the nationalist propaganda and Russian influences changed the peaceful character of public opinion in its broader aspects. Albert Malet

---

[102] *Lyon Républicain,* Aug. 22, 1913. All proposals for social reform, he declared, had been defeated.

[103] *Ibid.,* Aug. 29, 1913. The *Journal des Débats* (March 14, 1913; May 30, 1914), asserted that an entente with Germany would mean that France had sunk to the level of a vassal state: this point of view had always obstructed close relations between the two countries.

was eager for France to defend the interests of Serbia, but he was compelled to admit that the "immense majority of Frenchmen, . . . are entirely mistaken in regard to the significance of the great episodes of the Balkan drama . . ."[104] If the *Matin* (Nov. 25, 1912), one of the newspapers named by Isvolski as accepting his advice, acknowledged that the thought of a general war for Durazzo "was revolting to public opinion," it was eloquent testimony as to the general sentiment among the French people. The correspondent of the *Berliner Tageblatt* (Nov. 12, 1912) noticed the pacific character of public opinion. In August, 1913, Gabriel Trarieux, a leader of the Radical party, in a brief report of his contacts with the provincial population, wrote of the "quiet fatalism, the passive resignation" of the masses in regard to foreign affairs. "And war?" he asked. "Does any one think of it? . . . No, I have nowhere observed it. The noise of the Balkan cannons has not disturbed our peaceful fields. It is only a question for them of distant barbarians who are settling obscure quarrels."[105] The German ambassador commented upon the contrast between the attitude of the press and the definite opposition to war on the part of public opinion.[106]

Prolonged debates in parliament and a systematic and intense press campaign were required before the three-year service law could be passed. Early in 1913 the Reichstag had enacted a new military law providing for a notable increase in Germany's peace time army. It had doubtless been caused by the changed situation in the Balkans, but it inspired in France a general concern for her own security. Every group, with the possible exception of the Socialists, admitted that some kind of a reply was necessary. Even the few who believed that France could not hope in the long run to keep pace with Germany's armaments, in view of her increasing population, recognized the imperative need of maintaining equality for the immediate future.[107] It was known, of course, that in the event of war France would be called upon to resist the bulk of the German army until Russia, with her slower mobilization, could act. An intense press campaign was organized in support of the government's thesis that the only possible reply would be a return to the three-

[104] Malet, "Conflagration Generale," *Parlement et l'Opinion*, Nov. 10, 1912.
[105] *France de Bordeaux et du Sud-Ouest*, Aug. 16, 1913.
[106] Schoen to Bethmann-Hollweg, Paris, April 29, 1913. *G. P.*, XXXIX, 188–191.
[107] André Honnorat (Deputy), "Le Service de Trois Ans et la Natalité," *Grande Revue*, vol. 78, pp. 319, 320 (March, 1913).

year term of military service. The *Temps* (Feb. 16, 1913), which led it, at first affirmed its intention of avoiding an appeal to anti-German sentiment and of supporting the measure as justified without reference to Germany's action. France's decision, it declared (Feb. 19), had no connection with her foreign policy: "military action must not be confused with political intention. The political relations of Germany and France are at present as good as possible." These commendable purposes were promptly forgotten in the need of convincing a reluctant public opinion. On March 5, it undertook to prove that each step in the reduction of service in the French army and of its general strength had been followed by a threat from Germany. It was now a question of life and death for France to meet her action, and on March 11, it declared that "the military effort that France is going to impose upon herself constitutes the most eloquent testimony of her attachment to peace." Late in February, it printed the first of a series of articles from the provinces quoting various officials to the effect that public opinion approved the measure and that young men were eager to serve three instead of two years![108]

A determined opposition was organized by the parties of the left, and for this purpose a degree of union was restored between the two factions which had divided in regard to the Balkan questions.[109] The *Petit Comtois* (March 11, 1913), for example, wrote that "we must yield to the logic of numbers and resign ourselves as gracefully as possible to have fewer men than Germany, for her population will soon be the double of ours." This frankness was exceptional; the Socialists as well as the Radicals and the Radical-Socialists believed that the solution was to be found in the more effective training and use of the reserves. Since France's purposes were defensive, they argued, there was no need to equal the number of men which Germany had in her peace-time army. Jaurès proposed that every man subject to military service should keep his rifle

---

[108] *Temps*, Feb. 28, 1913. See Victor Augagneur's comments in the *Lyon Républicain*, May 30, 1913. The editorial policy of this important provincial newspaper in 1913–1914 was consistently in favor of a return to the law of 1905, but L. Berthet, its Paris correspondent, opposed this change.

[109] The *Petit Comtois* (Besançon), March 7, 11, 27, 1913, illustrates this tendency. The *Lanterne*, Feb. 19, May 10, 1913, although named in the Russian documents as sharing in the subsidies which were intended to overcome the opposition to the three-year service law, argued that the requirements of national defense could be met in some other way. Cf. *Radical*, May 19, Oct. 16. Camille Pelletan in the *Dépêche* (Toulouse), April 22. Professor Aulard, *ibid.*, April 24.

and equipment in his own home.[110] Russia, it was sometimes charged, had required Poincaré to promise the longer period of service when he had visited St. Petersburg in August, 1912.[111] "Is France Republican or cossack?" asked the *Dépêche* of Toulouse (June 1, 1913).

These groups welcomed an invitation from members of the Swiss national council to attend a Franco-German parliamentary conference in Berne, May 11–13, 1913, as perhaps containing the promise of better relations with Germany.[112] Their enthusiasm, in contrast to the hostility or skepticism of conservatives and nationalists, was almost certainly due, as von Schoen observed, to the hope that the conference, if successful, could be used for the purpose of defeating the three-year service bill, which was still pending.[113] The *Temps* (April 20, 1913), rather surprisingly, was not unfavorable, only insisting that the French delegation should be non-partisan, but it was seen at its preliminary meeting in Paris that the radical groups and the Socialists with a few pacifists had alone responded to the invitation. Even with this radical tendency, the French delegation decided that only such questions should come before the conference as could perhaps lead to an understanding.[114] This condition was, of course, intended to conciliate patriotic sentiment in France, but it necessarily eliminated the most serious questions which divided the two countries. Nevertheless, the radical press was enthusiastic. "Let us go to Berne," declared the *Radical* (May 10, 1913), "to prove that our ideas are sincerely peaceful, to prove to Europe and to the world that France does not desire war, but peace, to try to find a basis of understanding between us and Germany." When the conference met at Berne, more than 190 deputies and senators were present from the French parliament, whereas the German delegation included only the comparatively small number of thirty-four members of the Reich-

---

[110] Jean Jaurès, *L'Armée Nouvelle* (Paris, 1911). Victor Augagneur in the *Lyon Républicain,* April 4, 1913.

[111] The moderate *Journal de Rouen* (June 17, 1913) replied that this allegation was absurd because there had been no need of the longer period of service in 1912. A letter from St. Petersburg in the *Journal des Débats* (June 17, 1913) gave impressive statistics as to the present and future strength of Russia's peace-time army.

[112] *Radical,* April 18. *Lanterne,* May 2.

[113] Schoen to Bethmann-Hollweg, Paris, April 28, 1913. *G. P.,* XXXIX, 309–311.

[114] *Radical,* May 3, 1913. The *Temps* (May 4) regretted that patriotic (or nationalist?) deputies had not attended. Auguste Lalance, however, urged that the conference should discuss the Alsace-Lorraine question. *France,* May 10, quoting the *Journal d'Alsace-Lorraine.*

stag.[115] The elections of the Prussian parliament then in progress, according to a member of the German delegation, had prevented a larger attendance.[116] Neither delegation, it need scarcely be said, represented its government, and if the enterprise was in accord with the desire of peace among the two peoples, there was no adequate organization in either France or Germany to support whatever results the conference might accomplish. In accordance with the resolution adopted in Paris, a permanent Franco-German committee was authorized for the purpose of working for improved relations, the Bryan arbitration treaties were endorsed, and the will for peace among the French and German peoples was affirmed.[117]

It was a reference to Alsace-Lorraine in the resolution adopted by the conference at the close of its work and read by d'Estournelles de Constant which more than anything else determined the unfavorable reaction in France. Several incidents in 1913 had shown that Alsace wished to be heard in regard to the relations between France and Germany. Henri Kessler, the President of the Republican Committee of Alsace, wrote to the *Radical* (Jan. 10, 1913) that if Alsace still had for France "the respect and all of the affection which one has for a grandmother," her first love was for her own soil. Rather than remain the cause of a possible conflict which would inevitably lead to a European war, she preferred, wrote Kessler, to seek the status of an autonomous State within Germany. A similar opinion was stated by the representatives of all parties in Alsace meeting at Mulhouse, March 9, 1913.[118] The attitude of the *grande presse* in Paris toward this expression of opinion was one of interest. It was either systematically ignored or represented as the point of view of none but the German immigrants. "Do not listen, it is not Alsace that is speaking," was, according to Marcel Sembat, the characteristic reaction.[119] The *Dépêche* of Toulouse (March 20, 1913) protested against the comments or silence of the Parisian press. "In truth," it confessed, "I blushed when I read these perfidious insinuations. I was ashamed for all of us. . . ." The action

---

[115] Ten others sent regrets. The principal speeches, the final resolutions and the lists of participating members and of those who had expressed regrets are printed in G. Aubert, *La Folie Franco-Allemande*, pp. 234–256.

[116] *Ibid.*, p. 246 (Conrad Haussmann).

[117] *Ibid.*, pp. 249–251.

[118] *Dépêche* (Toulouse), March 20. *Lyon Républicain*, April 14.

[119] Sembat, *Faites un Roi*, p. 158.

of the Berne Conference had reference, however, to a resolution adopted by a group of deputies from the Alsatian Landtag under the direction of Dr. Ricklin, the president of the lower house, and of the Abbé Haegy, the clerical leader, which declared that Alsace did not wish to be the cause of another war. The conference, after announcing its intention of continuing the work for better relations between France and Germany, declared that "it heartily thanks the representatives of Alsace-Lorraine for having facilitated the *rapprochement* of the two countries in the interest of civilization." [120]

The disparity between the numbers of the French and German delegations had been at least the excuse of a first unfavorable reaction in France,[121] but it was chiefly this reference to Alsace-Lorraine and its desires which was decisive. Experience had shown that the moderate and conservative press was not disposed to accept as valid any expression of Alsatian opinion which did not accord with its own unchanging preconceptions.[122] At least one member of the French delegation was outraged by the action of the conference. Charles Leboucq returned, disillusioned and fearful. "We insist," he declared, "upon affirming our fidelity to our memories and declare that we place our hope, peacefully, but in a full sense of our national dignity, in the justice of the future, while reproving every warlike thought. We repeat with all our strength our horror of every brutal dream of a purposive *revanche*." [123] The true opinion of Alsace, wrote the *Temps* (May 13, 1913) should not be confused with that of "the representatives referred to in the resolution who include many Prussians, Saxons, and Badeners." The *Journal de Rouen* (May 13, 1913) thought that the French delegation "should have insisted upon silence, since none of them had the right to say a word which would have the appearance of a renunciation," and later it named the Abbé Wetterlé as the only qualified interpreter of Alsatian opinion. The nation should preserve the list of the French delegation, declared the *Patrie* (May 13, 1913), in order to defeat its members

---

[120] Aubert, *La Folie Franco-Allemande*, p. 250.

[121] *Journal des Débats,* May 12, 1913. Clemenceau in *Homme Libre,* May 10, 1913. Cf. Clemenceau, *Dans les Champs du Pouvoir* (Paris), p. 28.

[122] The *Journal de Rouen* (May 13, 1913) insisted that the true sentiment of Alsace-Lorraine was to be found in the novels of Bazin and Barrès. No attempt has been made in this study to weigh their influence, but it may be noted that the *République Française* (Jan. 20, 1911) characterized Barrès's *Au Service de l'Allemagne* as an historical document as well as a work of art.

[123] *France,* May 12, 13.

in the next election. The conference, however, was a success in the opinion of a number of radical newspapers.[124] "One must conclude," wrote the *Dépêche* of Toulouse (Aug. 8, 1913), "that it is not to the taste of all of our confrères to listen to Alsace. . . . Systematic misrepresentation or methodical omission is the fate of Alsace's goodwill, which is moving in its obstinate efforts." Even that section of the press which at first had given some attention to the conference soon became silent, and its results could scarcely be said to have improved the relations between the two countries.[125] If Germany had granted complete autonomy to Alsace-Lorraine, and if the two provinces had then expressed their satisfaction in such a form as to leave no doubt, it is difficult to see how the leaders of moderate public opinion in France could have continued their usual attitude: "Germany! O Germany! why will you not hear the despairing appeal, the peaceful appeal that comes from the heart of Alsace?"[126]

The Berne Conference had failed, of course, to enable the parties of the left to defeat the three-year service law, and after prolonged debates it passed in July, 1913. Their defeat, according to Jaurès, was "entirely provisional."[127] The Radical and Radical-Socialist groups reaffirmed their loyalty to the law of 1905 at Pau, October 17, 1913, and they declared again for a more effective training of the reserves as the proper reply to the increase of the German army.[128] Events were to show the difficulty of putting these purposes into effect even with governments of their own selection.[129] The radical Doumergue ministry did nothing to change the work of the Barthou cabinet under whose direction the law had been enacted. The normal division between the Radicals and the Radical-Socialists was reasserting itself with the result that the latter returned to their former policy of seeking a union with the United Socialists. *"Pas d'ennemis à gauche"*

---

[124] "For those to whom war is a terrible scourge," wrote the *Lanterne*, May 12, "the Berne conference will be honored by a happy page in the history of the world." *Ibid.*, May 13.

[125] The *Radical*, after approving the purposes of the conference, later scarcely referred to it. The measures taken by Germany against the French-language press in Alsace were interpreted as a reply to the conference. *France*, May 18.

[126] Bourdon, *German Enigma*, p. 339.

[127] *Dépêche* (Toulouse), July 23, 1913.

[128] See Max Clauss, *Das Politische Frankreich vor dem Kriege* (Karlsruhe, 1928), p. 117. *Journal des Débats*, Dec. 15, 1913.

[129] Lavisse predicted that the opponents of the law of 1913, once in power, would do nothing more than talk about an eventual return to the two-year basis. *Temps*, April 17, 1914. The *Petit Provençal* of Marseilles (July 8, 1914) thought that the opposition was merely a political maneuver.

again became their slogan for the sake of securing a return to the two-year service law.[130] The parliamentary elections of May, 1914, as they increased the Socialist group to about one hundred and maintained the Radicals and Radical-Socialists at their former strength, resulted in as clear a decision in favor of this purpose as apparently was possible in view of the conditions of French politics.[131] The temper of the new chamber was shown in its prompt disapproval of the attempt to create a Ribot cabinet in the Poincaré and Barthou tradition.[132] Nevertheless, when the Republican-Socialist Viviani formed a more satisfactory combination, he at once equivocated upon the essential question of military service by proposing that the law of 1913 should remain in effect until the suggested supplementary legislation had been satisfactorily applied. It would then perhaps be possible to discuss "a partial lightening of the military burdens. Until then the government intends to proceed, under the control of Parliament, with the exact and loyal application of the law." [133] The expression of public opinion in the elections had been nullified by the greater strength of the executive and by the failure of leaders of the radical groups to obey the instructions of their party congress. Under these circumstances, the prospects of an early return to the law of 1905 were not favorable, although the campaign was continued with undiminished zeal.

The two years 1912–1914 were a period of unusually intense and systematic propaganda. Efforts to arouse a nationalist spirit inspired the radical elements to a counter-agitation. The prospect of war explains much of the eagerness with which each element sought to impress its point of view upon public opinion. Since elections are the best means yet devised for testing it, although they are rarely decided by one factor, those of May, 1914, indicated that the policy of moderation and of peace had the greater numerical strength. Nevertheless, the nationalist point of view was actually the more significant because the government found it useful, and when Russia decided to interfere in French politics, it is worthy of note that she was as much concerned with maintaining in power Poincaré and men like him as

[130] Georges Ponsat (Senator), "Les Partis Politiques," Grande Revue, vol. 81, p. 667 (Oct., 1913). The socialist congress at Amiens required an unconditional repudiation of the three-year law as a condition to coöperation with the Radicals.
[131] Before the second tour de scrutin the Journal des Débats (May 7, 8, 1914) had insisted that the military law was the essential issue.
[132] Journal des Débats, June 13, 1914.
[133] Ibid., June 17, 1914.

with attempting to influence the expression of opinion. It was of course the propaganda which was intended to strengthen the confidence of public opinion in the policy of the equilibrium and in the value to the Triple Entente of a favorable situation in the Balkans which was most important from the government's point of view. War was implied as a possibility for the defense of this policy, but it was usually argued that the policy of the equilibrium was the best way to maintain peace. Serious differences of opinion existed as to the extent to which France should support Russia and as to the point of view which should prevail in France's relations with Germany, but there were none, naturally, as to the supreme necessity of self-defense.

CHAPTER XIII

THE FAILURE OF THE EQUILIBRIUM, JULY, 1914

La grande, la seule question est celle de savoir si la Triple Entente s'abaissera plus ou moins bas devant la Triple Alliance, ou si elle entend qu'on ne touche plus à elle. La question serbe sera la pierre de touche.

Journal des Débats, July 31, 1914.

With few exceptions, the policy of the balance of power had been accepted by public opinion as the most effective assurance of a peace which would be satisfactory to the security and interests of France. Each crisis since 1905 had apparently proved its worth, and its merits for years had been extolled by responsible statesmen and by the most influential sections of the press. The criticism by the Monarchists and by the Socialists had little effect, for it was generally believed that a danger of war would be averted by a close association with Russia and England in a common policy. Even war would be accepted in the defense of a policy which was considered essential to the security and interests of France. In so far as his policy served these purposes, Poincaré represented the general will of the nation.

Opinion was divided, however, in regard to other questions of importance. The response to the Franco-German Conference at Berne in 1913 had shown that other groups than the Socialists favored a specific effort to improve relations with Germany. The strong opposition to the military law of 1913, which perhaps represented a majority of the French people, testified to a general approval of a frankly defensive policy, and it had always been agreed that France should not assume again the responsibility of a declaration of war against Germany. The implicit contradiction between this state of mind and the general affirmation of loyalty to the Russian Alliance was not often seen. Nor had an agreement been reached as to the possibility of a European conflict developing from the Balkans, although the specific protest against this possibility in 1912–1913 was not continued when the immediate danger disappeared and when Serbia's value to the Triple Entente became apparent. The July crisis of 1914 was to revive this question in more tragic circumstances. It was then also necessary to consider France's action in the improbable event that Germany, while attacking Russia in support of Austria, would remain upon the defensive against France. Public opinion became an important factor during the crisis, although it had little influence upon the course of events.[1] Its leaders had always assumed that Germany would immediately attack France as well as Russia, but it was necessary to prepare public opinion for any eventuality. It is with the character of this preparation, and its adaptation to the underlying currents of public opinion, that this study of the crisis is chiefly concerned.

The assassination of the Archduke Francis Ferdinand and his wife at Sarajevo, June 28, was condemned in France,[2] as elsewhere, but the indignation it aroused was tempered by sympathy for Serbia as a small nation and by her value to the Triple Entente. Ernest Judet was rarely in accord with accepted opinion in regard to international affairs, but he noted with considerable acuteness the inability of the press to judge the situation fairly. It was committed, he wrote, to the idea of an "enormous Serbia." He referred to the earlier enthusiasm for an independent Poland and a united Italy, which, in each instance, had been followed by repentance, and he remarked, "It may be the same again."[3] It was almost unanimously agreed that Serbia could not be made responsible for the crimes of individuals.[4] Her government, it was said, was in no way involved.[5] Chabrinovitch's confession that he had been armed in Belgrade did not shake the *Temp*'s (July 4) confidence in her innocence: "the maneuver is self-evident; it is a question of destroying the high moral reputation which Serbia enjoys in Europe." An investigation, it was agreed, should be held in Serbia, but even the radical press insisted that Austria should have no part in it. Not a few warned Austria that her own interests required moderation. The Radical-Socialist *Aurore* (June 29) and the *Lanterne*

---

[1] The rapidity of events made the development of a clear opinion upon each phase of the crisis difficult. News of the Austrian ultimatum was almost immediately followed by the announcement that Austria had broken off relations with Serbia. Information was especially slow in reaching the provinces. The *Petit Marseillais*, for example, did not print Serbia's reply to Austria until July 28, and its first editorial comment upon the crisis appeared July 29.

[2] Gustave Hervé was one of the few to condone the crime. *Guerre Sociale*, July 1.

[3] *Éclair*, July 1. This editorial is not among those reprinted in his *Ma Politique, 1905–1917*.

[4] *République Française*, July 1. *Radical*, July 2. *Siècle*, July 8. *Action*, July 8. Austria was called upon to suppress the anti-Serbian riots at Sarajevo. *Petit Marseillais*, July 1. *Temps*, July 2. *Gaulois*, July 2. *Radical*, July 2.

[5] *Journal des Débats*, July 1. *Journal*, July 3. *Figaro*, July 3.

(June 29) thought that the assassination might lead to the revolt of her subject peoples and to a division of her territory between the Germanic and Slavic Empires. Her safety, it was said, depended upon the good-will of the Balkan Slavs. "Austria must choose," wrote the nationalist André Mévil, "between a war with the Slavic world and a policy of self-effacement." [6] "She can survive," declared the normally more moderate *Siècle* (July 2), "on the condition of having none but friends in Europe." "Her structure," observed the Radical-Socialist *Événement* (July 5), "is such, that she cannot exist, that she can only be strong on the condition of being peaceful and just." The press, almost without exception, at once aligned itself with Serbia in anticipation of a threat from her powerful neighbor. There was as yet no occasion, however, for a discussion of definite action by France.

The efforts of Berchtold, the Austrian foreign minister, during the weeks which followed the assassination to mislead Europe as to his plans were not entirely successful [7] so far as the French press was concerned. The *Matin* (July 6), it is true, announced that "fear of complications between Austria and Serbia appears unfounded." [8] It was observed, however, that a section of the Viennese press was demanding vigorous action, [9] and disquieting indications were found in German newspapers of a tendency to urge Austria on. Necessarily without information, it was then suspected, as is known to-day, that Germany had already given, or was about to give, her ally an unconditional assurance of support. [10] The "blank check," in fact, was handed to Austria on July 5. The French government was better informed as to impending difficulties than the press. On July 3, Dumaine, the ambassador to Austria, wrote that "it is intended to reopen almost the entire question of the Balkans." [11] The Paris press, until the Austrian ultimatum, did little to forewarn public opinion of the seriousness of the situation or to prepare it for the decisions which were later made. Two Radical newspapers of the provinces were more definite. France, according to the *Petit Comtois* of Besançon (July 4), could not remain neutral if Austria, pushed on by Germany, attacked Serbia: "this must be understood in Berlin and Vienna." The

[6] *Libre Parole*, July 2.
[7] Fay, *Origins of the World War*, II, 243–249.
[8] Cf. *Liberté*, July 6. *Radical*, July 7.
[9] *République Française*, July 2.
[10] *Journal des Débats*, July 3. *Temps*, July 3. *Liberté*, July 3.
[11] Poincaré, *L'Union Sacrée* (Paris, 1927), p. 189.

Petit Provençal of Marseilles (July 6) was more concerned with the prospective break-up of the Dual Monarchy, for France, it believed, should aid Serbia in acquiring an Adriatic port and in developing her power in other respects, while Germany's expansion to the Mediterranean should be prevented. "We should give our moral and material support to Serbia," it declared, "in order to prevent an aggression which can only succeed if our weakness, now traditional, alas!, permits it." These were preliminary notes of the press campaign which was to develop later. For the moment, they were not characteristic.

While the resistance of the Hungarian minister, Tisza, to an extremist policy was being surmounted in Vienna, the attention of public opinion in France turned to other matters. The dramatic details of the trial of Mme. Caillaux for the murder of Gaston Calmette, the editor of the *Figaro,* crowded the meager despatches relating to the Austro-Serbian situation from the first pages of the press. There is nothing to indicate that the strong opposition to a general strike as a means of averting war in the Socialist Congress in Paris was inspired by the fear of an immediate crisis.[12] The campaign against the three-year service law was continued. Early in July, representatives of the Radical and Radical-Socialist parties in southeastern France, meeting at Gap, declared their refusal "to permit the reactionary parties to make of France a militarist machine," and they resolved "that Parliament should reëstablish the law of 1905 as soon as possible." [13] A second regional assembly at Agen in southwestern France adopted a similar resolution a few weeks later in preparation for the approaching party congress at Brest.[14] Clemenceau, who approved the existing law, was confident that the divisions among its opponents would prevent their success.[15] Yet the *Lyon Républicain* (July 10) called for action to be taken after the parliamentary vacation. The most important members of the Viviani cabinet, it declared, including the President of the Council, had all gone on record against the law of 1913 at one time or another, and ten of the sixteen members of the chamber's budget committee were committed to the law of 1905. The persistence

---

[12] *Matin,* July 16, 17. Cf. Jonathan French Scott, *Five Weeks. The Surge of Public Opinion on the Eve of the Great War* (New York, 1927), pp. 182, 183.

[13] *Radical,* July 5.

[14] *Temps,* July 26.

[15] *Homme Libre,* July 6. A part of the Radical and Radical-Socialist press in fact defended the three-year period of service. *Petit Provençal* (Marseilles), July 8. *Action,* July 24. *Rappel,* July 26. Viviani later admitted that the majority of the chamber desired what he describes as a modification of the law of 1913. René Viviani, *Réponse au Kaiser* (Paris, 1923), pp. 74, 75.

with which the skilful politicians of these groups continued to make this the most important item of their platform is an excellent indication of its popular appeal.

Poincaré's proposed visit to St. Petersburg revived public interest in the international situation. It had been planned six months earlier, and he now argues that its delay might have alarmed Europe and increased the fears of a crisis.[16] Nevertheless, the opposition parties then feared that it would involve France in the Balkan question.[17] Jaurès's unsuccessful attempt in the chamber to defeat the necessary credits became the occasion for a vigorous defense of the Russian alliance.[18] The Socialists, according to the *Temps* (July 9), were working for the "disruption of our alliances, which would mean the end of diplomatic autonomy and of our national liberty." The plan, it was said, involved three objectives: the repeal of the three-year service law, the dissolution of the Russian alliance, and a *rapprochement* with Germany. Writing under the name of Georges Villiers in the *France de Bordeaux et du Sud-Ouest* (July 11), Tardieu conceded that the Socialists wished to include Germany rather than to dissolve the Triple Entente. "An enlargement of the Russian alliance and the Anglo-French entente by the inclusion of Germany," he wrote, "would . . . lead to catastrophe by delivering France without support to all of Germany's designs." The alleged Socialist campaign was the principal theme of Maurice Barrès's inaugural speech as the new president of the Ligue des Patriotes: ". . . it is clear," he declared, "that there is a conspiracy to break the Triple Entente and to substitute an alliance with Germany. It would mean that France, on her knees to Emperor William, would become the vassal of Germany." [19] It is possible that a desire to reaffirm France's diplomatic ties rather than fear of the Socialist campaign was the more important motive that inspired these assertions, for even the Radical-Socialists did not support Jaurès in this respect.[20]

Much remains obscure in regard to the conversations during Poincaré's visit to St. Petersburg (July 20–23), but the truth doubtless is somewhere between his own version [21] and that of his critics. They were neither entirely innocuous discussions of entente solidarity, nor

[16] Poincaré, *L'Union Sacrée,* p. 211.
[17] Paris correspondence, *Journal de Génève,* July 9.
[18] *Annales,* 1914, III, 414, 415 (July 7).
[19] He invited the Ligue to combat this danger. *Écho de Paris,* ,July 11.
[20] *Lyon Républicain,* July 12. *Lanterne,* July 15.
[21] Poincaré, *L'Union Sacrée,* pp. 237–280.

was war specifically planned by them. The French President used his influence to arrange recent differences which had arisen between England and Russia in Persia, but it was more significant that he gave satisfactory assurances to the Tsar and Sazonov of France's support in view of the impending difficulties in the Austro-Serbian question.[22] Although some alarm had been expressed in France as to the purposes of the visit and as to Russia's intentions, the press almost with one accord represented the event as serving the interests of peace.[23] The reports of the ceremonies in St. Petersburg contained no reference to any connection with the Austro-Serbian situation. Poincaré's disturbing remark to the Austrian ambassador that complications might follow any action by his government against Serbia was not known, nor was it possible for the press to enlighten public opinion as to the attitude of the war party in the Russian Court.[24] Few ventured to criticize the declaration of complete union betwen France and Russia in the toasts exchanged, July 21, by the President and Tsar at Peterhof.[25] "It is not the humiliating and precarious tranquility," wrote the *Progrès de la Côte d'Ôr* of Dijon (July 22), "that an all-powerful Empire imposes upon its weaker neighbors. . . . It is a peace based upon the equilibrium." The Radical and Radical-Socialist newspapers noted the reaffirmation of the alliance with satisfaction as an assurance of a peace that would not be disturbed by Germany's dictatorial methods. "With this shield which fears no sword, Europe will be able to pursue its work of civilization better than with bended knees and trembling souls." [26] The *Radical* (July 22) affirmed that "Autocratic Russia desires peace; war would not profit her in any way." Nevertheless, the *Lanterne* (July 21), remembering the rumor current some weeks earlier that Paléologue had threatened to resign as ambassador to Russia if the three-year service law were repealed, declared that Russia could not control France's policy.

[22] Buchanan to Grey, St. Petersburg, July 24, 1911. *Brit. War Docs.*, XI, 80. Fay, *Origins of the World War*, II, 277–286. See the favorable comments as to French policy during the crisis and as to these conversations in Baron Mikhail A. Taube, *La Politique Russe et la Fin de l'Empire des Tsars (1904–1917)* (Paris, 1928), pp. 370, 371.

[23] *Petit Journal*, July 20. *Journal*, July 20.

[24] Poincaré, *L'Union Sacrée*, pp. 253, 254. Poincaré's warning, reported to Vienna and Berlin, caused irritation there. P. Renouvin, *The Immediate Origins of the War* (New Haven, 1928), p. 81.

[25] Poincaré, *L'Union Sacrée*, pp. 241, 242. The reference to the maintenance of "peace in strength, honor, and dignity" appeared in Poincaré's toast, July 23, at the concluding dinner. *Ibid.*, p. 278.

[26] *Action*, July 22. Cf. *Rappel*, July 22. *République Française*, July 22.

In view of the sacrifices which France had recently accepted in the new law of 1913, it was natural that interest should be shown in the Russian army. The *Matin* and the *Temps* were especially responsible for exaggerated estimates of its present and prospective strength / which later helped to assure the acceptance of war. The *Novoïe Vremya,* it was observed, had announced "the preponderance of the Franco-Russian alliance over its rival," [27] with a criticism of France's purely defensive attitude.[28] Jules Hedeman, one of the most influential French correspondents, wrote from St. Petersburg that the Russian peace-time army would reach 2,545,000 by 1916. He added that it would then be superior to the combined German and Austrian armies, and that Russia in other respects stood supreme. "M. Poincaré arrives at the moment when this country is becoming the strongest military Power and when it is on the eve of becoming the leading nation from the agricultural, industrial and commercial points of view.[29] The *Temps* (July 16) wrote in somewhat the same strain, and in addition commented upon the probable effect of the enormous masses of the Russian army upon the balance of power. Mr. J. W. Headlam-Morley, the editor of the eleventh volume of the *British Documents on the Origins of the War,* writes that these articles did not represent "any fraction of French public opinion." [30] Nevertheless, they attracted considerable attention,[31] and it is reasonable to conclude that they contributed to the exaggerated confidence of the press in the superior strength of the Triple Entente during the crisis. "In truth," wrote the revolutionary *Bataille Syndicaliste* (July 19), "one has the impression in reading the *Temps* and the *Matin* that our patriots do not merely foresee a possible war but that they envisage a prompt conflict." Even the radical *Lyon Républicain* (July 24) was confident that the Triple Entente "holds the destinies of Europe in its hands," having control of the seas, two millions of soldiers under arms, and an inexhaustible man-power. This strength, it declared, should be used in the interests of peace. The attitude of the press and of public opinion after the Austrian ultimatum was in part influenced by this confidence in the armed superiority of the Triple Entente.

The Austrian ultimatum of July 23 had been prepared for the pur-

[27] *Matin,* July 17.
[28] *Éclair,* July 18.
[29] *Matin,* July 18.
[30] *Brit. War Docs.,* XI, X.
[31] *Événement,* July 19. *Siècle,* July 20.

pose of crushing Serbia as a danger to Austria's security and in order
to change the unfavorable balance of power in the Balkans. Its effect
upon the French press was immediate and practically unanimous.
There was doubtless much sincere sympathy for Serbia as a small
state threatened by a powerful neighbor, but it was not as significant
as the prompt assumption that the general equilibrium of Europe was
at stake. The *Temps* (July 25) declared that "the blow which
menaces the Balkans and Slavism also threatens the European equilibrium. . . . The balance of power is a bloc and . . . neither France
nor England can be indifferent to what is taking place in the Near
East." Serbia, according to the *Journal des Débats* (July 25), should
agree to open an investigation, to repudiate the anti-Austrian agitation and to punish those who were involved in the plot to assassinate
Francis Ferdinand. In regard to the other demands in the ultimatum,
"Serbia will not appeal in vain to the opinion of Europe and for the
support of the Great Powers who are determined at any price to
maintain the equilibrium." André Chéradame, the critic of Pan-
Germanism, attributed the ultimatum to Germany's inspiration, and
he maintained that her desire to localize the Austro-Serbian quarrel
should not be permitted "even if things must go to the point of war." The
Gaulois (July 25) was one of the few newspapers to print Austria's
evidence as to Serbia's suspected complicity, but it nevertheless insisted
that her refusal to accept a friendly settlement would amount to an
attack upon the Triple Entente. Certain nationalist newspapers were
too eager to announce the "inevitable" war to give much attention to the
diplomatic implications of the situation.[32]

Jacques Bainville was again one of the few to rationalize the
questions which France would have to answer. "Is public opinion," he
asked, "prepared to accept the idea of a continental war for the sake
of Serbia? Has the government of the Republic sufficiently considered
the consequences of the Russian alliance?"[33] The opinion of the
Siècle (July 25), for many years an ardent friend of Russia and
Serbia although it had not received a share of the Russian subsidies
in 1913, was clear. It would let Russia decide freely whether the
war would be localized or not. Acceptance of the balance of power
had become so complete, and Austria's position was so difficult to
support, that there was little prospect for the expression of a clearly
defined opinion that France should remain aloof, even among the

[32] *Paris-Midi,* July 25.
[33] *Action Française,* July 25.

Radical and Radical-Socialist press. The Radical *Rappel* (July 25) was certain that the Triple Entente could not be indifferent to Serbia's fate, and Senator Bérenger's *Action* (July 25) declared that France "must respect our ally's freedom of action." Nevertheless, there were some who did not permit their attachment to peace to be over-shadowed by concern for the unity of the Triple Entente. If the *Radical* (July 25) wrote, with a feeling akin to fatalism, that France could "only observe the course of events with agonizing attention," it also insisted that lack of direct interests should enable her to work for the maintenance of peace. The *Aurore* (July 25) believed that "European diplomacy" should restrain Austria, but it also insisted that "Serbia must be patient. Every one must set to work and impose peace." The first reaction of the *Événement* (July 25) was to suggest arbitration as a solution. Nor did all of the moderate and nationalist newspapers give first place to the interests of the Triple Entente. The *République Française* (July 25) urged a possible peaceful solution of the crisis, and the *Action Française* (July 25) hoped that means could be found for the arbitration of the difficulty as in other instances. The nationalist *Petit Marseillais* (July 25) even warned public opinion against Russia's aggressive purposes, adding that she had rarely been successful in offensive wars. "May she remain upon the defensive," it concluded, "since she has been successful in that policy."

Although a threat directed against the interests of the Triple Entente in the Balkans was interpreted by the press as a danger to France, public opinion in general could not be fully aroused unless Germany was represented as definitely involved. It was not easy to do this in connection with the Austrian ultimatum, but an incident occurred in Paris, July 24, which was used for this purpose. That afternoon, von Schoen, the German ambassador, read an important statement to Bienvenu-Martin, who was acting Minister of Foreign Affairs in Viviani's absence, announcing Germany's desire to localize the Austro-Serbian conflict. " 'Any intervention by another Power,' " it declared, " 'would lead, through the play of alliances, to incalulable consequences.' " [34] The French minister, according to Schoen's report, was favorably impressed. "The French government," he wrote, "sincerely shares the desire to localize the conflict, and it intends to

---

[34] Poincaré, *L'Union Sacrée*, p. 299. *Livre Noir*, II, 275, 276. Bienvenu-Martin to Viviani, Paris, July 24, 1914. *Livre Jaune: La Guerre Européenne, 1914*, pp. 48, 49.

act in this sense for the maintenance of peace." [35] But he had either misunderstood the position of the French government or he had been intentionally misled, for on the same day Paul Cambon skilfully diverted Grey's suggestion of intervention by the Powers not immediately interested between Austria and Russia to intervention between Austria and Serbia.[36] Moreover, the *Écho de Paris* (July 25), a newspaper which the British Ambassador identified as close to the Russian embassy, was permitted to publish in approximately accurate form a summary of von Schoen's communication [37] with comments which interpreted his purposes in the worst possible light. "The *démarche*," it declared, "amounts to this: 'Let Austria crush Serbia, otherwise you must deal with Germany.' Under the paradoxical pretext of localizing the conflict, there is a threat of a collective humiliation for the Triple Entente or the prospect of a general war." [38] Since Germany's attitude was watched with anxious concern, this revelation and comment was given much attention.[39] It was for the most part copied without additional comment, but the chauvinist *Libre Parole* (July 26) affirmed that "Germany has reserved for France the impertinence of a communication which contains an implicit threat of war." [40] Others insisted that, as the same statement had not been communicated to London or to St. Petersburg, it was a maneuver to separate France and Russia or to compel France to advise moderation to her ally.[41]

It was Germany, apparently, who acted first and most effectively to correct the unfortunate effect upon public opinion of the revelation

[35] Karl Kautsky, *Die Deutsche Dokumente zum Kriegsausbruch*, 4 vols. (Charlottensburg, 1919), I, 166, 167.

[36] Grey to Bertie, July 24, 1914. *Brit. War Docs.*, XI, 77, 78.

[37] Schoen to Foreign Office, Paris, July 25, 1914. Kautsky, *Die Deutsche Dokumente*, I, 183.

[38] According to the British ambassador, Schoen said that his communication was not a threat. Bertie to Grey, Paris, July 25, 1914. *Brit. War Docs.*, XI, 92. Schoen was assured that the government did not share the views of the *Écho de Paris* (*Livre Jaune: La Guerre Européenne, 1914*, pp. 55, 56), but he wrote after the war that the Quai d'Orsay really agreed. Wilhelm von Schoen, *Erlebtes. Beiträge zur Politischen Geschichte der Neuesten Zeit* (Stuttgart, 1921), pp. 165, 166. Cf. *Livre Noir*, II, 277 (12/25 July).

[39] *Matin*, July 25. *Petit Provençal* (Marseilles), July 26. *Action*, July 26. *Journal des Débats*, July 26, *Presse*, July 26. *France de Bordeaux et du Sud-Ouest*, July 26.

[40] The *Petit Comtois* of Besançon (July 27) characterized it as "the insolent, aggressive German menace." Bainville declared that France was placed under "a direct menace." *Action Française*, July 26.

[41] *Journal de Rouen*, July 27.

and comment of the *Écho de Paris*. A Havas despatch from Berlin, July 25, appeared in the *Matin* (July 26) containing a correction. "It is said, according to report, that it (Schoen's statement) was not menacing in character, and that it had no other purpose than to facilitate the coöperation of the Great Powers for the maintenance of peace." In Paris, Schoen also said as much to representatives of the press,[42] and late in the afternoon of July 26 he assured Bienvenu-Martin that Austria sought no territorial gains at Serbia's expense, that she intended no "attack upon the integrity of the Serbian monarchy," and that it would depend upon Russia to prevent war. These assurances were of questionable value in view of Berchtold's determination to crush Serbia, but it was significant that the German ambassador endorsed the principle of European solidarity for the maintenance of peace. "Germany," he declared, "feels herself in accord with France in an ardent desire that peace may be maintained." However, he refused to promise that Germany would advise moderation in Vienna, although he urged France to act in this sense upon her own ally.[43] Later on the same day, he returned to the Quai d'Orsai with the proposal to Philippe Berthelot, the political director, that the following note should be given to the press: "The German ambassador and the Minister of Foreign Affairs have had this afternoon a new interview during which they examined in a most friendly spirit and in a sentiment of peaceful solidarity the means which may be used for the maintenance of general peace." Berthelot refused his consent on the ground that it would give public opinion a false sense of security, but he was probably at least equally desirous of avoiding the impression in Russia that France was taking an "extra dance" with Germany.[44] Nevertheless, the *Journal* (July 27) reported that at

---

[42] *Matin*, July 26. *Journal de Genève*, July 28.

[43] Poincaré, *L'Union Sacrée*, pp. 329, 330. Pierre Renouvin, *Les Origines Immédiates de la Guerre* (Paris, 1927), pp. 24, 25. *Livre Noir*, II, 278 (13/26 July).

[44] *Livre Jaune: La Guerre Européenne*, 1914, pp. 74-76. Poincaré, *L'Union Sacrée*, pp. 330, 331. *Livre Noir*, II, 278 (13/26 July). Bertie hoped that his government would "urge the French government to issue notice suggested by German ambassador." The British ambassador had no sympathy for Russia's claim to be the protector of the Balkan Slavs. Bertie to Grey, Paris, July 27. *Brit. War Docs.*, XI, 127, 128. Permanent officials of the British Foreign Office, and Grey, believing that Germany was trying to divide France and Russia, refused to act upon this advice. See notes by Crowe and Nicolson. *Ibid.*, XI, 127, 128. Grey to Bertie, London, July 28. *Ibid.*, XI, 142. Schoen gained the impression that Bienvenu-Martin was willing to advise moderation at St. Petersburg after Austria-Hungary had affirmed that she sought no an-

11 P. M. of the preceeding day, "The German ambassador and the President of the Council *ad interim* had a new interview in the course of which they considered the means of action by the Powers for the maintenance of peace."[45] The authors of this note had carefully avoided the reference to the solidarity between France and Germany which had been the central point of Schoen's suggestion. Germany had acted promptly, and to a certain extent effectively to correct the unfortunate impression created by this incident. But the first effect, strengthened by instinctive suspicions of Germany's intentions, was not entirely neutralized, for many newspapers either omitted the later rectifications or printed them in obscure corners. Germany's supposed failure to advise moderation in Austria proved, it was said, the hypocrisy of her peaceful assurances.[46] In any event, Germany doubtless had hoped that Schoen's maneuvers would weaken the union between France and Russia.[47]

It is possible that French advice had some influence upon the preparation of Serbia's reply,[48] and its somewhat deceptive appearance of concessions upon almost every demand in the Austrian ultimatum, which would not weaken her independence as a sovereign State, insured its approval by the French press. But the Austro-Serbian quarrel became of secondary importance when Austria severed diplomatic relations with Serbia directly upon the receipt of her reply. The press at once developed the points of view which were in the main to persist throughout the crisis. On the first impression, it would seem that there were no differences of opinion.

nexations. Schoen to Foreign Office, Paris, July 26. Kautsky, *Die Deutsche Dokumente*, I, 230, 231.

[45] It was also reported from Berlin July 26 that Schoen's original communication had been made at London and St. Petersburg. *Progrès de la Côte d'Ôr* (Dijon), July 27. Jaurès believed that this assurance removed whatever appearance of unfriendliness the communication may have had. *Humanité*, July 27.

[46] *Événement*, July 27.

[47] Renouvin, *Immediate Origins of the War*, pp. 104–107. On July 27, acting upon his own responsibility, for he failed to report his proposal to his government, Schoen suggested to Abel Ferry that the two countries should intervene at St. Petersburg and Vienna. Ferry replied that France preferred action by the four Powers, referring to Grey's plan of intervention. France, it is to be noted, never encouraged intervention between Russia and Austria. Professor Schmitt thinks well of France's policy during this episode, but it is not easy to see what harm would have followed an open statement that France and Germany were coöperating in an effort to maintain peace. This, of course, is a matter of opinion. Schmitt, *Coming of the War*, II, 15.

[48] Fay, *Origins of the World War*, II, 340.

All were apparently agreed in backing Russia, in insisting upon the unity of the Triple Entente, and in accepting the prospect of a general war. Nevertheless, there were certain distinctions which, if implicit, were none the less real.

The small section of the press which had been for years most active in creating confidence in the balance of power, and whose discussions of foreign affairs enjoyed the greatest prestige, at once accepted Russia's intervention as inevitable. It insisted that the only hope of peace was in the moderation which the unity and strength of the Triple Entente should impose upon Germany and Austria.[49] "If Germany is silent at Vienna," declared the *Temps* (July 27), "it means the precipitation of the inevitable conflict." The *Journal des Débats* (July 29) asserted that Serbia's annihilation would mean the restoration of Germany's hegemony, and it called upon all classes to prevent this. "The German hegemony would weigh much more heavily upon the working classes . . . than upon the *bourgeoisie* or the financial aristocracy. It would lead promptly to the invasion of our factories, of our ship-yards, by German workmen and foremen, to the suppression of our merchant marine, to the absorption of our financial resources by German enterprises. . . ." On the next day (July 28), it promised that negotiations, if Austria should accept them, would be conducted "on our side in the greatest spirit of conciliation," but "it is not for us to take the initiative." It was Germany's duty to translate her peaceful assurances into such action as would restrain Austria. "The greater our coolness, our steadiness and firmness, the better we will defend the cause of peace." The right wing of the Radical press contributed to the feeling that neither France nor Russia could act effectively. Senator Bérenger's *Action* (July 26) admitted that Russia's defense of Serbia had been agreed upon during Poincaré's visit to Russia, yet it insisted that the Triple Entente could do nothing. "Russia," it affirmed, "has exhausted her diplomatic action," and France was not in a position to act. "Whether we desire it or not," wrote Bérenger, "our peace is at the mercy of a sudden attack by Germany." Forgetting its protest in 1912 against a general war arising from the Balkans, the *Lanterne* (July 27) accepted the prospect that the Russian alliance would involve France. "It is time," it affirmed, "to remember our most sacred duties. . . . Let us be ready."

---

[49] The Triple Entente, it was said, could only await the course of events. *Matin*, July 26, 27. *Siècle*, July 26.

The Radical press was, however, sometimes clearer in its insistence that the action of the Triple Entente should be in the interest of peace. The *Rappel* (July 26) was firm in its conviction that French interests were involved, but Steeg, a Radical senator, wrote in its columns that the Triple Entente should act in the interest of peace "before sentiments of pride, and explosions of rage . . . raise obstacles to the victory of good sense and reason." The *Radical* (July 26) would likewise have the Entente Powers use their greater solidarity in the interest of peace, although it was prepared to accept a war "which would be imposed upon France." The *Événement* (July 26) was one of the small minority of the press to urge that the Austro-Serbian conflict should be localized on the ground that Serbia would still have a good chance of success. Yet these newspapers did not see, as Bainville did, that the greatest danger to peace was precisely in the direct opposition between the two armed alliances.

Austria's delay of three days in declaring war (June 28) against Serbia strengthened for a moment the hope of peace. Here and there it was recognized that Germany was not aggressive and even that she was at last acting at Vienna in the interest of moderation.[50] But the first shot upon the Danube was answered by an even firmer dependence upon the Triple Entente. "After the *coup de Belgrade* as after the *coup d'Agadir*," Jean Herbette declared in the *Écho de Paris* (July 30), "peace perhaps can only be saved by the Triple Entente, united and ready for the conflict." War, wrote the *Temps* (July 29), was perhaps the only means of escape from the *impasse* into which the Triple Entente had been led by its weakness in dealing with Austria during the past two years. The real question, according to the *Journal des Débats* (July 29), was more concerned with the equilibrium of Europe and of the world than with Serbia. There was in prospect a rearrangement of Europe such as had followed Sadowa and Sedan, and if a single member of the Triple Entente weakened in its resolution to defend Serbia, it would mean the end of the independence of the Western Powers. "There is only one question," it concluded, "would Austria-Hungary and Germany be able in one form or another to restore the influence they have lost in the Near East during the past six years? If they are permitted to do this, the turn of the West will be next." As the danger of the situation increased, even the Radical press began to emphasize the military supe-

[50] *Événement*, July 28.

riority of the Triple Entente, not however to threaten war, but in the hope that it would persuade the Central Powers to yield. This, surprisingly, was the point of view of the *Lyon Républicain* (July 31), and the *Action* (July 30) believed that with the Triple Entente firmly united, a definite statement of its purposes at a critical moment would preserve peace.

The pressure of events gave importance to the attitude of the parties of the left, for it was from them that the only serious opposition could come. About fifty Socialist deputies meeting in Paris, July 28, protested against intervention by Russia and declared "'that France alone can dispose of France, that under no circumstances can she be drawn into a formidable conflict by the more or less arbitrary interpretation of secret treaties and of occult engagements and that she must keep her entire freedom of action in order to exercise a peaceful influence.'" [51] The authorities, however, had never accepted the advice of the socialist group in foreign affairs, and there was no prospect for a change during this crisis. The Radical and Radical-Socialist press had based its hope of peace upon the operation of the balance of power, but on July 29 the Radical-Socialist *Aurore* (July 29) expressed serious doubts as to the merits of Serbia's case and as to France's obligations to join Russia. "The Serbian government, in ordering the arrest of Major Voija Tankositch, has recognized the justice of the charges against her in the ultimatum." It seemed clear therefore that the Serbian government must have known of the plot. If her officials were involved, "who would say that the conditions imposed upon Serbia were excessive?" In any event, France should ask Austria for more information before she made her decision. As for France's obligations in the Russian alliance, it believed that the alliance was purely defensive. "Has Russia been attacked? It is certain that she has not been. . . ." It is impossible to estimate the extent to which the Radical-Socialist party, or public opinion in general, shared these doubts, but in any event they did not lead to any positive plan for imposing caution upon the government. On the contrary, the Radical and Radical-Socialist deputies then in Paris met on July 29, the date of Poincaré's and Viviani's return to Paris from St. Petersburg and adopted a resolution "recognizing the firmness and wisdom of the Government in the existing international situation" and declaring their solidarity

[51] *Radical,* July 29.

with it "in a sentiment of patriotic confidence." These groups had abdicated, under the pressure of patriotism, their function as the opposition.[52]

Even before this action by the radical groups, the government had of course enjoyed a free hand. It is safe to say that it had no intention of imposing effective restraint upon its ally. "The moment has passed," wrote Eyre Crowe, a permanent official of the British foreign office, as early as July 24, "when it might have been possible to enlist French support in an effort to hold back Russia. . . . It is clear," he concluded, "that France and Russia are decided to accept the challenge thrown out to them." [53] Evidently convinced that war was certain, Crowe was perhaps not in a position to judge France's purposes fairly, but she was in fact prepared to support Russia in defense of the interests of the Triple Entente. Schoen had received a distinctly favorable impression from his interviews with Bienvenu-Martin, but the latter assured Isvolski, in response to Russia's vigorous protest against a possible intervention at St. Petersburg, that he had not for a moment admitted the "possibility of exerting pressure in St. Petersburg in the interest of moderation." [54] On July 27, Viviani, probably with Poincaré's approval, informed Russia from the *France,* in which they were returning home, that "France is ready to second the action of the imperial government without reservation in the interest of peace." [55] These assurances apparently satisfied Isvolski and his government, for he acknowledged his gratitude, July 29, for France's unlimited support, adding that Russia was accelerating her military preparations.[56] These assurances were never withdrawn nor effectively qualified, but on July 30, perhaps for the purpose of giving

[52] *Radical,* July 30. "France," wrote the *Aurore* (Aug. 1) in commenting upon the assassination of Jaurès, ". . . does not desire war. But she is prepared for every eventuality. Calm and resolute, the nation waits, determined to follow those who direct its destinies in accord with allied and friendly countries. . . . If war must come, we will accept it." Gustave Hervé, who as late as July 28 had protested against war, invited Socialists to refrain from any action that would weaken France if war came. *Guerre Sociale,* July 30.

[53] Crowe's notes to a despatch from Buchanan to Grey, St. Petersburg, July 24, 1914. *Brit. War Docs.,* XI, 81, 82. Yet Bertie wrote, July 25, that France would probably advise against any excessive zeal on Russia's part in picking a quarrel with Austria, because public opinion in France would not support her. *Ibid.,* XI, 99.

[54] *Livre Noir,* II, 283, 284 (15/28 July).

[55] Poincaré, *L'Union Sacrée,* p. 385.

[56] *Livre Noir,* II, 289 (16/29 July).

an appearance of a defensive policy to the Triple Entente, Russia was advised to keep her military measures as secret as possible in order to avoid an excuse for mobilization by Germany.[57] The French government, interested chiefly in the defense of the diplomatic *status quo,* since this was favorable to the Triple Entente, had no reason to oppose Russia's suggestion of renewed negotiations based upon Austria's withdrawal of the two demands which Serbia had not accepted. It was even prepared to support an attempt to find a more satisfactory formula.[58] On July 31, the French Minister of War assured the Russian military attaché in "a tone of enthusiastic sincerity, the government's firm decision for war, asking me to confirm the hope of the general staff that our efforts will be directed against Germany and that Austria would be considered as *une quantité négligeable."* [59] In view of the minister's natural preoccupation with the responsibilities of his department, the second part of this statement was probably the more important—that is, from Messimy's point of view. There is little reason to doubt that the government of France, as well as the press and public opinion, preferred peace if the interests of the Triple Entente could be protected by peaceful means. The government's readiness to accept war rather than permit a reversal of the existing balance in the Balkans was equally certain.

The press, as a whole, reflected this point of view. War was therefore not only possible but probable, since a surrender by the Central Powers was scarcely to be expected. Measures were taken to convince public opinion that the members of the Triple Entente had exerted themselves to the utmost in the interest of peace, that England's aid was certain, and that conditions were favorable if war should come. Grey's suggestions of intervention were approved.[60] It was somewhat more difficult to attribute entirely peaceful activities

---

[57] *Livre Noir,* II, 290, 291 (17/30 July).

[58] Sazonov to the Russian Ambassador in Berlin, St. Petersburg, 17/30 July, 1914. *Ibid.,* II, 291, 292. Poincaré, *L'Union Sacrée,* pp. 402, 403.

[59] *Livre Noir,* II, 294 (18/31 July, 1914).

[60] The *Temps* (July 29) held that Germany's refusal would prove her desire for war. The *Journal des Débats* (July 29) was skeptical of any negotiation at this time. "If any one of the Powers of the Triple Entente weakens at this critical hour," it declared, "if it permits itself to be inveigled into dilatory conversations, if it wastes time in examining successive combinations intended to deceive and unnerve opinion, it means the end of the European equilibrium and of the independence of the Western Powers. The hour is decisive. Every official or leader in France and England as well as in Russia must realize that each sign of weakness, every gesture of lassitude would be a crime." But this important newspaper was more unbending than the great majority.

to Russia, but this feat was accomplished. She was represented as without fault. Her defense of Serbia was generally accepted as entirely legitimate, and it was said that her policy was free of all provocation. "France and England are certain," declared the *Temps* (July 30), "that Russia has done everything and continues to do everything to avoid precipitating the shock." "As for Russia," affirmed the *Matin* (July 29), "it is her calm which assures the security of Europe." The *Siècle* (July 29) referred to "Russia's evident and praiseworthy moderation." Stephen Pichon was puzzled by Germany's insistence that the real danger was in St. Petersburg "where, on the contrary, the government is resolutely and meritoriously peaceful." [61] Earlier, on July 27, the nationalist *Liberté* affirmed that "We have and we cherish the assurance that no provocation is to be feared from Russia." It was probably no mere oversight that the radical press had little to say on this point, although the *Action* (July 26) had assured its readers that Russia "would do everything" to obtain a peaceful settlement. Even her partial mobilization against Austria was interpreted as in no way affecting her desire of peace. The *Figaro* (July 30) added, after announcing it, that she was resolved to do everything to preserve the peace of Europe, and according to the *Gaulois* (July 30), this measure "would contribute more to safeguard peace . . . than any humiliating and useles diplomatic *démarches.*" The French government received word of Russia's order for general mobilization from Paléologue in St. Petersburg at 8:30 P. M. on July 31.[62] It appears that some delay occurred before it was communicated to Viviani and Poincaré, but they knew of it sometime that evening.[63] Russia's action was announced in the morning newspapers of August 1, based upon reports from London and Berlin, and in such a way as to represent it as a reply to the action of the Central Powers. The *Matin*'s headlines (Aug. 1) read "Mobilization in Austria became general yesterday, yesterday evening in Russia." [64] That afternoon, the *Journal des Débats* (Aug. 2) reported Russia's action in much the same way as it was announced in the falsified telegram from Paléologue of July 31 which appeared later

[61] *Petit Journal*, July 28.

[62] Fay, *Origins of the World War*, II, 476.

[63] Poincaré, *L'Union Sacrée*, pp. 455–457. Jaurès's assassination that evening was perhaps a disturbing factor.

[64] See the reproduction of these headlines, and of the long despatch from St. Petersburg, dated July 31, in which Russia's action was correctly reported as of July 30 in *Berliner Monatshefte für Internationale Aufklärung*, VIII (10), facing page 954 (Oct., 1930).

in the *Yellow Book*. "As a result of the official Austrian general mobilization and of the German mobilization concealed under the name of a state of siege, Russia has also been compelled to proclaim her general mobilization." It need scarcely be said that the Russian order in fact preceded that of any other Power.

If Russia desired peace and if her actions were directed to this end, as the press insisted, there was evidently no occasion for advising moderation. "The Paris cabinet," announced the *Journal des Débats* (July 31), "will not say a word to that of St. Petersburg to prevent it from taking the measures which are required for the defense of the vital interests of Russia and for the maintenance of the world equilibrium. . . . The moment has arrived for the Triple Entente to defend its existence by every means including force." Jules Hedeman, although reporting from Berlin that Germany desired peace, was convinced that Russia should be "the sole judge of her action." "Our rôle," declared the Radical *Action* (July 27), "is to follow them, and not to show them the route." The *Journal de Rouen* (July 31) agreed that "It is Russia who decides first. France then comes to her aid. This is required by an alliance in which the obligations are reciprocal." But this zeal in affirming Russia's peaceful purposes and the insistence that no steps would be taken to bring pressure to bear upon her suggests a doubt that public opinion was after all entirely convinced.

Supporting a policy which it was hoped would maintain peace while protecting the interests of France and of the Triple Entente, the press interpreted the international situation as unusually favorable in the event of war. It was at once recognized that England held the balance of power.[65] "Everything depends upon her," declared the chauvinist *Paris-Midi* (July 27). "If she notifies William that all of the ships of the Hamburg and North German lines will be sunk at the first sign of aggression, the Kaiser . . . will feel that the hour is badly chosen." The theory of the equilibrium, which colored the attitude of the press throughout the crisis, implied England's solidarity with France and Russia. It was said that England as well as France could not remain indifferent to events in the Balkans, but this was clearly a hope rather than a certainty. Public opinion had no dependable assurance of England's armed aid even in the event of a German attack upon France. The eagerness with which Churchill's order holding the Grand Fleet together after the annual review was

---

[65] *The Diary of Lord Bertie of Thame, 1914–1918,* 2 vols. (New York, 1924), I, 4, 5. Cf. *Guerre Sociale,* July 30.

welcomed betrayed a certain anxiety.[66] A definite word of England's intention to throw her lot with her friends, and to blockade the coast of Germany would, it was thought, finally persuade Germany to restrain Austria.[67] Grey, however, continued until almost the last moment to warn France through diplomatic channels that he could give no definite assurance. The situation, he said, differed radically from that of the Agadir crisis in 1911. France's own interests had then been involved, but under existing circumstances, British public opinion would not approve a war on behalf of Serbia or one resulting from a conflict between Russia and Austria for the control of the Balkans.[68] It was not until the morning of August 2, after Germany had presented her ultimatum to France, that he promised that the British fleet would protect the northern coast of France if the German fleet should appear in the English Channel.[69] "In fact," writes Poincaré, "the French government did not know what action England would take until the last moment." [70] This is perhaps too strong a statement, for without being certain, the French government probably was confident that England's eventual aid, envisaged since 1906 in the military conversations and in the Grey-Cambon letters of 1912, could be counted upon. The press, at any rate, gave the impression that her aid was assured. The *Journal* (Aug. 1) reported that "M. Francis Bertie demanded an audience with M. de Viviani yesterday (July 31) at 9:30 P. M.; and we can say that the result of this conversation is of such a nature as to give us complete security." [71] The next morning (Aug. 2), before Grey's limited commitment in regard to France's northern coast was known in Paris, an even more positive statement appeared in identical form in several Radical newspapers. "We are informed," it read, "that our government has received complete assurances as to the naval and military rôle of England in the event of a Franco-German war." [72] The confidence which it was

---

[66] *Matin*, July 28. *Patrie*, July 28. *Radical*, July 28. *Phare de la Loire*, July 29.

[67] *Journal*, July 29. *Figaro*, July 30. *Patrie*, July 30. *Journal de Rouen*, July 31.

[68] *Brit. War Docs.*, XI, 180, 200, 201, 203, 220, 226, 227, 258. A wire from London noting this tendency of public opinion was buried upon the last page of the *Journal*, July 27.

[69] Grey to Bertie, Foreign Office, Aug. 2, 1914, 4:45 P. M. *Brit. War Docs.*, XI, 274, 275.

[70] Poincaré, *L'Union Sacrée*, p. 437.

[71] Cf. *Journal des Débats*, Aug. 1. *Gaulois*, Aug. 2.

[72] *Action*, Aug. 2. *Rappel*, Aug. 2. *Homme Libre*, Aug. 2. Cf. *Figaro*, Aug. 2. It was on this date that Bertie wrote in his diary that "It will not be long now before it is 'Perfide Albion.'" *The Diary of Lord Bertie of Thame* (London, 1924), p. 8.

the evident purpose of this announcement to create was not justified by England's attitude at the moment.

It would be a mistake to conclude from the attitude of the press, from its support of Russia, from its refusal to approve pressure upon her in the interest of moderation, or from its unwarranted assurances of England's aid that public opinion desired war. The newspapers which evidently wished to stiffen public opinion and those who perhaps desired war represented war as probable regardless of France's attitude. The *Paris Midi* (July 25) announced it as imminent. The *Temps* (July 27), a more responsible newspaper, declared that there should be "no provocation, no nervousness, no panic, only the sentiment that grave dangers may arise against which it may be necessary to act."\ There was little evidence of the thoughtless chauvinism of 1870,[73] and it was significant that instead of encouraging its expression the authorities dispersed a small procession which was shouting "*À Berlin!*" Passers-by, it was reported, regarded the demonstration "with curiosity." [74] The police, however, were not more tolerant of the more imposing pacifist demonstration organized by the revolutionary *Bataille Syndicaliste* on the evening of July 27.[75] Not only did the *Paris-Midi*'s (July 30) false announcement of the mobilization of four classes (1908–1911) and the impending extension of this order to eight army corps, fail to arouse a war spirit,[76] but its editor, Maurice de Waleffe, was called to account by the authorities for his action.[77] The government, it is evident had no intention of stimulating a chauvinist spirit, for it only desired a public opinion which would be prepared for whatever decisions might be necessary. In spite of the normal suspicions of Germany's attitude and purposes, which had been strengthened by her apparent failure to restrain Austria, no incident had occurred since the Schoen episode of July 24 to embitter sentiment in regard to direct relations between France

[73] Arthur Meyer, the editor of the *Gaulois* (July 30), compared the temper of the crowds passing beneath his window with that of 1870 to the advantage of the former.

[74] *Journal*, July 27.

[75] *Figaro*, July 28.

[76] It must have appeared at about the same time as the special edition of the *Lokal Anzeiger* in Berlin which contained an equally false report of a German mobilization. The *Paris-Midi*'s sensational article is noted in Schmitt, *Coming of the War*, II, 234 (note). The Cabinet, however, had approved, under certain conditions, the moving of the covering troops to a distance of ten kilometers from the frontier (morning of July 30).

[77] *Gaulois*, July 31. Waleffe was a naturalized Frenchman of Belgian nationality.

and Germany. A section of the press, although stopping short of a direct demand for war, declared, however, that the Central Powers were facing war or humiliation. "If it is not war," according to the chauvinist *Patrie* (July 28), "it is the humiliation of Austria and behind Austria, that of Germany." "For every Serbian soldier killed by an Austrian bullet upon the Morava," wrote Jean Herbette, who believed that France should go to war in defense of Serbia regardless of Russia's action, "one more Prussian soldier will be able to advance to the Moselle." The British ambassador, however, insisted that these efforts to arouse a war spirit were unsuccessful.[78] The *Petit Parisien* (July 30) interpreted the general attitude of public opinion more accurately than the newspapers which were primarily concerned with the prestige and interests of the group of which France was a member. "This crisis," it exclaimed (July 30), "cannot end in a general war. It would be too monstrous that the peaceful purposes affirmed in all of the capitals of the continent—except Vienna—should lead to this result." Even Germany was sometimes credited with desiring peace, as Jules Hedeman reported from Berlin. "I repeat," he wrote in the *Matin* (July 30), "that Germany does not desire war. She desires it less to-day than yesterday, and yesterday less than day before yesterday." Gabriel Hanotaux felt that a solution might be found in "a Franco-German conversation, sincerely undertaken by French diplomacy. . . . One wonders if we did not lose a favorable occasion four days ago to enlist Germany in a moderating influence upon Vienna while we continued, on our side, to maintain contact with Russia."[79] The conservative *Gaulois* (July 31) was ready to accept Austria's occupation of Belgrade—the "halt in Belgrade" plan—as a satisfactory basis of negotiations.[80]

---

[78] "Many newspapers are writing about Germany in a way calculated to excite public opinion. . . . French public up to the present is disinclined to allow itself to be worked up to warlike excitement." Bertie to Grey, Paris, July 29, 1914. *Brit. War Docs.*, XI, 174. "The attitude of the population of Paris during the last five or six days has been admirable. Some papers, particularly the *Temps* and the Nationalist papers, began towards the middle of last week to publish very provocative articles, but the population has remained calm." Bertie to Grey, Paris, Aug. 2, 1914. *Ibid.*, XI, 332.

[79] *Figaro*, July 31. The same article appeared in the *Progrès de la Côte d'Or* (Dijon), Aug. 1.

[80] Malvy, the Minister of Interior, was reported to have informed the press on July 30 that "we have received from Germany news for which we dared not hope." *Progrès de la Côte d'Or* (Dijon), July 31. *Daily News* (London), July 31. This statement was either not reported by the Paris press or not given prominence.

The moderation of public opinion in Paris was sometimes interpreted as a cool determination to defend the cause of the Triple Entente,[81] but it as closely resembled a feeling of powerlessness to influence the course of events. By July 29, all groups, except the Socialists, had rallied to the support of the government. The *Radical* (July 29), however, indicated that it expected moderation and caution of those who represented France. It refused to endorse the Socialists's protest against a policy which would commit her under the terms of a secret alliance. "For the moment, we refuse to discuss this question. We are confident that the government will observe the proper measure in her conversations with Russia and Europe, that it will weigh the extent of our engagements, that it will conciliate the necessities of the alliance with the need of a dignified peace." As the time for final decisions approached, public opinion was assured that France was guiltless, and for this reason, it was said, war would be accepted. "It is because the government has demonstrated its repugnance for every provocation," affirmed the *France de Bordeaux et du Sud-Ouest* (July 31), "that it will have the support of all France if the peril becomes a reality." The nationalist *Presse* (Aug. 1) declared that "no one in France has desired war, it will be accepted as a cruel test."

Nevertheless, it is by no means certain that public opinion was prepared to approve a declaration of war if Germany acted only against Russia. The terms of the alliance committed France to this ultimate measure, and the government at least was undoubtedly determined to fulfil its obligations to the letter. Poincaré assured the perturbed Isvolski on August 1 that parliament would, if necessary, approve a declaration of war.[82] Jaurès's assassination, the night before, eliminated the one leader who might have organized an opposition, so that the government was more certain than ever of securing a majority.[83] Yet Poincaré, desiring that Germany should act first [84] in order to impress England and to avoid a public debate, told Isvolski and he preferred not to summon parliament.[85] The Socialists alone

[81] *Journal,* July 27.
[82] *Livre Noir,* II, 297, 298 (19 July/1 Aug.). Poincaré, *L'Union Sacrée,* pp. 495, 496.
[83] Georges Demartial, *L'Évangile du Quai d'Orsay* (Paris, 1926), p. 118.
[84] It was even insisted in the official order of mobilization on August 1 that this action did not mean war.
[85] *Livre Noir,* II, 297, 298. The cabinet confirmed Poincaré's assurance that France would fulfil her obligations in the alliance, but it also decided, for the

had asked for this action in the hope that it would help to maintain peace. Public opinion had been assured for years that France would not assume the responsibility for a declaration of war. "We are waiting," affirmed the *Phare de la Loire* of Nantes (July 28), "coldly resolved to sustain our allies and, if necessary, to resort to ultimate measures, but we are also determined to do nothing to precipitate the inevitable rupture." The Radical *Lanterne* (July 30) had approved a policy of complete loyalty to the alliance, but it had also declared that a "republican democracy cannot undertake an offensive war. It has however, the sacred duty of fidelity to its friendships and to its alliance." On August 1, the *Matin* affirmed that "we can make a solemn engagement before the assembly of civilized nations that we will not declare war, that we will not assume that responsibility before history." The *Journal des Débats* insisted on August 3, at the moment when Germany was about to take the final step, that France would not take the initiative. The Paris correspondent of the *Manchester Guardian* had already written (July 28) that an effort to secure a declaration of war from parliament might occasion "serious trouble in France, for a war on behalf of Russia, if France is not attacked, would be extremely unpopular." [86] The probability that an incident would present itself which could be interpreted as a German provocation, of course, weakened the force of this argument. The exact date when parliament was summoned (it met on August 4) is uncertain, but the order was probably sent on August 2.[87] Preceding Germany's final action on August 3, it may have meant that the government intended to ask for a declaration of war in the improbable event that Germany remained upon the defensive against France.

Germany unwisely, it is now clear, saved the French government from a most embarrassing position. Convinced that it was necessary to dispose of France as an inevitable enemy before turning against Russia, Germany, through her ambassador, asked France, July 31, to state her position as between Russia and Germany. The reply, eighteen hours later, was that France would consult her own interests. For the moment, Germany took no further action, doubtless hoping

moment, to delay the convocation of Parliament for ten days. Schmitt, *Coming of the War*, II, 338.

[86] Professor Scott believes, however, that the correspondent did not correctly understand public opinion at this time. Scott, *Five Weeks*, pp. 197, 198.

[87] Cambon, in Berlin, urgently advised French citizens to return to France immediately on the morning of August 2. François Charles-Roux, *Trois Ambassades Français à la Veille de la Guerre* (Paris, 1928), pp. 206, 207.

that France would assume the aggressive, or be guilty of a provocation. Before Schoen delivered the formal declaration of war on August 3, a considerable section of the press stiffened its tone. The favorable prospects of France and of the Triple Entente were now emphasized. "Will we ever find more favorable circumstances," asked the nationalist *Patrie* (Aug. 2), "for freeing ourselves from the German yoke? That is the reason why we accept war. . . ." "It seems that circumstances," declared the more moderate *Phare de la Loire* of Nantes (Aug. 2), "will never be so favorable, so critical even for Germany. If we were bellicose, it is we who should desire war; yet it is she who seems determined to throw herself into the horrible adventure." The *Petite Gironde* of Bordeaux (Aug. 2) was confident that France would never have a better moral and material situation. Those who wrote in this strain during the last hours of the crisis evidently wished to strengthen confidence rather than to create a demand for a declaration of war by France.

Until war was certain, the *revanche,* interpreted as a desire for the recovery of Alsace-Lorraine by force of arms, had little direct influence in the preparation of public opinion. A chauvinist newspaper or two had associated Serbia's aspirations in regard to Bosnia-Herzegovina with France's attachment to the lost provinces. No incident, however, occurred to occasion a definite campaign of hatred against Germany, and until August 1 the most specific attack upon her was directed against her failure to restrain Austria. The need of defending the unity of the Triple Entente, its interests in the Balkans, the security and influence of France contributed most to the formation of public opinion. It was not until August 1 that Stephen Pichon referred to the hope of recovering Alsace-Lorraine as a reason for accepting a war for which France was not responsible.[88] The self-questioning of some as to the responsibilities were silenced by this consideration. "Our oppressed brothers, lost since 1870: do we wish to recover them?" asked the editor of the *Aurore* (Aug. 2) in his last comments before joining his artillery regiment. "Do we wish to liberate them? to bring them back into the circle of the great family of France? Then, no more questions. Do not seek any longer the origins or the responsibility of the conflict. War has begun; it is not our fault; our conscience is clear." The people of France, like those of other countries, took up arms in the belief that the government had done everything in its power to preserve peace. "Let us face

[88] *Petit Journal,* Aug. 1. Cf. *Figaro,* Aug. 2.

events with courage," declared the *Humanité* (Aug. 2), "and only note that France has used every means in her power to prevent such a state of affairs."

For more than forty years, public opinion had refused either to approve a formal renunciation of Alsace-Lorraine or to sanction an offensive war for the recovery of the lost provinces. Serious conflicts of interest involving the direct relations between France and Germany had been arranged peacefully, although leaving a legacy of bad feeling in their wake. This state of affairs, chiefly responsible for increasing nervous tension, left much to be desired, but it was at least preferable to war. It has sometimes been said, in view of the tension in Franco-German relations on the eve of the World War, that a clash was inevitable. This is by no means certain, for experience had shown that public opinion always stopped short of demanding war in a crisis with Germany. The crucial test came as a result of the obligations France had assumed in the original Russian alliance and in its modification in 1899. Experience, aided by skilful propaganda, convinced public opinion that the maintenance of the balance of power was essential to peace, to France's security, and to the development of her interests. The instinctive caution observed in relations with Germany was lacking in regard to the Austro-Russian quarrel. Committed to the Russian alliance, the more effective sections of public opinion refused to sanction any pressure which might isolate France. When the moment arrived for the final decision, war was accepted because France, her ally, and her friends were said to have exhausted every means for the maintenance of peace, and it was then undertaken for the recovery of the lost provinces.

INDEX

INDEX

Abdul Aziz, 226

About, E., 97

Abyssinia, 144

Abzac, General d', 67

Académie Française, 9, 148, 191

Action, 10, 286, 288, 290, 294; Russian bribes and their effect, 1912, 1913, 274; France and Russia, 1914, 293; Russia's moderation, 1914, 297, 302; Triple Entente and peace, 299; attitude toward Russia, 303; England's aid, 304. See H. Bérenger

Action Française, 264; Monarchist society, 1905, 193

Action Française, 238 f., 292; arbitration in 1914, 293

Adam, Mme. Edmond, 75, 106; Gambetta's increasing moderation, 73 f., 76; Gambetta's Cherbourg speech, Aug. 9, 1881, 79; German press and Anglo-French relations, 1884, 97; *Nouvelle Revue,* 97, 137 f.; result of Schnaebelé affair, 1887, 133; Russian Alliance, 137; on Marchand, 1898, 173; attitude during Boer War, 198

Aderer, A., 190

Africa, 199; Berlin conference, 1884, 95

Agadir, 12; French land forces, 1910, 235

Agadir crisis, 1911, 250, 304; French military expedition to Fez, 236; negotiations with Germany and England, 236 f.; reaction in France to expedition, 237 ff.; Germany's policy, May 3, 239; dispatch of *Panther* to Agadir, July 1, 1911, 240; von Schoen's explanations, 240; French reaction to Agadir, 241 f.; Germany's demand, July 15, 243; England, Russia, and France during, 242 ff.; Lloyd-George's Mansion House speech, 244; direction of French and German policy, 245; effect of suspense, 246; agreements of Nov. 4, 246; reaction of public opinion to solution, 247 f.; publication of secret terms of Franco-Spanish entente, 1904, its effect, 249; debate on settlement of Nov. 4, 1911, 249 f.

Agathon (H. Massis, A. de Tarde), 255

Agen, 288

Ajam, M., Franco-German commercial relations, 256

Albert-Petit, A., 255

Albin, P., 146, 149, 240, 248

Alexander II, Tsar of Russia, interview with William I, Berlin, May, 1875, 59; London *Morning Post* on, 1875, 62; Gortchakov's comedy, 64; assassination of, 1881, 137

Alexander III, Tsar of Russia, 125, 140

Alexander, King of Serbia, 267

Alexandria, bombardment of, 1882, 93, 95

Alexis, Grand Duke, 154

Algeciras, Act of, 1906, 237, 238, 239, 240, 245

Algeciras, Conference of, 1906, 219 ff., 237, 242

Alliances, ententes, France and Prussia, 1866, 17; Prussia and South German states, 1867, 21; rumor of Catholic league, 1875, 55; Austro-German Dual Alliance, 1879, 84; Triple Alliance, 1882, 84, 154, 156 f., 198, 202, 225, 257; Reinsurance treaty, 1887, 139, 143; Franco-Russian Alliance, 1894, 73, 120, 135, 153 ff.; Franco-Italian entente, 1901, 202; *entente cordiale,* 202 f., 213, 294; Franco-Spanish entente, 1904, 249; Anglo-Russian entente, 1907, 204; Triple Entente, 258, *passim;* Grey-Cambon letters, 1912, 258, 304; Anglo-French Mediterranean agreement, 1912, 259; Franco-Russian naval treaty, 259; Serbo-Bulgarian Alliance, 1912, 263

Alsace, anti-German play, 254

Alsace-Lorraine, Question of, 5, 39, 65, 74, 97, 107, 109, 119, 134, 150, 166, 168, 178, 183, 196, 198, 234, 251, 256; effect of loyalty to France, 5; Prussia's peace terms, Sept., 1870, 37; preliminary terms of peace, 1871, 41; and French public opinion on Treaty of Frankfort, 1871, 44; German arguments for annexation, 44 f.; French opinion on, affected by domestic politics, 46; loyalty to, test of French patriotism, 47; recovery of, 47 f., 70, 147, 155, 178; prayers for return of, 52; and Franco-German relations, 68, 146; Gambetta and exchange for, 74; attitude of République Française, 75; Ligue des Patriotes's propaganda, 1882–1887, 112 passim; Bismarck and French colonial expansion, 86; Bismarck's speech, Jan. 11, 1887, 123; elections in, 1887, 126 f., 188; Leo XIII's plan of a buffer state, 1887, 128; Russia's attitude toward France's claims to, 154, 261; society, in Paris, 159; Delcassé's attitude toward, 171, 183; French public opinion and, 185 ff.; imprescriptible right, 188; autonomist movement, 188; proposals for peaceful solution, 189 ff.; J. Heimweh's pamphlets, 190; conditions in Alsace, 192; Germany and, 204 f.; Lavisse's attitude toward, 253; Poincaré's attitude, 258; C. René and autonomy, 259; Berne conference, 1913, and, 279 f.; Alsace-Lorraine and French public opinion during July crisis, 1914, 309

American Historical Review, 19 ff., 29 f., 33, 88, 208

Amiens, 283

Anderson, E. N., 201, 211

André, General, 112

Anglo-Russian entente (1907); Bülow and its relation to entente cordiale, 204; encouraged by French diplomacy, 222

Angra Pequena, 94

Annales de la Chambre des Députés, 67, 68, 76, 79, 82, 84, 90, 93, 94, 101, 102, 103, 106, 107, 158, 160, 171, 194, 196, 204, 207, 209, 219, 225, 250, 289

Annales de l'Assemblée Nationale, 41, 48, 50, 54

Annales du Sénat, 84

Annales du Sénat et du Corps Législatif, 18, 19, 21, 25, 27, 33 f.

Anthony, Prince, 29

Anti-Anglais, 97

Anti-militarism, 191

Aosta, Leper of, 103

Arabi Bey, 91

Archives Diplomatiques, 140

Archives Nationales, 7, 29

Arendt, O., 190

Army, reform of French, 1867, 20; reduction of annual contingent, 1870, 25; reorganization after 1871, 49; Gambetta on German, 74; review of July 14, 1886, 115; Boulanger and reduction of service, 115; increases in German, 1886, 1887, 121 ff.; Monarchist and clerical influences in, 191; two year service law, 1905, 191, 272, 283; increasing popularity of, 1906, 223; three-year service law, 1913, 253, 270 f., 277 f., 287 f., 291; strength of Russian, 291

Arndt, E., 114

Arnim, Count H. von, on strength of revanche group, 1872, 47 f.

Asquith, H., 244

Assemblée Nationale, 49

Atchinov, Cossack adventurer, 144

Aubert, C., 280, 281; Franco-German relations, 256 f.

Auerstadt, 223

Augagneur, V., 279; France and the Balkans, Oct. 1912, 273; French foreign policy, 1913, 276

Aulard, A., 190, 278; defensive attitude of French press, 1913, 256; French foreign policy, 1913, 257

Aurore, 8, 174, 184, 188, 206, 209, 212, 213, 214, 215, 216, 217, 220, 224, 261, 275; entente with Germany, 1898, 180 f.; Cassagnac's anti-English animus, 181; French policy during Algeciras Conference, 1906, 219; reaction to Act of Algeciras, 1906, 222; French press during Casablanca affair, 1908, 230; on balance of power, 1912, 272 f.; war over Balkans, 1912, 273; Russian bribes and their effect, 274 f.; break-up of Austria-Hungary, 1914, 286 f.; attitude toward Austria-Hungary and Serbia, 1914, 293; Serbia and France's obligations in Russian alliance, 299; attitude of public opinion, 1914, 300; Alsace-Lorraine and acceptance of war, 309. See G. Clemenceau

Austria-Hungary, 16, 72, 95, 138, 141, 157, 198, 225, 267, 294, 301; Napoleon III's letter, June 11, 1866, 18; Venice interview, Apr., 1875, 54; *Journal des Débats* on her Balkan interests, 1878, 77; Algeciras Conference, 1906, 221; attitude toward Franco-German Accord, 1909, 231; attitude toward Serbs, Oct., 1912, 260; understanding with Russia, 1897, 261; French loans to, 1911, 1912, 262; corruption of French press, 1912, 1913, 270; assassination of Francis Ferdinand, 1914, 286 f.; her ultimatum to Serbia, July 23, 291; her purposes, 295; severs diplomatic relations, 296; declaration of war vs. Serbia, July 28, 298; "halt in Belgrade plan," 306

Austro-Prussian War, 1866, 17; France's neutrality, 18; Peace of Nikolsburg, 19

Autorité, 151, 152, 164, 174, 175, 176, 178, 180, 184, 198; P. de Cassagnac on Frederick III, 1888, 145; P. de Cassagnac on William II, 1888, 145; reaction to anti-French campaign in English press, 1898, 173

Avant la Bataille, influence of, in Germany, 1886, 120

Bagdad Railway, 235, 245

Bahr-el-Gazel, 166 f., 174

Bainville, J., on balance of power, 1912, 252; Franco-Russian Alliance and Balkan War, 1912, 264; 1914, 292; Schoen's *démarche* of July 24, 1914, 294. See *Action Française*

Balkan League, 264, 266, 274

Balkan Wars, 1912, 1913, 6, 253, 256, 263, 277; France's attitude at beginning of, 263 ff.; effect of Balkan victories, 1912, 266

Bangkok, 158

Bank, Deutsche, 235

Bar-le-Duc, 260

Barclay, Sir Thomas, preparation for *entente cordiale*, 202 f.; purposes of *entente cordiale*, 203; unofficial mission to Berlin, 259

Bardo, Treaty of, 1881, 89; ratification of, 90

Barère, C., 104

Barrès, M., 36, 281; nationalist views, 192; president of Ligue des Patriotes, 1914, 252; Socialist campaign vs. Russian alliance, 1914, 289

Barthou, L., 283; speech at unveiling of monument to Déroulède, 110; his ministry and three-year service law, 1913, 282

Bataille Syndicaliste, attitude of *Temps, Matin*, 1914, 291; its peace demonstration, 305

Baudin, P., attitude toward Moroccan question, 1911, 241

Bayerische Zeitung (Munich), 21

Bazin, R., 281; his novels and interpretation of Alsatian opinion, 192

Beauregard, G. de, 115

Bebel, A., opposes sale of Alsace-Lorraine, 189

Bec du Canard, 246

Bienvenu-Martin, J. B., 295; Schoen's *démarche*, July 24, 1914, 293; Schoen on his attitude toward Russia, 295 f.; assurances to Isvolski, July 28, 300

Belfort, 145

Belgium, 87, 144, 198; Bismarck and her press laws, 1875, 57

Belgrade, 306

Belleville, Gambetta's speech, Oct. 27, 1876, 74

Benedetti, Count V. de, 25; negotiations, July 1870, 29 f.

Berchtold, Count, 295; on attitude of Paris press, Dec., 1912, 270; his attempt to mislead Europe, 1914, 287

Bérenger, H., 192, 274, 293; Triple Entente and the Balkan league, 1912, 214; attitude toward Germany, 1914, 297. See *Action*

Bergen, 199

Bergson, H., influence of his philosophy, 255

Berlin, 59, 128, 259; Congress of, 1878, 76; Treaty of, 1878, 232; conference of 1880, 81; 1884, 95 ff.; art exhibits, 1891, 148, 152; 1895, 165; 1899, 184 f.; *Journal's* aeronautical contest, 1911, 255

Berliner Monatshefte für Internationale Aufklärung, 302

Berliner Post, 124, 140; reasons for annexing Alsace-Lorraine, 45; moderation of French press, 1875, 56 f.; "Is War in Sight," Apr. 9, 1875, 55; war or peace, Jan., 1887, 125; "On the Razor Edge," Jan., 1887, 127; effect of Schnaebelé's arrest in France, 1887, 130

Berliner Tageblatt, 145, 185; Germany's advances to France, 1891, 152; England's and France's courtship of Germany, 1898, 177; improved feeling in France toward Germany, 1898, 178; insists on renunciation of Alsace-Lorraine, 1898, 181; Delcassé and French opinion, Apr., 1905, 209; Franco-German *rapprochement*, June 1905, 213; on French policy in Morocco, 1911, 239; French reaction to Agadir, 1911, 241; peaceful character of French public opinion, 1912, 277

Berne, Franco-German parliamentary conference, May, 1913, 279 f., 285

Berthelot, M., Franco-German intellectual relations, 1895, 186

Berthelot, P., Schoen's proposed public statement, July 26, 1914, 295

Berthet, L., 278

Bertie, Sir F., 304; Isvolski and Russian press-fund, 1913, 270; Schoen's *démarche* of July 24, 1914, 295; on Franco-German declaration of solidarity, 295; on French public opinion and Russia, July 25, 300; on efforts to arouse war spirit, 306

Bethmann-Hollweg, T. von, 259; French military expedition to Fez, 1911, 236; Kiderlen-Wächter's policy, 1911, 245

Beyens, Baron, 27, 33

Beyerlein, A., *La Retraite*, 185

Bihourd, Franco-German arrangement on Moroccan question, March, 1905, 209

Bismarck, Herbert von, 119; conversations with Ferry, 1884, 98; Boulanger's dismissal and chauvinist agitation, 1887, 143; moderate attitude toward France, March, 1889, 145

Bismarck, Prince Otto von, 62, 65, 79, 81, 89, 94, 97, 104, 126, 130, 137, 142, 161, 173; his manipulation of press, 11; and Hohenzollern candidature, 24 ff.; rumors of additional French

demands, July 12, 1870, 30; Ems despatch, 31, 33 f.; on continuation of war, Sept., 1870, 37 f.; negotiations with Favre, Sept., 1870, 39 f.; attitude after 1871 and moderate French opinion, 44 f.; manipulation of public opinion, 45; Gambetta on his understanding of France, 45; preference for republic in France, 47; attitude toward Thiers's government, 48; French army after 1871, 49; clerical government in France, 49 ff.; *Kulturkampf*, 49, 86, 52; pastoral letters of French bishops, 52; France's *Bündnisfähigkeit*, 53; his nervous irritation, 53; his intentions in warscare of 1875, 53, 56, 58; embargo on export of horses, 54; *Berliner Post's* article, Apr., 1875, 55; Belgian press laws, 57; his mistakes, 1875, 58; preventive war theory, 59 f.; Russia's advice, 63; Gortchakov's comedy, 1875, 64; French elections, Oct., 1877, 68; and Gambetta, 1878, 74; offer of Tunis to France, 76 f.; France and Dual Alliance, 1879, 84; and French colonial expansion, 86 f., 89; interpretation of French psychology, 86 f., 104, 134, 179; England and Tunis, 1879, 88; German colonial expansion, 94 f.; England's interests in Egypt, 95; France and China, Oct. 1884, 101, 104; failure of his French policy, 1885, 104 f., 107 f., 120; Caroline Islands affair, 1885, 105; test of Ligue des Patriotes's importance, 113; Boulanger as Minister of War, 117; Münster's reports, 1886, 120 f.; septennate, 121, 128; Freycinet and Egypt, 123, 127, 134, 139; Boulanger's removal, 1887, 127; Flourens's demands, 1887, 127; Schnaebelé's arrest and arguments for his release, 131 f.; his diplomacy and Franco-Russian Alliance, 136; his attitude during Boulanger crisis, Jan. 1889, 145; his dismissal, 1890, 153

Blanc, L., protest against cession of Alsace-Lorraine, 1871, 42

Blanqui, A., on public opinion in Paris, Sept., 1870, 39 f.

Blowitz, H. G. de, French reaction to Venice interview, Apr., 1875, 55; "A French War-Scare," article in *Times*,

May 6, 61 f.; proposed Gambetta-Bismarck interview, 75; on French chauvinists, 1891, 151; on Fashoda's value to France, 1898, 172
Blue Book, British, Fashoda crisis, 1898, 174
Blum, H., 45
Bocquillon, É., 195
Bodley, J. E. C., 69
Boer War, French opinion during, 198
Boland, H., 90
Bonaparte, Prince Jerôme, 18
Bosnian crisis, 1908, 1909, 231, 271; its relation to Casablanca affair, 227, 228 f., 231; French public opinion and, 262
Boulanger, General G., 134, 161, 188, 193, 224, 252, 256, 260; his military career, 114 f.; and Déroulède, 1883, 114; Clemenceau and his appointment as Minister of War, 1886, 114; review at Longchamps, 1886, 115; reasons for his popularity, 115; attitude of public opinion toward, 116 f.; opinions in speeches, 117 f.; Military Club, 118; Avant la Bataille, 120; his intentions, 1887, 127; and Schnaebelé affair, 1887, 127; removal from government, 133 f.; departure for Clermont-Ferrand, 134; Russia's attitude toward, 139; elections, May, 1887, 143; Paris election, Jan., 1889, 143 f.; failure of coup d'état, 144; his trial and suicide, 144
Bourdon, G., 282
Bourgeois, É., 17, 25, 33, 51, 53, 68, 76, 81, 87, 91, 92, 95, 117, 122, 127, 143, 162, 163, 167, 171, 199
Bourgeois, L., on French foreign policy, 1896, 165
Bourget, P., strength of nationalist movement, 1901, 192
Bourgogne, in German school atlas as Burgund, 111
Bourse, Paris, 235, 237; crisis of 1887, 126
Brame, J., 37
Brandenburg, E., 180, 213
Brest, 288
Bricard, E., 133
Brisson, H., protests against cession of Alsace-Lorraine, 1871, 42; ministry and Tonkin, 1885, 102
British Documents on the Origins of

the War, 159, 166, 171, 172, 174, 177, 181, 201, 202, 203, 207, 211, 220, 222, 290, 291, 294, 295, 300, 304, 306
Broglie, A., Duc de, 21, 24, 54, 58; ministry, 1873, and foreign policy, 51 f.; and clerical allies, 67; Republican propaganda in campaign of 1877, 68; and Russia, 136
Brunetière, F., 191; strength of nationalist movement, 192
Brussels, 200
Bryan, W. J., Berne conference and arbitration treaties, 1913, 280
Buckingham Palace, 224
Buckle, G. E., 61
Buisson, F., reaction to Act of Algeciras, 1906, 222
Buisson, G., 110, 112
Bulgaria, 87, 157; Russia's difficulties with, 1886, 1887, 120, 139; Serbian alliance, 1912, 263; Kavalla question, 1913, 275
Bulletin de l'Afrique Française, 206, 207
Bulletin de l'étranger, Temps's column on foreign affairs, 11
Bulletin des Instituteurs, 195
Bülow, Major von, effect of new military law, 1875, 54
Bülow, Prince B. von, 203; Franco-German interests in Africa, 1899, 199; attitude toward unofficial Franco-German conversations, 1901, 200; Holstein's watch-and-wait policy, 202; attitude toward entente cordiale, 204; policy during Moroccan crisis, 1904, 1905, 208, 215; effort to eliminate Delcassé, 209 f.; and opportunity to settle Moroccan question, 1905, 213 f., 218; J. Cambon and South German Courts, 1906, 225; William II's Daily Telegraph interview and Casablanca affair, 1908, 227; on French report on Casablanca affair, 228; attitude toward Franco-German understanding on Morocco, 1908, 231; significance of Franco-German Accord, 1909, 233
Bunau-Varilla, P., Matin and Franco-German understanding, 220
Busch, M., 11, 45, 87

Caillaux, J., 236, 241, 250; Petit Parisien, 13; Franco-German understanding, 1909, 231; Bagdad Railway shares in France, 235; his ministry and Kiderlen-Wächter's suggestion of compensations, 1911, 240; attitude after Agadir, July, 1911, 242; attitude toward de Selves, 1911, 245; policy of amicable negotiations, 258

Caillaux, Mme., 288

Caix, R. de, attitude during Boer War, 1899, 199; on Germany's interests in Morocco, 1904, 207

Calmette, G., 128, 288; defeat of Socialist view of foreign affairs, 1903, 197; France and Balkan War, 1912, 264 f.

Calonne, A. de, 19, 20

Cambon, J., 13, 236, 308; relations with South German states, 1906, 225; Casablanca affair, 1908, 227; Kiderlen-Wächter's suggestion of compensations, 1911, 240; Germany's demand, July 15, 1911, 243, 245; use of public opinion, 1911, 246; attitude under Poincaré government, 259

Cambon, P., 13; appointment as ambassador to England, 1898, 172; suggests compromise during Fashoda crisis, 173 f.; Germany's exclusion from Morocco, 1902, 201; Grey's proposed intervention, 1914, 294

Cameroons, 234

Campbell-Bannerman, Sir H., cabinet of, 220

Campenon, General, 101

Cann, A. H., 110, 112, 115

Cape Colony, 95

Card, É. B. de, 189

Caricatures, French, 5, 122, 198

Carnot, S., protests vs. cession of Alsace-Lorraine, 1871, 42; Ligue des Patriotes, 111

Caroline Islands, difficulty between Germany and Spain, 1885, 105

Carroll, E. M., 18

Carrousel, Place de, 78

Carthage, 119

Casablanca, 235, 245

⚹Casablanca affair, 1908, 231, 232; incident and negotiations, 226 f.; Daily Telegraph interview, Oct. 28, 227; reaction of French press and opinion to, 228 f.

Cassagnac, B. A. G., de, 21

Cassagnac, G. de, on German unity, March, 1867, 20

Cassagnac, P. de, 147, 181; on Frederick III, William II, 1888, 145; French artists and Berlin exposition, 1891, 149 f.; Franco-German rapprochement, 1891, 152; France and the opening of Kiel Canal, 1895, 163; on England's attitude, 1898, 174; his reaction to evacuation of Fashoda, 1898, 175; England and Germany, 1898, 176, 178; attitude during the Boer War, 198. See Autorité

Castarède, A. de, 18

Castilar, E., 189, 200 f.

Castillo, L., unofficial Franco-German conversations, 1901, 200

Caussette, J. B., 50

Castellane, Marquis de, Russian alliance and recovery of Alsace-Lorraine, 1891, 156

Ceccaldi, T. C., 47

Chabrinovitch, N., Temps on his confession, 1914, 286

Chamberlain, J., offer of alliance to Germany, 1898, 177, 180

Chambure, A. de, 12

Channel, English, 304

Channel Islands, 119

Chanzy, General, 114

Chants du Soldat, book of poems by Déroulède, 110

Charivari, 122

Charles V, Empire of, 17, 26

Charles-Roux, F., 308

Charmes, F., dinner with H. von Bismarck, 1884, 99; moderation of public opinion, 1895, 165; English anti-French campaign, 1898, 173

Charmes, G., 136; colonial expansion, 86; Anglo-French-German relations, 1884, 98 f.; dinner, with H. von Bismarck, 1884, 99. See Journal des Débats

Charnay, M., 161, 190, 194

Chaudordy, Count de, 38, 109

⚹Chauvinism, chauvinists, 65, 79, 99, 120; "revenge for Sadowa," 22; attitude of, after July 6, 1870, 29; hatred of England, 97, 119; reaction to Franco-German entente, 1884, 97 f.; in elections, Oct., 1885, 105 f.; analysis of, to 1886, 109; Boulanger agitation, 116 ff.; Bismarck's emphasis

of, 120 f.; Russo-Bulgarian controversy, 1886, 1887, 139; attitude
toward Russian alliance, 155; use of
improved Franco-German relations,
147; Empress Frederick's visit to
Paris, 1891, 149 ff.; intimidates moderate opinion, 149 ff., 186; alarmed
by moderate tendencies, 185; influence of, in nationalist movement after
1911, 254; situation in Paris, 1914,
305. See Déroulède; Boulanger;
Ligue des Patriotes; nationalist
movement
Chéradame, A., Germany and Austrian
ultimatum, 1914, 292
Cherbourg, 79
China, Ferry's Tonkin campaign, 1883–
1885, 101; treaty, Apr., 1885, 101,
104
Chincholle, C., 117
Chow, S. R., 3
Churchill, W., order to Grand Fleet,
1914, 303 f.
Civita-Vecchia, 51
Civrieux, Commandant, 254
"Clairon," Déroulède's poem, 110
Claretie, A. J., 109, 110, 111, 186
Clauss, M., 282
Claveau, A., 17
Clemenceau, G., 96, 261, 281; news-
paper connections, 13; on Russian
alliance, 13, 140; protests against ces-
sion of Alsace-Lorraine, 1871, 42;
Radicals' foreign policy, 1880, 80;
Tunis expedition and Bismarck,
1881, 89; attack on intervention in
Egypt, 1882, 93 f.; attack upon Ferry,
March, 1885, 102; evacuation of
Tonkin, 1885, 103; election, Oct.,
1885, 105 f.; memories of 1871, 107;
Boulanger's appointment as Minister
of War, 1886, 114; Franco-Russian
rapprochement, 1891, 156; charged
with accepting English money, 1893,
162; France and opening of Kiel
Canal, 1895, 163; Fashoda and Germany, 1898, 174; on Alsace-Lorraine
Question, 188; Pressensé's repudiation of the revanche, 1903, 196; attitude toward entente with England,
204; immediate negotiations with
Germany, March, 1905, 209; France's
allies and Delcassé's dismissal, June,
1905, 213; on international confer-

ence, July, 1905, 215; Germany's policy, 1905, 215 f., 220; on Björkö
meeting, 1905, 216; change in attitude
on Morocco, 1905, 217, 230; French
policy during Algeciras Conference,
1906, 219; Minister of Interior in
Sarrien cabinet, 1906, 220; President
of Council, 1906, his attitude, 224 f.;
attitude toward Russian alliance,
225; an inevitable war, 224 f.; on
opposition to three year service law,
1914, 288. See Justice; Aurore;
Homme Libre
Church, Roman Catholic, 17; attitude
of French clerical party, 49 ff., 50, 52,
66 ff.
Clermont-Ferrand, 134
Clubs, radical, siege of Paris, 1870,
1871, 38 f.
Cochery, 27
Cochin, D., favors entente with England, 1899, 181 f.
Colonial expansion, as means of national recovery, 84; public opinion on,
85 f.; Prévost-Paradol's vision of a
North African Empire, 85; P. Leroy-
Beaulieu's Colonisation chez les
Peuples Modernes, 85; propaganda
after 1881, 85 f.; criticism of continental policy, 86; opposition to colonial expansion, 86; Bismarck's support of French aims, 86 ff.; Ferry's
defeat and results, 102 ff.; revival of
interest in, 166 ff.; Delcassé's attitude toward, 171; relation to Continental policy, 182. See Tunis; Egypt;
Tonkin; Morocco
Comité du Commerce Français avec
l'Allemagne, 256
Commodus, William II compared to,
145
Commune, Paris, 9, 39, 67; strengthens
peace sentiment after 1871, 46
Condé, Princes of, 109
Congo, 104; French, 234, 239, 243, 244,
247
Congo Free State, 166
Congresses, conferences, Berlin, 1878,
76; Berlin, 1880, 81; Madrid, 1880,
88; Constantinople, 1882, 93; London,
1884, 94; Berlin, 1884, 95 ff.; Berlin
Labor Conference, 1890, 147; Algeciras Conference, 1906, 219 ff.; London Conference, 1913, 275; Franço-

German parliamentary conference at Berne, 1913, 279 f.

Constant, d'E. de, 279; Franco-German entente, 1899; as leader of moderate tendencies, 193

Constantinople, 93

Constitutionnel, on Hohenzollern candidature, 26

Continental union, against England, 92 f., (1884) 98; Bismarck and secondary naval powers, 95; *France Militaire* on, 119; Holstein on, 1895, 168; intervention in Boer War, 199; William's hope for, 1904, 208

Copenhagen, 170

Corbier, D., 47

Correspondant, 8, 68, 70, 75, 76, 78, 84, 102, 114, 116, 144, 145, 162, 213; movement for German entente, 1898, 178; Delcassé's control of foreign policy, 198

Coubertin, P., 185, 214

Coulanges, F., de, 40

Courcel, Baron de, 92; Egypt and Franco-German understanding, 1884, 95; visit to Varzin, 1884, 98

Courrier de France, 56

Cremin, 265

Cri du Peuple, 119; France and Bismarck's colonial ambitions, 97; Brisson's Tonkin policy, 103

Crimean War, 62

Crisis of 1887, Bismarck's speech of Jan. 11, 1887, 123 f.; represented as provocation, 124; Reichstag's defeat of septennate, 125; attitude of influential Paris newspapers, 125; *Daily News*'s note, Jan. 24, 125; Havas Agency's misrepresentation, 126 f.; *Berliner Post*'s "On the Razor Edge," article, 126; elections in Alsace-Lorraine, 1887, 126 f.; Flourens's demands, 1887, 127; Boulanger's intentions, 1887, 127; passage of septennate, 128. See Schnaebelé affair

Crispi, F., Decaze's foreign policy, 67

Correspondance Française, news-agency, Russian propaganda for French alliance, 1887, 142

Cromer, Earl, on Germany's probable action in Morocco, 1904, 207

Crowe, Sir Eyre, on France's attitude toward Russia, July 24, 1914, 300

Crozier, P., Pichon and annexation of Bosnia, 1908, 231 f.

Cruppi, J. C. M., 250; military expedition to Fez, 1911, 236; questions England, 236 f.

Cyon, É. de, 91, 126, 136, 138, 139, 142; propagandist for Russian alliance, 137 f.; editor of *Gaulois,* 1881, 138; and Boulanger, 1886, 139; Rochefort's conversion to Russian alliance, Aug., 1887, 140; France's support for Russia vs. England, 1890, 142; peaceful revision of Treaty of Frankfort, 1891, 155; Russian fleet and Egypt, 1890, 157; Franco-Russian negotiations, 1893, 159

Cyprus, Anglo-Turkish agreement, June 4, 1878, 76

Dahomey, 166

Daily News (London), 34, 124; reaction of French press to Bismarck's speech, Jan. 11, 1887, 124; French patriotic demonstrations, 133; note on Germany's intentions, 1887, 125; Malvy's statement, July 31, 1914, 306

Daily Telegraph (London), 34, 123, 124, 126; Boulanger's intentions, 1887, 127; peace sentiment in France and press, 1887, 128; French reaction to evacuation of Fashoda, 1898, 175; policy during discussion of Franco-German entente, 1898, 1899, 180; William II's interview, Oct. 28, 1908, 227

Daniel, A., 197

Danube, 298

Darimon, A., 32, 33

Daudet, E., 58, 89, 91, 120

Daudet, L., on Franco-German alliance, 1899, 179; public's lack of patriotic sentiment, 1905, 185

Davidov, special Russian agent, 268 f.

Decazes, Duc de, 57, 85; effect of Commune on French policy, 46; withdrawal of *Orénoque,* 52; revives crisis, Apr., 1875, 58; confidence in Russia's friendship, 1875, 58; appeals to England and Russia, 1875, 59, 62; proposes understanding with Germany, 1875, 60; motives in second phase of war-scare, 61; fears inspired by, 63; Crispi on his foreign policy, 1877, 67; on German interference in

French politics, 67; Tunis, 88; and Russia, 136; correspondence with Le Flô, 1875, 140

Decorations affair, 1887, 143

Delafosse, J., 207; colonial expansion, 84; attack upon Ferry, March, 1885, 102; on German danger, 1895, 164; Russia and *entente cordiale*, 1904, 204; England and Agadir crisis, 1911, 244

Delaisi, F., 12

Delane, J. T., editor of London *Times*, 61

Delcassé, T., 174, 206, 208, 209, 217, 223, 268; relations with *Matin*, 13; attitude toward Germany's offer of understanding, 1898, 171, 199; his intentions and foreign policy, 171 f.; his policy during Fashoda affair, 172 ff.; reaction to proposed Franco-German entente, 1898, 177 f.; offers to negotiate with England, 1899, 181; control of foreign policy, 1898–1905, 197 ff.; his revision of Russian alliance, 1899, 198; Russia's proposal for intervention in Boer War, 1900, 199; and the *entente cordiale*, 1904, 203; and crises after 1904, 205; Germany and his diplomatic preparations in Moroccan question, 207; attitude of public opinion toward, 1905, 208; Rouvier's support in Chamber, Apr., 1905, 210; von Donnersmarck and his dismissal, June, 1905, 211 f.; German press on his dismissal, 214; interview in *Gaulois*, July 12, 1905, 216; connection with *Matin* and *Gaulois*, 218; on Germany's policy, 1905, 219; his defense, 1908, 222; his diplomatic system, 257 f. See Fashoda; *entente cordiale;* Moroccan crisis

Delescluze, C., 39

Denbourg, H., 189

Dépêche (Toulouse), 10, 143, 190, 195, 219, 222, 256, 257, 275, 278; Venice interview, Apr. 5, 1875, 55; Bismarck's demand to Belgium, Apr. 1875, 57; alarm in Paris, 1875, 63; Germany's purpose during Casablanca affair, 1908, 229; Isvolski's estimate of its importance, 1913, 271; Russian influence upon French politics, 1913, 279; reaction of Paris

press to Alsatian autonomist opinion, 1913, 280, 282

Derby, Lord, 59; war-scare of 1875, 61; reply to Decaze's appeal, 62; instructions to ambassadors, 1875, 64

Déroulède, P., 134, 140, 147, 177, 254, 256; his birth and youth, 109 f.; resignation from army, 47; his *Chants du Soldat*, 110; qualities as leader of *revanche*, 110; founds Ligue des Patriotes, 110; Ferry's colonial policy, 97, 110, 113; report as president of the Ligue, 111; on education of youth and *revanche*, 111; Rochefort on his influence, 113; Germany's attitude toward, 1886, 119; preface to *Avant la Bataille*, 120; resignation as president of Ligue des Patriotes, 128 f.; Paris election, Jan., 1889, 143 f.; Boulanger's attempted coup d'état, Jan., 1889, 144; Empress Frederick's visit, 1891, 150 ff.; discredited by attack upon Clemenceau, 1893, 162; his retirement, 165; on Delcassé during Fashoda crisis, 1898, 174; reorganizes Ligue des Patriotes, 1898, 192; his exile, 1899, 192; attitude toward entente with England, 202, 204, 218; on England's aid, 1905, 215; death of, 1914, 252, 254; his influence after 1900, 254

Désastre, novel by Paul and Victor Margueritte, 187

Des Idées Napoliennes, 16

Desmoulins, C., 146

Deschanel, P., 36, 72, 78

Desorges, Abbé, Catholic view of War of 1870, 50

Detaille, J., 149

Deutsche Revue, 90

Determinism, 15

Dicey, E., France's attitude toward war, 1887, 121

Die Belgischen Dokumente, 154, 222, 235, 254

Die Deutsche Dokumente zum Kriegsausbruch, 294, 296.

Die Grosse Politik, 11, 46, 48, 53, 54, 55, 60, 64, 87, 88, 91, 95, 96, 98, 99, 100, 101, 104, 105, 120, 121, 122, 125, 128, 132, 139, 143, 145, 148, 151, 152, 162, 164, 165, 167, 168, 169, 178, 185, 186, 199, 200, 201, 204, 208, 210, 211, 213, 214, 215, 218, 219, 220, 221, 223,

225, 226, 227, 228, 231, 232, 233, 235, 236, 238, 239, 240, 242, 243, 244, 247, 250, 260, 264, 266, 267, 270, 277, 279
Dilke, Sir C., 78
Dimnet, Abbé, attitude toward nationalist movement, 255
Diplomacy, secret, protest against, 1906, 219 f.
Diplomatische Aktenstücke (Austria-Hungary), 225, 229, 232, 258, 262, 270
Disarmament, *Figaro* and Leo XIII's intervention, 1887, 128; France and first Hague Conference, 1899, 184; Jaurès's proposal for simultaneous disarmament, 1902, 196 f.
Disraeli, B., Lord Beaconsfield, on Bismarck in War-Scare of 1875, 61
Documents Diplomatiques Français, 49, 51, 52, 53, 58, 60, 61, 77, 84, 88, 200, 232, 249; official influence on press, 12; proposed Gambetta-Bismarck interview, 1878, 75; Salisbury's offer of Tunis, 1878, 77
Dollfus, C., 15
Dongola, English expedition to, 1896, 169
Doniol, H., 48
Donnersmarck, Prince H. von, Gambetta's knowledge of Germany, 73; proposed Bismarck-Gambetta interview, 1878, 75; Bismarck's intentions in Schnaebelé affair, 1887, 130; alleged demand for Delcassé's dismissal, 1905, 211
Doumergue, Gaston, 261; reaction to Franco-German agreements, Nov. 4, 1911, 247; Poincaré's foreign policy, 1912, 273 f.; his ministry and three-year service law, 1913, 282
Douniol, 22
Drapeau, 129; propagandist organ of Ligue des Patriotes, 111
Drapeyron-Seligmann, L., 32
Dréo, M., 37
Dreux, A., 53, 56, 57, 58, 61, 67
Dreyfus affair, 197; connection with Fashoda crisis, 172, 180; political significance of, 191, 272
Dreyfus, C., demands war, 1890, 147; Empress Frederick's visit, 1891, 151
Driault, É., 81
Drumont, É., chauvinist pressure in 1895, 165

Ducroy, C., 110, 116, 144
Dufferin, Marquis of, on anti-English sentiment, 1893, 159
Duhoureau, F., 36
Dumaine, 287
Dupin, G., (Ermenonville), 253
Durazzo, 277
Duvernois, C., 21, 35

Ebray, A., 196
Écho de Paris, 10, 175, 178, 180, 197, 237, 238, 243, 253, 254, 257, 259, 262, 267, 289, 295; on Fashoda crisis, 1898, 174; attitude toward England and Germany, 1898, 176; peace sentiment in 1903, 183; on plebiscite as solution of Alsace-Lorraine Question, 190; publication of secret Franco-German letters of 1909, 249; Poincaré's speech, Nantes, Oct., 1912, 260; Isvolski's influence upon, 1912, 271; version of Schoen's *démarche* of July 24, 1914, 294
Écho du Nord (Lille), 10; Casablanca incident and relations with Germany, 1908, 226; on solution of Casablanca affair, 1908, 230; Poincaré's speech, Nantes, Oct., 1912, 260
Éclair (Montpellier), proposed statement of French policy, Jan. 1887, 124
Éclair, 216, 232, 244, 262, 286, 291. See E. Judet
École des Beaux Arts, 150
École Läique, 195
École Normale, 253
École Nouvelle, 195
Économiste Française, 88
Edward VII, King of England, 224; dinner with Gambetta, 1878, 77; visit to Paris, 1902, 203
Edwards, establishes *Matin,* 9
Egypt, Egyptian question, 93, 94, 107, 154, 157, 158, 176; Bismarck and French interests, 88; Arabi Bey and nationalist revolt, 1882, 91; Anglo-French co-operation, 91 ff.; political situation in France and intervention, 93 f.; defeat of French credits, 94; French claims after 1882, 94; Franco-German conversations on, 1884, 98; 1886, 122, 139; French demand for financial investigation, 1885, 100; Franco-German negotia-

tions, 1896, 168; *entente cordiale,* 1904, 203

Électeur, 8

Elections, May, 1869, 23; National Assembly, Feb. 8, 1871, 40 f.; Oct., 1877, 67 ff., 71; Oct., 1885, 104, 106 f.; May, 1887, 1888, 143; Paris election, Jan., 1889, 143 f.; Oct., 1889, 145; in Alsace-Lorraine, 1887, 188; parliamentary, 1893, 194; Paris, May, 1900, 192; parliamentary, 1906, 192; parliamentary, 1914, 283

Élysée Menilmontant, 91

Elzbacher, P., 13

Émancipateur (Cambrai), 67

Ems, interview, July 13, 1870, 30

Ems despatch, effect in Paris, 25; Gramont's reaction to, 31; publication and an additional paragraph, 32 f.; Bismarck's circular, 31, 33; effect upon decision for war, 33 f.

England, 70, 85, 94, 154, 179, 188, 215, 221, 259, 262, 285, 307; Bismarck's demand to Belgium, 1875, 57; attitude during war-scare of 1875, 58 f., 64; Anglo-Turkish agreement, June 4, 1878, 76; Greco-Turkish boundary question, 81; Tunis, 88; co-operation with France in Egypt, 91 f., 93; Egypt and Gambetta's attitude, 92; continental union vs. England, 92 f., 119, 180, 181; *entente cordiale,* 94, 202 f.; Bismarck's policy in 1884, 95; moderate French press, 1884, 97 f.; anti-English sentiment, 1886, 1887, 119, 127; Cyon's anti-English propaganda, 1890, 142; relations with Triple Alliance, 1891, 155, 157 f.; Franco-Russian *rapprochement* directed against, 156 ff.; friction with France over Siam, 1893, 158; Anglo-Congo Treaty, 1894, 166 f.; popular demand for French evacuation of Fashoda, 172 f.; attitude of French nationalists after Fashoda, 1898, 6, 176 ff.; implications of Franco-German conversations, 1898, 193; French opinion during Boer War, 198 f.; Anglo-German agreements, 199; proposed continental intervention in Boer War, 199 f.; preparation of opinion for entente with France, 202 f.; alleged offer of military aid to France, 1905, 211, 218 f.; conditional promise of diplomatic support, Apr., 1905, 211; policy during Algeciras Conference, 1906, 220; Anglo-Franco-Belgian military conversations, 1906, 220, 258 f.; Tardieu and Anglo-French military alliance, 1908, 224; William II's *Daily Telegraph* interview, Oct. 28, 1908, 227; and the Agadir Crisis, 1911, 242; Anglo-French Mediterranean agreement, 259; differences with Russia in Persia, 1914, 290; her relation to crisis of 1914, 303 ff.; British public opinion and France, 1914, 304 f.

English Historical Review, 27

Entente cordiale, 208, 213, 220; preparation of opinion for, 202 ff.; terms, 1904, 203; England's sacrifices, 203; reaction to, in France, 203 f.; Barclay on purposes of, 203; opinion on addition of Russia, 204; communication to Germany, 207; Germany's attempt to break, 217 ff., 230; Tardieu and military alliance, 1908, 224

Enquête Parlementaire, 27, 30, 32, 34, 38

Equilibrium, balance of power, 233, 297, 298, 303, 309; Tardieu's campaign in *Temps,* 10 f., 222 f.; Franco-Russian Alliance and, 155; Germany's fear of encirclement, 223; Sembat's criticism of, 1913, 257; R. Poincaré's foreign policy, 258 f.; during Balkan Wars, 1912, 1913, 264 ff., 284; effect of Balkan Wars upon Triple Entente, 1912, 1913, 276; public opinion and, 285; French government and the, 301

Est Républicain (Nancy), 275; Poincaré and France's aspirations, 1913, 258

Étienne, E., Russia and *entente cordiale,* 1904, 204; proposed warning to England, 1902, 207

Eugénie, Empress, fears for succession of Prince Imperial, 23; attitude, July 1870, 28; influence on decision for war, 33

Europe Nouvelle, 189

Eustis, J. B., 164

Événement, 101, 107, 159, 291, 296; Germany's attitude, Aug., 1885, 105; on Déroulède, 114; Russian bribes and their effect, 1912, 1913, 274;

Austria-Hungary's need of moderation, 1914, 287; arbitration in 1914, 293; attitude toward Austro-Serbian quarrel, 298

Faites un Roi, sinon faites la Paix, book by M. Sembat, 257
Fallières, President, 224
Famille, 116
Farrar, J. A., 224
Fashoda crisis, 1898, 203; Anglo-French-German relations in first phases of, 168 f.; English expedition to Dongola, 1896, 168; Marchand's mission, 169; Russia's attitude during, 169, 175, 177; Delcassé's policy, 172 ff., 177; England's attitude, 172 f., 175; attitude of French public opinion, 173; attitude of inspired press, 174; evacuation, Nov. 4, 175, 180; movement in favor of Franco-German entente, 1898, 1899, 6, 176 ff., 180 ff.; debate in Chamber of Deputies, Jan. 1899, 181; Anglo-French Accord, Mar. 1899, 182
Faure, F., Ligue des Patriotes, 111; opening of Kiel Canal, 1895, 162; public opinion on relations with Germany, 1896, 168; Déroulède's demonstration at funeral of, 1899, 192
Favre, Jules, 45; opposition to war. July, 1870, 33; committee of national defense, Sept. 3, 1870, 36; Minister of Foreign Affairs, 37; circular of Sept. 6, 1870, 37, 40, 42 f.; negotiations with Bismarck, Sept. 19, 1870, 39 f.; armistice, Jan. 28, 1871, 40
Fay, S. B., 53, 120, 121, 160, 202, 211, 216, 239, 245, 258, 287, 290, 296, 302
Ferry, A., 296
Ferry, J., 71, 80, 91, 94, 104, 105, 112, 155, 161, 224; contributor to *Temps,* 13; on German Confederation, 16; on greater Prussia, 18; colonies and surplus capital, 85; parliament and his colonial policy, 86; Tunis, 88 ff.; his defeat, Nov., 1881, 90; second ministry, 1882–1885, 94 ff.; difference with Déroulède on patriotic instruction, 1882, 110; conversations with Germany, 1884, 94 ff., 98; Bismarck's support of French colonial expansion, 1884, 1885, 100 ff., 120; beginning of Tonkin campaign, 1883, 101; his

defeat, Mar. 30, 1885, 101 ff., 136 f.
Figaro, 10, 56, 105, 115, 152, 155, 164, 168, 175, 179, 180, 196, 197, 218, 220, 221, 222, 226, 233, 240, 241, 242, 259, 265, 266, 286, 304, 305, 306; continental union vs. England, 1884, 98; on Franco-German understanding, 1884, 99; Tonkin and elections, Oct. 1885, 106; Déroulède and Ligue des Patriotes, 114; attitude toward Boulanger, 1886, 116; peace policy, 1886, 122; on Alsace-Lorraine, 1887, 126; Leo XIII's proposed intervention, 1887, 128; Déroulède's resignation, 1887, 128 f.; Russia's attitude toward France, 1887, 140; publication of Decazes-Le Flô letters, 1887, 140; Russian diplomat on Germany's amiabilities, interview, 1887, 142; German opinion on Alsace-Lorraine, 185; Morocco and Franco-German entente, 1901, 202; Russia and the *entente cordiale,* 1904, 204; Germany's policy, July, 1905, 215, 217; reaction to Act of Algeciras, 1906, 222; Casablanca affair and Germany's policy, 1908, 228; publication of Franco-Spanish entente of 1902, 249; decline of Déroulède's influence, 254; Poincaré's speech, Nantes, Oct., 1912, 260; annexation of Bosnia-Herzegovina, 1908, 262; Russian bribes and their effect, 1913, 274 f.; Russia's mobilization, July, 1914, 302; England's aid, 304
Figurey, E., 47
Fischer, C., on popular understanding of Alsatian opinion, 192
Flaissières, Dr., 257
Flandre, in German school atlas as *Flandern,* 111
Flourens, E. L., 59, 140, 212; asks explanations from Germany, 1887, 127; Schnaebelé affair, 129 f.; Schnaebelé's release, 132; England and Russian visit, 1893, 159
Flotow, Baron, effect of Moroccan crisis, 1905, 1906, upon French public opinion, 221
Fontainebleau, 109
Foreign Legion, 226
✳Foreign policy, French, popular or parliamentary control of, 3; France and political division of Central

Europe, 15 f.; Republicans and Monarchists on, 69 ff.; criticism of continental policy, 86; end of Franco-German co-operation, 1885, 104 ff.; views of Radicals in election, Oct., 1885, 105; Russian alliance and, 165; continental and colonial policy, 66, 182; French traditions and moderate tendencies, 183; *Journal des Débats* on domestic politics and, 191; Republicans' point of view, 193; Delcassé's control of, 1898-1905, 197 ff.; revision of Russian alliance, 1899, 198; national spirit as moral support for, 255; V. Augagneur on, 1913, 276. See equilibrium; French statesmen

Français, 26, 51, 52; on Gramont's declaration of July 6, 1870, 28; on preliminary terms of peace, 41; appeal for coolness, 1875, 63; Gambetta's political influence, 1878, 72; results of Congress of Berlin, 1878, 78; on Franco-German alliance, 1884, 99; on Brisson's Tonkin policy, 1885, 103; on Germany's point of view, Oct., 1885, 104

France, Napoleon III and Austro-Prussian War, 1866, 17 ff.; Gramont's statement, July 6, 1870, 27 f.; Gramont's demand of guarantees, July 12, 30; declaration of war, July 15, 34; fall of Empire, Sept., 1870, 35; terms of peace, 1871, 41; Thiers, Chief of Executive Power, 1871, 48; Thiers's fall, 1873, 49; Organic Laws, 1875, 53; MacMahon's coup d'état, May 16, 1877, 66; establishment of Republic, 68 f.; Boulanger, 114 ff.; Dreyfus affair, 191, 272; See French statesmen and leaders; diplomatic crises; foreign policy; public opinion; newspaper press; alliances and ententes; Monarchists; Republicans; Radicals; Radical-Socialists; Socialists

France, Anatole, protest against secret diplomacy, 1906, 219 f.

France, 26, 33, 112, 122, 126, 139, 256, 279; Boulanger's intentions, 1886, 117; attitude during Schnaebelé Affair, 1887, 121; war inevitable, 1887, 133; Hugonnet on danger of Pan-Slavism, 1886, 138; Russian bribes and their effect, 1912, 1913, 274;

Germany's reply to Berne conference, 1913, 282; ten kilometer order, July 30, 1914, 305

France de Bordeaux et de Sud-Ouest, 257, 275, 277, 289, 294; Delcassé's dismissal, 1905, 212; reaction to Franco-German agreements, Nov. 4, 1911, 247; public opinion and government's policy, July 31, 1914, 307

France Herself Again, book by Abbé Dimnet, 255

France Militaire, 122, 126; boycott of German labor, 112; army's self-confidence restored, 115; inevitable war, 1886, 118; continental league vs. England, 119; peaceful return of Alsace-Lorraine, 1887, 127; demand for guarantees and apology, 1887, 133; Russia and Franco-German War, 1887, 141

Franche Comté, in German school atlas as *Freigrafschaft*, 111

Francis Joseph II, advice to William II during Casablanca affair, 1908, 229, 232

Francis Ferdinand, Archduke, assassination of, June 28, 1914, 286

Franco-German Accord, 1909, 237, 240, 250; Austria-Hungary's influence, 231 f.; fear of complications, 232; terms, 232 f.; interpretation of, in France, 233 f.; interpretation of, in Germany, 234

Franco-German conversations, in 1884, 95 ff.; political use of, 1884, 1885, 107; for revision of Anglo-Congo Treaty, 1894, 167; before Fashoda crisis, 169 ff.; press discussion of entente, 1898, 1899, 176 ff.; anti-English implications, 193; unofficial conversations, 1901, 1902, 200 f.; leading to Accord of 1909, 231 f.

Franco-Prussian War, 9, 85, 109, 114, 163, 178, 187, 254; causes of, 16, 25 ff.; Gramont's declaration, July 6, 27 f.; Leopold's renunciation, July 12, 29 f.; demand of guarantees, July 12, 30; meeting of French council, July 14, 31; Ems despatch, 31; official influence on demand for war, 32; Bismarck's circular and *Corps Legislatif*, 33 f.; declaration of war, July 15, 34; French war-aims, 35; continuation of war, Sept., 1870,

36 ff.; Favre's circular, Sept. 4, 1870, 37; danger of revolution in Paris, 38 f.; efforts to end war, 39 f.; armistice and preliminary terms of peace, 40 f.; Bismarck on its cause, 45; *Univers*'s explanation of defeat, 50
Franco-German parliamentary conference, Berne, May, 1913, 279 ff., 285
Franco-Russian Alliance, 73, 120, 147, 170, 196, 258, 285, 310; effect of Schnaebelé affair, 1887, 135; Clemenceau on reaction of public opinion to, 136; attitude of Monarchists and Republicans, 136 f.; Radicals and Russian autocracy, 137 f.; propaganda for, 137, 142; attitude of public opinion, 1886, 138; 1887, 140; Rochefort's conversion, 1887, 140; effect of Empress Frederick's visit to Paris, 1891, 152 f.; preliminaries of, 153; dangers involved for France, 156, 160, 261; diplomatic entente, 1891, 157; Russia's anti-English purposes, 157 f.; negotiation of military alliance, 1894, 159 f.; terms of, 160 f.; and Alsace-Lorraine, 162; existence of, admitted, 1895, 164; relation to French foreign policy, 165; Jaurès's attitude, 1898, 176; and sense of security, 183; Socialists' attitude, 194 f.; Delcassé's revision of, 1899, 198; public opinion and France's obligations in, 261 f., 264 ff.; French loans, 263; attitude of French Socialist deputies, 1914, 299; French government and obligations in, 300
Frankfort, Treaty of, 44, 84, 155, 164, 186, 187; Ligue des Patriotes' use of Article II, 112
Frankfurter Zeitung, 264, 272; attitude toward *entente cordiale,* 1905, 219
Frederick, Empress, her Paris visit, Feb. 1891, 148 ff., 161, 163
Frederick II, King of Prussia, William II's hero, 145
Frederick III, Emperor of Germany, 120, reaction to, in France, 1888, 145
Freppel, Bishop, 189; colonial expansion, 84
Freycinet, C. de, 71, 72, 79, 91, 94, 157; Greco-Turkish boundary question, 81 f.; co-operation with England in Egypt, 92; continues Ferry's policy,

1885, 104; concentration of army on continent, 114; Bismarck and Egypt, 1886, 122, 139; Russia's proposals for an alliance, 1886, 122; regrets occasioned by Empress Frederick's visit, 1891, 151; end of France's isolation, 1891, 155
Fuller, J. V., 59, 122, 125, 127

Gabriac, Marquis de, on first interview with Bismarck, 1871, 45
Gaillard, L. de, 24
Galli, H. (H. Gallichet), 41, 46, 75, 111, 114
Gambetta, L., 24, 40, 71, 123; opposition to war, July, 1870, 33; public opinion, Sept. 4, 1870, 36; protest of Alsatian deputies, 1871, 41; on Bismarck's understanding of France, 45; Alsace-Lorraine and the *revanche,* 1871, 45, 72, 73, 74, 120; Republican foreign policy, 69; political influence after Oct. 1877, 72, 74; influence on foreign affairs, 72 ff.; relation to public opinion, 72; relations with Bismarck and Germany, 72 ff.; on possible alliances, 72; St. Quentin speech, Nov. 16, 1871, 73; Mme. Léon's influence upon, 73; his papers, 73; on German army, Sept., 1876, 74; proposed interview with Bismarck, 1878, 74 f.; Russia in Russo-Turkish War, 1877, 1878, 76; on Anglo-Turkish agreement, June 4, 1878, 76; dinner with Prince of Wales, 1878, 77; on Franco-Russian alliance, 1878, 77; on more active foreign policy, 1879, 78 f.; his Cherbourg speech, Aug. 9, 1881, 78; attitude of Radicals toward, 79 f.; basis of his popularity, 82; on colonial expansion, 85; on effect of silence in regard to *revanche,* 87, 120; Tunis, 91; *le grand ministère,* 91; alleged trip to Varzin, 91; French interests in Mediterranean, 92; co-operation with England in Egypt, 92; member of Ligue des Patriotes, 111; French police and Russian nihilists, 137. See *République Française*
Gap, 288
Garnier-Pagès, L. A., 32, 37
Gaulois, 8, 11, 13, 136, 179, 180, 185, 213, 233, 237, 240, 244, 248, 260, 262, 264,

267, 286, 292, 304, 305; É. de Cyon, editor of, 1881, 138; Russia's aid in 1887, 140; Radical-Monarchist coalition, 1885, 106; von Donnersmarck and Delcassé's dismissal, 1905, 211 f.; Delcassé's interview, July 12, 1905, 216; Germany's policy in Moroccan crisis, Sept., 1905, 218; French policy and Casablanca affair, 1908, 228; reaction to Franco-German agreements, Nov. 4, 1911; attitude toward Balkan League, 1912, 266; Russian bribes, their effect, 1913, 274 f.; Russia's partial mobilization, 1914, 302; on "halt in Belgrade" plan, 306

Gautsch, German police commissioner, 129; statement to correspondent of *Daily News*, Apr. 29, 1887, 131

Gauvain, A., Franco-German Accord, 1909, 234, 235; nationalist point of view, 253

Gavard, C., 53, 62

Gazette de France, 75, 77, 78, 79, 122, 163; preliminary terms of peace, 41 f.; France and Italian unity, 50; on moderation of Republican press, 1875, 56; Bismarck's demands to Belgium, Apr., 1875, 57; French foreign policy, 70; Tunis expedition, 1881, 89; Franco-German entente, 1884, 97, 98 f.; Radical-Monarchist coalition, Oct., 1885, 106; description of Déroulède, 113 f.; on Bismarck's speech, Jan. 11, 1887, 124; effect of Russian alliance, 1895, 164; plebiscite as solution of Alsace-Lorraine question, 1895, 190

Geffcken, H. H., 56

German Confederation, 16, 19

German unity, French attitude toward, as cause of war of 1870, 16 f., 44; debate in French parliament, March, 1867, 21; disunion predicted by *Journal de Marseille,* 47; attack by *Univers,* 1873, 51

Germany, 5 f., 47, 64, 65, 74, 94, 101, 103, 107, 119, 143, 179, 183, 198 f., 214, 216, 217 f., 223, 254, 275, 285, 297, 301, 307; France and unification of, 17 ff., 44; recovery of, after 1919, 39; proclamation of German Empire at Versailles, Jan. 18, 1871, 44; justification of annexation of Alsace-Lorraine,

44 f.; evacuation of French territory, Sept., 1873, 49; attitude of French clericals, 50; Decazes's attitude, 1875, 60; Gambetta and, 72 f.; increasing population of, and French colonization, 85 f., 89; increasing population and *revanche,* 86 f.; Saint-Hilaire's letter, 90; her colonial expansion, 94 f.; Franco-German conversations, 1884, 95; 1898, 176 ff.; and French claims in Egypt, 99; and anti-German demonstrations in France, 1885, 104 f.; trade with France, 1882–1886, 112; attitude toward French chauvinism, 1886, 119; Bismarck's speech, Jan. 11, 1887, 123 f.; conservative party after defeat of septennate, 1887, 125; Leo XIII's proposed intervention and Alsace-Lorraine, 1887, 128; Schnaebelé's arrest, 1887, 129; and Franco-Russian *rapprochement,* 159 ff.; Anglo-Congo treaty, 1894, 167; Kruger Telegram, 1896, 168; Chamberlain's offer of alliance, 1898, 177, 180; insists on renunciation of Alsace-Lorraine, 183; and Paris exposition, 1900, 185; proposed solutions of Alsace-Lorraine question, 190 ff.; hatred of, in French text-books, 195; proposed intervention in Boer War, 1900, 199 f.; Anglo-German-French relations, 1901, 201; Delcassé's diplomatic preparations in Morocco, 207; her Moroccan policy, 208, 221; and Delcassé's dismissal, June, 1905, 211 ff.; Tardieu on fear of encirclement, 223; Clemenceau's attitude toward German people, 224; attitude toward Clemenceau ministry, 1906, 125; during Agadir crisis, 1911, 236 ff.; effect of her Moroccan policy, 252; attitude of, toward balance of power policy, 257; military increases, 1913, 277; delegation to Berne conference, 1913, 279 f.; her "blank check," July 5, 1914, 287; Schoen's *demarche,* July 24, 293 ff.; her refusal to restrain Austria-Hungary, 296; her action at Vienna after July 27, 298; her ultimatum to France, July 31, 308; her declaration of war vs. France, Aug. 3, 309. See Bismarck; Bülow; Bethman-

Hollweg; German newspapers; diplomatic crises
Gheusi, P. B., 92
Gibraltar, 119
Gide, C., exchange of French and German students, 1895, 186
Giffen, M. B., 175, 178
Giers, N. de, 138; Bismarck's request for free hand vs. France, 1887, 139 f.; entente with France, 1891, 153
Giornale d'Italia, 172
Girardin, É. de, 8, 79; on public opinion and war, 1868, 23; official influence on press, July, 1870, 26
Gladstone, W., intervention in Egypt, 92
Gleize, J., 185
Goblet, R., 195; circulation of *Revanche,* 1886, 117; policy during Schnaebelé affair, 1887, 129 f., 132
Gohier, U., 191
Gontant-Biron, Vicomte de, 51, 57 f., 61, 67
Gooch, G. P., 75, 77, 110, 113, 115, 122, 148, 149, 159
Gordon, General, 166
Gorlov, V. de, 138
Gortchakov, Alexander, Prince, 73; jealousy of Bismarck, 58; Broglie's appeal to, 58; Decaze's appeal to, Apr., 1875, 59; assurances to Le Flô, 60; advice to Bismarck, 64
Goulette, L., 116
Goyau, G., 52, 113
Gramont, Duc de, 227; declaration of July 6, 1870, 6, 27 f., 38, 43; significance of appointment as Foreign Minister, May, 1870, 24; references to public opinion July, 1870, 25; directions for press campaign, July 3, 1870, 26; his intentions, 27 f.; note of apology, July 12, 1870, 30; demand of guarantees, 30; Ems despatch, 31 f.; testimony to committee, July 15, 1870, 34
Grande Revue, 178, 252, 255, 257, 261, 274, 277, 283
Grandlieu, P. de (Léon Lavedan), 79, 91, 122
Granville, Lord, intervention in Egypt, 92; delay in replying to Bismarck, 94 f.
Gravelotte, 152
Greece, in Congress of Berlin, 1878, 77;

Greco-Turkish boundary question, 81 f.; Kavalla question, 1913, 275
Grèvy, J., 79, 91; on renunciation of Alsace-Lorraine, 47; election as president of France, 78; attitude during Schnaebelé affair, 1887, 129 f.; attitude during Boulanger agitation, 143
Grey, Sir Edward, 237, 259; statement in House of Commons, March 28, 1895, 167, 207; policy during Algeciras Conference, 1906, 220; Anglo-Franco-Belgian military conversations, 1906, 220, 258 f.; attitude during Agadir Crisis, 1911, 242, 244 f.; Grey-Cambon letters, Nov., 1912, 258, 304; Poincaré's note, Oct. 30, 1912, 266; his proposal for intervention, 1914, 294, 301; on aid to France, 1914, 304
Gricourt, Marquis de, 21
Grisson, G., 116
Gueronnière, Comte de la, 19
Guéroult, A., 19, 40
Guerre Sociale, 286, 300, 303. See G. Hervé
Guinea, 87
Gwinner, von, 235

Haegy, Abbé, 281
Hague Conferences, 1899, France's point of view, 184
Haldane mission, 1912, R. Poincaré and, 258
Halévy, D., 17, 21, 27, 67
Halévy, É., 233, 263
Hammann, O., 209; effect of Moroccan Crisis, 1905, 1906, upon French public opinion, 221
Hanotaux, G., 58 ff., 81, 84, 91, 262, 265; as a contributor to press, 13; opening of Kiel Canal, 1895, 162; reply to Grey, 1895, 168; on Egyptian question, 1896, 169; William II's estimate of, 170; France and opening of Straits, 1912, 265; Balkan League and Russia's interests, 1912, 267; on Franco-German conversation, 1914, 306
Hansen, J., 73, 139 f., 142, 155; seeks Prussia's terms, Sept., 1870, 38; conversations with A. von Huhn, 1896, 169 f.; 1898, 177; Delcassé-Radolin conversations, 1901, 200 f.
Hartung, F., 235, 237

Haussmann, C., 280

Haussonville, Comte d', 40 f.

Havas Agency, official connections, 12; Bismarck's circular, July, 1870, 34; its note, May 5, 1875, 63; correction of Boulanger's statement, 1886, 117; misrepresentation of *Daily News*, Jan., 1887, 126; on Schnaebelé's arrest, 1887, 130; Berlin wire, July, 1914, 295

Headlam-Morley, J. W., 291

Hedemann, J., 9; unofficial mission to Berlin, Apr., 1905, 209 f.; on condition of army, 1911, 216; his nationalist point of view, 253; estimate of Russian army, 1914, 291; on Russia's freedom of action, 303; Germany and peace, 306

Heimweh, J., (Fernand de Dartein), reopening of Alsace-Lorraine question, 188; solution of Alsace-Lorraine Question, 190

Heinrich, G. A., 46

Helgoland, 119

Henriot, É., 255

Henry, Colonel, 172

Henry IV, King of France, 80

Herbette, Ambassador to Germany, 119, 127, 132, 143, 148

Herbette, J., France's interests and Balkan League, 1912, 267; Balkans and the Russian alliance, 1912, 274; peace and the Triple Entente, 1914, 298; France and Austro-Serbian War, 306

Herbette, M., 267

Herkenberg, K. O., 14

Hervé, É., 56

Hervé, G., 221; pacifist educational movement, 195; on assassination of Francis Ferdinand, 1914, 286; appeal to Socialists, 1914, 300

Herzfeld, H., 41, 54

Hippeau, E., 92

Hoettschau, Lt.-Col. C., 120

Hohenlohe, Prince C. von, 55, 58, 68, 75, 87, 104, 170; Decazes's proposal for understanding, 1875, 60; proposed Franco-German understanding, 1884, 95; Franco-German co-operation, 1896, 96 ff.

Hohenzollern candidature, 6, 24 f., 42, 174

Holborn, H., 19, 53

Holland, 198; Leo XIII's plan of a buffer state, 1887, 128; proposed union with Alsace-Lorraine, 189

Holstein, Baron F. von, on continental league, 1895, 168; Delcassé and Franco-German entente, 1902, 201; his policy during the Moroccan Crisis, 1905, 1906, 202, 208, 215; reaction in France to his dismissal, 1906, 221

Homme Libre, 13, 281, 288; on England's aid, 1914, 304. See G. Clemenceau

Honorat, A., 277

Hôtel de Ville, 40

Houssaye, H., 186; on the *revanche*, 1897, 187

Hroumirs, 89

Hübner, 37

Hugo, V., protest against cession of Alsace-Lorraine, 1871, 42; Ligue des Patriotes, 111

Hugonnet, L., 86, 87; attacks upon England in *France*, 119; danger in Pan-Slavism, 138

Huhn, A. von, conversations with J. Hansen, 1896, 169 f.; conversations with French officials, 1898, 177 f.

Huhne, Captain von, 120

Humanité, 8, 11, 197, 209, 215 f., 217, 219, 224, 229, 231, 233, 238, 248 f., 255, 261, 264, 268 f., 270 f., 296, 309 f., See J. Juarès

Hutin, M., 259

Imminent justice, Gambetta's Cherbourg speech, Aug. 9, 1881, 78

Impartiale du Finisterre, 67

Indépendance Belge (Brussels), 33, 34, 35

Indépendance de la Moselle (Metz), 38

India, 158

Inevitable war, 15, 249, 292; fear of, 1867–1870, 23; and public opinion, July 1870, 35; denial of, 47; *France Militaire* on, 1886, 117; *France* on, 1887, 133; C. Dreyfus, 147; G. Clemenceau on, 1905, 224; Déroulède on occasion for, 1912, 254

Intransigeant, 93, 106, 113, 123, 131 ff., 139, 140, 152, 158, 174; on Gambetta's Cherbourg speech, Aug. 9, 1881, 78; on Tunis expedition, 1881, 89; denial of impending ultimatum, Jan., 1887,

125; attitude during Schnaebelé affair, 1887, 131; France and opening of Kiel Canal, 1895, 163; Franco-German intellectual relations, 186. See H. Rochefort

Iphigenia, French training ship, 199

Isaac, A., 166

Isambert, G., 22

Isvolski, A., 250, 300; on French military expedition to Fez, 1911, 236; Russia's attitude during Agadir Crisis, 1911, 244 f.; on Serbo-Bulgarian alliance, 1912, 263; desire for revenge after Bosnian crisis, 1908, 1909, 268; interpretation of France's and 'Poincaré's points of view, 1912, 268; concern for French public opinion, 268; Kokovtsev on his venality, 269; on provincial French press, 1913, 272; Poincaré's assurances to, Aug. 1, 1914, 307

Italy, 16, 65, 67, 72, 119, 160, 188, 222, 286; Napoleon III and Venice, 1866, 18; attitude of French clericals, 1871, 50; the *Orénoque,* 50 f.; Venice interview, Apr., 1875, 54; L. Bourgeois on colonial accord with, 1896, 165; Franco-Italian entente, 202; Algeciras Conference, 1906, 221; and corruption of French press, 1912, 1913, 270

Jameson raid, 168

Japan, 163 f.; war with Russia, 216, 221

Japikse, N., 55

Jaurès, J., 9, 221, 254, 257, 272, 279; on evacuation of Fashoda, 1898, 176; as leader of moderate tendencies, 193, 195; attitude toward Alsace-Lorraine, 194; repudiation of *revanche* in Chamber, 1902, 195; letter to Andrea Costa, 1902, 195 f.; proposal for simultaneous disarmament, 1902, 196; defeated for re-election as vice-president, 1904, 197; Russia and *entente cordiale,* 1904, 204; his interpellation, Apr., 1905, 209; Germany's threat to *entente cordiale,* 1905, 214 f.; Björkö meeting, 1905, 217; attitude during Algeciras Conference, 1906, 219; attitude during Casablanca affair, 1908, 231; on Franco-German Accord, 1909, 233; on expedition to Fez, 1911, 238; effect of publication

of Franco-Spanish accord of 1904, 249; defense of Franco-German agreements, Nov. 4, 1911, 249; Europe and Balkan War, 1912, 264; substitute for three-year service law, 1913, 278 f.; on passage of three-year service law, 1913, 282; attitude toward Poincaré's St. Petersburg visit, 1914, 289; his assassination, July 31, 302. See *Humanite;* Socialism

Jena, 223

Joan of Arc, 159

Journal, 9, 36, 286, 290, 304, 305, 307; on Franco-German Accord, 1909, 233; its aeronautical contest, 1911, 255; Russia and the Serbs, 1908, 262

Journal (Mans), 67

Journal d'Alsace-Lorraine, 279

Journal de Génève, 295; France's attitude toward compromise, 1911, 246 f.; ratification of Franco-German agreements of Nov. 4, 1911, 250, 289

Journal de Paris, 56 f.

Journal de Marseille, 34, 47

Journal de Rouen, 8, 10, 175 f., 178, 212, 279, 294, 304; Franco-German reconciliation, 1891, 152; its point of view after Fashoda, 1898, 176; Germany's threat to *entente cordiale,* 1905, 215; French delegation at Berne, 1913, 281; attitude toward Russia, 1914, 303

Journal des Débats, 10 f., 12, 17, 25 f., 28, 32 f., 38, 40, 44, 49, 53 f., 86, 90, 93, 105, 110, 114, 123, 126, 143, 152, 155, 164 f., 167, 175, 192, 196, 199, 206, 208, 220, 221 f., 231, 248 f., 253, 257, 259, 262, 281 f., 286, 287, 294; on the *revanche,* 1871, 42; Broglie's foreign policy, 51; on *Time's* war-scare letter, 1875, 62; on Anglo-Turkish agreement, June 4, 1878, 77; on Austria's policy in Balkans, 1878, 77; Greco-Turkish boundary question, 81 f.; on colonial expansion, 85; Waddington and Tunis, 89; cooperation with England in Egypt, 92; Ferry's Tonkin campaign, 1885, 101; Ferry's defeat, 1885, 103; elections, Oct., 1885, 106; English press and Franco-German relations, 1886, 119; on Bismarck's speech, Jan. 11, 1887, 124; attitude during Schnaebelé affair, 1887, 131; advice to Bulgarian deputies, 1887, 139; on Empress Frederick's visit, 1891, 151; Kronstadt and Franco-Russian entente, 1891, 154; attitude during Fashoda affair, 1898, 173 ff.; on French understanding of Germany, 1895, 185; on domestic politics and foreign policy, 1904, 191; Jaurès's proposal for disarmament, 1902, 196; defeat of Socialists on disarmament, 1903, 197; preparation of public opinion for *entente cordiale*, 1905, 215, 217; Björkö meeting, 1905, 217; French policy during Algeciras Conference, 1906, 219; on annexation of Bosnia-Herzegovina, 1908, 232; attitude during Casablanca affair, 1908, 229; expedition to Fez, 1911, 238 f.; official interpretation of Schoen's *démarche*, July, 1911, 240; nationalists and Agadir, 1911, 241; decline of Déroulède's influence, 254; attitude during Balkan War, 1912, 264, 266; Isvolski's influence upon, 1912, 275; Radical and Radical-Socialist attitude toward Balkans, 273; significance of a Franco-German entente, 1913, 276; strength of Russian army, 1913, 279; three-year service law and elections, 1913, 283; chief issue in 1914, 285; Serbia and Germany hegemony, 1914, 297; 1914 and the balance of power, 298, 301; report of Russia's general mobilization, 302 f.; on advice to Russia, 303 f. See G. Charmes; R. de Caix

Journal Illustré, 116
Journal Officiel, 102
Journalists, and diplomatic service, 13
Jouvenel, H., 223
Jouvenel, R., de, 12
Judet, E., 9, 216, 244; French interests and Russian alliance, 1891, 156; anti-English editorials in *Petit Journal,* 202 f.; on press reaction to assassination of Francis Ferdinand, 286. See *Petit Journal; Éclair*
Jupilles, F. de, 116
Justice, 13, 89, 91, 93, 105 f., 107, 113, 115, 122 f., 126, 139, 155 f., 159, 163; on Ferry and Germany, 97; on French policy and Tonkin, 1885, 101 f.; on Bismarck's speech, Jan.

11, 1887, 124; on official statement of French policy, Jan., 1887, 126; attitude toward Russian alliance, 138 f., 141, 164. See G. Clemenceau; C. Pelletan; C. Longuet

Karlsruhe Zeitung, 64
Katkof, M., relations with É. de Cyon, 138
Kautsky, K., 294, 296
Kavalla, 275
Kératry, Comte É. de, 34
Kerner, 114
Kessler, H., Alsace-Lorraine's point of view, 1913, 280
Khartoum, 166
Keudell, R. von, 23
Khevenhüller, 228 f.; Paris press in 1908, 262
Kiderlen-Wächter, A. von, 236; his Moroccan policy, May 3, 1911, 239; Kissengen conversations with J. Cambon, 240; dispatch of *Panther,* July 1, 240; Germany's demands, July 15, 1911, 242; change in policy, July 20, 1911, 245
Kiel Canal, 162 f., 165, 167
Kirk Kilisse, 266
Kissengen, Cambon-Kiderlen-Wächter's conversations, 1911, 240, 242 f.
Kitchener, Earl, 170, 172
Klotz, Russian press-fund, 1912, 1913, 269 ff.
Kohl, H., 75
Kokovtsev, V. N., Poincaré on corruption of French press, 1912, 268; Isvolski's venality, 269
Kölnische Zeitung, 34, 112, 124, 170, 180, 233; war-scare of 1875, 54, 63; its Vienna letter, Apr. 4, 1875, 55; Anglo-French relations, 1884, 97; radical French press, 1884, 99; on war or peace, Jan., 1887, 125; Germany's control of Alsace-Lorraine, 1887, 128; "echoes from a madhouse," 131; effect in France of William II's advances, 1891, 148; on French chauvinists, 1891, 152; possibility of Franco-German entente, 1898, 176, 178 f.; insists on renunciation of Alsace-Lorraine, 1898, 181; reaction to Casablanca incident, 1908, 226; Paris press on compensations,

1911, 241; inspired Paris newspapers, 1912, 267
Kreuzzeitung (Berlin), 214, 233
Kronberg, 148
Kronstadt, visit of French naval squadron, 1891, 153 f., 157; Franco-Russian toasts, 1897, 166
Kruger, President, William II's telegram, 1896, 168, 170; visit to France, 1900, 200

Laffitte, L., 184
Laffon, E., Russian influence upon *Temps*, 271
La Gorce, P. de, 20
Lalance, A., 73, 171, 189, 190; Alsace-Lorraine and Franco-German relations, 146; exchange of colony for Alsace-Lorraine, 178; French editorial opinion on *revanche*, 185 f.; Berne Conference and Alsace-Lorraine, 1913, 279
Lamy, É., 86
Landtag, Alsatian, resolution vs. Franco-German war, 281
Lanessan, J. L. de, solution of Moroccan question, 1906, 220. See *Siècle*
Lang-Son, 101 f.
Langer, W. L., 77, 88, 89, 146, 149, 152, 153, 160
Langlois, E., 147
Lanterne, 257, 279, 289, 290; France and opening of Kiel canal, 1895, 163; Russian bribes and their effect, 1912, 1913, 274 f.; Russia and Balkan War, 1912, 275; attitude toward three-year service act, 1913, 278; on Berne conference, 1913, 282; break-up of Austria-Hungary, 1914, 286 f.; France and Russian alliance, 1914, 297, 308; on aggressive war, 1914, 308. See Millerand
Lascelles, Sir F., 181
Laur, F., 147; Empress Frederick's visit, 1891, 150; attitude toward England, 1891, 158
Laurent, P., 255
Lautier, E., attitude during Casablanca affair, 1908, 229. See *Figaro*
Lauzanne, S., 9; revelations in *Matin*, Oct., 1905, 218 f.
Laveleye, E. de, on German unification, 16
Lavisse, E., Germany and *Avant la*

Bataille, 1886, 120; on patriotic demonstrations and relations with Germany, 121; Germany's desire of peace, 1892, 185; on discussion of Alsace-Lorraine Question, 1891, 188; his nationalist point of view, Alsace-Lorraine, 253; on opposition to three-year service law, 1914, 282
Le Flô, General, 49, 58, 59; Gortchakov's assurances, 1875, 60; correspondence with Decazes, 140
League of the Three Emperors, 53
Leboucq, C., effect of Berne conference, 1913, 281
Lehautcourt, P., (pseud. General Palat), 27
Leipzig, 129; Schnaebelé's condemnation, 129
Lemaître, J., Alsace-Lorraine and a European conference, 178; strength of nationalist movement, 1901, 192
Lemoinne, J., 9; *revanche* in 1887, 124
Lenoir, connection with Russian press-fund, 270, 275
Leo XIII, Pope, proposed intervention between France and Germany, 1887, 127
Léon, Mme. Léonie, 73 ff.
Leopold II, King of Belgium, Anglo-Congo Treaty, 1894, 166
L'Hèritier, M., 81
Leopold, Prince of Hohenzollern-Sigmaringen, 24 ff.
Leroy-Beaulieu, A., 143; public opinion on Russian alliance, 1887, 141
Leroy-Beaulieu, P., 85, 90; on the *revanche*, 87 f.
Les Danicheffs, play by A. Dumas fils, 136, 137
Les Oberlé, R. Bazin's novel, 192
Les Origines Diplomatiques, 19
Lesseps, F. de, unofficial mission to Berlin, 1887, 128
Leygues, G., peace sentiment, 1903, 183
Lhuys, D. de, his advice, 1866, 18
Liberté, 23, 26, 32, 33, 63, 181, 222, 224, 244, 262, 287; arrangement with Germany, 1905, 209; on Delcassé's dismissal, 1905, 212; Germany's threat to *entente cordiale*, 1905, 214; on *Panther* at Agadir, 1911, 241 f.; Germany's policy, 1911, 246; reaction to Franco-German agreements,

Nov. 4, 1911, 247; Russian bribes, their effect, 274 f.; Russia's moderation, 1914, 302

Libre Parole, 165, 216, 219, 287; Russian bribes and their effect, 1913, 274 f.; Schoen's *démarche*, July 24, 1914, 294

Libreville, 243

Ligue de la Patrie Française, 177; revival of nationalism, 190 f.; membership of, 192; bankruptcy of, 1905, 193

Ligue des Droits de l'Homme, 191

Ligue des Patriotes, 105, 109, 134, 161, 177, 193, 202, 289; its organization, 1882, 110 f.; its propaganda, 111 f.; its membership, 113; Germany's and Bismarck's attitude toward, 113, 119 ff.; its spectacular exploits and public opinion, 113 ff.; dissolution of, 1889, 121, 144, 188 f.; Déroulède's resignation as president, 1887, 128 f.; Paris election, 1889; and Boulanger, 143 f.; and Empress Frederick's visit to Paris, 1891, 149 f.; its reorganization by Déroulède, 1898, 174; M. Barrès as president, 1914, 254. See P. Déroulède; M. Barrès; chauvinism

Lille, 143

Lippmann, W., 4 f.

Littré, E., 70 f.

Livres Jaunes, 81, 82, 83, 92, 93, 94, 98, 153, 157, 158, 160, 174, 198, 209, 236, 240, 242, 243, 244, 263, 266, 293, 303

Livre Noir, 236, 245, 260, 261, 266, 268, 269, 275, 294, 295, 300, 301, 307

Lloyd-George, David, his Mansion House Speech, 1911, 244

Lockroy, É., Germany's economic progress, 186

Lokal-Anzeiger (Berlin), 305

London, 294, 296, 302; Conference of, 1884, 94; William II's visit, 1891, 153; Loubet's and Delcassé's visit, 1903, 203

Longchamps, 260

Longuet, C., on French foreign policy, 80

Lord, R. H., 26, 29, 30, 34, 35

Lorraine, in German school atlas as *Lothringen,* 111

Loubet, President, 198, 211; projected meeting with William II, 1904, 208

Louis, G., 225, 259

Louis XIV, King of France, 80, 151

Lüderitz, German consul, 226

Lule Burgas, 266, 268

Luxemburg, Leo XIII's plan of a buffer state, 1887, 128

Lyon Républicain (Lyons), 10, 123, 151, 228, 275 f., 280, 289; on Alsace-Lorraine's loyalty, 1887, 127; value of favorable foreign public opinion, 1887, 132; on result of Schnaebelé affair, 133; on Russia's vogue, 1891, 154; end of France's isolation, 1891, 155; dangers in Russian alliance, 1891, 156; Paris opinion during Casablanca affair, 1908, 230; on effect of publication of Franco-Spanish entente of Oct., 1904, 1911, 249; attitude toward three-year service law, 1913, 278, 288; preponderance of Triple Entente, 1914, 291; Triple Entente and peace, 299. See V. Augagneur

Lyons, 26

Lyons, Lord, 28, 59, 76, 82; on effect of Ems despatch, 31

Macedonia, 264

MacMahon, Marshal, 49, 67, 78

Madagascar, 166; proposed exchange for Alsace-Lorraine, 189

Madelin, L., 248

Madrid, 29; Moroccan Conference, 1880, 88

Main, as southern limit to German unity, 20, 24

Malet, A., France's interests and Serbia, 1912, 267; French public opinion on Balkan crisis, 1912, 276 f.

Malon, resigns from National Assembly, 41

Malta, 119

Malvy, 306

Manchester Guardian, French public opinion and aggressive war, 1914, 308

Mannesmann brothers, 234

Manteuffel, Marshal, telegram to Thiers, 1877, 67

Manuel General, 195

Manufacturers, effect of economic depression, 1867-1870, 22

Marcère, E. de, 103

Marchand, Colonel, 173; instructions and purposes, 169

Marcus Aurelius, Frederick III compared to, 145

Maret, H., weakness of public opinion, 1897, 186 f.

Margaine, 157

Marguerite, P., on the *revanche*, 1897, 187

Marguerite, V., on the *revanche*, 1897, 187

Marignani, and *Petit journal*, 8

Marini, H., 189

"Marseillaise," 32, 154, 157

Marseilles, 71, 287

Martial, R., 189

Martin, H., 110

Masonic Order, 97

Mathiez, A., on Delcassé's revision of Franco-Russian alliance, 1899, 198

Matin, 9, 13, 37, 123 f., 165, 167, 171 f., 180, 209, 219, 220, 223, 240, 253, 275, 288, 294 f., 297, 304, 306; Leo XIII's proposed mediation, 1887, 128; Déroulède's influence, 1886, 129; on Russia's aid, 1887, 140; on Empress Frederick's visit, 1891, 149 f.; France and Kiel Canal, 1895, 163; on results of Russian alliance, 1895, 164; mission of correspondent to Berlin, 169; on value of Fashoda, 174; reaction to evacuation of Fashoda, 1898, 175, 180; on Tangier incident, 1905, 208; Delcassé's dismissal and public opinion, 1905, 212; and change of French policy, June, 1905, 213; on Björkö meeting, 1905, 216; Germany's policy in Moroccan crisis, 218; on Morocco-Congo exchange, May, 1911, 239, 241; reply to Agadir, 1911, 242; and Germany's demand of Congo, 1911, 243; publication of Franco-Spanish entente, Oct., 1904, 249; reply to *Journal's* aeronautical contest, 1911, 255; public opinion and general war, 1912, 277; on fear of Austro-Serbian complications, 1914, 287; its estimate of Russian army, 1914, 291; on Russia's moderation, 302; Russia's general mobilization, 302; on France's defensive attitude, Aug. 1, 1914, 308. See Delcassé; J. Lemoinne; S. Lauzanne; J. Hedeman

Maurras, C., 212, 257; Morocco and Alsace-Lorraine, 238

Maury, A., 17

Mediterranean, 224, 288; Gambetta and French interests in, 92; Franco-Russian naval co-operation, 158

Mehemet Ali, 92

Meinecke, F., 177, 200

Meissonier, J., 148, 149

Méline, J., 209

Mémorial des Deux Sèvres (Niort), 24

Mémorial Diplomatique, 33

Mercereau, A., 255

Merchants, effect of economic depression, 1867-1870, 22

Mercure de France, questionnaire on Franco-German intellectual relations, 1895, 186; questionnaire on *revanche*, Dec. 1897, 186 f.

Mermeix (B. Terrail), 235, 243, 245

Mermet, circulation of *France Militaire*, 1886, 118

Messimy, A., statement to Russian military attache, July 31, 1914, 301

Metternich, Prince, 24, 27; on public opinion, July 14, 1870, 31

Metz, 40, 68, 113, 124, 129, 156, 163, 174, 190, 234, 254, 267

Mévil, André, 171; attitude during Boer War, 198 f.; Germany and expedition to Fez, 1911, 237; his nationalist point of view, 253; on Germany and the "next war," 253 f.; on Austria-Hungary's future, 1914, 287. See *Écho de Paris, Libre Parole* (1914)

Mexican adventure, 18

Meyer, A., on temper of crowds, 1914, 305

Michon, G., 138, 141, 153, 166, 198, 225, 263; effect of Russian alliance on French politics, 161

Middle classes, and military reforms, 1867, 22; political views, 69.

Mielle, P., 194

Military Club, founded by Boulanger, 117

Millaud, E., 115

Millerand, A., 194, 268; compromise with Germany, 1884, 97; attitude toward Alsace-Lorraine, 164; annual spring review, 260; connection with *Lanterne*, 274

Millet, R., 171; parliament and foreign affairs under Delcassé, 197 f.

Millevoye, L., 140; Russian propaganda for French alliance, 1887, 142; attitude toward England, 1891, 157; discredited by attack on Clemenceau, 1891, 162; his reaction to evacuation of Fashoda, 1898, 175; attitude toward entente with England, 202; relations with England and Germany, 1905, 215; on expedition to Fez, 1911, 238; on reply to Germany's demand of Congo, 1911, 243; Russia and Bosnian crisis, 1908, 1909, 262

"Mission civilisatrice," 85

Moabite, Déroulède's play, 110

Mobilization, significance of, 1894, 160

Moch, G., 190

Molenaar, H., 190

Molinari, G., 38

Moltke, H., Count von, 30, 59

Monarchists, 84, 114, 194; and political use of foreign policy, 1867, 21, 67; National Assembly, 1871, 40 f.; their struggle with Republicans, 46 f., 65; and Bismarck's preference for Republic, 46; and payment of indemnity, 49; Thiers' defeat, 1873, 49; and national traditions, 65; their propaganda in 1877, 67; France and Congress of Berlin, 76 f.; combine with Radicals, 79, 89, 92, 96, 163; on colonial expansion, 86; and Gambetta ministry, 1881, 91; and Boulanger, 116, 122; elections, Oct., 1885, 106; on Russian alliance, 136; and Dreyfus affair, 191; on policy of equilibrium, 272, 285

Monde, 50, 56

Moneypenny, A. F., 61

Monis, 259; President of Council, 1911, 236

Moniteur Universel, 18; war-scare of 1875, 63

Monod, G., character of Boulangist leaders, 144

Monson, Sir E., 172, 174, 177, 181; strength of French colonial group, 1898, 166; Russia and Fashoda Crisis, 1898, 175

Montenegro, 175

Montesquiou, L. de, 25

Montpellier, 186

Moon, P. T., 85

Monteil, Colonel, 167

Morel, E. D., 201

Morning Post (London), 32, 34; war-scare letter from St. Petersburg, 62; attitude during discussion of Franco-German entente, 1898-1899, 180

Morocco, 88, 201, 210, 231, 234, 242, 244, 249 f., 250, 252; Delcassé and 1899, 199; P. Cambon and Germany in, 1902, 201; and Franco-German understanding, 1901, 202; secret terms of entente cordiale, 203; attitude of French public opinion, 206; Delcassé's policy, 206 f.; crisis, 1905, 1906, 208 ff.; settlement of, 1906, 221; Casablanca crisis, 1908, 226 f.; becomes a national issue, 230; Franco-German Accord, 1909, 232; Franco-German co-operation, 1909-1911, 234; Germany's attitude toward policy of peaceful penetration, 235; expedition to Fez, 1911, 235; agreements of Nov. 4, 1911, 246

Moroccan crisis, 1905, 1906, Germany's policy, 208; William II at Tangier, March, 1905, 208; French public opinion and change of policy, 208 f., 213; Rouvier's offer of entente, 210 f.; Bülow's reply, 211; public opinion on Delcassé's dismissal, 1905, 212 f.; Bülow and conference, 214; threat vs. entente cordiale, 214 f.; preliminary agreement July 8, 1905, 215; effect of Germany's manœuvres in, 217; agreement of Sept. 25, 1905, 218; Algeciras Conference, 1906, 219 ff.; England and France, 220; Act of Algeciras, 1906, 221; effect of Act upon public opinion, 221 f.

Moskovskija Vedomosti (Moscow), 138

Mulai Hafid, 226, 239

Mulhouse, 68; autonomist resolution adapted at, Mar., 1913, 280

Mun, Count A. de, Germany and expedition to Fez, 1911, 237; public opinion and war, 1911, 241

Münster, Count, 151, 162; reports on French public opinion, 1886, 120; 1891, 148; lectured by Bismarck,

1886, 120 f.; France's refusal of Russian alliance, 1886, 139; French reaction to coronation of Nicholas II, 1896, 165; French reaction to Kruger telegram, 1896, 168 f.; *Mercure de France*'s questionnaire on the *revanche*, 1897, 186
Murat, P., 30

Nancy, 52, 156, 254
Nantes, 6, 26, 260, 266, 269
Napoleon I, 15, 92, 116
Napoleon III, 27, 123; his public statements and French policy, 6; and nationalism, 16 f.; his letter, June 11, 1866, 18; and Austro-Prussian War, 1866, 19; on Gramont, 24; attitude in July, 1870, 28
Napoleonic legend, and peasants, 24
National, 71, 104
National Assembly, election of, Feb. 8, 1871, 40; and preliminary terms of peace, 41; clerical petitions, 1871, 50; war-scare of 1875, 55
National Defense, Government of, 36 f.; peace in Sept., 1870, 37 f.; attack on Hôtel de Ville, Oct. 31, 1870, 40; shares blame with Prussia, 42
National Review, 218
National Zeitung (Berlin), war-scare of 1875, 54; French press and official influence, 56
Nationalism, nationalist movement, nationalists, 194, 213; French intervention and German, 16; and Napoleon III, 17; resisted by government and moderate opinion, 192 f.; revival of, in 1911, 252; government's attitude after 1911, 257 f.; significance of, 1912-1914, 283 f. See Boulanger; Ligue des Patriotes; Ligue de la Patrie Française; Poincaré; Déroulède; etc.
Near Eastern Crisis, 1878, 74; public opinion during, 76
Nevers, Bishop of, 66
Newspapers, see press
Newton, Lord, 38, 41, 59, 76, 78, 82, 101, 115
Nicholas II, Tsar of Russia, 261, 290; coronation of, a French holiday, 165; calls First Hague Conference, 1899, 184; Björkö meeting with

William II, 1905, 216; Port Baltic interview, 259
Nicot, L., anti-German articles in *France*, 119
Nigra, 52
N'goko-Sangha, 234
Nikolsburg, Peace of, 1866, 19
Nile, 166 f., 172
Nineteenth Century, 121
Nord, department of, 143
Nord (Brussels), Russia and a Franco-German War, 1887, 140; Russia's vogue in France, 1891, 154
Norddeutsche Allgemeine Zeitung (Berlin), 12, 55, 79, 114; Ems despatch, July 13, 1870, 31; on continuation of war, Sept. 1870, 37; "war in the air," Jan. 1874, 52; collection of chauvinist excerpts from French press, 56; *Temps*'s cavalry article, 1885, 104; denial of impending ultimatum, Jan. 1887, 125; Germany's interests in Morocco, 1905, 208; on expedition to Fez, 1911, 238
North American Review, 164
North German Confederation, 19
Norton papers, 162
Notovich, editor of *Novosti*, 154
Nouvelle Revue, 86, 97 f., 106, 122, 133, 138, 142 f., 145, 198
Nouvion-en-Thierache, 253
Novoïe Vremya (St. Petersburg), 291
Novosti (St. Petersburg), 154
Nyström, Dr. A., 194

Ollivier, É., 26, 31; on German unity, March, 1867, 20; his ministry, Jan. 1870, 24; on prospect of peace, June, 1870, 25; his attitude, July 6, 1870, 28; on pressure of public opinion, July 14, 31; session of *corps législatif*, July 15, 33
Ollivier, Marie Thérèse, 33
Omedurman, 172,
Oncken, H., 15, 18, 19, 20, 21, 22, 24, 27, 28, 35
Opinion Nationale, 17, 35, 40
Ordre, against immediate war, 1875, 48; *Times*'s war-scare article, 1875, 62
Orénoque (French war-ship), 51 f.

Organic Laws of 1875, 53, 114
Oubril, P., Count, 30

Pagès, G., 51, 53, 68, 76, 87, 91, 95, 122, 127, 162, 163, 167, 171, 199
Pagny-sur-Moselle, 129
Paix, 156, 158; Empress Frederick's visit, 1891, 149; Franco-Russian entente, 1891, and Alsace-Lorraine, 155
Paladines, General de, 37
Paléologue, M., 290, 302
Palestine, 201
Palikao, Marshal, 36
Pallain, 201; dinner with H. von Bismarck, 1884, 99
Pan-Germanism, 266
Pan-Islam, 94
Pan-Slavism, 266, 270; Gambetta and, 72; and alliance with France, 1886, 138
⚓ Paris, 73, 81, 95, 97, 190, 214, 232, 239, 258, 270, 293, 299; siege of, 1870-1871, 17, 36; illumination of, 1866, 18; opposition's control of, 1863-1870, 24; attitude of crowds, July 13, 14, 32; danger of revolution, 1870, 1871, 38 f.; attack on Hôtel de Ville, Oct. 31, 1870, 40; election of National Assembly, Feb. 8, 1870, 40 f.; preliminary terms of peace, 41; proposed conference on Egypt, 1884, 98; effect of French defeat in Tonkin, 1885, 102; climax of Boulangism, Jan., 1889, 143 f.; Exposition of 1889, 145; Empress Frederick's visit, 1891, 148 ff.; visit of Russian naval officers, 1893, 157; Nicholas II's visit, 1896, 165; municipal council and evacuation of Fashoda, 1898, 174 f.; German visitors to Paris Exposition, 1900, 185; municipal elections, May, 1900, 192; reaction of Paris delegation to repudiation of revanche, 1903, 196; Edward VII's visit, 1902, 203; chauvinism in, after 1911, 254, 273; demonstrations, 1914, 305
Paris, 106
Paris-Midi, 292; England's strategic position, 1914, 303; partial mobilization, July 30, 305. See M. de Waleffe
Parlement et l'Opinion, 277

Parliament, French debates and public opinion, 7; interpellations on foreign affairs, 7 f.; Delcassé and, 212
Parliamentary Debates, 59, 167, 244
Parti-Ouvrier, 159
Passy, F., leadership of moderate tendencies, 193
Pastoral letters, and German Catholics, 52
Patrie, 32 f., 56, 105, 114 f., 117, 127, 139, 174, 192, 215 f., 219 f., 224, 238, 242 f.; 244, 248 f., 251, 262, 267, 304, 306; on preliminary terms of peace, 42; on Venice interview, Apr., 1875, 55; England and war-scare, 1875, 64; French defeat in Tonkin, 1885, 102; Brisson's Tonkin policy, 1885, 103; recovery by diplomacy, 1886, 122; on peace policy, 1886, 123; on the revanche, 1887, 124; French policy in 1887, 126; organ of Ligue des Patriotes, 1898, 175; Alsace-Lorraine and public opinion, 1908, 185; Socialist defeat, 1903, 187; attitude toward entente with England, 202; on negotiations with Germany, 1905, 209; on Delcassé's dismissal, 1905, 212; Triple Alliance and Moroccan crisis, 1905, 1906, 222; on Franco-German Accord, 1909, 233; government and Fez expedition, 1911, 235; Germany and Agadir, 1911, 241; reaction to Franco-German agreements, Nov. 4, 1911, 247; public opinion and Balkan War, 1912, 265; appeal to confidence, Aug. 2, 1914, 309
Patrie en Danger, 39, 40
✳Patriotism, Alsace-Lorraine as a test of, 47; attitude of Socialists, 194; E. Lavisse on, 253
Pau, 282
Pays, 21, 26, 36, 38; on Gambetta's Cherbourg Speech, Aug. 9, 1881, 78; French defeat in Tonkin, 1885, 102; on German press, 1885, 104 f.; coalition of Radicals and Monarchists, election of Oct., 1885, 106
Peasants, and military reforms, 1867, 22; Napoleonic legend, 24
Pellet, M., 73
Pelletan, C., 12, 212, 278; Radicals' foreign policy, 1880, 80; official policy in Tunis affair, 1881, 89;

Tunis and memory of Alsace-Lorraine, 90; on credits for Tonkin, Dec., 1885, 107; on memories of 1871, 107; on Ligue des Patriotes, 113; true patriotism, 114; Germany and *revanche*, 1886, 123; on Schnaebelé's arrest, 1887, 130; on Russian autocracy, 1881, 137; on Russo-Bulgarian controversy, 1886, 139

Perchot, Senator, 273. See *Radical*

"Père de la Victoire," 154

Père Lachaise, 194

Persia, 290

"Pertinax," defeat of Socialist view of foreign affairs, 1903, 197. See *Écho de Paris*

Peterhof, 290

Petit Champenois (Rheims), 171

Petit Comtois (Besançon), 10, 232, 249, 257, 275; Poincaré on settlement with Germany, 1911, 247; effect of Agadir crisis on public opinion, 1911, 251; Triple Entente and Balkan War, 1912, 265; three-year service law and German population, 1913, 278; France's action in Austro-Serbian War, 1914, 287; Schoen's *démarche*, July 24, 1914, 294

Petit Journal, 8, 9, 13, 117, 123, 126, 128, 150, 156, 159, 164, 167, 175, 290, 302; attitude toward Boulanger, 1886, 116; anti-English campaign, 119, 202; Boulanger, and its circulation, 143; French artists and Berlin exposition, 1891, 149. See E. Judet, S. Pichon

Petit Marseillais (Marseilles), 256, 267, 286; Russia and the defensive, 1914, 293

Petit Parisien, 9, 133, 140, 242 f., 262; Bülow's interview in, Oct. 2, 1905, 218; Casablanca affair, 1908, 229 f.; on Franco-German Accord, 1909, 233; Germany and expedition to Fez, 1911, 237 f., 239; Russia and the Serbs, 1908, 262; attitude toward crisis, 1914, 306. See J. Caillaux

Petit Provençal (Marseilles), 8, 189, 257, 294; on Tangier incident, 1905, 209; Germany's threat to *entente cordiale*, 1905, 215; on opposition to three-year service law, 1914, 282;

France's interests and Serbia, 1914, 288

Petit Gironde, (Bordeaux), 10, 121, 153, 159; on the *revanche*, 1887, 124 f.; reaction to Franco-German agreements, Nov. 4, 1911, 247; advantages of France's position, Aug. 2, 1914, 309

Petit République, 159, 176, 195 f., 261; on Delcassé's dismissal, 1905, 212; secret terms of *entente cordiale*, 1911, 249; war over Balkans, 1912, 273. See J. Juarès

Petite République Française, 112, 167

Peuple Français, 21, 35, 38

Peyramont, editor of *Revanche*, Boulanger and *revanche*, 117; prosecution and acquittal, 1887, 121

Phare de la Loire (Nantes), 9, 26, 267, 304; Poincaré's Nantes speech, Oct., 1912, 260; on aggressive declaration of war, 1914, 308 f.

Pichon, S., 13, 250; France and peace policy, 1886, 122; Casablanca affair, 1908, 228; annexation of Bosnia-Herzegovina and, 231 f.; Franco-German economic agreement in Morocco, 1909, 234; on Russia's attitude, 1914, 302; Alsace-Lorraine and acceptance of war, 1914, 309. See *Petit Journal*

Pingaud, A., 17

Pinon, R., 253

Place de la Concorde, 154

Playne, C. E., 255

Plebiscite, of May, 1870, 24; of Nov. 2, 1870, 40

Poincaré, R., 162, 232, 283, 287, 289, 293, 295, 300 f., 302; speech of Oct. 27, 1912, 6, 260, 266, 269; on agreement with Germany, 1911, 248; his foreign policy, 258 f.; co-operation with Germany in Balkans, 1912, 259; on revival of military spirit, 1912, 260; political support for foreign policy, 261; attitude toward Serbo-Bulgarian Alliance, 1912, 263; attitude toward Isvolski and Russia during the Balkan Wars, 1912, 1913, 263 f.; Isvolski's interpretation of his point of view, 1912, 268; visit to St. Petersburg, 1912, and the three-year service law, 1913, 279; attitude toward corruption of

French press, 1912, 1913, 268 ff.; on newspapers accepting Russian bribes, 274; visit to St. Petersburg, 1914, 289 f., 297; return to Paris, 299; on England's aid, 304; assurances to Isvolski, Aug. 1, 1914, 307

Pointu, J., 29

Poirier, M., 252

Poland, 286

Polignac, de, 57

Ponsat, G., 282

Ponsonby, Sir F., 148

Port Baltic, interview at, 259

Portsmouth, visit of French naval squadron, 1891, 157

Potsdam, 185

Prefects, reports, 6 f., 18; reports of, on economic depression, 22; on war or peace, July, 1870, 29

Press, newspaper (French), and hatred of Germany, 5; publication of parliamentary debates, 7; development of, in relation to public opinion, 8 ff.; provincial press, 9 f., 22; power of repetition, 10 f.; official influence upon, 11 ff.; and German troops in Paris, 1871, 41; *National Zeitung* on use of official influence upon, 1875, 56; Republican press and German influence, 68; moderate press and Franco-German entente, 1884, 97 f.; 1898, 180; chauvinist press, 116, 119 ff.; sensational Paris press in South and the telegraph, 143; moderate, and chauvinist pressure, 1891, 150; 1895, 163 f.; and *Mercure de France*'s questionnaires, 186 ff.; silence of, on Alsace-Lorraine Question, 188; radical Republican, and foreign affairs, 198; failure to prepare opinion as to Germany's attitude, 1905, 207; 1911, 250; corruption of, by Russia, 1905, 1906, 261; 1912, 1913, 268 ff.; attitude of Paris press toward autonomist opinion in Alsace, 1913, 280; preparation of opinion by, 1914, 286 ff.; 301 ff.; publication of news, July, 1914, 286. See Havas Agency; public opinion

Presse, 8, 26, 216, 217 f., 219, 259, 294; on Gramont's declaration of July 6, 1870, 28; on Franco-German entente, July, 1905, 217; public opinion and war, Aug. 1, 1914, 307

Pressensé, F. de, 257, 272; dismissal by *Temps*, 11; leader of moderate tendencies, 193; becomes a Socialist, 196; attitude toward Alsace-Lorraine and the *revanche*, 1903, 196 f.

Prévost-Paradol, L. A., on German unification, 16; French North African Empire, 85

Progrès (Lyons), 9, 26, 34, 35; *Times*'s war-scare article, 62; alarm in Paris, 1875, 63

Progrès de la Cote d'Or (Dijon), 9, 24, 62, 154, 158, 290, 306

Proust, A., 82

Provinzialkorrespondenz (Berlin), reasons for annexing Alsace-Lorraine, 45; assurances of peace, Apr. 14, 1875, 57

Prussia, 25, 26, 46; Napoleon III and moderate expansion of, 17; war with Austria, 1866, 18; Gramont's warning, July 1, 1870, 24; Gramont's declaration, July 6, 1870, 28; peace terms in Sept., 1870, 37; becomes aggressor, 40. See Bismarck

Public opinion, and international relations, 3; meaning of, 4; and stereotypes, 5; sources of, 6 ff.; reports of prefects, 6 f.; influence of parliamentary debates, 7 f.; value of, to foreign policy, 13 f.; on German unification, 16 f.; fear of inevitable war, 1867-1870, 23; passiveness of, 4 f., 23; effect of national resistance on later development of, 39; influence of, in 1870, 1871, 42; problems after Treaty of Frankfort, 44; influences toward moderation, 45 ff.; Alsace-Lorraine, a test of patriotism, 47 f.; conclusions, 1871-1875, 64 f.; fear of complications, 71 f., 81 ff., 107, 127, 232; opportunist Republican point of view, 82 f.; Bismarck's interpretation of French psychology, 86, 123 f.; effect of Gambetta's advice of silence, 87; on colonial expansion, 107 f.; chauvinist propaganda, 110 f.; conclusions as to *revanche*, 109, 134 f.; and Russian alliance, 160 f.; resistance to chauvinist pressure, 165; moderate tendencies, 183 ff., 193, 197; investigations of, 185 ff.; *fin de siècle* mood,

187 f., 255; Alsace-Lorraine question after 1871, 188 f.; resistance to revived nationalism, 191 ff.; hatred of Germany in text-books, 195 f.; on France's diplomatic arrangements, 220 f.; Tardieu's campaign for equilibrium, 10 f., 222; effect of suspense, 1911, 246; on nationalist movement after 1911, 255 ff.; effect of corruption of press, 261, 268; attitude toward Alsace-Lorraine, 1913, 276; and the balance of power, 285, 310; preparation of, by press, 1914, 286 ff., 301 ff.; attitude toward aggressive war, 307 ff., 310. See press; inevitable war; equilibrium

Public, 26 f.; Gramont's declaration, July 6, 1870, 29

Pyat, F., resigns from National Assembly, 1871, 41

Quai d'Orsay, 40, 77, 91, 165, 177, 198, 208, 228, 238, 240, 243, 267, 294, 295

Questions Diplomatiques et Coloniales, 208

Quinet, E., on cession of Alsace-Lorraine, 1871, 42

Radical, 57, 233, 242, 244, 261 f., 264, 273, 278 f.; 280, 282, 286 ff., 290, 304; on Kronstadt, 1891, 154; Russian friendship and French opinion, 1891, 155; Socialists and Russian visit to Paris, 1893, 159; on Kiel Canal, 1895, 163; on conditions in Morocco, 1911, 235; Germany and Agadir, 1911, 241; M. Barrès as president of Ligue des Patriotes, 1914, 252; on balance of power, 273; Russian bribes and their effect, 1913, 274 ff.; on Berne conference, 1913, 279; France and peace, 1914, 293; Triple Entente and peace, 1914, 298; on official policy, July 29, 307. See Senator Perchot

* Radical party, effect of Russian bribery upon its press, 1912, 1913, 270 ff.; attitude of its press toward three-year service law, 1913, 271; attitude toward foreign affairs, 1912, 1913, 272; attitude toward Alsace-Lorraine, 1913, 276; substitute for three-year service act, 1913, 278; and Berne conference, 1913, 279 f.;

Pau Congress and three-year-service law, 1913, 282; parliamentary elections, 1914, 283; resolutions adopted at Gap and Agen, 1914, 288; resolution of confidence, July 29, 299

* Radical-Socialist party, 272; peace resolution at Congress of Tours, Oct., 1912, 264 f.; effect of Russian bribes upon its press, 270; attitude of its press toward three-year service law, 1913, 271; attitude toward foreign affairs, 272; on general war over Balkans, 1913, 276; attitude toward Alsace-Lorraine, 1913, 276; substitute for three-year service act, 1913, 278; and Berne conference, 1913, 279 f.; Pau Congress on three-year service law, 1913, 282; co-operation with United Socialists, 1913, 1914, 282 f.; parliamentary elections, 1914, 283; resolution adopted at Gap and Agen, 1914, 288; and Jaurès's hostility to Russian alliance, 1914, 289; resolution of confidence, July 29, 299 f.

* Radicals, and amnesty, 79; and Gambetta, 80; on foreign policy, 80; on Tunis and Germany, 90; combine with Monarchists, 89, 92, 96, 101 f., 163; non-intervention in Egypt, 1882, 93; division on evacuation of Tonkin, 1885, 102; election of Oct., 1885, 105 ff.; use of Germany's support of French colonial policy, 107; attitude toward Ligue des Patriotes, 113, 116; change after Oct., 1885, on foreign policy, 122, 134; attitude toward Boulanger, 122; Russo-Bulgarian controversy, 1886-1887, 139; and Socialists's attitude toward patriotism, 194

Radolin, Prince, 210, 227; and Parisian society, 200; policy of silence, June, 1905, 213; Casablanca incident, 226 f.; attitude of French public opinion toward entente with Germany, 1908, 231

Radowitz, J. M. von, 19, 55, 64; preventive war theory, 59 f.

Raffalovitch, Russian financial agent, 269 ff.; Isvolski's influence upon *Temps*, 271

Rambaud, A., 102

Ranc, A., 45; leaves National Assembly, 1871, 41; on cession of Alsace-Lorraine, 1871, 42

Ranke, L., 67

Rappel, 8, 239, 290; preliminary terms of peace, 1871, 41; on cession of Alsace-Lorraine, 1871, 42; *Times*'s war-scare article, 62; England's aid in war-scare, 1875, 64; Russian bribes and their effect, 1912, 1913, 274 f.; Triple Entente and Serbia, 1914, 293; French interests and Austro-Serbian quarrel, 298

Reclus, M., 37

Recouly, R., 144; Germany and expedition to Fez, 1911, 237; reaction of public opinion to Agadir, 1911, 241; reply to Agadir, 1911, 242; Balkan League and Macedonia, 1912, 264; balance of power and Balkan War, 1912, 265 f.

Reinach, J., 66, 75, 79, 81, 85, 90, 186; foreign policy and fear of complications, 71; Gambetta's political influence, 72; traditions in Republic's foreign policy, 80; France's relation to Greece, 81; public opinion and foreign affairs, 83; von Donnersmarck's assurances, 1887, 130; on the *revanche,* 1897, 187

Reinsurance Treaty, non-renewal of, 1890, 153

Renan, E., on German nationalism, 16

Renard, G., 257

René, C., Franco-German *rapprochement* and Poincaré, 1912, 259

Renouvin, P., 290, 295, 296

Republican-Socialists, 272

Republicans, 194; decline of hatred of Germany, 6; and election of National Assembly, 1871, 40 f.; conflict with Monarchists, 46, 66; and payment of indemnity, 49, 65; in campaign of 1877, 68; on foreign policy and Alsace-Lorraine, 69; and moderate diplomatic activity, 71; increasing confidence, 78; elections, Oct., 1885, 106; and Dreyfus Affair, 191 ff.; resistance to revived nationalism, 192 f.; on relations with Germany. See L. Gambetta; J. Ferry; J. Reinach; C. Freycinet, etc.

République Française, 13, 49, 67, 75, 77, 84, 106, 119, 126, 141, 164, 171, 195, 212, 216, 224, 236, 244, 248, 262,

281, 286, 287, 290; Venice interview, 1875, 54 f., 93; Bismarck's demand to Belgium, 57; on *Times*'s war-scare article, 1875, 62; to the Monarchists, 66; German garrisons in Alsace-Lorraine, 1877, 68; on international democratic propaganda, 69; fear of complications and foreign policy, 71; on Alsace-Lorraine, 76; on Anglo-Turkish agreement, June, 1878, 76 f.; France's recovery, 79; Greco-Turkish boundary question, 82; Waddington and Tunis, 89; co-operation with England in Egypt, 92; Franco-German relations, 1884, 97; France and Kiel Canal, 1895, 163; on Grey's statement, Mar., 1895, 167; Russia and *entente cordiale,* 1904, 204; attitude toward Morocco, 206; on relations with Germany, June, 1905, 213; acceptance of conference, July, 1905, 215; growth of national feeling, 1905, 217; effect of Moroccan crisis, 1905, 1906, 221; Casablanca incident and acceptance of war, 1908, 228 f.; on Franco-German Accord, 1909, 233 f.; on expedition to Fez, 238 f.; on Germany's demand for Congo, 1911, 243; "The Eventual War," 1911, 246; on peaceful solution, 1914, 293. See L. Gambetta; J. Reinach; J. Méline

Reuss, A., 189

Reuter Agency, Bismarck's circular, 34

Revanche, 73, 90, 183; in 1871, 45; and Gambetta in 1871, 45 f.; discouraged by Grévy and Thiers, 47; Gambetta's St. Quentin speech, Nov., 1871, 73; effect of Gambetta's advice of silence, 87; P. Leroy-Beaulieu on, 8/ f.; and election, Oct., 1885, 104; analysis of, 109; Paul Déroulède, 109 f.; Ligue des Patriotes, 110 ff.; Déroulède's ideas as to education, 111, Boulanger in 1886, 115 ff.; attitude of French government, 1886, 121; Déroulède's resignation as president of Ligue des Patriotes, 1887, 128 f.; *Vossische Zeitung* on, 1891, 149; Russia's attitude toward, 154, 162, 165; at close of nineteenth century, 184; A. Lalance's census of editorial opinion on, 185; influence during July crisis, 1914, 309. See nationalism; public

opinion; Ligue des Patriotes; Déroulède; Boulanger; chauvinism
Revanche (newspaper), 122; Boulanger and the *revanche,* 117; prosecution and acquittal of Peyramont, 1887, 121; France and Austro-Russian War, 1887, 124; election in Alsace-Lorraine, 1887, 127; limited appeal, 134
Réveil, 8, 32, 35
Revolution of 1789, 15
Revue Blanche, 163
Revue Bleue, 188
Revue Catholique des Institutions et du Droit, 189
Revue de France, 73, 232
Revue de l'Enseignement Primaire, 195, 254
Revue de Paris, 73, 74, 78, 148
Revue des Deux Mondes, 38, 46, 48, 51, 84, 87, 113, 121, 141, 165 f., 167, 181, 191, 206, 218, 240, 253
Revue des Revues, 194
Revue des Sciences Politiques, 120
Revue du Foyer, 267
Revue d'Histoire Moderne, 30
Revue et Revue des Revues, 192
Revue Hebdomadaire, 265
Revue Politique et Parlementaire, 129, 130, 171, 189, 196
Regnault, H., 150 f.
Rey, É., 252
Reynauld, G., 171
Rhine, 15, 18, 71, 76, 86
Ribot, A., England and Franco-Russian negotiations, 1891, 157; on Franco-Russian alliance, 160, 164; defeat of his cabinet, 1914, 283
Richecour, A. de, 51
Riker, T. W., 167, 172
Ricklin, Dr., 281
Riou, G., 255
Rire, attitude during Boer War, 198
Robiquet, P., 80
Rochefort, H., 24, 79, 142; resigns from National Assembly, 41; on Ligue des Patriotes and Déroulède's influence, 113; Germany's intentions, 1886, 123; ostracism of all Germans, 1887, 131; on Bismarck's provocations, 1887, 132; on Russo-Bulgarian controversy, 1886, 139; conversion to Russian Alliance, Aug. 1887, 140 f.; on Empress Frederick's

visit, 1891, 152; attitude toward England, 1891, 158; Dreyfus and Fashoda, 1898, 174; expedition to Fez, 1911, 238; reaction to Agadir, 1911, 242; on Franco-German agreements, Nov. 4, 1911, 248; attitude after Agadir crisis, 1911, 251. See *Intransigeant*
Rome, 119, 208
Roon, A., Count von, 30
Rosen, Dr., 218, 219
Rosen, G., 47
Rothan, G., exclusion from Alsace, 1885, 105
Rouher, 19; on results of Austro-Prussian War, 20
Roumania, France's support in Congress of Berlin, 1878, 77
Rousset, Colonel, 260
Routier, G., 149, 153, 185
Rouvier, ministry, 1887, omission of Boulanger, 133 f.; end of France's isolation, 1891, 155; supports Delcassé, Apr. 19, 1905, 210; Delcassé's dismissal, June 6, 1905, 211; and cooperation with Germany, 1905, 212; renewed suggestion of understanding with Germany, Sept., 1905, 218; change of attitude, Oct., 1905, 219; Moroccan policy, 1905, 219; policy of amicable negotiations, 258
Rouyer, A., 132, 142
Roux, C. de, 75
Rue de la Paix, 118
Rue de l'Opéra, 118
Russell, Lord John, 59
Russell, Lord Odo, advises moderation to Bismarck, 64
Russia, 70, 122, 144, 180, 199, 231, 253, 259, 271, 277, 283, 285, 294 f., 296, 301, 307; and French conservatives, 51; Bismarck's irritation against, 53; and war-scare of 1875, 58 ff.; Gambetta and Gortchakov, 1875, 73; Near Eastern crisis, 76; her colonial expansion, 86; and French argument in Egyptian finances, 1884, 96; popularity of in France after 1875, 136; Bulgarian controversy, 1886, 1887, 139; attitude during crisis of 1887, 139 f.; and Empress Frederick's visit to Paris, 1891, 149, 153; alliance with France, 77, 122, 147, 153 ff.; attitude toward *revanche,* 154; and

Franco-German relations, 1895, 162 f.; and Fashoda crisis, 1898, 175; change in French alliance, 1899, 198; and Boer War, 199; war with Japan, 216, 221; attitude during Agadir crisis, 1911, 242 ff.; Russo-German agreement, 1911, 245; Franco-Russian naval treaty, 259; and Austro-Serb relations, Oct., 1912, 260; Revolution of 1905, 261; and corruption of French press, 261, 268 ff.; Kavalla question, 1913, 275; and French three-year service law, 1913, 279; strength of army, 1914, 291; and Austro-Serb relations, 1914, 296; French loans, 263; negotiations with Austria, 1914, 301; her mobilization, 1914, 302. See Gortchakov; de Giers; Isvolski; Sazonov

Russo-Japanese War, 216; results of Russia's defeat, 221

Sadowa, 20, 21, 22, 298
Sagallo, 144
St. Cloud, 31, 33, 150
Saint-Hilaire, B., 82; letter to *Deutsche Revue*, 90; opposition to Russian alliance, 1891, 156
Saint-Ogan, L., 86
St. Petersburg, 38, 59, 259, 261, 270, 279, 288, 290, 294, 295, 296, 300, 302
St. Quentin, Gambetta's speech, Nov. 16, 1871, 73
St. Sebastian, 73
Saint-Vallier, Comte de, 95; Tunis, 84 f.; Alsace-Lorraine in conversations with Bismarck, 87
Salisbury, R., Marquis of, 174; and Tunis, 1878, 77; Fashoda crisis and French *Yellow Book,* 1898, 174
Salomon, H., 25
Samoan Islands, 199
Sarajevo, 286
Sarraut, M., on Germany's policy in 1905, 219
Sarrien, ministry of, 1906, 220
Say, L., 77
Sazonov, S. D., Russia and Balkan War, 1912, 265; Poincaré's note, Oct. 30, 1912, 266; Poincaré's visit to St. Petersburg, 1914, 290
Schefer, C., 88
Scheurer-Kestner, A., 47, 72

Schiemann, T., attitude toward *entente cordiale,* 1905, 214
Schmitt, B. E., 256, 296, 305, 307 f.
Schnaebelé affair, 1887, 129 ff., 140, 152
Schoen, W., Baron von, and Casablanca affair, 1908, 227 f.; on French public opinion, 1913, 256; on Poincaré's policy, Nov., 1912, 264; press and public opinion in France, 267; his *démarche,* July 24, 1914, 293 ff.; 296, 305; Austria-Hungary's purposes, July 26, 295; on Franco-German solidarity, 295; on French advice to Russia, 295; intervention between Russian and Austria, July 27, 1914
Schouvalov, P., 139 f.
Scott, J. F., 288, 308
Schwertfeger, B., 154
Scutari, 275
Second Empire, 69
Security, 252; French policy in Central Europe, 15; uncertainty, 1867–1870, 22 f.; loss of Alsace-Lorraine, its effect upon, 44; Franco-Russian Alliance, 161, 183; solution of Alsace-Lorraine Question, 190; and the equilibrium, 285
Sedan, 36, 87, 110, 152, 163, 298
Siegnobos, C., 40, 69; protest against secret diplomacy, 1906, 219 f.
Selves, de, loans to Austria-Hungary, 1911, 232; Caillaux's attitude toward, 1911, 245; attitude toward Franco-German agreements of Nov. 4, 1911, 250
Sembat, M., 272, 276; defense of Franco-German agreements, Nov. 4, 1911, 249; *Faites un Roi, sinon faites la Paix,* its significance, 257; reaction to Alsatian opinion, 1913, 280
Serbia, 271, 258, 294, 295, 298; attitude of public opinion during Near-Eastern crisis, 1875-1878, 76; Bosnian crisis, Russia and France's attitude, 1908, 1909, 262 f.; Bulgarian alliance, 1912, 263; assassination of Francis Ferdinand, 286 f.; her reply to ultimatum, July 25, 1914, 296; Austro-Hungarian declaration of war, July 28, 298
Siam, Anglo-French friction, 1893, 158
Siècle, 17, 26, 34, 36, 46, 102, 107, 123, 224, 232, 239, 242, 249, 286, 291, 297;

on preliminary terms of peace, 1871, 41; on *Time*'s war-scare article, 1875, 63; on French foreign policy, 1881, 69; on Tunis and Germany, 90; attitude toward Morocco, 206; on Germany's attitude, Mar., 1905, 209; de Lanessan's articles, 1906, 220; results of Algeciras conference, 1906, 223; Germany's fear of encirclement, 223; and military measures, 1911, 246; reaction to agreements, Nov. 4, 1911, 247; diplomatic value of national union, 1912, 255 f.; Russia and the Serbs, 1908, 262; on Austria Hungary's future, 1914, 287; attitude toward Russia, 1914, 292 f.; on Russia's moderation, 302

Sigmaringen, 29

Simon, J., 32, 37, 48, 76; Berlin Labor Conference, 1890, 148

Sino-Japanese War, 1894–1895; Franco-Russian-German intervention, 163, 165

✳ Socialism, Socialists, 194; on Russian visit to Paris, 1893, 159; on peaceful solution of Alsace-Lorraine question, 190; leadership of moderate tendencies, 193 ff., 204, 197; parliamentary elections, 1893, 194; on patriotism and the *patrie,* 194; in pedagogical reviews, 195; co-operation with Republican *bloc,* 195; defeat of disarmament motion, 1903, 197; attitude toward Delcassé's foreign policy, 202; Jaurès founds *Humanité,* 1904, 197; union with Italy and England, 202; on *entente cordiale,* 1906, 220; on Russia's weakness, 263; attitude on war over Balkans, 272; France's choice in foreign policy, 276; substitute for three-year service act, 1913, 278 f.; on Berne conference, 1913, 279 f.; parliamentary elections, 1914, 283; Amiens Congress and three-year service law, 283; criticism of equilibrium, 285; Paris Congress, 1914, 288; action of Socialist deputies, 1914, 299; on convoking parliament, 307. See J. Jaurès; F. de Pressensé; M. Sembat; *Petite Republique; Humanité*

Société Française de la Sauvetage, 117

Soir, Ems despatch, 31 f.

Soleil, increasing frontier incidents, 1885, 105

Sontag, R. J., 208

Sorel, A., 34, 38; on Gambetta's motives, 1870-1871, 36; on Favre's circular, Sept. 4, 1870, 38; Ligue de la Patrie Française, 191

Sosie, character in Moliére's *Amphitryon,* 74

Soudan, 166, 168

South German states, 18, 33

Spahn, M., on value of newspapers as historical source, 14

Spain, 119, 178, 188, 242; occupation of Larache, 1911, 239; secret terms of Franco-Spanish entente, 1904, 249

Staats-Anzeiger (Berlin), 21

Standard (London), on Franco-German relations, 1884, 98; French press and military spirit, 1886, 118; Bismarck's intentions, Jan., 1887, 127; effect in France of Schnaebelé's arrest, 1887, 129 f.

Stannard, H., 73, 91

Steeg, T., Triple Entente and peace, 1914, 298

Stereotypes, 5, 179, 184, 192

Stern, A., 18, 30

Stieve, F., 259, 268

Stoffel, Colonel, 190; relations with Germany and Russia, 146 f.

Straits Question, in 1887, 139; negotiation of Franco-Russian alliance, 157; Agadir crisis and, 1911, 245

Strassburg, 40, 68, 71, 97, 113, 124, 129, 150, 154 f., 174, 267

Stuart, G. H., 212

Suez Canal, 93, 104

Switzerland, 58; Leo XIII's plan of buffer state, 128; proposed union with Alsace-Lorraine, 189

Szécsen, Count, 258, 270

Taine, H., Socialism after 1871, 193 f.

Talhouët, 34

Talmeyr, M., 134

Tanganyika, Lake, 166

Tangier, 255

Tardieu, André, 10 f., 212, 219; succeeds F. de Pressensé as foreign editor of *Temps,* 1904, 196; effect of Franco-Italian entente on Triple Alliance, 202; Delcassé's failure to communicate *entente cordiale* to

Germany, 208; effect of Germany's insistence upon conference, June, 1905, 214; on France's diplomatic arrangements, Oct., 1905, 218; 1906, 221; his campaign for equilibrium, 10 f., 222; aims of French diplomacy, 223; Germany's fear of encirclement, 223; Anglo-French military alliance, 1908, 224; Casablanca incident and public opinion, 1908, 228; on annexation of Bosnia-Herzegovina, 1908, 232; on Franco-German Accord, 1909, 233, 237; N'goko-Sangha enterprise, 234; conditions in Morocco, 1911, 235; Germany and necessary changes in Morocco, 1911, 237; *Norddeutsche Allgemeine Zeitung*'s warning, 1911; 238; reaction to Agadir, 1911, 241; on Germany's demand of Congo, 1911, 243; reaction to Franco-German agreements, Nov. 4, 1911, 247 f.; nationalist point of view, 253; attitude at beginning of Balkan Wars, 1912, 265; equilibrium and Balkan War, 1912, 266; Socialists and Russian alliance, 1914, 289. See *Temps;* G. Villiers

Taube, A., 290

Télégraphe, 113; public opinion on Franco-German entente, 1884, 100

Temperley, H., 27, 159

Temps, 10 f., 12 f., 16, 18, 20, 26, 36, 38, 56, 62, 70, 89 f., 93, 113, 121, 125, 129, 144 f., 149, 152 f., 158 f., 164, 167 f., 170, 172, 186, 192 f., 214, 216, 220 f., 223 f., 228, 232 f., 236, 238 f., 241, 247 f., 253, 255, 266 f., 275, 287 f.; on German Question, 15; results of war of 1866, 19; public opinion and Empire's foreign policy, 23; on preliminary terms of peace, 1871, 42; on Alsace-Lorraine's loyalty, 1871, 46; on clericals' foreign policy, 1874, 52; on *Time*'s war-scare article, 1875, 63; Russia and England in war-scare, 1875, 64; Europe and election, Oct., 1877, 68; on Anglo-Turkish agreement, June 4, 1878, 77; Gambetta's Cherbourg speech, Aug., 1881, 79; on Greco-Turkish boundary question, 1881, 82; and colonial expansion, 85; on colored colonial army, 86; on co-operation with England in Egypt, 92; on Franco-

German alliance, 1884, 99; on Ferry's defeat, 1885, 103; cavalry article, July, 1885, 104; on Bismarck's speech, Jan. 11, 1887, 124; on Havas Agency, Jan., 1887, 126; on French policy, 126; attitude during Schnaebelé affair, 131; on Russian alliance, 1887, 141; on Kronstadt, 1891, 153 f.; end of France's isolation, 1891, 155; peaceful revision of Treaty of Frankfort, 1896, 161; France and Kiel Canal, 1895, 163; public opinion and colonial expansion, 1894, 166; on Kruger telegram, 1896, 169; on evacuation of Fashoda, 1898, 174 f.; on entente with Germany, 1899, 181; Jaurès and disarmament, 1902, 196; Pressensé's repudiation of *revanche,* 1903, 196 f.; attitude during Boer War, 1898, 200; preparation of opinion for *entente cordiale,* 202; Morocco and Franco-German entente, 1901, 202; Germany and *entente cordiale,* 1904, 203; Russia and *entente cordiale,* 1904, 204; France's need of Morocco, 1901, 207; Germany and Tangier incident, 1905, 208; and change of French policy June, 1905, 213; on Björkö meeting, 1905, 218; French policy during Algeciras Conference, 1906, 219; Tardieu's campaign for equilibrium, 10 f., 222 f.; on Fez expedition, 1911, 237, 258; publication of secret terms of *entente cordiale,* 1911, 249; attitude during Bosnian crisis, 1908, 1909, 262; attitude during Balkan Wars, 1912, 1913, 271 f.; Russian bribes and their effect, 1913, 274 f.; campaign for three-year service law, 1913, 278; and Berne conference, 1913, 279; on Alsatian opinion, 1913, 281; on Chabrino-vitch's confession, 1914, 286; on Socialists and Franco-Russian Alliance, 1914, 289; estimate of Russian army, 1914, 291; Serbia and balance of power, 1914, 292; Germany's silence at Vienna, 296; Triple Entente and war, 298; Germany and Grey's mediation proposal, 301; on Russia's attitude, 302; its appeal to public opinion, 305. See de Pressensé; Tardieu

Thessaly, 81
Theirs, A., 24; speech of May 3, 1866, 7, 17; on French foreign policy, March, 1867, 20 f.; and Cochery's interpellation, July 6, 1870, 27; on Paris public opinion, July 13, 14, 32; his opposition to war, July, 1870, 33; and committee of national defense, Sept. 3, 1870, 36; his mission to neutral courts, 1870, 39; on armistice, Oct., 1870, 40; election of Feb. 8, 1871, 41; on preliminary terms of peace, 41; Chief of the Executive Power, 41; his liking for Bismarck, 41; on the *revanche,* 47; his foreign policy, 1871–1873, 48 ff.; and reorganization of army, 49; his defeat, 1873, 49; and clerical petitions for intervention in Italy, 50; and Conservative Republic, 69; his death, 72

Thomassin, head of proposed mission to Greece, 1880, 82

Times (London), 55, 57, 124, 125; on French war party, July, 1870, 29; Ems despatch, 31 f.; French version of Bismarck's circular, July 16, 1870, 34; on Paris opinion, Sept., 1870, 38 f.; Blowitz's war-scare article, 61 f.; Paris press during Fashoda Crisis, 1898, 173; on Franco-German arrangement, 1898, 180; on French opinion during Casablanca Affair, 1908, 228; Poincaré's Nantes speech, Oct., 1912, 260

Tisza, Count, 288

Togoland, 243, 246

Tonkin, 106, 134; beginning of Ferry's campaign, 1883, 101; Monarchist-Bonapartist-Radical opposition, 1885, 102; question of evacuation, 103, 107; credits for, 103, 107; Ferry's defeat, 102 ff.; Treaty of Apr., 1885, 101; proposed exchange for Alsace-Lorraine, 189

Toulon, visit of Russian naval squadron, 1893, 158

Tours, 38; Radical-Socialist Congress, Oct., 1912, 264

Toury, F. G. de, 255, 267

Trarieux, G., peace sentiment in providences, 1913, 277

Treaties, agreements, of 1815, 17; Nikolsburg, 1866, 19; Westphalia, 1648, 19; preliminary terms of peace, 1871, 41; Anglo-Turkish agreement, June 4, 1878, 76; Frankfort, 1871, 44, 84, 186; Bardo, 1881, 89; Franco-Chinese, Apr., 1885, 101, 170; Re-insurance Treaty, 1887, 153; Anglo-Congo Treaty, 1894, 166; Anglo-German Treaty, 1898, 177; Björkö, 1905, 216; Berlin, 1878, 81, 232; Russo-German agreement, 1911, 245; Franco-Spanish entente, 1902, 249; Franco-German Accord, 1909, 232; Franco-German agreements, Nov. 4, 1911, 246

Tribune, 8

Tridon, resigns from National Assembly, 1871, 41

Trochu, General, 40

Tunis, 86, 87, 88, 90, 134; Salisbury and Bismarck, Congress of Berlin, 1878, 77; expedition of 1881, 85; France's delay, 89; loans to, 88 f.; Treaty of Bardo, ratification of, 90

Turkey, 94, 138, 242, 243; Cyprus agreement with England, June 4, 1878, 76; Greco-Turkish boundary question, 81 f.; proposed intervention in Egypt, 1882, 92 f.; Franco-Russian negotiations, 157; corruption of French press, 1912, 1913, 270

Ubanghi, Upper, approach to Bahr-el-Gazel, 166

Union de la Presse Radicale-Socialiste, election, Oct., 1885, 106

Union des Mines, 234

Union Republicaine, Ferry and Gambetta's policies, 103

Univers, 26, 32, 71; campaign for temporal power, 50; on Broglie ministry, 1873, 51 f.; suspended, 52; attitude during war-scare, 1875, 56

Vacherot, E., 69, 81

Valary, E., 93

Valdrôme, C. de, 26

Valfrey, J., 38; breakfast with von Huhn, 1898, 177; contributes as Whist to *Figaro,* 177; exchange of articles with *Kölnische Zeitung,* 178 f.; on basis for Franco-German entente, 1899, 179 f.

Vandal, 186

Vanne, Bishop of, 67

Vannes, 109

Varzin, 98

Vatican, 50
Vattier, É., 45
Vaucluse, department, 22
Vaudière, Mme. Jane de la, youth and the *revanche*, 1897, 187
Venetia, 18
Venice, interview of Apr., 1875, 54
Versailles, 44, 109, 150
Veuillot, L., on Paris public opinion, Sept., 1870, 36 f. See *Univers*
Victoria, Queen of England, 61, 64
Vienna, 24, 33, 287 f., 298
Villaume, Lieutenant, reports on French chauvinism, 1886, 120
Villiers, Georges, A. Tardieu's pseudonym, 214, 289
Villot, Colonel, 147
Vincennes, 260
Viviani, R., 189, 293, 302, 304; ministry of 1914, 256; Tsar and Revolution of 1905, 261; on three-year service law, 1914, 283; on opposition to three-year law in Chamber, 1914, 288; return to Paris, 1914, 299; France's support of Russia, 1914, 300
Volks-Zeitung (Berlin), 45
Voltaire, 102, 103, 105, 106
Volume, 195
Vosges, 76, 77, 105, 238
Vossische Zeitung (Berlin), 149

Waddington, Mary K., 69
Waddington, W. H., Salisbury, Bismarck, and Tunis, 1878, 77; friendly press and offer of Tunis, 89; Russia's advances, 1879, 137
Wahl, A., 53
Waldteuffel, E., purchase of Alsace-Lorraine, 1893, 189
Waleffe, M. de, 305
War-scare of 1875, 130; clericals and foreign affairs, 49 f.; Bismarck's intentions, 53, 56, 58; moderation of French policy on eve of, 53; Bismarck's embargo on export of horses, 54; Art. 3 of military law, 54; French press on Venice interview, Apr. 5, 54 f.; Vienna letter, *Kölnische Zeitung*, Apr. 4, 55; *Berliner Post*'s "Is War in Sight" article, 55; French press and German alarmist articles, 55 f.; end of first phase, Apr. 14, 57; Bismarck and Belgian press laws, 57; French opinion at end of first period, 58; Decazes revives crisis, 58; Russia and England, 58 f.; preventive war theory, 59 f.; Blowitz's "A French War-Scare" article in *Times*, 61 f.; *Morning Post*'s War-scare letter, 62; attitude of French press to *Times*'s war-scare article, 62 f.; pressure upon Bismarck, 64
Waterloo, 87
Weill, G., 8, 194
Welschinger, H., 28
Wemyss, Mrs. R., 60
Werther, K., Baron von, 29
Wetterlé, Abbé, 281
White Nile, 174
Wickersheimer, E., 86
William I, King of Prussia, Emperor of Germany, 60, 126; and Prince Leopold's renunciation, 29; and continuation of war, Sept., 1870, 37; interview with Alexander II, May, 1875, 59; Münster's letter, 1886, 120
William II, Emperor of Germany, 176, 217; and France, 1888, 145; his courtship of France, 145 f., 161; and Berlin Labor Conference, 1890, 148; Empress Frederick's visit to Paris, 1891, 148 ff.; and Kruger Telegram, 1896, 168; his estimate of Hanotaux, 170; suggested visit to French port, 1898, 177; press discussion of Franco-German entente, 1899, 180; attitude toward possible Anglo-French war, 1898, 181; visits French training ship *Iphigenia*, 1899, 199; hope for a Continental league, 1904, 208; influences back of Tangier demonstration, 1905, 208; on Rouvier's offer of entente, 213; Björkö meeting with Nicholas II, 1905, 216; opinion of Jules Cambon, 225; *Daily Telegram* interview, Oct. 28, 1908, 227; on French report of Casablanca affair, 1908, 228; Port Baltic interview, 259
Winterfeldt, 256
Wirth, F., 190
Witte, S., Count, 217
Wolff, T., William II's courtship of France, 145 f.; attitude of French public opinion toward Germany, 185
World War, 195, 252, 310
Worms, É., 112

Worth, 152

Wolff agency; Bismarck's circular, 34

Wuttke, H., 11

XIX Siècle, 113; Anglo-French-German relations, 1884, 97 f.

Yellow Book, French, published during Fashoda crisis, 1898, 174. See Livres Jaunes

Zévaès, A., 130, 172, 194

Ziekursch, J., 113

Zurlinden, General, 13